D1522077

Advances

in COMPUTERS
VOLUME 62

Advances in
COMPUTERS

Advances in Software Engineering

EDITED BY

MARVIN V. ZELKOWITZ

Department of Computer Science
and Institute for Advanced Computer Studies
University of Maryland
College Park, Maryland

VOLUME 62

ELSEVIER
ACADEMIC
PRESS

Amsterdam Boston Heidelberg London New York Oxford
Paris San Diego San Francisco Singapore Sydney Tokyo

ELSEVIER B.V.
Sara Burgerhartstraat 25
P.O. Box 211, 1000 AE Amsterdam
The Netherlands

ELSEVIER Inc.
525 B Street, Suite 1900
San Diego, CA 92101-4495
USA

ELSEVIER Ltd
The Boulevard, Langford Lane
Kidlington, Oxford OX5 1GB, UK

ELSEVIER Ltd
84 Theobalds Road
London WC1X 8RR, UK

First edition 2004

Library of Congress Cataloging in Publication Data
A catalog record is available from the Library of Congress.

British Library Cataloguing in Publication Data
A catalogue record is available from the British Library.

ISBN: 0-12-012162-X
ISSN (Series): 0065-2458

⊗ The paper used in this publication   of ANSI/NISO Z39.48-1992 (Permanence of Paper).

Printed in Great Britain.

Contents

An Introduction to Agile Methods

David Cohen, Mikael Lindvall, and Patricia Costa

The Timeboxing Process Model for Iterative Software Development

Pankaj Jalote, Aveejeet Palit, and Priya Kurien

A Survey of Empirical Results on Program Slicing

David Binkley and Mark Harman

Challenges in Design and Software Infrastructure for Ubiquitous Computing Applications

Guruduth Banavar and Abraham Bernstein

Introduction to MBASE (Model-Based (System) Architecting and Software Engineering)

David Klappholz and Daniel Port

Software Quality Estimation with Case-Based Reasoning

Taghi M. Khoshgoftaar and Naeem Seliya

Data Management Technology for Decision Support Systems

Surajit Chaudhuri, Umeshwar Dayal, and Venkatesh Ganti

Contributors

Guruduth Banavar is the Senior Manager of the Pervasive Computing Infrastructure group at the IBM TJ Watson Research Center in Hawthorne, New York. Dr. Banavar's group works on several aspects of pervasive computing, such as context-based systems, wearable computing, disconnectable application infrastructure, security, and programming tools for pervasive applications. Prior to this, he led the group that conceived and built Multi-Device Authoring Technology, an Eclipse-based tool for targeting web applications to multiple pervasive devices. He has previously worked on middleware for content delivery, publish-subscribe, and synchronous collaboration. Dr. Banavar received a Ph.D. in Computer Science in 1995 from the University of Utah.

Abraham Bernstein is an Associate Professor of computer science and information technology at the University of Zurich, Switzerland. His current research focuses on various aspects of support for dynamic (intra- and inter-) organizational processes in areas such as knowledge discovery, service discovery/matchmaking, mobile/pervasive computing and enterprise resource planning systems. His work is based on both social science (organizational psychology/sociology/economics) and technical (computer science, artificial intelligence) foundations. Prior to joining the University of Zurich Dr. Bernstein was on the faculty at New York University and was a project manager as well as research scientist at Union Bank of Switzerland. Dr. Bernstein has a Ph.D. from MIT and also holds a Diploma in Computer Science (comparable to a M.S.) from the Swiss Federal Institute in Zurich (ETH).

David Binkley is a Professor of Computer Science at Loyola College in Baltimore Maryland where he has been a member of the faulty since 1991. His research interests include slice-based metrics, testing, slicing and recently amorphous slicing, currently supported by NSF, and software maintenance cost reduction tools. Dr. Binkley has recently served as the general chair and subsequently program co-chair for the annual workshop on source code analysis and manipulation.

Surajit Chaudhuri is a senior researcher and manager of the Data Management, Exploration, and Mining Group at Microsoft Research. His research interests include self-tuning database systems, decision support systems, and integration of text, relational, and semi-structured information. He received a PhD in computer science from Stanford University. Chaudhuri is a member of the ACM and the IEEE Computer Society. Contact him at surajitc@microsoft.com.

David Cohen is a Junior Scientist at Fraunhofer Center for Experimental Software Engineering Maryland. He specializes on the software development lifecycle, including hands-on agile development experience, and user interface usability modeling. Currently, David is working on development of collaborative, internet-based tools to facilitate knowledge transfer between individuals and organizations and build experience bases supporting the Experience Factory Model. David may be contacted at dcohen@fc-md.umd.edu.

Patricia Costa is a scientist at the Fraunhofer Center for Experimental Software Engineering, Maryland. She has a B.Sc. and a M.Sc. in Computer Science from the Federal University of Minas Gerais, Brazil, awarded in 1996 and 1999, respectively, and a M.Sc. in Telecommunications Management from University of Maryland University College in 2001. Her research interests include: software architecture, agile methods and knowledge management. Contact her at pcosta@fc-md.umd.edu.

Umeshwar Dayal is Director of the Intelligent Enterprise Technologies Laboratory at Hewlett-Packard Laboratories. His research interests are data mining, business process management, distributed information management, and decision support technologies, especially as applied to e-business. He received a PhD in applied mathematics from Harvard University. Dr. Dayal is a member of the ACM and IEEE. Contact him at umeshwar.dayal@hp.com.

Venkatesh Ganti is a researcher in the Data Management, Exploration, and Mining group at Microsoft Research. His research interests include infrastructure support for developing and maintaining decision support systems, infrastructure for improving data quality in data warehouses, and mining and monitoring large datasets. He received a PhD in Computer Sciences from the University of Wisconsin-Madison. Find more details about Ganti at http://research.microsoft.com/~vganti and contact him at vganti@microsoft.com.

Mark Harman is a Reader in Computing at Brunel University, UK. Dr. Harman has worked on program slicing and testing, and in particular amorphous and conditioned slicing since 1994. More recently he has been active in championing role of search-based techniques in software engineering. Dr. Harman is funded by the UK Engineering and Physical Sciences Research Council (EPSRC) and Daimler-Chrysler, Berlin. He is program chair for several conferences and workshops including the 20th international conference on software maintenance and the search-based software engineering track of the genetic and evolutionary computation conference.

Pankaj Jalote is a Professor of Computer Science at IIT Kanpur. He did his B.Tech. from IIT Kanpur and Ph.D. from University of Illinois at Urbana–Champaign. From 1985 to 1989 he was an Assistant Professor at University of Maryland at College Park. Since 1989 he is at IIT Kanpur. From 1996 to 1998, he was Vice President (quality) at Infosys Technologies Ltd., a large Bangalore-based software house. He is the author of *Software Project Management in Practice* (Addison Wesley, 2002), CMM *in Practice—Processes for Executing Software Projects at Infosys* (Addison Wesley, SEI Series on Software Engineering), *An Integrated Approach to Software Engineering* (Springer Verlag), and *Fault Tolerance in Distributed Systems* (Prentice Hall, 1994). He has published over 60 research articles. His areas of interest are software engineering and fault tolerance.

Taghi M. Khoshgoftaar is a professor of the Department of Computer Science and Engineering, Florida Atlantic University and the Director of the Empirical Software Engineering Laboratory. His research interests are in software engineering, software metrics, software reliability and quality engineering, computational intelligence, computer performance evaluation, data mining, and statistical modeling. He is a member of the Association for Computing Machinery, the IEEE Computer Society, and IEEE Reliability Society. He served as the general chair of the 1999 International Symposium on Software Reliability Engineering (ISSRE'99), and the general chair of the 2001 International Conference on Engineering of Computer Based Systems. He has served as North American editor of the Software Quality Journal, and is on the editorial boards of the journals Empirical Software Engineering, Software Quality, and Fuzzy Systems.

David Klappholz is Associate Professor of Computer Science at Stevens Institute of Technology and Associate Director of the New Jersey Center for Software Engineering. His current research interests include the assessment of individual and team skills in software development, pedagogic methods for overcoming aversion toward software development process, and empirical studies of the software development process. Earlier research interests have included the architecture of shared memory multiprocessors, implicitly parallel programming languages, and compiler optimizations. NSF, DoE, and IBM Research have funded his work, among others.

Priya Kurien is a Senior Technical Architect at Infosys Technologies Limited. She has a Masters in Information Systems from the Birla Institute of Technology and Sciences, Pilani and a Bachelors in Electronics and Communication from the College of Engineering, Guindy. Her experience includes over eight years of defining, designing and implementing IT solutions for clients across a range of industries, as well as involvement in the definition and design of processes and metrics for Infosys and its clients.

Mikael Lindvall is a scientist at Fraunhofer Center for Experimental Software Engineering, Maryland (http://fc-md.umd.edu). He specializes in work on software architecture and impact analysis as well as experience and knowledge management in software engineering. He is currently working on defining cost-efficient approaches to evaluate software architectures. He received his PhD in computer science from Linköpings University, Sweden. His PhD work was based on a commercial development project at Ericsson Radio and focused on the evolution of object-oriented systems. Contact him at mmlindvall@fc-md.umd.edu.

Aveejeet Palit is a Principal Architect with Infosys Technologies Limited. He received his Masters in Physics and Bachelors in Electrical and Electronics Engineering from Birla Institute of Technology and Science. Aveejeet has more that 13 years of industry experience in the field of Information Technology. He has consulted to organizations across US, Europe and Australia in areas of IT Strategy, Enterprise Architecture and Knowledge Management. His area of specialization is in Internet and related emerging technologies and methodologies.

Daniel Port is an Assistant Professor of Information Technology Management at the University of Hawaii, Monoa and Research Assistant Professor of Computer Science at the University of Southern California Center for Software Engineering. Research interests include Strategic Software Engineering, Empirical Software Engineering methods and models, and Software Engineering Education.

Naeem Seliya received the M.S. degree in Computer Science from Florida Atlantic University, Boca Raton, FL, USA, in 2001. He is currently a PhD candidate in the Department of Computer Science and Engineering at Florida Atlantic University. His research interests include software engineering, computational intelligence, data mining and machine learning, software measurement, software reliability and quality engineering, software architecture, computer data security, and network intrusion detection. He is a student member of the IEEE Computer Society and the Association for Computing Machinery.

Preface

In this volume, the 62nd volume in the *Advances in Computers* series, we present seven chapters that survey the ever-changing face of software development. Subtitled "Advances in Software Engineering," this volume describes new methods that are now being used to help improve the quality of software products and the efficiency of the process to produce it.

Chapter 1, entitled "An introduction to agile methods" by David Cohen, Mikael Lindvall and Patricia Costa, surveys the emerging field of agile methods. For years software development has been modeled on complex processes, such as the "waterfall model" or the "spiral model," which were expensive and time-consuming activities. The advent of the World Wide Web and the ever shortening of software development time have required companies to produce products on an ever decreasing development cycle. Companies now are required to be nimble and "agile." Along with this agility are a series of processes now known under the general term "agile methods." This chapter surveys the agile landscape.

Pankaj Jalote, Aveejeet Palit, and Priya Kurien in Chapter 2 "The Timeboxing process model for iterative software development" discuss Timeboxing. This is a process that addresses the same problem addressed by the agile methods of Chapter 1. Often development is late due to increasing and changing requirements that causes each development activity to take an increasing length of time. With Timeboxing, new software features are scheduled as part of multiple releases. Schedules are fixed with requirements for each software release being the dependent variable. This provides a way to schedule releases in a timelier manner.

Testing of software has always been the most time consuming (and expensive) activity in software development. Slicing is a technique developed about 20 years ago that simplifies some of these testing activities by subdividing the source program into just those statements that can affect the location of a programming error. In Chapter 3, David Binkley and Mark Harman survey the current slicing scene in "A survey of empirical results on program slicing."

Today, just about everything is electronic and computer controlled—from your automobile, microwave oven, television, to probably your toothbrush. Computers are ubiquitous. What sort of interface will users need for all of these devices? Chapter 4,

"Challenges in design and software infrastructure for ubiquitous computing applications" by Guruduth Banavar and Abraham Bernstein discusses how computers (and their software) may evolve in the future, as this ubiquity becomes part of the everyday social landscape of society.

In Chapter 5, "Introduction to MBASE (Model-Based [System] Architecting and Software Engineering)" by David Klappholtz and Daniel Port, the authors describe a process for again tackling some of the problems with waterfall or spiral development that were described in Chapters 1 and 2. One consistent problem is that different stakeholders (e.g., customer, developer, user) of a system have a different view of the system, which results in "model clashes" among these stakeholders. These clashes show up as incorrect specifications, design and coding defects, and testing problems. MBASE is a process for identifying such model clashes and a series of activities that clearly delineates such problems for their elimination.

Chapter 6, "Software quality estimation with case-based reasoning" by Tahgi Khoshgoftaar and Naeem Seliya looks at the problem of estimating software quality using a case-based reasoning approach. Case-based reasoning (CBR) develops a solution to a problem based upon knowledge of past cases kept in a knowledge base. In this chapter, several clustering models are used to predict the occurrence of faults in software, and CBR is used to identify the better approaches.

A data warehouse contains data consolidated, from multiple databases, over long periods of time. In the final chapter, "Data management technology for decision support systems," Surajit Chaudhuri, Umeshwar Dayal and Venkatesh Ganti survey the various components—tools to consolidate data into the data warehouse, systems to store and manage a large data warehouse, analytical tools leveraging the data warehouse—that a successful decision support system must contain. They briefly discuss the key issues underlying each one of these components, current research on these issues, and the support provided by commercial database and data warehousing systems.

The *Advances in Computers* has been published continuously since 1960, and each year from 1 to 3 volumes are published that contain some of the latest advances in the information technology area. I hope that you find the chapters in this book of interest and of value in your work or studies. If you have any suggestions of topics for future chapters, or if you wish to contribute such a chapter, I can be reached at mvz@cs.umd.edu.

Marvin Zelkowitz
University of Maryland,
College Park, MD, USA

An Introduction to Agile Methods

DAVID COHEN, MIKAEL LINDVALL, AND
PATRICIA COSTA

Fraunhofer Center for Experimental Software Engineering
4321 Hartwick rd, Suite 500
College Park, MD 20742
USA
dcohen@fc-md.umd.edu
mlindvall@fc-md.umd.edu
pcosta@fc-md.umd.edu

Abstract

Agile Methods are creating a buzz in the software development community, drawing their fair share of advocates and opponents. While some people consider agile methods the best thing that has happened to software development in recent years, other people view them as a backlash to software engineering and compare them to hacking.

The aim of this chapter is to introduce the reader to agile methods allowing him/her to judge whether or not agile methods could be useful in modern software development. The chapter discusses the history behind agile methods as well as the agile manifesto, a statement from the leaders of the agile movement. It looks at what it means to be agile, discusses the role of management, describes and compares some of the more popular agile methods, provides a guide for deciding where an agile approach is applicable, and lists common criticisms. It summarizes empirical studies, anecdotal reports, and lessons learned from applying agile methods and concludes with an analysis of various agile methods.

The target audiences for this chapter include practitioners, who will be interested in the discussion of the different methods and their applications, researchers who may want to focus on the empirical studies and lessons learned, and educators looking to teach and learn more about agile methods.

1. Introduction

The pace of life is more frantic than ever. Computers get faster every day. Start-ups rise and fall in the blink of an eye. And we stay connected day and night with our cable modems, cell phones, and Palm Pilots. Just as the world is changing, so too is the art of software engineering as practitioners attempt to keep in step with the turbulent times, creating processes that not only respond to change but embrace it.

These so-called Agile Methods are creating a buzz in the software development community, drawing their fair share of advocates and opponents. The purpose of this report is to address this interest and provide a comprehensive overview of the current State-of-the-Art, as well as State-of-the-Practice, for Agile Methods. As there is already much written about the motivations and aspirations of Agile Methods (e.g., [1]), we will emphasize the latter. Section 1 discusses the history behind the trend, as well as the Agile Manifesto, a statement from the leaders of the Agile movement [12]. Section 2 represents the State-of-the-Art and examines what it means to be Agile, discusses the role of management, describes and compares some of the more popular methods, provides a guide for deciding where an Agile approach is applicable, and lists common criticisms of Agile techniques. Section 3 represents State-of-the-Practice and summarizes empirical studies, anecdotal reports, and lessons learned. The report concludes with an Appendix A that includes a detailed analysis of various Agile Methods for the interested reader.

It is interesting to note that there is a lack of literature describing projects where Agile Methods failed to produce good results. There are a number of studies reporting poor projects due to a negligent implementation of an Agile method, but none where practitioners felt they executed properly but the method failed to deliver on its promise. This may be a result of a reluctance to publish papers on unsuccessful projects, or it may in fact be an indication that, when implemented correctly, Agile Methods work.

1.1   History

Agile Methods are a reaction to traditional ways of developing software and acknowledge the "need for an alternative to documentation driven, heavyweight software development processes" [12]. In the implementation of traditional methods, work begins with the elicitation and documentation of a "complete" set of requirements, followed by architectural and high-level design, development, and inspection. Beginning in the mid-1990s, some practitioners found these initial development steps frustrating and, perhaps, impossible [28]. The industry and technology move too fast, requirements "change at rates that swamp traditional methods" [31], and customers have become increasingly unable to definitively state their needs up front while, at the same time, expecting more from their software. As a result, several consultants have independently developed methods and practices to respond to the inevitable change they were experiencing. These Agile Methods are actually a collection of different techniques (or practices) that share the same values and basic principles. Many are, for example, based on iterative enhancement, a technique that was introduced in 1975 [9].

In fact, most of the Agile practices are nothing new [19]. It is instead the focus and values behind Agile Methods that differentiate them from more traditional methods. Software process improvement is an evolution in which newer processes build on the failures and successes of the ones before them, so to truly understand the Agile movement, we need to examine the methods that came before it.

According to Beck, the Waterfall Model [48] came first, as a way in which to assess and build for the users' needs. It began with a complete analysis of user requirements. Through months of intense interaction with users and customers, engineers would establish a definitive and exhaustive set of features, functional requirements, and non-functional requirements. This information is well-documented for the next stage, design, where engineers collaborate with others, such as database and data structure experts, to create the optimal architecture for the system. Next, programmers implement the well-documented design, and finally, the complete, perfectly designed system is tested and shipped [10].

This process sounds good in theory, but in practice it did not always work as well as advertised. Firstly, users changed their minds. After months, or even years, of collecting requirements and building mockups and diagrams, users still were not sure of what they wanted—all they knew was that what they saw in production was not quite "it." Secondly, requirements tend to change mid-development and when requirements are changed, it is difficult to stop the momentum of the project to accommodate the change. The traditional methods may well start to pose difficulties when change rates are still relatively low [14] because programmers, architects, and managers need to meet, and copious amounts of documentation need to be kept up to date to accommodate even small changes [13]. The Waterfall model was supposed to fix the problem of changing requirements once and for all by freezing requirements and not allowing any change, but practitioners found that requirements just could not be pinned down in one fell swoop as they had anticipated [10].

Incremental and iterative techniques focusing on breaking the development cycle into pieces evolved from the Waterfall model [10], taking the process behind Waterfall and repeating it throughout the development lifecycle. Incremental development aimed to reduce development time by breaking the project into overlapping increments. As with the Waterfall model, all requirements are analyzed before development begins; however, the requirements are then broken into increments of stand-alone functionality. Development of each increment may be overlapped, thus saving time through concurrent "multitasking" across the project.

While incremental development looked to offer time savings, evolutionary methods like iterative development and the Spiral Model [13] aimed to better handle changing requirements and manage risk. These models assess critical factors in a structured and planned way at multiple points in the process rather than trying to mitigate them as they appear in the project.

Iterative development breaks the project into iterations of variable length, each producing a complete deliverable and building on the code and documentation produced before it. The first iteration starts with the most basic deliverable, and each subsequent iteration adds the next logical set of features. Each piece is its own waterfall process beginning with analysis, followed by design, implementation, and finally testing. Iterative development deals well with change, as the only complete requirements necessary are for the current iteration. Although tentative requirements need to exist for the next iteration, they do not need to be set in stone until the next analysis phase. This approach allows for changing technology or the customer to change their mind with minimal impact on the project's momentum.

Similarly, the Spiral Model avoids detailing and defining the entire system upfront. Unlike iterative development, however, where the system is built piece by piece prioritized by functionality, Spiral prioritizes requirements by risk. Spiral and iterative development offered a great leap in agility over the Waterfall process, but some practitioners believed that they still did not respond to change as nimbly as necessary in the evolving business world. Lengthy planning and analysis phases, as well as a sustained emphasis on extensive documentation, kept projects using iterative techniques from being truly Agile, in comparison with today's methods.

Another important model to take into account in these discussions is the Capability Maturity Model (CMM)[1] [43], "a five-level model that describes good engineering and management practices and prescribes improvement priorities for software organizations" [41]. The model defines 18 key process areas and 52 goals for an organization to become a level 5 organization. Most software organizations' maturity level is 'Chaotic' (CMM level one) and only a few are 'Optimized' (CMM level five). CMM focuses mainly on large projects and large organizations, but can be tailored to fit small as well as large projects due to the fact that it is formulated in a very general way that fits diverse organizations' needs. The goals of CMM are to achieve process consistency, predictability, and reliability ([41]).

Ken Schwaber was one practitioner looking to better understand the CMM-based traditional development methods. He approached the scientists at the DuPont Chemical's Advanced Research Facility posing the question: "Why do the defined processes advocated by CMM not measurably deliver?" [52]. After analyzing the development processes, they returned to Schwaber with some surprising conclusions. Although CMM focuses on turning software development into repeatable, defined, and predictable processes, the scientists found that many of them were, in fact, largely unpredictable and unrepeatable because [52]:

- Applicable first principles are not present.
- The process is only beginning to be understood.
- The process is complex.
- The process is changing and unpredictable.

Schwaber, who would go on to develop Scrum, realized that to be truly Agile, a process needs to accept change rather than stress predictability [52]. Practitioners came to realize that methods that would respond to change as quickly as it arose were necessary [56], and that in a dynamic environment, "creativity, not voluminous written rules, is the only way to manage complex software development problems" [19].

Practitioners like Mary Poppendieck and Bob Charette[2] also began to look to other engineering disciplines for process inspiration, turning to one of the more innovate

---

[1]We use the terms CMM and SW-CMM interchangeably to denote the Software CMM from the Software Engineering Institute (SEI).

[2]Bob Charette's "Lean Development" method will be discussed later.

industry trends at the time, Lean Manufacturing. Started after World War II by Toyoda Sakichi, its counter-intuitive practices did not gain popularity in the United States until the early 1980s. While manufacturing plants in the United States ran production machines at 100% and kept giant inventories of both products and supplies, Toyoda kept only enough supplies on hand to run the plant for one day, and only produced enough products to fill current orders. Toyoda also tightly integrated Dr. W. Edwards Deming's Total Quality Management philosophy with his process. Deming believed that people inherently want to do a good job, and that managers needed to allow workers on the floor to make decisions and solve problems, build trust with suppliers, and support a "culture of continuous improvement of both process and products" [45]. Deming taught that quality was a management issue and while Japanese manufacturers were creating better and cheaper products, United States manufacturers were blaming quality issues on their workforce [45].

Poppendieck lists the 10 basic practices which make Lean Manufacturing so successful, and their application to software development [45]:

(1) Eliminate waste—eliminate or optimize consumables such as diagrams and models that do not add value to the final deliverable.
(2) Minimize inventory—minimize intermediate artifacts such as requirements and design documents.
(3) Maximize flow—use iterative development to reduce development time.
(4) Pull from demand—support flexible requirements.
(5) Empower workers—generalize intermediate documents, "tell developers what needs to be done, not how to do it."
(6) Meet customer requirements—work closely with the customer, allowing them to change their minds.
(7) Do it right the first time—test early and refactor when necessary.
(8) Abolish local optimization—flexibly manage scope.
(9) Partner with suppliers—avoid adversarial relationships, work towards developing the best software.
(10) Create a culture of continuous improvement—allow the process to improve, learn from mistakes and successes.

Independently, Kent Beck rediscovered many of these values in the late 1990s when he was hired by Chrysler to save their failing payroll project, Chrysler Comprehensive Compensation (C3). The project was started in the early 1990s as an attempt to unify three existing payroll systems ([55]) and had been declared a failure when Beck arrived. Beck, working with Ron Jeffries [31], decided to scrap all the existing code and start the project over from scratch. A little over a year later, a version of C3 was in use and paying employees. Beck and Jeffries were able to take a project that had been failing for years and turn it around 180 degrees. The C3 project became the first project to use eXtreme Programming [31] (discussed in detail later), relying on the same values for success as Poppendiek's Lean Programming.

Similar stories echo throughout the development world. In the early 1990s, the IBM Consulting Group hired Alistair Cockburn to develop an object-oriented development method [31]. Cockburn decided to interview IBM development teams and build a process out of best practices and lessons learned. He found that "team after successful team 'apologized' for not following a formal process, for not using high-tech [tools], for 'merely' sitting close to each other and discussing while they went," while teams that had failed followed formal processes and were confused why it hadn't worked, stating "maybe they hadn't followed it well enough" [31]. Cockburn used what he learned at IBM to develop the Crystal Methods (discussed in detail later).

The development world was changing and, while traditional methods were hardly falling out of fashion, it was obvious that they did not always work as intended in all situations. Practitioners recognized that new practices were necessary to better cope with changing requirements. And these new practices must be people-oriented and flexible, offering "generative rules" over "inclusive rules" which break down quickly in a dynamic environment [19]. Cockburn and Highsmith summarize the new challenges facing the traditional methods:

- Satisfying the customer has taken precedence over conforming to original plans.
- Change will happen—the focus is not how to prevent it but how to better cope with it and reduce the cost of change throughout the development process.
- "Eliminating change early means being unresponsive to business conditions—in other words, business failure."
- "The market demands and expects innovative, high quality software that meets its needs—and soon."

1.2   The Agile Manifesto

"[A] bigger gathering of organizational anarchists would be hard to find" Beck stated [12] when seventeen of the Agile proponents came together in early 2001 to discuss the new software developments methods. "What emerged was the Agile 'Software Development' Manifesto. Representatives from Extreme Programming (XP), SCRUM, DSDM, Adaptive Software Development, Crystal, Feature-Driven Development, Pragmatic Programming, and others sympathetic to the need for an alternative to documentation driven, heavyweight software development processes convened" [12]. They summarized their viewpoint, saying that "the Agile movement is not anti-methodology, in fact, many of us want to restore credibility to the word methodology. We want to restore a balance. We embrace modeling, but not in order to file some diagram in a dusty corporate repository. We embrace documentation, but not hundreds of pages of never-maintained and rarely used tomes. We plan, but recognize the limits of planning in a turbulent environment" [12]. The Manifesto itself reads as follows [12]:

> We are uncovering better ways of developing software by doing it and helping others do it. Through this work we have come to value:
>
> - Individuals and interaction over process and tools,
> - Working software over comprehensive documentation,
> - Customer collaboration over contract negotiation,
> - Responding to change over following a plan.
>
> That is, while there is a value in the items on the right, we value the items on the left more.

The Manifesto has become an important piece of the Agile Movement, in that it characterizes the values of Agile methods and how Agile distinguishes itself from traditional methods. Glass amalgamates the best of the Agile and traditional approaches by analyzing the Agile manifesto and comparing it with traditional values [25].

On *individuals and interaction over process and tools*: Glass believes that the Agile community is right on this point: "Traditional software engineering has gotten too caught up in its emphasis on process" [25]. At the same time "most practitioners already know that people matter more than process" [25].

On *working software over comprehensive documentation*: Glass agrees with the Agile community on this point too, although with some caveat: "It is important to remember that the ultimate result of building software is product. Documentation matters ... but over the years, the traditionalists made a fetish of documentation. It became the prime goal of the document-driven lifecycle" [25].

On *customer collaboration over contract negotiation*: Glass sympathizes with both sides regarding this statement: "I deeply believe in customer collaboration, and ... without it nothing is going to go well. I also believe in contracts, and I would not undertake any significant collaborative effort without it" [25].

On *responding to change over following a plan*: Both sides are right regarding this statement, according to Glass: "Over the years, we have learned two contradictory lessons: (1) [C]ustomers and users do not always know what they want at the outset of a software project, and we must be open to change during project execution" and (2) Requirement change was one of the most common causes of software project failure" [25].

This view, that both camps can learn from each other, is commonly held, as we will see in the next section.

1.3 Agile and CMM(I)

As mentioned above, Agile is a reaction against traditional methodologies, also known as rigorous or plan-driven methodologies [14]. One of the models often used to represent traditional methodologies is the Capability Maturity Model (CMM)[3] [43] and its replacement[4] CMMI, an extension of CMM based on the same values.[5] Not much has been written about CMMI yet, but we believe that for this discussion, what is valid for CMM is also valid for CMMI.[6]

As mentioned above, the goals of CMM are to achieve process consistency, predictability, and reliability. Its proponents claim that it can be tailored to also fit the needs of small projects even though it was designed for large projects and large organizations [41].

Most Agile proponents do not, however, believe CMM fits their needs at all. "If one were to ask a typical software engineer whether the Capability Maturity Model for Software and process improvement were applicable to Agile Methods, the response would most likely range from a blank stare to a hysterical laughter" [57]. One reason is that "CMM is a belief in software development as a defined process ... [that] can be defined in detail, [that] algorithms can be defined, [that] results can be accurately measured, and [that] measured variations can be used to refine the processes until they are repeatable within very close tolerances" [29]. "For projects with any degree of exploration at all, Agile developers just do not believe these assumptions are valid. This is a deep fundamental divide—and not one that can be reconciled to some comforting middle ground" [29].

Many Agile proponents also dislike CMM because of its focus on documentation instead of code. A "typical" example is the company that spent two years working (not using CMM though) on a project until they finally declared it a failure. Two years of working resulted in "3500 pages of use cases, an object model with hundreds of classes, thousands of attributes (but no methods), and, of course, no code" [29]. The same document-centric approach resulting in "documentary bloat that is now endemic in our field" [23] is also reported by many others.

While Agile proponents see a deep divide between Agile and traditional methods, this is not the case for proponents of traditional methods. Mark Paulk, the man behind CMM, is surprisingly positive about Agile Methods and claims that "Agile Methods address many CMM level 2 and 3 practices" [42]. XP,[7] for example, addresses most

---

[3]We use the terms CMM and SW-CMM interchangeably to denote the Software CMM from the Software Engineering Institute (SEI).

[4]CMM will be replaced by CMMI; see "How Will Sunsetting of the Software CMM® Be Conducted" at http://www.sei.cmu.edu/cmmi/adoption/sunset.html.

[5]The Personal Software Process (PSP) [33] is closely related to the CMM.

[6]E-mail conversation with Sandra Shrum, SEI.

[7]As XP is the most documented method, it often is used as a representative sample of Agile Methods.

level 2^8 and 3^9 practices, but not level 4 and 5 [41]. As a matter of fact, "most XP projects that truly follow the XP rules and practices could easily be assessed at CMM level 2 if they could demonstrate having processes for the following:" [26]

- Ensuring that the XP Rules and Practices are taught to new developers on the project.
- Ensuring that the XP Rules and Practices are followed by everyone.
- Escalating to decision makers when the XP Rules and Practices are not followed and not resolved within the project.
- Measuring the effectiveness of the XP Rules and Practices.
- Providing visibility to management via appropriate metrics from prior project QA experience.
- Knowing when the XP Rules and Practices need to be adjusted.
- Having an independent person doing the above.

Glazer adds, "with a little work on the organizational level, CMM level 3 is not far off" [26].

So according to some, XP and CMM *can* live together [26], at least in theory. One reason is that we can view XP as a software development methodology and CMM as a software management methodology. CMM tells us *what* to do, while XP tells us *how* to do it.

Others agree that there is no conflict. Siemens, for example, does not see CMM and Agility as a contradiction. Agility has become a necessity with increasing market pressure, "but should be built on top of an appropriately mature process foundation, not instead of it" [40]. Many make a distinction between "turbulent" environments and "placid" environments, and conclude that CMM is not applicable to the "turbulent" environments. These claims are based on misconceptions. "In fact, working under time pressure in the age of agility requires even better organization of the work than before!" [40].

Regarding the criticism about heavy documentation in CMM projects, Paulk replies: "over-documentation is a pernicious problem in the software industry, especially in the Department of Defense (DoD) projects" [42]. "[P]lan-driven methodologists must acknowledge that keeping documentation to a minimum useful set

---

[8]XP supports the following level 2 practices according to [41]: *requirements management, software project planning, software project tracking and oversight, software quality assurance,* and *software configuration management,* but not *software subcontract management.*

[9]XP supports the following level 3 practices according to [41]: *organization process focus, organization process definition, software product engineering, inter-group coordination,* and *peer reviews.* XP does not support the level 3 practices *training program* and *integrated software management.*

is necessary. At the same time, "practices that rely on tacit knowledge[10] ... may break down in larger teams ..." [42]. Others claim that "CMM does not require piles of process or project documentation" and there are "various organizations that successfully can manage and maintain their process with a very limited amount of paper" [40].

CMMI is the latest effort to build maturity models and consists of Process Areas (PA) and Generic Practices (GP). CMMI is similar to CMM, but more extensive in that it covers the discipline of system engineering. In an attempt to compare Agile and CMMI, Turner analyzed their values and concluded that their incompatibilities are overstated and that their strengths and weaknesses complement each other [57].

While many tired of traditional development techniques are quick to show support for the Agile movement, often as a reaction against CMM, others are more skeptical. A common criticism, voiced by Steven Rakitin, views Agile as a step backwards from traditional engineering practices, a disorderly "attempt to legitimize the hacker process" [46]. Where processes such as Waterfall and Spiral stress lengthy upfront planning phases and extensive documentation, Agile Methods tend to shift these priorities elsewhere. XP, for example, holds brief iteration planning meetings in the Planning Game to prioritize and select requirements, but generally leaves the system design to evolve over iterations through refactoring, resulting in hacking [46]. This accusation of Agile of being no more than hacking is frenetically fought [15] and in response to this criticism, Beck states: "Refactoring, design patterns, comprehensive unit testing, pair programming—these are not the tools of hackers. These are the tools of developers who are exploring new ways to meet the difficult goals of rapid product delivery, low defect levels, and flexibility" [31]. Beck says, "the only possible values are 'excellent' and 'insanely excellent' depending on whether lives are at stake or not ... You might accuse XP practitioners of being delusional, but not of being poor-quality-oriented hackers" [31]. "Those who would brand proponents of XP or SCRUM or any of the other Agile Methodologies as 'hackers' are ignorant of both the methodologies and the original definition of the term hacker" [12]. In response to the speculation that applying XP would result in a Chaotic development process (CMM level 1), one of the Agile proponents even concluded that "XP is in some ways a 'vertical' slice through the levels 2 through 5" [34].

The question whether Agile is hacking is probably less important than whether Agile and CMM(I) can co-exist. This is due to the fact that many organizations need both to be Agile and show that they are mature enough to take on certain contracts. A model that fills that need and truly combines the Agile practices and the CMM key processes has not, that we are aware of, been developed yet.

---

[10]Agile Methods rely on undocumented (tacit) knowledge and avoid documentation.

2. State-of-the-Art

This section discusses what it means to be Agile, describes a selected set of Agile Methods, and concludes with a discussion on whether an organization is ready to adopt Agile Methods.

2.1   What Does It Mean to be Agile?

The goal of Agile Methods is to allow an organization to be agile, but what does it mean to be Agile? Jim Highsmith says that being Agile means being able to "Deliver quickly. Change quickly. Change often" [31]. While Agile techniques vary in practices and emphasis, they share common characteristics, including iterative development and a focus on interaction, communication, and the reduction of resource-intensive intermediate artifacts. Developing in iterations allows the development team to adapt quickly to changing requirements. Working in close location and focusing on communication means teams can make decisions and act on them immediately, rather than wait on correspondence. Reducing intermediate artifacts that do not add value to the final deliverable means more resources can be devoted to the development of the product itself and it can be completed sooner. "A great deal of the Agile movement is about what I would call 'programmer power'" [25]. These characteristics add maneuverability to the process [18], whereby an Agile project can identify and respond to changes more quickly than a project using a traditional approach.

Cockburn and Highsmith discuss the Agile "world view," explaining "what is new about Agile Methods is not the practices they use, but their recognition of people as the primary drivers of project success, coupled with an intense focus on effectiveness and maneuverability" [19]. Practitioners agree that being Agile involves more than simply following guidelines that are supposed to make a project Agile. True agility is more than a collection of practices; it's a frame of mind. Andrea Branca states, "other processes may *look* Agile, but they won't *feel* Agile" [18].

2.2   A Selection of Agile Methods

Agile Methods have much in common, such as what they value, but they also differ in the practices they suggest. In order to characterize different methods, we will examine the following Agile Methods: Extreme Programming, Scrum, Crystal Methods, Feature Driven Development, Lean Development, and Dynamic Systems Development Methodology. We will attempt to keep the depth and breadth of our discussion consistent for each method, though it will naturally be limited by the amount of material available. XP is well-documented and has a wealth of available

Build a features list: Next, the team identifies a collection of features representing the system. Features are small items useful in the eyes of the client. They are similar to XP story cards written in a language understandable by all parties. Features should take up to 10 days to develop [28]. Features requiring more time than 10 days are broken down into subfeatures.

Plan by feature: The collected feature list is then prioritized into subsections called "design packages." The design packages are assigned to a chief programmer, who in turn assigns class ownership and responsibility to the other developers.

Design by feature & build by feature: After design packages are assigned, the iterative portion of the process begins. The chief programmer chooses a subset of features that will take 1 to 2 weeks to implement. These features are then planned in more detail, built, tested, and integrated.

Team size: Team size varies depending on the complexity of the feature at hand. DeLuca stresses the importance of premium people, especially modeling experts.

Iteration length: Up to two weeks.

Support for distributed teams: FDD is designed for multiple teams and, while it does not have built-in support for distributed environments, it should be adaptable.

Criticality: The FDD prescription does not specifically address project criticality.

2.2.5   Lean Development

Lean Development (LD), started by Bob Charette, draws on the success Lean Manufacturing found in the automotive industry in the 1980s. While other Agile Methods look to change the development process, Charette believes that to be truly Agile you need to change how companies work from the top down. Lean Development's 12 principles focus on management strategies [28]:

(1) Satisfying the customer is the highest priority.
(2) Always provide the best value for the money.
(3) Success depends on active customer participation.
(4) Every LD project is a team effort.
(5) Everything is changeable.
(6) Domain, not point, solutions.
(7) Complete, do not construct.
(8) An 80 percent solution today instead of 100 percent solution tomorrow.
(9) Minimalism is essential.
(10) Needs determine technology.

(11) Product growth is feature growth, not size growth.
(12) Never push LD beyond its limits.

Because LD is more of a management philosophy than a development process, team size, iteration length, team distribution, and system criticality are not directly addressed.

2.2.6   *Dynamic Systems Development Method*

Dynamic Systems Development Method (DSDM), according to their website,[11] is not so much a method as it is a framework. Arising in the early 1990s, DSDM is actually a formalization of RAD practices [28]. As depicted in Fig. 4, the DSDM lifecycle has six stages: Pre-project, Feasibility Study, Business Study, Functional Model Iteration, Design and Build Iteration, Implementation, and Post-project.

Pre-project: The pre-project phase establishes that the project is ready to begin, funding is available, and that everything is in place to commence a successful project.

Feasibility study: DSDM stresses that the feasibility study should be short, no more than a few weeks [54]. Along with the usual feasibility activities, this phase should determine whether DSDM is the right approach for the project.

Business study: The business study phase is "strongly collaborative, using a series of facilitated workshops attended by knowledgeable and empowered staff who can quickly pool their knowledge and gain consensus as to the priorities of the development" (http://www.dsdm.org). The result of this phase is the Business Area Definition, which identifies users, markets, and business processes affected by the system.

Functional model iteration: The functional model iteration aims to build on the high-level requirements identified in the business study. The DSDM framework works by building a number of prototypes based on risk and evolves these prototypes into the complete system. This phase and the design and build phase have a common process:

(1) Identify what is to be produced.
(2) Agree how and when to do it.
(3) Create the product.
(4) Check that it has been produced correctly (by reviewing documents, demonstrating a prototype or testing part of the system).[12]

---

[11] http://www.dsdm.org.
[12] http://www.dsdm.org.

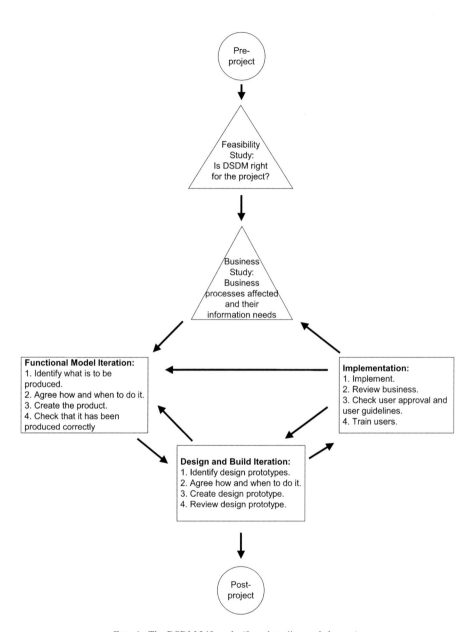

FIG. 4. The DSDM Lifecycle (from http://www.dsdm.org).

Design and build iteration: The prototypes from the functional model iteration are completed, combined, and tested and a working system is delivered to the users.

Implementation: During this phase, the system is transitioned into use. An Increment Review Document is created during implementation that discusses the state of the system. Either the system is found to meet all requirements and can be considered complete, or there is missing functionality (due to omission or time concerns). If there is still work to be done on the system, the functional model, design and build, and implementation phases are repeated until the system is complete.

Post-project: This phase includes normal post-project clean-up, as well as ongoing maintenance.

Because of DSDM's framework nature, it does not specifically address team size, exact iteration lengths, distribution, or system criticality.

2.2.7   Agile Modeling

Agile Modeling (AM) is proposed by Scott Ambler [2]. It is a method based on values, principles and practices that focus on modeling and documentation of software. AM recognizes that modeling is a critical activity for a project success and addresses how to model in an effective and Agile manner [3].

The three main goals of AM are [3]:

(1) To define and show how to put into practice a collection of values, principles and practices that lead to effective and lightweight modeling.
(2) To address the issue on how to apply modeling techniques on Agile software development processes.
(3) To address how you can apply effective modeling techniques independently of the software process in use.

AM is not a complete software development method. Instead, it focuses only on documentation and modeling and can be used with any software development process. You start with a base process and tailor it to use AM. Ambler illustrates, for example, how to use AM with both XP and Unified Process (UP) [2].

The values of AM include those of XP—communication, simplicity, feedback and courage—and also include humility. It is critical for project success that you have effective communication in your team and also with the stakeholder of the project. You should strive to develop the simplest solution that meets your needs and to get feedback often and early. You should also have the courage to make and stick to your decisions and also have the humility to admit that you may not know everything and that others may add value to your project efforts.

Following is a summary of the principles of AM [2]:

(1) *Assume simplicity*: Assume that the simplest solution is the best solution.

(2) *Content is more important than representation*: You can use "post it" notes, whiteboard or a formal document. What matters is the content.

(3) *Embrace change*: Accept the fact that change happens.

(4) *Enabling your next effort is your secondary goal*: Your project can still be a failure if you deliver it and it is not robust enough to be extended.

(5) *Everyone can learn from everyone else*: Recognize that you can never truly master something. There is always an opportunity to learn from others.

(6) *Incremental change*: Change your system a small portion at a time, instead of trying to get everything accomplished in one big release.

(7) *Know your models*: You need to know the strengths and weaknesses of models to use them effectively.

(8) *Local adaptation*: You can modify AM to adapt to your environment.

(9) *Maximize stakeholder investment*: Stakeholders have the right to decide how to invest their money and they should have a final say on how those resources are invested.

(10) *Model with a purpose*: If you cannot identify why you are doing something, why bother?

(11) *Multiple models*: You have a variety of modeling artifacts (e.g., UML diagrams, data models, user interface models, etc.).

(12) *Open and honest communication*: Open and honest communications enable people to make better decisions.

(13) *Quality work*: You should invest effort into making permanent artifacts (e.g., code, documentation) of sufficient quality.

(14) *Rapid feedback*: Prefer rapid feedback to delayed feedback whenever possible.

(15) *Software is your primary goal*: The primary goal is to produce high-quality software that meets stakeholders' needs.

(16) *Travel light*: Create just enough models and documents to get by.

(17) *Work with people's instincts*: Your instincts can offer input into your modeling efforts.

Here is a summary of the AM practices [2]:

(1) *Active stakeholder participation*: Project success requires a significant level of stakeholder involvement.

(2) *Apply modeling standards*: Developers should agree and follow a common set of modeling standards on a software project.

(3) *Apply the right artifact(s)*: Modeling artifacts (UML diagram, use case, data flow diagram, source code) have different strengths and weaknesses. Make sure you use the appropriate one for your situation.

(4) *Collective ownership*: Everyone can modify any model and artifact they need to.

(5) *Consider testability*: When modeling, always ask the question: "how are we going to test this?"

(6) *Create several models in parallel*: By creating several models you can iterate between them and select the best model that suits your needs.

(7) *Create simple content*: You should not add additional aspects to your artifacts unless they are justifiable.

(8) *Depict models simply*: Use a subset of the modeling notation available to you, creating a simple model that shows the key features you are trying to understand.

(9) *Discard temporary models*: Discard working models created if they no longer add value to your project.

(10) *Display models publicly*: Make your models accessible for the entire team.

(11) *Formalize contract models*: A contract model is always required when you are working with an external group that controls an information resource (e.g., a database) required by your system.

(12) *Iterate to another artifact*: Whenever you get "stuck" working on an artifact (if you are working with a use case and you are struggling to describe the business logic), iterate with another artifact.

(13) *Model in small increments*: Model a little, code a little, test a little and deliver a little.

(14) *Model to communicate*: One of the reasons to model is to communicate with the team or to create a contract model.

(15) *Model to understand*: The main reasons for modeling is to understand the system you are building, consider approaches and choose the best one.

(16) *Model with others*: It is very dangerous to model alone.

(17) *Prove it with code*: To determine if your model will actually work, validate your model by writing the corresponding code.

(18) *Reuse existing resources*: There is a lot of information available that modelers can reuse to their benefit.

(19) *Update only when it hurts*: Only update a model or artifact when you absolutely need to.

(20) *Use the simplest tools*: Use the simplest tool that works in your case: a napkin, a whiteboard and even CASE tools if they are the most effective for your situation.

Since AM is not a complete software process development method and should be used with other development methods, the team size, exact iteration lengths, distribution and system criticality will depend on the development process being used.

TABLE I
PRESCRIPTIVE CHARACTERISTICS

	XP	Scrum	Crystal	FDD	LD	DSDM	AM
Team size	2–10	1–7	Variable	Variable			
Iteration length	2 weeks	4 weeks	< 4 months	< 2 weeks		N/A	
Distributed support	No	Adaptable	Yes	Adaptable			
System criticality	Adaptable	Adaptable	All types	Adaptable			

2.3 Characteristics of Selected Agile Methods

Table I presents the collected prescriptive characteristics of the discussed methods. As we have seen, different Agile Methods have different characteristics. A brief comparison of Crystal Clear and XP resulted, for example, in the following [31]:

- XP pursues greater productivity through increased discipline, but it is harder for a team to follow.

- Crystal Clear permits greater individuality within the team and more relaxed work habits in exchange for some loss in productivity.

- Crystal Clear may be easier for a team to adopt, but XP produces better results if the team can follow it.

- A team can start with Crystal Clear and move to XP; a team that fails with XP can move to Crystal Clear.

2.4 Is Your Organization Ready for Agile Methods?

As we have seen, there are many Agile Methods to select from, each bringing practices that will change the daily work of the organization. Before an organization selects and implements an Agile Method, it should ponder whether or not it is ready for Agile or not. Scott Ambler discusses factors affecting successful adoption in his article *"When Does(n't) Agile Modeling Make Sense?"* [7]. Number one on his list, "Agile adoption, will be most successful when there is a conceptual fit between the organization and the Agile view. Also important for adoption are your project and business characteristics. Is your team already working incrementally? What is the team's motivation? What kind of support can the team expect?" [7]. Are there adequate resources available? How volatile are the project requirements? Barry Boehm suggests using traditional methods for projects where requirements change less than 1% per month [14].

Ambler also suggests the importance of an Agile champion—someone to tackle the team's challenges so they can work easily [7]. Boehm stresses the importance of having well-trained developers, since Agile processes tend to place a high degree of reliance on a developer's tacit knowledge [14]. The customer also needs to be devoted to the project, and must be able to make decisions. "Poor customers result in poor systems" [19]. Boehm adds, "Unless customer participants are committed, knowledgeable, collaborative, representative, and empowered, the developed products typically do not transition into use successfully, even though they may satisfy the customer" [14].

Alistair Cockburn lists a few caveats when adopting an Agile process:

- As the number of people on a project grows, there is an increased strain on communications.
- As system criticality increases, there is decreased "tolerance for personal stylistic variations."

If Agile Methods do not seem to be a good fit for your project or organization right off the bat, Ambler suggests partial adoption [7]. Look at your current development process, identify the areas that need the most improvement, and adopt Agile techniques that specifically address your target areas. After successful adoption of the chosen practices and, even better, a demonstrated improvement to your overall process, continue selecting and implementing Agile techniques until you have adopted the entire process.

3.   State-of-the-Practice

Agile Methods are gaining popularity in industry, although they comprise a mix of accepted and controversial software engineering practices. In recent years, there have been many stories and anecdotes of industrial teams experiencing success with Agile Methods. There is, however, an urgent need to empirically assess the applicability of these methods, in a structured manner, in order to build an experience base for better decision-making. In order to reach their goals, software development teams need, for example, to understand and choose the right models and techniques to support their projects. They must consider key questions such as "What is the best life-cycle model to choose for a particular project? What is an appropriate balance of effort between documenting the work and getting the product implemented? When does it pay off to spend major efforts on planning in advance and avoid change, and when is it more beneficial to plan less rigorously and embrace change?"

While previous sections of this report discussed Agile Methods from a state-of-the-art perspective, this section addresses these questions and captures the state-of-the-practice and the experiences from applying Agile Methods in different settings.

The section starts with results from an eWorkshop on Agile Methods followed by other empirical studies.

3.1   eWorkshop on Agile Methods

The goal of the Center for Empirically-Based Software Engineering (CeBASE) is to collect and disseminate knowledge on software engineering. A central activity toward achieving this goal has been the running of "eWorkshops" (or on-line meetings). The CeBASE project defined the eWorkshop [8] and has, for example, used it to collect empirical evidence on defect reduction and COTS [53]. This section is based on a paper that discusses the findings of an eWorkshop in which experiences and knowledge were gathered from, and shared between, Agile experts located throughout the world [36]. The names of these 18 participants are listed in the acknowledgments of this report.

3.1.1   Seeding the eDiscussion

For this eWorkshop, Barry Boehm's January 2002 IEEE Computer article [14], Highsmith and Cockburn's articles [30,20], and the Agile Manifesto[13] served as background material, together with material defining Agile Methods such as Extreme Programming (XP) [11], Scrum [52], Feature Driven Development (FDD) [16], Dynamic Systems Development Method (DSDM) [54], Crystal [17], and Agile Modeling [2].

Boehm brings up a number of different characteristics regarding Agile Methods compared to what he calls "Plan-Driven Methods," the more traditional Waterfall, incremental or Spiral methods. Boehm contends that Agile, as described by Highsmith and Cockburn [30], emphasizes several critical people-factors, such as amicability, talent, skill, and communication, at the same time noting that 49.99% of the world's software developers are below average in these areas. While Agile does not require uniformly highly capable people, it relies on tacit knowledge to a higher degree than plan-driven projects that emphasize documentation. Boehm argues that there is a risk that this situation leads to architectural mistakes that cannot be easily detected by external reviewers due to the lack of documentation [14].

Boehm also notes that Cockburn and Highsmith conclude that "Agile development is more difficult for larger teams" and that plan-driven organizations scale-up better [30]. At the same time, the bureaucracy created by plan-driven processes does not fit small projects either. This, again, ties back to the question of selecting the right practices for the task at hand [14].

[13]http://www.agileAlliance.org.

Boehm questions the applicability of the Agile emphasis on simplicity. XP's philosophy of YAGNI (You Aren't Going to Need It) [11] is a symbol of the recommended simplicity that emphasizes eliminating architectural features that do not support the current version. Boehm feels this approach fits situations where future requirements are unknown. In cases where future requirements are known, the risk is, however, that the lack of architectural support could cause severe architectural problems later. This raises questions like "What is the right balance between creating a grandiose architecture up-front and adding features as they are needed?" Boehm contends that plan-driven processes are most needed in high-assurance software [14]. Traditional goals of plan-driven processes such as predictability, repeatability and optimization are often characteristics of reliable safety critical software development. Knowing for what kind of applications different practices (traditional or Agile) are most beneficial is crucial, especially for safety critical applications where human lives can be at stake if the software fails.

Based on background material, the following issues were discussed:

(1) The definition of Agile.
(2) Selecting projects suitable for Agile.
(3) Introducing the method.
(4) Managing the project.

Each of these will be discussed in the following section. The full discussion summary can be found on the FC-MD web site (http://fc-md.umd.edu).

3.1.2   Definition

The eWorkshop began with a discussion regarding the definition of Agile and its characteristics, resulting in the following working definition.

Agile Methods are:

- *Iterative*: Delivers a full system at the very beginning and then changes the functionality of each subsystem with each new release.

- *Incremental*: The system as specified in the requirements is partitioned into small subsystems by functionality. New functionality is added with each new release.

- *Self-organizing*: The team has the autonomy to organize itself to best complete the work items.

- *Emergent*: Technology and requirements are "allowed" to emerge through the product development cycle.

All Agile Methods follow the four values and twelve principles of the Agile Manifesto.

3.1.3   Selecting Projects Suitable for Agile Methods

The most important factor that determines when Agile is applicable is probably project size. From the discussion it became clear that there is [28]:

- Plenty of experience of teams with up to 12 people.
- Some descriptions of teams of approximately 25 people.
- A few data points regarding teams of up to 100 people, e.g., 45 and 90-person teams.
- Isolated descriptions of teams larger than 100 people. (e.g., teams of 150 and 800 people were mentioned and documented in.

Many participants felt that any team could be Agile, regardless of its size. Alistair Cockburn argued that size is an issue. As size grows, coordinating interfaces becomes a dominant issue. Face-to-face communication breaks down and becomes more difficult and complex past 20–40 people. Most participants agreed, but think that this statement is true for any development process. Past 20–40 people, some kind of scale-up strategies must be applied.

One scale-up strategy that was mentioned was the organization of large projects into teams of teams. On one occasion, an 800-person team was organized using "scrums of scrums" [51]. Each team was staffed with members from multiple product lines in order to create a widespread understanding of the project as a whole. Regular, but short, meetings of cross-project sub-teams (senior people or common technical areas) were held regularly to coordinate the project and its many teams of teams. It was pointed out that a core team responsible for architecture and standards (also referred to as glue) is needed in order for this configuration to work. These people work actively with the sub-teams and coordinate the work.

Effective ways of coordinating multiple teams include yearly holding conferences to align interfaces, rotation of people between teams in 3-month internships, and shared test case results. Examples of strategies for coping with larger teams are documented in Jim Highsmith's Agile Software Development Ecosystems [28], in which the 800-person team is described.

There is an ongoing debate about whether or not Agile requires "good people" to be effective. This is an important argument to counter since "good people" can make just about anything happen and that specific practices are not important when you work with good people. This suggests that perhaps the success of Agile Methods could be attributed to the teams of good folks, rather than practices and principles. On the other hand, participants argued that Agile Methods are intrinsically valuable. Participants agreed that a certain percentage of experienced people are needed for a successful Agile project. There was some consensus that 25%–33% of the project personnel must be "competent and experienced."

"Competent" in this context means:

- Possess real-world experience in the technology domain.
- Have built similar systems in the past.
- Possess good people and communication skills.

It was noted that experience with actually building systems is much more important than experience with Agile development methods. The level of experience might even be as low as 10% if the teams practice pair programming [59] and if the makeup of the specific programmers in each pair is fairly dynamic over the project cycle (termed "pair rotation"). Programmers on teams that practice pair rotation have an enhanced environment for mentoring and for learning from each other.

One of the most widespread criticisms of Agile Methods is that they do not work for systems that have criticality, reliability and safety requirements. There was some disagreement about suitability for these types of projects. Some participants felt that Agile Methods work if performance requirements are made explicit early, and if proper levels of testing can be planned for. Others argue that Agile best fits applications that can be built "bare bones" very quickly, especially applications that spend most of their lifetime in maintenance.

There was also some disagreement about the best Agile Methods for critical projects. A consensus seemed to form that the Agile emphasis on testing, particularly the test-driven development practice of XP, is the key to working with these projects. Since all tests have to be passed before release, projects developed with XP can adhere to strict (or safety) requirements. Customers can write acceptance tests that measure nonfunctional requirements, but they are more difficult and may require more sophisticated environments than Unit tests.

Many participants felt that Agile Methods render it easier to address critical issues since the customer gives requirements, makes important issues explicit early and provides continual input. The phrase "responsibly responding to change" implies that there is a need to investigate the source of the change and adjust the solution accordingly, not just respond and move on. When applied right, "test first" satisfies this requirement.

3.1.4   Introducing Agile Methods: Training Requirements

An important issue is how to introduce Agile Methods in an organization and how much formal training is required before a team can start using it. A majority (though not all) of the participants felt that Agile Methods require less formal training than traditional methods. For example, pair programming helps minimize what is needed in terms of training, because people mentor each other. This kind of mentoring (by some referred to as tacit knowledge transfer) is argued to be more important than explicit training. The emphasis is rather on skill development, not on learning Agile Methods. Training on how to apply Agile Methods can many times occur as self-training. Some participants have seen teams train themselves successfully. The participants concluded that there should be enough training material available for XP, Crystal, Scrum, and FDD.

3.1.5   Project Management: Success Factors and Warning Signs

One of the most effective ways to learn from previous experience is to analyze past projects from the perspective of success factors. The three most important success factors identified among the participants were culture, people, and communication.

To be Agile is a cultural matter. If the culture is not right, then the organization cannot be Agile. In addition, teams need some amount of local control. They must have the ability to adapt working practices as they feel appropriate. The culture must also be supportive of negotiation, as negotiation forms a large part of Agile culture.

As discussed above, it is important to have competent team members. Organizations using Agile use fewer, but more competent people. These people must be trusted, and the organization must be willing to live with the decisions developers make, not consistently second-guess their decisions.

Organizations that want to be agile need to have an environment that facilitates rapid communication between team members. Examples are physically co-located teams and pair programming.

It was pointed out that organizations need to carefully implement these success factors in order for them to happen. The participants concluded that Agile Methods are most appropriate when requirements are emergent and rapidly changing (and there is always some technical uncertainty!). Fast feedback from the customer is another factor that is critical for success. In fact, Agile is based on close interaction with the customer and expects that the customer will be on-site to provide the quickest possible feedback, a critical success factor.

A critical part of project management is recognizing early warning signs that indicate that something has gone wrong. The question posed to participants was "How can management know when to take corrective action to minimize risks?"

Participants concluded that the daily meetings provide a useful way of measuring problems. As a result of the general openness of the project and because discussions of these issues are encouraged during the daily meeting, people will bring up problems. Low morale expressed by the people in the daily meeting will also reveal that something has gone wrong that the project manager must deal with. Another indicator is when "useless documentation" is produced, even though it can be hard to determine what useless documentation is. Probably the most important warning sign is when the team is falling behind on planned iterations. As a result, having frequent iterations is very important to monitor for this warning sign.

A key tenet of Agile Methods (especially in XP) is refactoring. Refactoring means improving the design of existing code without changing the functionality of the system. The different forms of refactoring involve simplifying complex statements, abstracting common solutions into reusable code, and the removal of duplicate code.

Not all participants were comfortable with refactoring the architecture of a system because refactoring would affect all internal and external stakeholders. Instead, frequent refactoring of reasonably-sized code, and minimizing its scope to keep changes more local, were recommended. Most participants felt that large-scale refactoring is not a problem, since it is frequently necessary and more feasible using Agile Methods. Participants strongly felt that traditional "Big Design Up Front (BDUF)" is rarely on target, and its lack of applicability is often not fed back to the team that created the BDUF, making it impossible for them to learn from experience. It was again emphasized that testing is the major issue in Agile. Big architectural changes do not need to be risky, for example, if a set of automated tests is provided as a "safety net."

Product and project documentation is a topic that has drawn much attention in discussions about Agile. Is any documentation necessary at all? If so, how do you determine how much is needed? Scott Ambler commented that documentation becomes out of date and should be updated only "when it hurts." Documentation is a poor form of communication, but is sometimes necessary in order to retain critical information. Many organizations demand more documentation than is needed. The organizations' goal should be to communicate effectively, and documentation should be one of the last options to fulfill that goal. Barry Boehm mentioned that project documentation makes it easier for an outside expert to diagnose problems. Kent Beck disagreed, saying that, as an outside expert who spends a large percentage of his time diagnosing projects, he is looking for people "stuff" (like quiet asides) and not technical details. Bil Kleb said that with Agile Methods, documentation is assigned a cost and its extent is determined by the customer (excepting internal documentation). Scott Ambler suggested his Agile Documentation essay as good reference for this topic [4].

3.2   Lessons Learned

Several lessons can be learned from this discussion that should prove to be useful to those considering applying Agile Methods in their organization. These lessons should be carefully examined and challenged by future projects to identify the circumstances in which they hold and when they are not applicable.

Any team could be Agile, regardless of the team size, but should be considered because greater numbers of people make communication more difficult. Much has been written about small teams, but less information is available regarding larger teams, for which scale-up strategies are necessary.

- Experience is important for an Agile project to succeed, but experience with actually building systems is much more important than experience with Agile Methods. It was estimated that 25%–33% of the project personnel must be "competent and experienced," but the necessary percentage might even be as low as 10% if the teams practice pair programming due to the fact that they mentor each other.

- Agile Methods require less formal training than traditional methods. Pair programming helps minimize what is needed in terms of training, because people mentor each other. Mentoring is more important than regular training that can many times be completed as self-training. Training material is available in particular for XP, Crystal, Scrum, and FDD.

- Reliable and safety-critical projects can be conducted using Agile Methods. Performance requirements must be made explicit early, and proper levels of testing must be planned. It is easier to address critical issues using Agile Methods since the customer gives requirements, sets explicit priorities early and provides continual input.

- The three most important success factors are culture, people, and communication. Agile Methods need cultural support, otherwise they will not succeed. Competent team members are crucial. Agile Methods use fewer, but more competent, people. Physically co-located teams and pair programming support rapid communication. Close interaction with the customer and frequent customer feedback are critical success factors.

- Early warning signs can be spotted in Agile projects, e.g., low morale expressed during the daily meeting. Other signs are production of "useless documentation" and delays of planned iterations.

- Refactoring should be done frequently and of reasonably-sized code, keeping the scope down and local. Large-scale refactoring is not a problem, and is more feasible using Agile Methods. Traditional "BDUF" is a waste of time and doesn't lead to a learning experience. Big architectural changes do not need to be risky if a set of automated tests is maintained.

- Documentation should be assigned a cost and its extent be determined by the customer. Many organizations demand more than is needed. The goal should be to communicate effectively and documentation should be the last option.

In another eWorkshop, the following experiences were reported regarding Agile and CMM:

- At Boeing, XP was used before CMM was implemented and they were able to implement the spirit of the CMM without making large changes to their software processes. They used XP successfully, and CMM helped introduce the Project Management Discipline.

- Asea Brown Boveri (ABB) is introducing XP while transitioning from CMM to CMMI worldwide. They are in the opposite position from Boeing: CMM(I) was introduced several years before XP, which is true for their corporate research centers as well as for business units.

- NASA Langley Research Center reported a better match with CMM and Agile when the CMM part is worded generally, as in "follow a practice of choice," and not delving into specifics such as, "must have spec sheet 5 pages long."

- ABB added that their organization has adopted the CMMI framework and they are incorporating Agile practices into the evolutionary development lifecycle model. They believe that there is a clear distinction between life cycle models and continuous process improvement models such as CMMI and both are not incompatible. No incompatibilities between Agile and CMM were reported [37].

3.3   Case Studies

Another important source of empirical data is case studies. In this section, we report from a selected number of case studies on different aspects of applying Agile Methods.

3.3.1   Introducing XP

Karlström reports on a project at Online Telemarketing in Lund, Sweden, where XP was applied [35]. The report is based both on observation and interviews with the team that applied XP. The project was a success despite the fact that the customer had a very poor idea of the system at the beginning of the project. All XP practices were practically introduced. The ones that worked the best were: planning game, collective ownership, and customer on site. They found small releases and testing difficult to introduce.

Online Telemarketing is a small company specializing in telephone-based sales of third party goods. It had recently been expanded internationally and management realized that a new sales support system would be required. COTS alternatives were investigated and discarded because they were expensive, and incorporating desired functionality was difficult. The lack of detailed requirements specifications from management, and the lack of a similar system, motivated the use of XP.

The system was developed in Visual Basic, and it had 10K lines of code. The development started in December 2000 and the first functional system was launched in April 2001. The product has been in operation since August 2001.

The senior management at Online Telemarketing assumed the role of a customer. Configuration management started without a tool and developers were supposed to copy the files to a directory. This worked when they had two developers. When the team grew, they added a text file to manage copies to checkout directory. This solution still presented problems when the developers were out or working different schedules. Once the communication issues were resolved the solution worked.

The following experiences were reported:

(1) *The planning game*: In total, 150 stories were implemented. Stories were added during the whole project. In the beginning, time estimates were inaccurate, but became better after a few weeks passed. Breaking the stories into tasks was hard for the developers, causing them to create too detailed stories. It was hard to set a common level of detail for the stories. In the end, this practice proved to be one of the greatest successes.

(2) *Small releases*: The first iteration took too long because of the lack of experience with XP. Once a complete bare system was implemented, it was easier to implement small releases. During the long initial release, they tried to maintain the communication between the developers and the customer, to avoid mistakes in development.

(3) *Metaphor*: They used a document that was an attempt at a requirements document, before they decided to use XP and their metaphor. As the project progressed, the document was not updated.

(4) *Simple design*: The development team stressed implementing the simplest possible solution at all times. They thought that this practice saved them time when a much larger solution would be implemented, avoiding unnecessary code.

(5) *Testing*: Test-first was difficult to implement at first and VBUnit was hard to learn and set up. When the time pressure increased, the developers started to ignore test-first. Although they saw the benefits, it involved too much work. Since it was hard to write tests for the GUI and the team thought that mastering a GUI testing tool would take too long, they decided to test the GUI manually. The customer tested the functionality of the system before each release, and when a problem was found a correction card was created.

(6) *Refactoring*: No tools for refactoring were used, and the team performed minor refactoring continuously. No major refactoring of the code was performed.

(7) *Pair programming*: They used pair programming at all times. At first the developers were not comfortable, but later they started to work naturally and

efficiently in pairs. The developers were inexperienced, which might be why they felt uncomfortable. The lead developer thought that they produced code faster in pairs than they would have if working alone.

(8) *Collective ownership*: This practice worked well. The developers avoided irritations by thinking of bugs as group issues instead of as someone's defect. The configuration management, however, was not very effective and sometimes developers were afraid to change code if not in direct contact with others.

(9) *Continuous integration*: This practice was natural in the development environment. As soon as the code was finished, it was integrated.

(10) *40-hour week*: Since the developers were part-time, this practice was adjusted and followed.

(11) *On site-customer*: This practice worked well, despite some schedule conflicts because the developers were part-time and the customer was played by busy senior managers.

(12) *Coding standards*: A coding standard document was developed in the beginning of the project and updated when needed. Over time, developers became a little relaxed in following the standards, but once this was identified as an issue, it was reinforced.

3.3.2 Launching XP at a Process-Intensive Company

Grenning reports experiences from the introduction of an adaptation of XP in an organization with a large formal software development process [27]. The task was to build a new system to replace an existing safety-critical legacy system. The new system was an embedded-systems application running on Windows NT.

The system was divided into subsystems developed by different units. The author was called to help one of these units. The author was very enthusiastic about XP and decided to convince the team to apply some of the techniques.

The company already had a process in place that added a lot of overhead to the development because requirements were partially defined and deadlines were tight.

Recognizing that the organization culture believed in up-front requirements and designs followed by reviews and approvals, the team decided to "choose their battles" and introduce the practices that would be most beneficial for the project. One major issue was documentation. How much documentation was sufficient? The team would be developing a piece that was supposed to work with pieces being developed by other teams using the standard process at the organization. They identified that they needed enough documentation to define the product requirements, sustain technical reviews and support the system's maintainers. Clean and understandable source code and some form of interface documentation was necessary due to the need to collaborate with other teams. XP recognizes that documentation has a cost and that incomplete documentation might be cost-effective, but choosing not to create any documentation would be unacceptable in this environment.

When proposing the new approach to management, story cards appeared unacceptable and the team decided to use cases instead of story cards. The management was concerned with future maintenance of the system; if the system was transitioned to another team, more than readable code would be needed. After some discussions, the team decided to create high-level documentation at the end of the project, instead of documenting in the beginning followed by updates during the project. The management, however, still wanted to be able to review the design. The proposed solution was to document the design decisions and have them reviewed at the end of every month. This removed the review from the critical path of the project.

Despite compromising on a few issues, the team got permission to apply test-first, pair programming, short iterations, continuous integration, refactoring, planning, and team membership for the customer.

According to Grenning, at the project's conclusion, the programmers were happy with their creation. After the fourth iteration the project manager was satisfied. The reason is that they already had working code at a point when their regular process would have produced only three documents. The project manager also recognized that dependencies between the features were almost non-existent since they followed the customer's priorities and not the priorities dictated by a big design up front. The team was Agile and able to adapt to other subsystems' changing needs.

Grenning points out the importance of including senior team members because they "spread the wealth of knowledge, and both they (senior people) and their pair partners learn" [27]. Despite the fact that the project was terminated due to changes in the market, the management was very pleased with results and two other pilot projects were started.

At the end of the report, the author gives advice to management and developers willing to try XP. For managers, it is important to try XP on a team with open-minded leaders, encourage XP practices, and recruit a team that wants to try XP instead of forcing a team to use XP. For developers, the advice is to identify the problems that they might solve, develop a sales pitch and do a pilot project [27].

3.3.3   Using XP in a Maintenance Environment

Poole and Huisman report their experience with introducing XP in Iona Technologies [44]. Because of its rapid growth and time-to-market pressures, the engineering team often ignored engineering practices. As a result, they ended up with a degenerated code that was salvaged in reengineering efforts that led to XP.

As part of the improvement effort, they used a bug-tracking tool to identify problem areas of the code. The code was cleaned through the elimination of used code and the introduction of patterns that made it easier to test, maintain and understand the code. As part of this effort, one lead engineer promoted stronger engineering practices making engineers constantly consider how they could improve the quality of their code. Testing of the whole system was also automated. After all these transformations, the company saw a lot of improvement. Despite their progress, however, they still had issues to resolve regarding testing, visibility, morale and personal work practices. They already had a maintenance process in place that had a lot in common with XP practices, so they decided to apply XP in order to solve the remaining issues.

All bugs reported by customers, enhancement requirements, and new functional requirements are documented. That documentation is accessible by both customers and the team. They do not use index cards for the requirements and the requirements are not in the form of user stories yet. Index cards are used to track tasks and those tasks are added to storyboards. The developers estimate the tasks, and the customers prioritize them. When the tasks are finished, they are removed from the storyboard, recorded in a spreadsheet and the cards are archived in the task log. They also introduced daily stand-up meetings to increase visibility and also stimulate communication among the team members.

They automated their whole testing process, making it possible to test the whole system with the click of a button. All engineers are supposed to test the whole system after changes are made to ensure nothing was broken.

They report that convincing programmers to do pair programming is extremely difficult. Luckily, their pair programming experience came to them by accident. In 2000, a customer engineer working with them paired with the developers. The experience was good, the team felt that they worked more effectively, the overall productivity was high and morale improved. They are now trying to formally introduce pair programming.

Increments are kept short and they continuously produce small releases. Refactoring has also been extensively applied, which can be seen in the code reviews. Engineers are encouraged to identify areas of the code that are candidates for refactoring, and they follow up after delivery with a refactoring task in the storyboard. In order to improve communications, they also changed the workspace to make pair programming easier and facilitate discussions of their ideas on whiteboards.

The effort seemed to pay off and the productivity increase is noticeable. In their point of view the greatest benefit to the team has been the increase in visibility. The storyboards let people see what others are doing and help management track progress and plan.

They conclude the paper pointing out that the application of pair programming and collection of metrics can improve their process. They believe that improving the pair programming initiative can improve their lack of cross-training among the code base's many modules. The metrics are critical to the planning game, since estimating how long a story will take requires finding a similar story in the past and researching how long it took. Currently they are tracking estimates and actuals on a spreadsheet and are working to integrate this into their defect tracking system.

3.3.4   XP's "Bad Smells"

In an attempt to provide early warning signals ("bad smells") when applying XP, Elssamadisy and Schalliol analyzed a three-year project involving 30 developers (50 in total) that produced about 500,000 lines of executable code [24]. The project switched to XP due to previous experiences with ineffective traditional methods. The lessons learned from the experience of applying XP can be useful to others:

- Customers are typically happy during early iterations but later begin to complain about many things from all iterations. The customer needs to be coached to provide early and honest feedback. Elssamadisy and Schalliol suggest they think like buying a tailored suit in which you cannot just have measurements taken at the beginning.

- Programmers are typically not sure of how functionality works together. Large complex systems require a good metaphor or overview.

- Everyone claims the story cards are finished, yet it requires weeks of full-time development to deliver a quality application. The solution is to create a precise list of tasks that must be completed before a story is finished, and make sure programmers adhere to the rules: Acknowledge poorly estimated stories and reprioritize. Do not rush to complete them and cut corners with refactoring or testing.

The authors concluded pointing out that the team needs to be conscious of the process the whole time, and that laziness will affect the whole team.

3.3.5   Introducing Scrum in Organizations

Cohn and Ford [22] have successfully introduced Scrum to seven organizations over a period of four years. They discuss their lessons learned, as well as mistakes.

In several cases they encountered resistance from developers who preferred to develop non-code artifacts and from those who "valued their contribution to a project by the number of meetings attended in a given day" [22]. Some even tried to put more documentation back into the process. The solution used by the authors is to not intervene and instead let peers decide whether to adopt suggestions or not.

The authors were surprised to find that many developers view Agile Methods as micromanagement. In traditional projects, developers meet the project manager once a week, but in an Agile environment they meet daily. To change developers' perceptions, the project manager has to show that he is there to remove obstacles, not to complain about missed deadlines and must not be judgmental when developers report that they will be delayed with their tasks.

Distributed development has been successful, and the authors believe that methods other than Scrum can also be used in distributed environments. They propose waiting two or three months until developers get used to Agile development before implementing distributed development. In order for distributed development to work, many people must be brought together for the first few weeks of the project.

Experience shows that Agile Methods require good developers and that "productivity difference matters most when two programmers are writing code ... [it is] irrelevant during those times when both are, for example, trapped in an unnecessary meeting" [22]. When fully engaged, a team will move quickly. If there are too many slow people, the whole team will slow down or move forward without them.

One team was overly zealous and did not anticipate productivity decrease during transition and did not use forethought well enough. The conclusion is that "this team did not have the discipline required for XP and, while paying lip service to XP, they were actually doing nothing more than hacking" [22].

The authors' experience is that testers are even more prone to view Agile as micromanagement. In typical organizations, testers do not receive much attention from managers and are not used to the extra attention they get in Agile processes. Involving testers in the daily routine as soon as possible poses one solution, but they should not write code or unit tests for programmers.

A common experience is that managers are reluctant to give up the feeling of control they get from documents typically generated by document-driven methodologies. The solution is to show where past commitments have been incorrect (time/date/cost/functionality), so that management can be convinced to try Agile Methods.

A surprising experience is that the Human Resource (HR) department can be involved in a project adopting Agile processes. The authors experienced several cases where HR received complaints by developers who did not like the process. For example, they received specific complaints regarding pair programming. Working with and informing HR beforehand so that they are prepared to deal with issues that might appear, can prevent this situation.

3.3.6   Lessons in Agility from Internet-Based Development

Scott Ambler describes two different approaches for developing software in two successful Internet startups that provided insights to what later became Agile Modeling [6].

The two companies were growing and needed to redesign their systems. They wanted to use an accredited software development process like Rational Unified

Process (RUP) to gain the trust of investors, while at the same time they wanted a process that would not impose a lot of bureaucracy that might slow them down. In both organizations, management and some members of the development team wanted more modeling; others thought it was a waste of time. Ambler calls the companies XYZ and PQR.

XYZ used an approach of modeling in teams. The team would design by whiteboarding. In the beginning, they were uncomfortable with whiteboarding and tried to use CASE tools instead, but they later discovered that whiteboarding was more efficient because a modeling language did not limit them and they could more quickly express their ideas.

PQR decided to hire a chief architect. The architect talked to members of the team, and designed privately. Later he published his results on the web and members of the team gave him feedback.

Both organizations developed in a highly interactive manner and released incrementally in short cycles. Both generated documentation in HTML and learned that design and documentation are separate activities. XYZ's architecture was developed more quickly, since lots of people worked in parallel. XYZ's architecture found greater acceptance since the development team participated in the architectural team. PQR's approach led to lower costs, since the chief architect worked alone. The chief architect also provided a single source control that sometimes caused a bottleneck in the process. Both approaches resulted in scalable architecture that met the needs of the organization, and both approaches worked well within a RUP environment.

Ambler shares the lessons learned from these approaches:

- People matter and were key to the success, in accordance with the Agile Manifesto: "value of individuals over processes and tools" [12].

- You do not need as much documentation as you think. Both organizations created only documentation that was useful and needed.

- Communication is critical. Less documentation led to greater communication.

- Modeling tools are not as useful as you think. The organizations tried to use UML modeling tools, but the tools generated more documentation than needed and were limited to the UML language. White boards and flipcharts, on the other hand, were very useful.

- You need a variety of modeling techniques in your toolkit. Since UML was not sufficient, both companies needed to perform process-, user interface- and data-modeling.

- Big up-front design is not required. Both organizations quickly began work without waiting months for detailed modeling and documentation before they started.

- Reuse the wheel, do not reinvent it. At XYZ, they took advantage of open source whenever possible.

3.3.7   Agile Modeling and the Unified Process

Ambler presents a case study of the introduction of a combination of Agile Modeling and Rational Unified Process [5]. The method was introduced in a small project. Failure would be noticeable, but would not jeopardize the whole organization. Ambler points out the importance of the organization's will to change in the success of the introduction.

Different people on the team with different backgrounds had various reactions to the method. For example, one member of the team was used to Big Design Up Front and had a hard time doing an incremental design and development. Others felt more comfortable. Management was involved and interested in the effort and satisfied to see constant progress in the project.

While whiteboards made sense to the team members, they were not comfortable with index cards and post it notes. They needed a document using the appropriate tools (Together/J, Microsoft Visio, etc.). In Ambler's opinion, the team produced too much documentation. This is, however, not necessarily negative since documenting increased their comfort level during the transition.

3.4   Other Empirical Studies

In this section we discuss a selected set of experiments and surveys on Agile Methods.

3.4.1   XP in a Business-to-Business (B2B) Start-up

In the paper "Extreme adoption experiences of a B2B start-up" [32], the authors report from a case study in which two nearly identical projects used XP and non-XP practices. The XP-project delivered the same amount of functionality during a shorter period of time and required considerably less effort than the non-XP project. The XP project also increased code quality with test-first, resulting in a 70% reduction in bugs and increased architectural quality. The value of the study is questionable, however, as the non-XP project was stopped 20 months into the project "because of excessive costs of ownership" [32] and the XP project "was suspended after nine months of development" [32]. The conclusions are thus based on extrapolations of the unfinished projects and not on complete projects.

3.4.2 Empirical Experiments with XP

In order to compare XP and traditional methodologies, the authors ran a pilot XP experiment [39]. The study involved eighty 2nd year undergraduate students as part of a project for real clients. The students were divided into fifteen teams working for three clients. During five weeks, each of the three clients described what their software needs were. After that, the software was developed. Some teams used XP while others did not. At the end of the semester, five versions of the system that each of the clients had specified were produced. The clients evaluated the quality of the systems without knowing which systems were developed using XP and which ones were not.

This experiment demonstrated that the XP teams generated more useful documentation and better manuals than the other teams. Two of the three clients found that the best external factors were in the products produced by the XP teams. The lecturers concluded that the products delivered by the XP teams possessed better internal qualities.

3.4.3 Survey Conducted by Cutter Consortium

Cockburn and Highsmith mention results from a survey conducted by the Cutter Consortium in 2001. Two hundred people from organizations all over the world responded to the survey [20]. The findings pointed out by Cockburn and Highsmith are:

- Compared to a similar study in 2000, many more organizations were using at least one Agile Method.
- In terms of business performance, customer satisfaction and quality, Agile Methods showed slightly better results than traditional methods.
- Agile Methods lead to better employee morale.

3.4.4 Quantitative Survey on XP Projects

Rumpe and Schröder report the results of a survey conducted in 2001 [49]. Forty-five participants involved in XP projects from companies of various sizes and different international locations completed the survey. Respondents had different levels of experience and participated in finished and in-progress projects using XP.

The main results of the survey indicate that most projects were successful and all of the developers would use XP on the next project if appropriate. The results also indicate that most problems are related to resistance to change: developers refused to do pair programming and managers were skeptical, etc. Common code ownership, testing and continuous integration were the most useful practices. Less used and most difficult to apply were metaphor and on-site customer. The success factors most often mentioned were testing, pair programming and the focus of XP on the right goals.

The authors point out potential problems with the survey. XP might be deemed successful due to the fact that the respondents were happy with XP. Others that had bad experiences with XP might not have been reached or did not answer. Also, early adopters tend to be highly motivated, which may be responsible for projects' success.

Interestingly, the results showed that there are larger projects that use XP. From the total of responses:

- 35.6% teams had up to 5 people,
- 48.9% teams had up to 10 people,
- 11.1% teams had up to 15 people, and
- 4.4% teams had up to 40 people.

The survey asked respondents to rate project progress and results relative to traditional approaches on a scale from 5 (much better) to −5 (much worse). On average, respondents rated the cost of late changes, the quality of results, the fun factor of work, and on-time delivery higher than a three on this scale. No negative ratings were given. The authors divided the results between the finished and ongoing projects. It is interesting to note that both the cost of change and quality were deemed less positive by the finished projects than the ongoing ones. The authors suggest that this sustains the fact that changes in later phases still have higher costs.

3.4.5   How to Get the Most Out of XP and Agile Methods

Reifer reports the results of a survey of thirty-one projects that used XP/Agile Methods practices [47]. The goals of the survey were to identify the practices being used, their scope and conditions, the costs and benefits of their use and lessons learned.

Most projects were characterized by small teams (less than ten participants), with the exception of one project that had thirty engineers. All projects were low-risk and lasted one-year or less. The primary reason for applying XP/Agile Methods was to decrease time-to-market.

Startup seemed most difficult for the majority of the organizations: Enthusiastic staff that wanted to try new techniques needed to convince management. Practices introduced in pilot projects represented low-risk to the organization.

The projects noticed an average gain of 15%–23% in productivity, 5%–7% cost reduction on average and 25%–50% reduction in time to market.

The paper also points out 4 success factors:

- *Proper domain fit*: XP/Agile Methods have been recognized as working best on small projects, where systems being developed are precedent, requirements are stable and architecture is well established.

- *Suitable state of organizational readiness*: XP/Agile requires a cultural change. Make sure the workforce is well trained and educated.

- *Process focus*: Adapt and refine instead of throwing away what you have. Agile projects work best when integrated into an existing framework.

- *Appropriate practice set*: Do not be afraid to put new practices in place when they are needed to get the job done.

3.4.6   Costs and Benefits of Pair Programming

Pair Programming, one of the key practices of XP, marks a radical departure from traditional methods and has been the focus of some controversy. Pair programming has been argued to improve quality of software and improve successes of projects by increasing communication in the teams. Others, however, are skeptical because it seems to take two people to do the work of one, and some developers do not feel comfortable working in pairs. Pros and cons, as well as main concepts, best practices, and practical advice to successfully apply Pair Programming, are discussed in a paper based on an experiment at the University of Utah where one third of the class developed the projects individually and the rest developed in pairs. The results were analyzed from the point of views of economics, satisfaction, and design quality [21].

- *Economics*: The results showed that the pairs only spent 15% more time to program than the individuals and the code produced by pairs had 15% fewer defects. Thus, pair programming can be justified purely on economic grounds since the cost of fixing defects is high.

- *Satisfaction*: Results from interviews with individuals who tried pair programming were analyzed. Although some were skeptical and did not feel comfortable at first, most programmers enjoyed the experience.

- *Design quality*: In the Utah study, the pairs not only completed their projects with better quality but also implemented the same functionality in fewer lines of code. This is an indication of better design.

Other benefits of pair programming are continuous reviews, problem solving, learning, and staff and project management [21]:

- *Continuous reviews*: Pair programming serves as a continual design and code review that helps the removal of defects.

- *Problem solving*: The teams found that, by developing in pairs, they had the ability to solve problems faster.
- *Learning*: The teams emphasized how much they learned from each other by doing pair programming. Pair programmers often mention that they also learned to discuss and work together, improving team communications and effectiveness.
- *Staff and project management*: From the staff and project management point of view, since people are familiar with each piece of code, staff-loss risks are reduced.

Pair programming is further discussed in a new book by Williams and Kessler [58].

4. Conclusions

Agile Methods are here to stay, no doubt about it. Agile Methods will probably not "win" over traditional methods but live in symbiosis with them. While many Agile proponents see a gap between Agile and traditional methods, many practitioners believe this narrow gap can be bridged. Glass even thinks that "[t]raditionalists have a lot to learn from the Agile folks" and that "traditional software engineering can be enriched by paying attention to new ideas springing up from the field" [25].

Why will Agile Methods not rule out traditional methods?

Agile Methods will not out rule traditional methods because diverse processes for software engineering are still needed. Developing software for a space shuttle is not the same as developing software for a toaster [38]. Not to mention that the need to maintain software, typically a much bigger concern than development, also differs according to the circumstances [50]. Software maintenance is, however, not an issue discussed in Agile circles yet, probably because it is too early to draw any conclusions on how Agile Methods might impact software maintenance.

So what is it that governs what method to use?

One important factor when selecting a development method is the number of people involved, i.e., project size. The more people involved in the project, the more rigorous communication mechanisms need to be. According to Alistair Cockburn, there is one method for each project size, starting with Crystal Clear for small projects and, as the project grows larger, the less Agile the methods become [17].

Other factors that have an impact on the rigor of the development methods are application domain, criticality, and innovativeness [25]. Applications that may endanger human life, like manned space missions, must, for example, undergo much stricter quality control than less critical applications. At the same time, a traditional method might kill projects that need to be highly innovative and are extremely sensitive to changes in market needs.

In conclusion, the selection of a method for a specific project must be very careful, taking into consideration many different factors, including those mentioned above. In many cases, being both Agile and stable at the same time will be necessary. A contradictory combination, it seems, and therefore extra challenging, but not impossible. As Siemens states, "We firmly believe that agility is necessary, but that it should be built on top of an appropriately mature process foundation, not instead of it" [40].

Where is Agile going?

Agile is currently an umbrella concept encompassing many different methods. XP is the most well known Agile Method. While there may always be many small methods due to the fact that their proponents are consultants who need a method to guide their work, we expect to see some consolidation in the near future. We compare the situation to events in the object-oriented world in the 1990s, where many different gurus promoted their own methodology. In a few years, Rational, with Grady Booch, became the main player on the method market by recruiting two of the main gurus: James Rumbaugh (OMT) and Ivar Jacobsson (Objectory). Quickly the "three amigos" abandoned the endless debates regarding whose method was superior, which mainly came down to whether objects are best depicted as clouds (Booch), rectangles (OMT), or circles (Objectory), and instead formed a unified alliance to quickly become the undisputed market leader for object-oriented methods. We speculate that the same can happen to the Agile Methods, based, for example, on the market-leader XP. Even if the Agile consolidation is slow or non-existent, what most likely will happen, independent of debates defining what is and is not Agile, practitioners will select and apply the most beneficial Agile practices. They will do so simply because Agile has proven that there is much to gain from using their approaches and because of the need of the software industry to deliver better software, faster and cheaper.

ACKNOWLEDGEMENTS

This book chapter was based on a State-of-the-Art Report entitled "Agile Software Development" authored by the same authors and produced by DoD Data & Analysis Center for Software (DACS).

We would like to recognize our expert contributors who participated in the first eWorkshop on Agile Methods and thereby contributed to the section on State-of-the-Practice:

Scott Ambler (Ronin International, Inc.),
Ken Auer (RoleModel Software, Inc.),
Kent Beck (founder and director of the Three Rivers Institute),
Winsor Brown (University of Southern California),
Alistair Cockburn (Humans and Technology),
Hakan Erdogmus (National Research Council of Canada),
Peter Hantos (Xerox), Philip Johnson (University of Hawaii),
Bil Kleb (NASA Langley Research Center),
Tim Mackinnon (Connextra Ltd.),
Joel Martin (National Research Council of Canada),
Frank Maurer (University of Calgary),
Atif Memon (University of Maryland and Fraunhofer Center for Experimental
    Software Engineering),
Granville (Randy) Miller (TogetherSoft),
Gary Pollice (Rational Software),
Ken Schwaber (Advanced Development Methods, Inc. and one of the developers
    of Scrum),
Don Wells (ExtremeProgramming.org),
William Wood (NASA Langley Research Center).

We also would like to thank our colleagues who helped arrange the eWorkshop and
co-authored that same section:

Victor Basili, Barry Boehm, Kathleen Dangle, Forrest Shull, Roseanne Tesoriero,
Laurie Williams, Marvin Zelkowitz.

We would like to thank Jen Dix for proof reading this chapter.

Appendix A: An Analysis of Agile Methods

'Agile' has become a buzzword in the software industry. Many methods and processes are referred to as 'Agile,' making it difficult to distinguish between one and the next. There is a lack of literature on techniques with which to compare software development methods, so we have developed processes through which to draw this comparison. This technique will not be the focus of this section, nor do we guarantee its comprehensiveness, but we found it adequate for our analysis, which we will discuss in detail below.

While conducting our research, we found it difficult to distinguish between methods in respect to which aspect of software development each method targeted. To help with our own understanding, we decided to examine each method in terms of what activities it supports, and to what extent. All methods, whether traditional or Agile, address the following project aspects to varying degrees: development support, management support, communications support, and decision-making support.

Although critics may find more project areas missing from this list, these are the four we felt were most critical for Agile Methods.

The next obstacle was to find a basis for comparison between methods. For this, we decided to use each method's core practices or rules. This method for comparison does have its drawbacks:

- Some methods, like XP, have a discrete collection of practices while others, like Scrum, are not as clearly delineated.

- Processes such as Lean Development (LD) present more principles than practices. LD's "Satisfying the customer is the highest priority" principle, for instance, is stated at a much more abstract level than Scrum's Constant Testing practice.

- Relying on a method's stated core practices naturally leaves a lot of the method behind. Daily standup meetings practiced in XP are not explicitly stated in the 12 practices but, nonetheless, emphasize XP's attention to communication.

Despite these acknowledged limitations, we feel each method's core practices or principles provide a good representation of the method's focus. Researchers interested in pursuing further this line of analysis may want to explore how to adequately represent and compare methods and processes.

We began by breaking the support groups (development, management, communication, decision-making) into smaller subsections for easier analysis. Development was redefined as requirements collection/analysis, design, coding, testing/integration, and maintenance. Management was clarified as project management. Communication was split into developer-customer, developer-manager, and developer-developer communication. Decision-making was separated into release planning, design & development, and project management.

A survey was conducted asking five experts to classify the core practices of XP, Scrum, Lean Development, FDD, and DSDM. The results were averaged and color-coded in an attempt to create easily readable results. Support agreement of more than 60% is black, 0–59% is white, and 0% (all experts agreed there is no support) is gray. A brief explanation of well-supported (black) aspects follows each chart.

A.1 Extreme Programming

XP was the method best understood by our experts; all five responded. XP's practices are abbreviated as: The Planning Game (PG), Small Releases (SR), The Metaphor (M), Simple Design (SD), Test-First Development (TF), Refactoring (R), Pair Programming (PP), Continuous Integration (CI), Collective Code Ownership (CO), On-Site Customer (OC), 40-Hour Work Week (WW), and Open Workspace (OW).

TABLE II
XP DEVELOPMENT SUPPORT

	PG	SR	M	SD	TF	R	PP	CI	CCO	OSC	WW	OW
Requirements												
Design												
Coding												
Testing/ Integration												
Maintenance												

PG: The Planning Game is used for Requirements collection and clarification at the beginning of each iteration and is also employed to address Maintenance issues between iterations.

SR: Small Releases force developers to Design-in components and Test after each release.

M: Interestingly, our experts found Metaphor, the oft-cited least understood practice, to provide support for all phases of development. By creating one or a set of metaphors to represent the system, decisions involving Requirements, Design, Coding, Testing/Integration, and Maintenance can be easily evaluated for relevance and priority.

SD: Simple Design helps a developer choose their Design, tells them how to Code sections when presented with multiple alternatives, and makes Maintenance easier than a complicated design.

TF: Test-First is a way of Coding as well as a Testing approach, and makes Maintenance easier by providing a test suite against which modifications can be checked.

R: Refactoring tells a developer to simplify the Design when she sees the option, affects Coding in the same way, and facilitates Maintenance by keeping the design simple.

PP: Pair Programming has two developers code at the same computer, and lets them collaborate with Designing and Coding. Maintenance is affected because two developers working together will usually produce less, and better written code than a single developer working alone.

CI: Continuous Integration is an approach to Coding, and obviously effects how and when developers Integrate new code.

CCO: Collective Code Ownership is a way for developers to program, giving them the option to modify other's Code.

OSC: On-Site Customer impacts Requirements because developers may discuss and clarify requirements at any time.

OW: Open Workspace allows all developers, even those beyond the pair programming team, to collaborate with Coding and Integration.

TABLE III
XP MANAGEMENT SUPPORT

	PG	SR	M	SD	TF	R	PP	CI	CCO	OSC	WW	OW
Management	■		▒		▒	▒	■	▒	■	■	■	■

PG: The Planning Game allows the project manager to meet with all the project stakeholders to plan the next iteration.

SR: Small Releases tell the manager how often to iterate.

CI: Continuous Integration allows the project manager (PM) to see the current state of the system at any point in time.

OSC: On-Site Customer enables the manager to better interact with the customer than she would be able to with an offsite customer.

WW: The 40 hour Work Week provides a philosophy on how to manage people.

OW: Open Workspace tells the PM how the work environment should be set up.

TABLE IV
XP COMMUNICATION SUPPORT

	PG	SR	M	SD	TF	R	PP	CI	CCO	OSC	WW	OW
Developer-Customer	■	■	■	▒				▒	▒	■	▒	
Developer-Manager	■	■	■	▒		▒	▒	■	▒	▒		■
Developer-Developer	■	■	■	■	■	■	■	■	■	▒		■

PG: The Planning Game helps the Developers communicate with the Customer, the Manager, and other Developers, in the beginning of each iteration.

SR: Small Releases provide instant project progress assessment for Customers, Managers, and Developers between iterations.

M: Using a Metaphor or a set of metaphors allows Customers, Managers, and Developers to communicate in a common, non-technical language.

SD: Simple Design encourages Developers to communicate their ideas as simply as possible.

TF: Test-First allows Developers to communicate the purpose of code before it is even developed.

R: Refactoring encourages Developers to simplify code, making the design simpler and easier to understand.

PP: Pair Programming allow sets of Developers to communicate intensely while coding.

CI: Continuous Integration allows the Managers and Developers to check the current state of the system at any time.

CCO: Collective Code Ownership allows Developers to communicate through code, comments, and documentation.

OSC: On-Site Customer facilitates quick communication between the Customer and the Developers.

OW: Open Workspace enables Developers and Managers to communicate quickly and freely.

TABLE V

XP DECISION-MAKING SUPPORT

	PG	SR	M	SD	TF	R	PP	CI	CCO	OSC	WW	OW
Release Planning	■	■		▒		▒	▒		▒			
Design and Development			■	■	■		■	■	■			
Project Management	■		▒		▒		▒		▒	■		

PG: The Planning Game assists decision making for Releases and helps Project Managers plan the project.

SR: Small Releases dictates how often to iterate which affects Release Planning and Project Management.

M: Metaphor guides Design decisions based on how well the design fits the metaphor.

SD: Simple Design guides Design decisions when presented with multiple choices.

TF: Test-First tells the developer that before he Designs and Develops any new code, he must first write the test.

PP: Pair Programming lets programmers collaborate on Design and Development decisions.

CI: Continuous Integration instructs the programmers to integrate on a regular basis, which affects how Design and Development is conducted.

CCO: Collective Code Ownership encourages developers to make changes to parts of the code that they did not author instead of waiting for the original developer to get around to it, and affects how Design and Development is conducted.

OSC: On-Site Customer allows the customer and PM to interact frequently, enabling quick decision-making.

A.2 Scrum

Only three experts felt comfortable answering about Scrum. The core practices are abbreviated: Small Teams (ST), Frequent Builds (FB), Low-Coupling Packets (LCP), Constant Testing (CT), Constant Documentation (CD), Iterative Controls (IC), Ability to declare the project done at any time (DPD).

TABLE VI
SCRUM DEVELOPMENT SUPPORT

	ST	FB	LCP	CT	CD	IC	DPD
Requirements	▨	▨	▨	▨	■	■	■
Design	■	☐	■	▨	■	■	■
Coding	☐	■	■	■	■	■	■
Testing/ Integration	☐	■	■	■	■	■	■
Maintenance	☐	■	■	■	■	▨	■

ST: Breaking the development group into Small Teams affects how the system is Designed and distributed between teams.

FB: Frequent Builds affects Coding practices and means that new code needs to be Integrated on a regular basis. Maintenance is also affected, as a current version of the system is always available for testing, catching errors earlier.

LCP: Low-Coupling Packets influences the system Design and Coding practices. Testing, Integration, and Maintenance should be made easier due to relative component independence.

CT: Constant Testing changes the way developers need to Code, Test and Integrate, and should make Maintenance easier by catching more bugs during development.

CD: Constant Documentation affects the way Requirements, Design, and Coding are conducted. The presence of up-to-date documentation should facilitate testing and maintenance.

IC: Iterative Controls help prioritize and guide Requirements collection and Design. They also affect how Coding, and Testing and Integration are conducted.

DPD: The ability to declare a project done at any time has far reaching consequences; every step in the development process should be treated as if it were in the last iteration.

TABLE VII
SCRUM MANAGEMENT SUPPORT

	ST	FB	LCP	CT	CD	IC	DPD
Management							

ST: Small Teams means Managers have to manage and distribute work between teams and team leaders.

FB: Frequent Builds allows Managers to see the state of the system at any given time to track progress.

LCP: Low Coupling Packets influences how Managers distribute work.

CT: Constant Testing provides the Manager with a system he can demo or ship at any time.

CD: Constant Documentation provides an up-to-date snapshot of the system and its progress, which can be used by the Manager for tracking or for bringing new people up to speed.

IC: Iterative Controls help the Manager gauge requirements, functionality, risk, and plan iterations.

DPD: The ability to declare a product done at any time is a Management philosophy placing emphasis on usability and correctness of the system rather than strict feature growth.

TABLE VIII
SCRUM COMMUNICATION SUPPORT

	ST	FB	LCP	CT	CD	IC	DPD
Developer-Customer							
Developer-Manager							
Developer-Developer							

ST: Small Teams help break down communications barriers, allowing easy, informal communication between all parties in the teams.

FB: Frequent Builds enables Developers to communicate the status of the system with other Developers and Managers at any time.

LCP: Low Coupling Packets reduce the need for technical communications between Developers.

CT: Constant Testing allows Developers to know the current state of the system at any point in time.

CD: By providing comprehensive up-to-date documentation, any stakeholder can learn about their respective interests in the system.

IC: Iterative Controls provide a means through which Customers, Management, and Developers collaborate to plan iterations.

TABLE IX
SCRUM DECISION MAKING SUPPORT

	ST	FB	LCP	CT	CD	IC	DPD
Release Planning	■	■			■	■	■
Design and Development	■	■	■	■	■		
Project Management	■	■			■	■	■

ST: Small Teams make all levels of decision-making easier by involving a smaller number of individuals on lower level decisions.

FB: Frequent Builds help Managers plan and monitor Releases and Development.

LCP: Low-Coupling Packets help guide Design decisions.

CT: Constant Testing tells developers to test as they Code.

CD: Constant Documentation dictates that documentation should be produced and kept up to date not only for code but also for Requirements and Release Planning. The produced documentation helps guide the PM.

IC: Iterative Controls help guide the PM with respect to Release Planning decisions.

DPD: The ability to declare a project done at any time affects what kind of features or fixes are incorporated into the next Release, and also affects the mentality with which the PM Manages the Project.

A.3 Lean Development

The 12 principles of LD are abbreviated as: Satisfying the Customer is the highest priority (SC), always provide the Best Value for the money (BV), success depends on active Customer Participation (CP), every LD project is a Team Effort (TE), Everything is Changeable (EC), Domain not point Solutions (DS), Complete do not construct (C), an 80 percent solution today instead of 100 percent solution tomorrow (80%), Minimalism is Essential (ME), Needs Determine Technology (NDT), product growth is Feature Growth not size growth (FG), and Never Push LD beyond its limits (NP). 3 experts contributed to the LD survey.

TABLE X
LEAN DEVELOPMENT SUPPORT

	SC	BV	CP	TE	EC	DS	C	80%	ME	NDT	FG	NP
Requirements	▒	■		■	▒			▒		▒		▒
Design	▒	■	■			■				▒		▒
Coding	▒	■	▒			■	■			▒		▒
Testing/ Integration			▒			■			▒	▒		▒
Maintenance			▒		▒				▒	▒		▒

BV: Always provide the Best Value for the money means that during requirements analysis, easy-to-implement features that provide a quick win are implemented, rather than hard to implement features that do not provide immediate value. Similarly, this affects Coding and Design. They should be done with optimal trade-off between quality and time.

CP: Requirements collection and analysis works best with active Customer Participation.

TE: Every phase of development is a Team Effort.

DS: By focusing on Domain Solutions, Design and Coding should look to create reusable components. Domain solutions will be pre-tested and should be easier to Integrate and Maintain than brand new code.

C: When Designing to Construct a new system, LD teams look to purchase parts of the system that may already be commercially available. By doing so, Testing and Integration should be easier, as the shrink-wrapped portion is, ideally, bug-free.

TABLE XI
LEAN DEVELOPMENT MANAGEMENT SUPPORT

	SC	BV	CP	TE	EC	DS	C	80%	ME	NDT	FG	NP
Management	■	■	■	■				■				

SC: The PM needs to change her frame of mind to make Customer Satisfaction the highest priority, as opposed to budget, politics, and other concerns.

BV: The PM also needs to manage the project with the goal to build and prioritize the system to provide the Best Value for the money.

CP: It becomes the PM's responsibility to keep the Customer Participating in the project.

TE: The PM needs to include the entire Team in decision-making processes.

80%: Instead of making everything perfect, the PM should focus on providing the best system she can at the moment.

ME: The PM should focus on keeping team size, code size, documentation, and budget as small as necessary for a successful project.

TABLE XII
LEAN DEVELOPMENT COMMUNICATIONS SUPPORT

	SC	BV	CP	TE	EC	DS	C	80%	ME	NDT	FG	NP
Developer-Customer	■		■	■			▨	▨	▨	▨	▨	▨
Developer-Manager			▨		▨		▨	▨		▨	▨	▨
Developer-Developer	▨	▨	▨	■			▨	▨	▨	▨	▨	▨

SC: Ensuring Customer Satisfaction entails enhanced communication between the Developers and Customers.

CP: Active Customer Participation gives Customers more incentive to work with the Developers.

TE: The 'everything is a Team Effort' philosophy encourages communication between all members of the team.

TABLE XIII
LEAN DEVELOPMENT DECISION MAKING SUPPORT

	SC	BV	CP	TE	EC	DS	C	80%	ME	NDT	FG	NP
Release Planning	■	■	▨	■	▨	▨	■	■		▨	■	▨
Design and Development	■		▨		■		■		■	■		▨
Project Management	■	■	▨				■	■	■	■	■	▨

SC: Prioritizing Customer Satisfaction means that during Release Planning, Design and Development, and Project Management, the interest of the customer may have to be put before that of the team.

BV: Providing the Best Value for the money is a management philosophy, affecting mostly what requirements get prioritized for what release.

CP: Active Customer Participation provides decision support for PM's, and is also instrumental in prioritizing Release features.

EC: Having the ability to Change Everything means that Release and Design decisions are not set in stone, letting them be made more quickly and changed later if necessary.

C: An emphasis on Constructing based on already-built components has a large effect on Design decisions.

80%: Having an 80% solution today means that, from a Release, Design, and PM perspective, adding a new feature today is a better decision than completing an old one.

ME: Minimalism helps a PM decide what artifacts to produce during development.

NDT: The Needs Determine Technology philosophy helps the PM and designers decide on an appropriate solution rather than a high-tech solution for high-tech's sake.

FG: By emphasizing Feature Growth, Releases and PM's tend to push features more than other requirements.

A.4 Feature Driven Development

The core practices of FDD are abbreviated: problem domain Object Modeling (OM), Feature Development (FD), Component/class Ownership (CO), Feature Teams (FT), Inspections (I), Configuration Management (CM), Regular Builds (RB), and Visibility of progress and results (V). Only 2 experts felt comfortable enough with FDD to complete the survey.

TABLE XIV
FEATURE DRIVEN DEVELOPMENT SUPPORT

	OM	FD	CO	FT	I	CM	RB	V
Requirements			▒			▒	▒	▒
Design	█	█	█	█	▒	▒	▒	▒
Coding	▒	█			▒	█	█	▒
Testing/ Integration	▒	█	█	█	█	█	█	
Maintenance	▒	█			█	█	█	

OM: Object Modeling provides a different approach to Design.

FD: Feature Development provides a development methodology that effects the way Design, Coding, and Integration are approached. Maintenance is also affected as the system is considered as a collection of features rather than lines of code.

CO: Individual Code Ownership means that Design, Coding, and Integration become individual efforts.

FT: Feature Teams means that the feature as a whole becomes a team effort.

I: Inspections are a testing technique that should produce better and more bug-free code that is easier to Maintain.

CM: Configuration Management is established for support of Testing, Integration, and Maintenance.

RB: Regular Builds affect coding procedures, help to integrate testing and integration during the development process, and make maintenance easier with more bug-free code.

TABLE XV
FEATURE DRIVEN DEVELOPMENT MANAGEMENT SUPPORT

	OM	FD	CO	FT	I	CM	RB	V
Management	▦	■			▦		■	

FD: Feature Development allows the PM to manage teams by easily separating development workload.

CO: Code Ownership gives the PM a point of contact about any piece of the system.

FT: Feature Teams allow the PM to break the team effort into more easily manageable sections.

RB: Regular Builds give the PM a snapshot of the system at any point in time.

V: Visibility of progress allows easy tracking of the project.

TABLE XVI
FEATURE DRIVEN DEVELOPMENT COMMUNICATION SUPPORT

	OM	FD	CO	FT	I	CM	RB	V
Developer-Customer	▦	■	▦		▦	▦		■
Developer-Manager	■		■	■	▦	■	■	
Developer-Developer	■		■	■	■	■	■	■

OM: Object Modeling allows Developers to communicate with Managers and other Developers specifically, and in detail, about small components of the system.

FD: Feature Development allows the Developer to prototype and display working units of the system to Managers and Customers.

CO: Code Ownership gives Managers and other Developers a point of contact about specific sections of code in the system.

FT: Feature Teams allow easy collaboration and communication between Developers and Managers.

I: Inspections allow Developers to read, explain and understand the code.

CM: Configuration Management provides a vehicle for communication for Developers and Managers.

RB: Regular Builds let Developers and Managers see the current state of the system.

V: Progress Visibility allows the Customer to track the project with ease.

TABLE XVII

FEATURE DRIVEN DEVELOPMENT DECISION MAKING SUPPORT

	OM	FD	CO	FT	I	CM	RB	V
Release Planning	▨	■	▨	■	▨	▨	▨	
Design and Development	■			■		▨	■	
Project Management		■	■		■	■		■

OM: Object Modeling allows for a flexible framework for Design.

FD: Feature Development allows for easy distribution of features in releases. Prototyped features can be tested, designed, and developed, and Project Managers can manage the system as a set of features.

CO: Code Ownership gives PM's a point of contact for specific pieces of code.

FT: By building a small team to handle Features, decision-making for release, design and development is delegated to the group. It also guides the PM's resource allocation.

I: Inspections correct and reshape design and code.

CM: Configuration Management provides a resource and reference for PM's.

RB: Regular Builds provide feedback during Development.

V: Visibility allows the project manager to track the project and make changes when necessary.

A.5 Dynamic Systems Development Methodology

Only one expert felt comfortable enough with DSDM to complete the survey. DSDM's principles are abbreviated: Active User Involvement is imperative (AUI), DSDM teams must be Empowered to make decisions (E), focus is on Delivery Of Products (DOP), Fitness for business purpose is the essential criterion for acceptance of deliverables (F), Iterative and incremental development is necessary to converge on an accurate business solution (I), all changes during development are Reversible (R), requirements are baselines at a High Level (HL), Testing is Integrated throughout the life cycle (TI), and a Collaborative and Cooperative approach between all stakeholders is essential (CC).

TABLE XVIII

DYNAMIC SYSTEMS DEVELOPMENT METHODOLOGY DEVELOPMENT SUPPORT

	AUI	E	DoP	F	I	R	HL	TI	CC
Requirements	■	▒	▒	▒	■	▒	■	▒	■
Design	▒	■	▒	▒	■	■	▒	▒	▒
Coding	▒	■	▒	▒	■	■	▒	▒	▒
Testing/ Integration	▒	▒	■	▒	■	■	▒	■	▒
Maintenance	▒	▒	▒	▒	■	▒	▒	▒	▒

AUI: Active User Involvement is important for good Requirements collection.

E: Team Empowerment allows developers to make the right decisions during Design and Coding.

DOP: Frequent Delivery Of Products gives the customer a system they can Test while it is still under development.

I: Incremental development affects the entire development process, breaking Requirements collection, Design, Coding, Testing, Integration, and Maintenance into short cycles.

R: Reversible decisions means developers can feel freer to commit to decisions during Design and Coding. During Testing or Integration these decisions can be reversed, if necessary.

HL: High Level requirements keep Requirements collection at an abstraction high enough for participation from all stakeholders.

TI: Constant Testing and Integration allows bugs to be caught and fixed earlier in the development lifecycle.

CC: A Collaborative approach between stakeholders will assist in accurate Requirements collection.

TABLE XIX

DYNAMIC SYSTEMS DEVELOPMENT METHODOLOGY MANAGEMENT SUPPORT

	AUI	E	DoP	F	I	R	HL	TI	CC
Management	■	■	■	■	■	▒	▒	▒	■

AUI: The Project Manager needs to manage collaboration between users and the Customer and Developers.

E: Empowering teams means Management has to be more flexible.

DOP: Focus on the Delivery Of Products is a Management mindset.

F: Management needs to consider Fitness for purpose over other factors.

I: Iterative development breaks Management into smaller, more intense cycles.

R: The project manager needs to feel free to make decisions without worrying about irReversible consequences.

CC: Managers need to facilitate Collaboration between stakeholders.

TABLE XX

DYNAMIC SYSTEMS DEVELOPMENT METHODOLOGY COMMUNICATION SUPPORT

	AUI	E	DoP	F	I	R	HL	TI	CC
Developer-Customer	■		■			■	■		■
Developer-Manager			■			■	■	■	
Developer-Developer						■		■	

AUI: Active User Involvement ensures good communication between Developers and the Customer.

DOP: Frequent Delivery Of Products allows Managers and Customers to keep up-to-date on the status of the system.

I: Incremental development gives Developers, Managers, and Customers frequent opportunities to interact.

HL: High Level requirements provide Developers with a vehicle for non-technical requirements communication with Managers and Customers.

TI: Integrated Testing allows Developers and Managers to see the state of the system at any point in time.

CC: A Collaborative approach keeps the Customer actively involved.

TABLE XXI

DYNAMIC SYSTEMS DEVELOPMENT METHODOLOGY DECISION MAKING SUPPORT

	AUI	E	DoP	F	I	R	HL	TI	CC
Release Planning			■		■				
Design and Development		■						■	
Project Management	■								

AUI: Management needs to keep users actively involved.

E: Teams can feel free to make design and development decisions as they see fit.

DOP: Management philosophy needs to reflect the frequent delivery of products and plan releases accordingly.

F: Management needs to evaluate decisions on fitness for the business purpose.

I: Iterative development makes decision-making cycles shorter and deals with smaller, more frequent decisions.

R: Reversible decisions means that decision making does not have to be 100% complete or hold up the process until made.

TI: Developers learn to test frequently during development.

REFERENCES

[1] Abrahamsson P., Salo O., Ronkainen J., Warsta J., "Agile software development methods", *VTT Publications* **478** (2002).

[2] Ambler S., *Agile Modeling*, John Wiley and Sons, 2002.

[3] Ambler S., "Introduction to agile modeling (AM)". Available: http://www.ronin-intl.com/publications/agileModeling.pdf, 2002.

[4] Ambler S., "Agile documentation", http://www.agilemodeling.com/essays/agileDocumentation.htm, 2001, 12-4-2002.

[5] Ambler S., "Agile modeling and the unified process", http://www.agilemodeling.com/essays/agileModelingRUP.htm, 2001, 12-4-2002.

[6] Ambler S., "Lessons in agility from internet-based development", *IEEE Software* **19** (2) (Mar. 2002) 66–73.

[7] Ambler S., "When does(n't) agile modeling make sense?", http://www.agilemodeling.com/essays/whenDoesAMWork.htm, 2002, 12-4-2002.

[8] Basili V.R., Tesoriero R., Costa P., Lindvall M., Rus I., Shull F., Zelkowitz M.V., "Building an experience base for software engineering: A report on the first CeBASE eWorkshop", in: *Proc. Profes (Product Focused Software Process Improvement)*, 2001, pp. 110–125. Available: http://citeseer.nj.nec.com/basili01building.html.

[9] Basili V.R., Turner A.J., "Iterative enhancement: A practical technique for software development", *IEEE Transactions on Software Engineering* **1** (4) (1975) 390–396.

[10] Beck K., "Embrace change with extreme programming", *IEEE Computer* (Oct. 1999) 70–77.

[11] Beck K., *Extreme Programming Explained: Embracing Change*, Addison–Wesley, 1999.

[12] Beck K., Cockburn A., Jeffries R., Highsmith J., "Agile manifesto", http://www.agilemanifesto.org, 2001, 12-4-2002.

[13] Boehm B., "A spiral model of software development and enhancement", *IEEE Computer* **21** (5) (1988) 61–72.

[14] Boehm B., "Get ready for agile methods, with care", *IEEE Computer* (Jan. 2002) 64–69.

[15] Bowers P., "Highpoints from the agile software development forum", *Crosstalk* (Oct. 2002) 26–27.

[16] Coad P., deLuca J., Lefebvre E., *Java Modeling in Color with UML*, Prentice Hall, 1999.

[17] Cockburn A., "Selecting a project's methodology", *IEEE Software* **17** (4) (2000) 64–71.

[18] Cockburn A., "Agile software development joins the 'would-be' crowd", *Cutter IT Journal* (Jan. 2002) 6–12.

[19] Cockburn A., Highsmith J., "Agile software development: The business of innovation", *IEEE Computer* (Sept. 2001) 120–122.

[20] Cockburn A., Highsmith J., "Agile software development: The people factor", *IEEE Computer* (Nov. 2001) 131–133.

[21] Cockburn A., Williams L., "The costs and benefits of pair programming", in: *Proc. eXtreme Programming and Flexible Processes in Software Engineering—XP2000*, 2000. Available: http://collaboration.csc.ncsu.edu/laurie/Papers/XPSardinia.PDF.

[22] Cohn M., Ford D., "Introducing an agile process to an organization", http://www.mountaingoatsoftware.com/articles/IntroducingAnAgileProcess.pdf, 2002, 8-2-2002.

[23] DeMarco T., Boehm B., "The agile methods fray", *IEEE Computer* (June 2002) 90–92.

[24] Elssamadisy A., Schalliol G., "Recognizing and responding to 'bad smells' in extreme programming," 2002, pp. 617–622.

[25] Glass R., "Agile versus traditional: Make love, not war", *Cutter IT Journal* (Dec. 2001) 12–18.

[26] Glazer H., "Dispelling the process myth: Having a process does not mean sacrificing agility or creativity", *Crosstalk* (Nov. 2001).

[27] Grenning J., "Launching extreme programming at a process-intensive company", *IEEE Software* **18** (6) (Nov. 2001) 27–33.

[28] Highsmith J., *Agile Software Development Ecosystems*, Addison–Wesley, Boston, MA, 2002.

[29] Highsmith J., "What is agile software development?", *Crosstalk* (Oct. 2002) 4–9.

[30] Highsmith J., Cockburn A., "Agile software development: The business of innovation", *IEEE Computer* (Sept. 2001) 120–122.

[31] Highsmith J., Orr K., Cockburn A., "Extreme programming", in: *E-Business Application Delivery*, Feb. 2000, pp. 4–17. Available: http://www.cutter.com/freestuff/ead0002.pdf.

[32] Hodgetts P., Phillips D., "Extreme adoption experiences of a B2B start-up", http://www.extremejava.com/eXtremeAdoptioneXperiencesofaB2BStartUp.pdf, 12-4-2002.

[33] Humphrey W.S., *A Discipline for Software Engineering*, Addison–Wesley, Reading, MA, 1995.

[34] Jeffries R., "Extreme programming and the capability maturity model", http://www.xprogramming.com/xpmag/xp_and_cmm.htm, 12-4-2002.

[35] Karlström D., "Introducing extreme programming—an experience report", in: *Proc. 3rd International Conference on eXtreme Programming and Agile Processes in Software Engineering—XP2002*, 2002, pp. 24–29. Available: http://www.xp2002.org/atti/DanielKarlstrom--IntroducingExtremeProgramming.pdf.

[36] Lindvall M., Basili V.R., Boehm B., Costa P., Dangle K., Shull F., Tesoriero R., Williams L., Zelkowitz M.V., "Empirical findings in agile methods", in: *Proc. Extreme Programming and Agile Methods—XP/Agile Universe 2002*, 2002, pp. 197–207. Available: http://fc-md.umd.edu/mikli/Lindvall_agile_universe_eworkshop.pdf.

[37] Lindvall M., Basili V.R., Boehm B., Costa P., Shull F., Tesoriero R., Williams L., Zelkowitz M.V., *Results from the 2nd eWorkshop on agile methods*, Fraunhofer Center for Experimental Software Engineering, College Park, Maryland 20742, Aug., 2002. Technical Report 02-109.

[38] Lindvall M., Rus I., "Process diversity in software development", *IEEE Software* **17** (4) (Aug. 2000) 14–71. Available: http://fc-md.umd.edu/mikli/LindvallProcessDiversity. pdf.

[39] Macias F., Holcombe M., Gheorghe M., "Empirical experiments with XP", in: *Proc. 3rd International Conference on eXtreme Programming and Agile Processes in Software Engineering—XP2002*, 2002, pp. 225–228. Available: http://www.xp2002.org/atti/ Macias-Holcombe--EmpiricalexperimentswithXP.pdf.

[40] Paulisch F., Völker A., "Agility—build on a mature foundation", in: *Proc. Software Engineering Process Group Conference—SEPG 2002*, 2002.

[41] Paulk M.C., "Extreme programming from a CMM perspective", *IEEE Software* **18** (6) (2001) 19–26.

[42] Paulk M.C., "Agile methodologies and process discipline", *Crosstalk* (Oct. 2002) 15–18.

[43] Paulk M.C., "Key practices of the capability maturity model, version 1.1", Technical Report CMU/SEI-93-TR-25, 1993.

[44] Poole C., Huisman J., "Using extreme programming in a maintenance environment", *IEEE Software* **18** (6) (Nov. 2001) 42–50.

[45] Poppendieck M., "Lean programming", http://www.agilealliance.org/articles/articles/ LeanProgramming.htm, 2001, 4-12-2002.

[46] Rakitin S.R., "Manifesto elicits cynicism", *IEEE Computer* **34** (12) (Dec. 2001) 4.

[47] Reifer D., "How to get the most out of extreme programming/agile methods", in: *Proc. Extreme Programming and Agile Methods—XP/Agile Universe 2002*, 2002, pp. 185–196.

[48] Royce W.W., "Managing the development of large software systems: Concepts and techniques", in: *Proc. WESCON*, 1970, pp. 1–9.

[49] Rumpe B., Schröder A., "Quantitative survey on extreme programming project". Available: http://www.xp2002.org/atti/Rumpe-Schroder-- QuantitativeSurveyonExtremeProgrammingProjects.pdf, 2002.

[50] Rus I., Seaman C., Lindvall M., "Process diversity in software maintenance—guest editors' introduction", *Software Maintenance Research and Practice*, Dec. 2002, in press.

[51] Schwaber K., Beedle M., *Agile Software Development with SCRUM*, Prentice Hall, 2002.

[52] Schwaber K., "Controlled chaos: living on the edge", http://www.agilealliance.org/ articles/articles/ap.pdf, 2002, 4-12-2002.

[53] Shull F., Basili V.R., Boehm B., Brown A.W., Costa P., Lindvall M., Port D., Rus I., Tesoriero R., Zelkowitz M.V., "What we have learned about fighting defects", in: *Proc. 8th International Software Metrics Symposium*, 2002, pp. 39–42. Available: http:// fc-md.umd.edu/fcmd/Papers/shull_defects.ps.

[54] Stapleton J., *DSDM: The Method in Practice*, Addison–Wesley, 1997.

[55] The C3 Team, "Chrysler goes to "extremes"", in: *Distributed Computing*, Oct. 1998, pp. 24–28.

[56] Turk D., France R., Rumpe B., "Limitations of agile software processes", in: *Proc. 3rd International Conference on eXtreme Programming and Agile Processes in Software Engineering—XP2002*, 2002. Available: http://www4.informatik.tu-muenchen. de/~rumpe/ps/XP02.Limitations.pdf.

[57] Turner R., Jain A., "Agile meets CMMI: Culture clash or common cause?", in: *Proc. eXtreme Programming and Agile Methods—XP/Agile Universe 2002*, 2002, pp. 153–165.

[58] Williams L., Kessler R.R., *Pair Programming Illuminated*, Addison–Wesley, 2003.

[59] Williams L., Kessler R.R., Cunningham W., Jeffries R., "Strengthening the case for pair programming", *IEEE Software* **17** (4) (2000) 19–25.

The Timeboxing Process Model
for Iterative Software Development

PANKAJ JALOTE

Department of Computer Science and Engineering
Indian Institute of Technology
Kanpur 208016
India
jalote@iitk.ac.in

AVEEJEET PALIT AND PRIYA KURIEN

Infosys Technologies Limited
Electronics City
Bangalore 561 229
India

Abstract

In today's business where speed is of essence, an iterative development approach that allows the functionality to be delivered in parts has become a necessity and an effective way to manage risks. In an iterative process, the development of a software system is done in increments, each increment forming of an iteration and resulting in a working system. A common iterative approach is to decide what should be developed in an iteration and then plan the iteration accordingly. A somewhat different iterative approach is to time box different iterations. In this approach, the length of an iteration is fixed and what should be developed in an iteration is adjusted to fit the time box. Generally, the time boxed iterations are executed in sequence, with some overlap where feasible. In this paper we propose the *timeboxing* process model that takes the concept of time boxed iterations further by adding pipelining concepts to it for permitting overlapped execution of different iterations. In the timeboxing process model, each time boxed iteration is divided into equal length stages, each stage having a defined function and resulting in a clear work product that is handed over to the next stage. With this division into stages, pipelining concepts are employed to have multiple time boxes executing concurrently, leading to a reduction in the delivery time for product releases. We illustrate the use of this process model through

ADVANCES IN COMPUTERS, VOL. 62
ISSN: 0065-2458/DOI 10.1016/S0065-2458(03)62002-4

67

an example of a commercial project that was successfully executed using the proposed model.

1. Introduction

The main objective of a software project can be stated as follows—deliver a high quality software product within schedule and within budget. A successful project is the one that satisfies the constraints on all the three fronts of cost, schedule, and quality (we are including functionality or features as part of quality, though they could be treated as another driver). Consequently, when planning and executing a software project, the decisions are mostly taken with a view to ultimately reduce the cost or the cycle time, or for improving the quality.

A software project has to execute a number of engineering and management tasks for delivering a software product that satisfies the user requirements. Software projects utilize a process to organize the execution of the tasks to achieve the goals on the cost, schedule, and quality fronts. A process typically specifies the tasks that should be performed and the order in which they should be performed. Processes so utilized frequently conform to a process model—a general process structure for the lifecycle of software development. A process model generally specifies the set of stages in which a project should be divided, the order in which the stages should be executed, and any other constraints and conditions on the execution of stages.

The basic premise behind any process model is that, in the situations for which the model is applicable, using the process model for a project will lead to low cost, high quality, or reduced cycle time. In other words, a process is a means to reach the goals of high quality, low cost, and low cycle time, and a process model provides generic guidelines for developing a suitable process for a project.

Software development is a large and complex task. As with any complex problem, the solution approach relies on the "divide and conquer" strategy. For software it means that this complex problem of developing software should be divided into parts that can be solved separately. At the top level, this division is typically done by breaking the overall project into key phases, with each phase focusing on a separate task. In other words, phases help in "separation of concerns." This partitioning of the whole problem into a set of phases is typically what a process model does. A process model specifies the phases such that this set of phases executed in the specified order leads to a successful execution of the project.

It should be pointed out that typically within each phase also methodologies or mini-processes are used to further apply the divide-and-conquer approach. However, process models usually focus only on the top level, phase-wise organization. Frequently, the major phases are requirements analysis and specification, design, build, and test. Process models specify how these tasks are partitioned and organized, keeping in view the project constraints.

The most influential process model is the waterfall model, in which the different phases of requirements specification, design, coding, and testing are performed in sequence. In this process model, the overall task of developing software is broken into a few phases, with a phase getting initiated when the previous phase ended. The linear organization of phases in this model requires that the requirements be frozen early in the requirements phase.

Due to the current scenario of changing requirements and need for shortening the cycle time, iterative process models have now become more common. In an iterative model, the software is developed in a series of iterations, with each iteration acting like a "mini-waterfall" and delivering some software. In a typical iterative development project, the first iteration builds some core system and subsequent iterations add new features and functionality on the existing software. A different shade of iterative development is to have time boxed iterations in which each iteration is fixed in time and the functionality to be developed in an iteration is adjusted to fit the time box.

In an iterative development, generally the different iterations are executed in sequence. This form of iterative development does not directly help reduce the cycle time. However, iterative development also opens the possibility of executing different iterations in parallel and thereby reducing the average cycle time of an iteration. To exploit this potential of parallel execution of iterations, suitable process models are needed to structure the execution of different tasks in different iterations. In this chapter we describe the timeboxing process model that enhances the time boxed iterations by concepts of pipelining, thereby allowing parallel execution of iterations in a structured manner, resulting in a reduction in the cycle time for deliveries.

The chapter is organized as follows. In the next section we discuss the iterative development approaches in general and see how the timeboxing model relates to them. In Section 3, we describe the timeboxing process model in more detail, execution of a project using this process model, and issues like team size and impact of unequal stages or exceptions on the execution. In Section 4, we discuss some aspects of applying the process model on projects—the nature of projects for which this is suitable, how changes are handled, project management issues, etc. In Section 5 we discuss a real commercial project in which we applied this model, and discuss how we dealt with some of the constraints that the project presented. The chapter ends with conclusions.

2.   Iterative Development Models

One cannot discuss the iterative models without first discussing the waterfall model, as it is the shortcomings of this model that lead to the development of the iterative models. The waterfall model for software development was first proposed by Royce [26] to suggest that there should be many distinct stages in a project execution. Though the waterfall model suggests a linear execution of stages, Royce had in fact suggested that, in practice, there is a need for feedback from testing to design and from design to early stages of requirements. In any case, waterfall model as a linear sequence of stages became the most influential process model—it was conceptually simple and was contractually somewhat easier to administer (e.g., each stage can be defined as a milestone at which some output is obtained and some payment is made.)

Waterfall model has some well known limitations [7]. The biggest drawback with the waterfall model is that it assumes that requirements are stable and known at the start of the project. Unchanging requirements, unfortunately, do not exist in reality, and requirements do change and evolve. In order to accommodate requirement changes while executing the project in the waterfall model, organizations typically define a change management process which handles the change requests. Another key limitation is that it follows the "big bang" approach—the entire software is delivered in one shot at the end. This entails heavy risks, as the users do not know till the very end what they are getting. These two key limitations can be alleviated through the use of an iterative development model.

In an iterative development, software is built and delivered (either for production use or for feedback) in iterations—each iteration delivering a working software system that is generally an increment to the previous delivery. The concept of iteratively developing software has been around for a long time and for a history of iterative development, the reader is referred to the paper by Larman and Basili [21].

Iterative enhancement [1] and spiral [6] are two well-known early process models that support iterative development. In iterative enhancement, in each iteration software is delivered and feedback from using the software is a key input in deciding what to build in the next iteration. In the spiral model, what is to be built in an iteration is influenced heavily by the risk perception at that stage, and activities of the iteration also help mitigate or better understand the risks.

More recently, agile methods [10] and XP [4] also promote iterative development—iterative development is a part of the agile manifesto and small iterations is a key practice in the XP methodology. Iterative development is also a foundation for methodologies like RUP [19] and DSDM [27]. In most of these, small iterations are recommended, along the lines of the "daily build" concept utilized in organizations like Microsoft. In this approach, the entire system is built almost daily, and much of the testing is then done with the built system. In other words, all the code that is ready to be incorporated in the system is checked in during the day and at the end of the day, a new version of the software is created. In this model, the development and software build are separated—a new software build is created daily incorporating whatever software modules have been delivered. The software development, on the other hand, proceeds separately and teams developing different modules make their modules available for a build as and when they are ready.

With iterative development, the release cycle becomes shorter, which reduces some of the risks associated with the "big bang" approach. Requirements need not be completely understood and specified at the start of the project—they can evolve over time and can be incorporated in the system in any iteration. Incorporating change requests is also easy as any new requirements or change requests can be simply passed on to a future iteration. Overall, iterative development is able to handle some of the key shortcomings of the waterfall model, and is well suited for the rapidly changing business world, despite having some of its own drawbacks. (E.g., it is hard to preserve the simplicity and integrity of the architecture and the design.)

The commonly used iterative development approach is organized as a sequence of iterations, with each of the iterations delivering parts of the functionality. Features to be built in an iteration are decided in the start and then the iteration is planned for delivering them (an approach called *feature boxing* in [22]). Though the overall de-livered functionality is delivered in parts, the total development time is not reduced. In fact, it can be argued that if the requirements are known then for the same amount of functionality, iterative development might take more time than a waterfall model-based development. Furthermore, for each iteration, the risk of over-committing and not being able to deliver in time is still there, though it is reduced as the scope of each iteration is smaller.

One approach to alleviate the schedule risk is to time box the iterations. With time boxing of each iteration, the duration of each iteration, and hence the delivery time, is fixed. The functionality that can be delivered in a time box is what is negotiated for an iteration while keeping the delivery time fixed. In contrast, in feature boxing, the functionality is selected and then the time to deliver is determined. Time boxing changes the perspective of development and makes the schedule as a non-negotiable and a high priority commitment. As the delivery date is sacrosanct, this approach also helps sharpen the focus on important requirements since only limited require-ments can be accommodated and there is no flexibility to increase them. Time boxed development is a natural extension of an iterative development approach and has been proposed for use in RUP [20], in DSDM [27], and is a key strategy for rapid application development [18,23].

Even with time boxed development, the total time of development remains the same, if different iterations are executed in sequence. Time boxing helps in reducing development time by better managing the schedule risk and the risk of "gold plating," which is a major cause of cost and schedule overruns.

To reduce the total development time, one approach is to use components and em-ploy reuse—a technique that is employed frequently. With components and reuse, time to build an application is reduced as less software is being developed to deliver the desired functionality by leveraging existing software. However, components and reuse can be employed to reduce the delivery time even if the underlying develop-ment process model is waterfall-like and is not iterative.

Another natural approach to speed up development that is applicable only when iterative development process is used, is to employ parallelism between the different iterations. That is, a new iteration commences before the system produced by the current iteration is released, and hence development of a new release happens in parallel with the development of the current release. By starting an iteration before the previous iteration has completed, it is possible to reduce the delivery time for successive iterations (after the first iteration). The Rational Unified Process (RUP) uses this approach by suggesting that the final stages of an iteration may overlap with the initial stages of the next [19]. In practice, many products evolve this way—the development of the next version starts well before the development of the earlier version has completed. However, this type of overlapping of iterations is unstructured and is not systematic.

In this chapter, we discus in detail the *timeboxing* process model that takes the concept of parallelism between different iterations further and structures it by using the pipelining concepts [13]. In this model, iterative development is done in a set of fixed duration time boxes. Each time box is divided into stages/phases of approximately equal duration, and the work of each stage is done by a dedicated team. Multiple iterations are executed concurrently by employing pipelining—as the first stage of the first time box completes, the team for that stage starts its activities for the next time box, while the team for the next stage carries on with the execution of the first time box. This model ensures that deliveries are made with a much greater frequency than once every time box, thereby substantially reducing the cycle time for each delivery. How execution of a project proceeds when using the waterfall, iterative, or the timeboxing process model proceed is shown in Fig. 1.

As mentioned above, the concept of using time boxes for iterations has been around for quite some time, though mostly for predefining the delivery times and deriving the benefits that come from it. Overlapping of iterations also has been talked about and has been used in practice by many product vendors. The timeboxing process model formalizes this concept of overlapping iterations by structuring the iterations to facilitate the use of pipelining concepts to reduce software delivery time. It provides a conceptual framework that is grounded in the pipelining concepts developed to speed up execution of instructions in processors. The discussion of the timeboxing model is based on our earlier paper [16].

Note that this overlapping is different from the overlapping of different phases within an iteration, as is proposed in RUP [19]. Overlapping the different phases means that an earlier phase in an iteration does not have to completely finish before the next phase of that iteration starts. This overlapping of phases avoids the hard "hand-over" from one phase to another and allows, for example, requirements to evolve even while design is being done. Though this approach for overlapping has clear practical benefits in handling evolving requirements it, however, does not provide any direct benefit in reducing the delivery time.

Note that the concept of pipelining the execution of different iterations in a software development is also quite different from the concept of software pipelines [13]. Software pipelines are used to apply some techniques to the source code of a program such that the transformed program is better suited for pipelined execution of the instructions in the hardware.

We believe that the timeboxing process model is a viable approach for executing projects when there is a strong business need to deliver working systems quickly. Due to the constraints the model imposes, this model is likely to work well for medium sized projects which have a stable architecture and have a lot of feature requirements

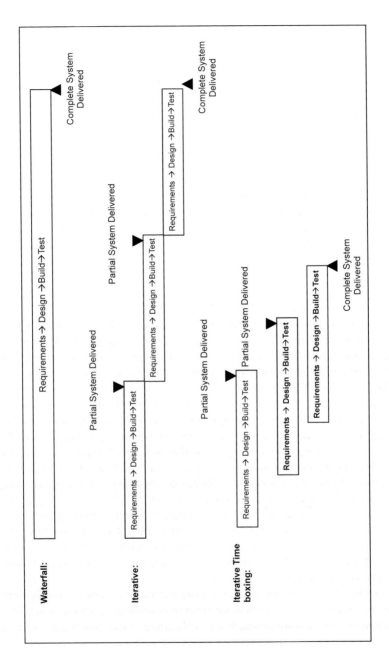

FIG. 1. Waterfall, iterative, and timeboxing process models.

that are not fully known and which evolve and change with time. Application of the model is eased if there is flexibility in grouping the requirements for the purpose of delivering meaningful systems that provide value to the users. The model is not likely to work well for projects where flexible grouping of requirements for the purpose of delivery is not possible. It is also not likely to work well where development within an iteration cannot be easily divided into clearly defined stages, each of which ending with some work product that form the main basis for the next stage.

3.   The Timeboxing Process Model

In the timeboxing model, as in other iterative development approaches, some software is developed and a working system is delivered after each iteration. However, in timeboxing, each iteration is of equal duration, which is the length of the time box. In this section we discuss the various conceptual issues relating to this process model.

3.1   A Time Box and Stages

In the timeboxing process model, the basic unit of development is a time box, which is of fixed duration. Within this time box all activities that need to be performed to successfully release the next version are executed. Since the duration is fixed, a key factor in selecting the requirements or features to be built in a time box is what can be "fit" into the time box.

Each time box is divided into a sequence of *stages*, like in the waterfall model. Each stage performs some clearly defined task of the iteration and produces a clearly defined output. The output from one stage is the only input from this stage to the next stage, and it is assumed that this input is sufficient for performing the task of the next stage. When the output of one stage is given to the next stage, the development activity is *handed over* to the next stage, and for this time box, the activity shifts to the next stage. Note that handing over will require some artifacts to be created by a stage which provide all the information that is needed to perform the next stage.

The model also requires that the duration of each stage, that is, the time it takes to complete the task of that stage, is approximately the same. (Impact of exceptions to this are discussed later.) Such a time box with equal stages in which the task is handed over from one stage to the next is shown in Fig. 2. In the figure, the time box is the outer box, and stages are represented by boxes within the time box. In this figure, we have explicitly shown the handing over from one stage to another by showing an output of a stage which forms the input to the next. Later, we will dispense with this and just show a time box divided into stages.

FIG. 2. A time box with equal stages.

There is a dedicated team for each stage. That is, the team for a stage performs only tasks of that stage—tasks for other stages are performed by their respective teams. With dedicated teams, when an iteration is handed over from one stage to the next as shown in Fig. 2, in effect, the responsibility for further development of that iteration is being handed over to another team. This is quite different from most other models where the implicit assumption is that the same team performs all the different tasks of the project or the iteration. In such resource models where the same team performs the entire task, the phases in the development process are logical tasks that are performed by the same team and completion of a task ending with a work product is primarily for review and control purposes. There is really no handing over to another resource group as the development moves from stage to stage.

As pipelining is to be employed, the stages must be carefully chosen. Each stage performs some logical activity which may be communication intensive—that is, the team performing the task of that stage needs to communicate and meet regularly. However, the stage should be such that its output is all that is needed from this stage by the team performing the task of the next stage. In other words, the output should be such that when the iteration is handed over from one stage to another, the team to which the iteration has been handed over needs to communicate minimally with the previous stage team for performing their task. Note that it does not mean that the team for a stage cannot seek clarifications with teams of earlier stages—all it means is that the communication needs between teams of different stages are so low that their communication has no significant effect on the work of any of the teams. However, this approach disallows parallelism between the different stages within a time box— it is assumed that when a stage finishes, its task for this iteration is completely done and only when a stage finishes its task, the activity of the next stage starts.

3.2   Pipelined Execution

Having time boxed iterations with stages of equal duration and having dedicated teams renders itself to pipelining of different iterations. Pipelining is one of the most powerful concepts for making faster CPUs and is now used in almost all processors [13]. Pipelining is like an assembly line in which different pipe-segments execute different parts of an instruction. The different segments execute in parallel, each working on a different instruction. The segments are connected to form a pipe—new instructions enter one end of the pipe and completed instructions exit from the other end. If each segment takes one clock cycle to complete its task, then in a steady state, one instruction will exit in each clock cycle from the pipeline, leading to the increased throughput and speedup of instruction execution. We refer the reader to [13] for further details on the concepts of pipelining in hardware.

In timeboxing, each iteration can be viewed like one instruction whose execution is divided into a sequence of fixed duration stages, a stage being executed after the completion of the previous stage. In general, let us consider a time box with duration T and consisting of n stages—$S_1, S_2, \ldots, S_n$. As stated above, each stage S_i is executed by a dedicated team (similar to having dedicated segment for executing a stage in an instruction).

The team of each stage has T/n time available to finish their task for a time box, that is, the duration of each stage is T/n. When the team of a stage i completes the tasks for that stage for a time box k, it then passes the output of the time box to the team executing the stage $i + 1$, and then starts executing its stage for the next time box $k + 1$. Using the output given by the team for S_i, the team for S_{i+1} starts its activity for this time box. By the time the first time box is nearing completion, there are $n - 1$ different time boxes in different stages of execution. And though the first output comes after time T, each subsequent delivery happens after T/n time interval, delivering software that has been developed in time T.

Another way to view it is to consider the basic time unit as the duration of a stage. Suppose that a stage takes one stage-time-unit (STU) to complete. Then a n-stage time box will take n STUs to complete. However, after the completion of the first iteration, an iteration will complete after each STU. Once an STU is chosen, the time box will have to be divided into stages such that each stage takes only one STU to complete. With pipelining, if all the stages are properly balanced, in the steady state, on an average it will take one STU to complete an iteration.

As an example, consider a time box consisting of three stages: requirement specification, build, and deployment. The requirement stage is executed by its team of analysts and ends with a prioritized list of requirements to be built in this iteration. The requirements document is the main input for the build team, which designs and develops the code for implementing these requirements, and performs the testing. The tested code is then handed over to the deployment team, which performs pre-deployment tests, and then installs the system for production use.

These three stages are such that in a typical short-cycle development, they can be of equal duration (though the effort consumed is not the same, as the manpower deployed in the different stages is different.) Also, as the boundary between these stages is somewhat soft (e.g., high level design can be made a part of the first stage

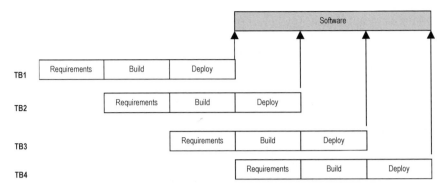

FIG. 3. Executing the timeboxing process model.

or the second), the duration of the different stages can be made approximately equal by suitably distributing the activities that lie at the boundary of two adjacent stages.

With a time box of three stages, the project proceeds as follows. When the requirement team has finished requirements for timebox-1, the requirements are given to the build-team for building the software. Meanwhile, the requirement team goes on and starts preparing the requirements for timebox-2. When the build for the timebox-1 is completed, the code is handed over to the deployment team, and the build team moves on to build code for requirements for timebox-2, and the requirements team moves on to doing requirements for timebox-3. This pipelined execution of the timeboxing process is shown in Fig. 3.

With a three-stage time box, at most three iterations can be concurrently in progress. If the time box is of size T days, then the first software delivery will occur after T days. The subsequent deliveries, however, will take place after every $T/3$ days. For example, if the time box duration T is 9 weeks (and each stage duration is 3 weeks), the first delivery is made 9 weeks after the start of the project. The second delivery is made after 12 weeks, the third after 15 weeks, and so on. Contrast this with a linear execution of iterations, in which the first delivery will be made after 9 weeks, the second will be made after 18 weeks, the third after 27 weeks, and so on.

3.3   Time, Effort and Team Size

It should be clear that the duration of each iteration has not been reduced—in fact it may even increase slightly as the formality of handing over between stages may require extra overhead that may not be needed if the strict partitioning in stages was not there. The total work done in a time box also remains the same—the same amount of software is delivered at the end of each iteration as the time box undergoes the same stages. However, the delivery time to the end client (after the first iteration) reduces by a factor of n with an n-stage time box if pipelining is employed. As in hardware, let us define the *speedup* of this process model as the ratio of the number of stage-time-units it takes to deliver one time box output if development is done without overlapping with the number of stage-time-units it takes on an average to deliver one time box output when pipelining is used. It is clear that, in ideal conditions, with a n-stage time box, the speedup is n. In other words, the development is n times faster with this model as compared to the model where the iterations are executed serially.

We can also view it in terms of throughput. Let us define the throughput as the amount of software delivered per unit time. Note that throughput is different from productivity—in productivity we compute the output per unit effort while in throughput we are interested in the output per unit time. We can clearly see that in steady state, the throughput of a project using timeboxing is n times more than what is achieved if serial iterations were employed. In other words, n times more functionality is being delivered per unit time. If in an iteration the team can develop S size units (in lines of code, function points, or some other unit) and the duration of the time box is T, then the throughput of a process in which the iterations are executed serially will be S/T size units per unit time. With the timeboxing process model, however, the throughput is $n * S/T$. That is, the throughput also increases by a factor of n.

If the size of the team executing the stage S_i is R_i, then the effort spent in the stage S_i is

$$E(S_i) = R_i * T/n.$$

Note that the model only requires that the duration of the stages be approximately the same, which is T/n in this case (or one stage-time-unit.) It does not imply that the amount of effort spent in a stage is same. The effort consumed in a stage S_i also depends on R_i, the size of the team for that stage. And there is no constraint from the model that the different R_is should be the same.

The total effort consumed in an iteration, i.e., in a time box, is

$$E(\text{TB}) = \sum_{i=1}^{n} E(S_i).$$

This effort is no different than if the iterations were executed serially—the total effort for an iteration is the sum of the effort for its stages. In other words, the total effort for an iteration remains the same in timeboxing as in serial execution of iterations. Note also that the productivity of the timeboxing process model (assuming no extra overhead) is same as without pipelining of iterations. In each of the cases, if S is the output in each iteration, the productivity is $S/E(\text{TB})$ size units per person-day (or whatever unit of effort we choose.)

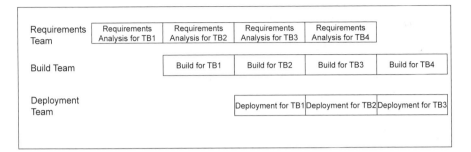

FIG. 4. Tasks of different teams.

If the same effort and time is spent in each iteration and the productivity also remains the same, then what is the cost of reducing the delivery time? The real cost of this increased throughput is in the resources used in this model. With timeboxing, there are dedicated teams for different stages. Each team is executing the task for that stage for a different iteration. This is the main difference from the situation where there is a single team which performs all the stages and the entire team works on the same iteration. With timeboxing process model, different teams are working on different iterations and the total team size for the project is $\sum_{i=1}^{n} R_i$. The team-wise activity for the 3-stage pipeline discussed above is shown in Fig. 4.

Let us compare the team size of a project using timeboxing with another project that executes iterations serially. In a serial execution of iterations, it is implicitly assumed that the same team performs all the activities of the iteration, that is, they perform all the stages of the iteration. For sake of illustration, let us assume that the team size is fixed throughout the iteration, and that the team has R resources. So, the same R people perform the different stages—first they perform the tasks of stage 1, then of stage 2, and so on. Assuming that even with dedicated resources for a stage, the same number of resources are required for a stage as in the linear execution of stages, the team size for each stage will be R. Consequently, the total project team size when the time box has n stages is $n * R$. That is, the team size in timeboxing is n times the size of the team in serial execution of iterations.

For example, consider an iterative development with three stages, as discussed above. Suppose that it takes 2 people 2 weeks to do the requirements for an iteration, it takes 4 people 2 weeks to do the build for the iteration, and it takes 3 people 2 weeks to test and deploy. If the iterations are serially executed, then the team for the project will be 4 people (the maximum size needed for a stage)—in the first 2 weeks two people will primarily do the requirements, then all the four people will do the task of build, and then 3 people will do the deployment. That is, the team size is likely to be the peak team size, that is, four people. If the resources are allocated to the project as and when needed (that is, there is a resource ramp-up in the start and ramp-down in the end), the average team size is $(2 + 4 + 3)/3 = 3$ persons.

If this project is executed using the timeboxing process model, there will be three separate teams—the requirements team of size 2, the build team of size 4, and the deployment team of size 3. So, the total team size for the project is $(2 + 4 + 3) = 9$ persons. This is three times the average team size if iterations are executed serially. It is due to this increase in team size that the throughput is also 3 times the throughput in serial-iterations.

Hence, in a sense, the timeboxing provides an approach for utilizing additional manpower to reduce the delivery time. It is well known that with standard methods of executing projects, we cannot compress the cycle time of a project substantially by adding more manpower [8]. This principle holds here also within a time box—we cannot reduce the size of a time box by adding more manpower. However, through the timeboxing model, we can use more manpower in a manner such that by parallel execution of different stages we are able to deliver software quicker. In other words, it provides a way of shortening delivery times through the use of additional manpower.

The above example can be used to illustrate another usefulness of the timeboxing model. We know that in a project, typically the manpower requirement follows a Rayaleigh curve [2], which means that in the start and end, the project typically requires less resources (even if there are more resources available, it can gainfully consume only the required number), and the peak is reached somewhere in the middle. This poses a challenge for staffing in a project—if the team size is fixed, then it means that in the start and the end, they may be underutilized (or in the middle, the progress is slower than it could be as not enough resources are available). To avoid this underutilization, resources can be ramped-up on a need basis in the start and then ramped-down towards the end.

The same sort of resource requirement can be expected within an iteration, as an iteration is essentially a small project. However, though in a waterfall process model adding the resources slowly and then slowly removing them from the project can be done relatively easily, this ramp-up and ramp-down will not be always feasible in an iterative development as it will have to be done for each iteration, which can make resource management very difficult. Furthermore, as iterations may not be very large, the benefit of allocating resources when needed and freeing them when they are not needed might not be worth the effort as the slack time may be of short durations. Overall, optimum resource allocation in serial iterations is difficult and is likely to result in underutilization of resources.

The situation with the timeboxing process model is different. The team sizes for the different stages need not be same—in fact, they should be of the size needed to complete the task in the specified duration. Hence, we can allocate the "right" team size for the different phases, which generally will mean smaller team size for the initial and end phases and larger team size for the middle phases. These resources are "permanently" allocated to the project, which simplifies resource allocation and management. And the resources have, in the ideal case, a 100% utilization.

3.4   Unequal Stages

Clearly, the reality will rarely present itself in such a clean manner such that iterations can be fit in a time box and can be broken into stages of equal duration. There will be scenarios where these requirements will not hold. And the first possibility of a non-ideal situation is where the duration of the different stages is not the same—different stages take different time to complete.

As the pipelining concepts from hardware tell us [13], in such a situation the output is determined by the slowest stage, that is, the stage that takes the longest time. With unequal stages, each stage effectively becomes equal to the longest stage and therefore the frequency of output is once every time period of the slowest stage. In other words, the stage-time-unit is now equal to the duration of the longest stage, and the output is delivered once for each of this stage-time-unit. As each stage effectively becomes equal to the longest stage, the team for smaller stages will have slack times, resulting in resource under-utilization in these stages while the team with longest stage will be fully occupied.

As an example, let us consider a 3-stage pipeline of the type discussed above in which the different stages are 2 weeks, 3 weeks, and 4 weeks—that is, the duration of the time box is 9 weeks. For pipelined execution, such an iteration will first be transformed into an iteration of 12 weeks and 3 stages, each stage taking 4 weeks. Then, the iterations will be executed in parallel. The execution of different iterations from the perspective of different teams is shown in Fig. 5 (W represents "work" and S represents "slack").

Note, however, that even with the output frequency being determined by the slowest stage, a considerable speedup is possible. In a serial iterative development, software will be delivered once every 9 weeks. With the timeboxing model, the slowest stage will determine the speed of execution, and hence the deliveries are done every 4 weeks. This delivery time is still less than half the delivery time of serial iterations!

However, there is a cost if the stages are unequal. As the longest stage determines the speed, each stage effectively becomes equal to the slowest stage. In this example, as shown in Fig. 4, it means that the first and second stages will also get 4 weeks each, even though their work requires only 2 and 3 weeks. In other words, it will result in "slack time" for the teams for the first and the third stage, resulting in under utilization of resources. So, the resource utilization, which is 100% when all the stages are of equal duration, will reduce resulting in underutilization of resources. Of course, this wastage can easily be reduced by reducing the size of the teams

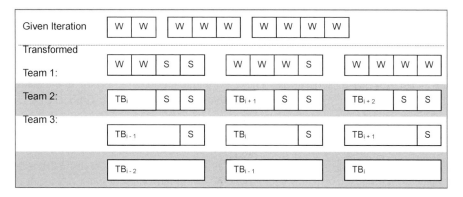

FIG. 5. Execution with unequal stages.

for the slower stages to a level that they take approximately the same time as the slowest stage. Note that elongating the cycle time by reducing manpower is generally possible, even though the reverse is not possible.

3.5   Exceptions

What happens if an exceptional condition arises during the execution of a stage of some time box? The most common exception is likely to be that a stage in an iteration finishes either before or after its time. If a stage of an iteration completes before time, there is no problem—the team for the stage will have to wait for the remaining period (or till the previous stage of the next iteration finishes). In other words, if the team for a stage I of an iteration K finishes ΔT time before its completion time, then in the worst case it will wait for this amount of time without any work (assuming that other stages do not slip.) Of course, if the stage $I - 1$ of the iteration $K + 1$ also completes before its time and is able to handover the work to the team for the stage I, then this team can start working and will have ΔT extra time to complete the task for the iteration $K + 1$.

If the stage completes late, then there can be a cascade effect on other stages leading to each of the future stages getting delayed. Suppose that the stage I is late by ΔT. This means that the team for stage $I + 1$ will have to wait for ΔT without any work, assuming that it finished its task for the earlier iteration in time. If the team for stage $I + 1$ can complete the task in this reduced time, then there is no further effect on the execution. In other words, if one team is late, it can be compensated by the next team (or the next few teams) doing their tasks in lesser time.

If, however, each team continues to work for their fully allotted time, then there will be a cascading effect. The team for each stage, after completing its task for the previous iteration, will have to wait for ΔT to get the work for this iteration. This cascades to the last stage also, which starts and completes ΔT late. In other words, the net effect of the exception is that the delivery of this iteration is late by ΔT. After the delayed iteration, all future deliveries will come after every T/n time units (for a n-stage time box of T duration.) The effect on team utilization is that all the teams for stages subsequent to where the exception occurred have to wait without work for ΔT time, leading to reduced utilization of resources.

The timeboxing process model assumes that the resources for the different stages are separate, so there is no resource contention. In fact, as discussed above, this is one of the key features of this model—most other models share the resources in different stages. Situations can arise in which two concurrently executing iterations, each in a different stage, require some common resources. For example, for the requirement analysis of one iteration and deployment of another iteration, the same resources may be required. If timeboxing is to be used, such a situation should be avoided. However, in some exceptional conditions, this situation might arise.

If the shared resource that has caused this "conflict" is only a part of one team, then the net result of this sharing will be that the stage will be left with fewer resources and hence may take a longer time to complete. The effect of this we have discussed above. However, if the conflicting resources form the complete team of a stage, then we have a peculiar situation—there is no resource to execute the stage for the iteration. This case will finally translate to a "null" iteration being executed—this iteration consumes the time but no resources and produces no output. The effect of such a null iteration is that there will be no output when this null iteration completes. Also, the null iteration will cause the other teams which were not being shared or which had no conflicts to waste their time for this null iteration.

Other exceptional conditions must be possible. In each such case, one has to examine and see how to deal with it within the timeboxing framework. Note, however, all such exceptional situations will lead to some loss in terms of output or benefits. Consequently, if the exception is likely to occur very frequently—a situation implying that the process model was probably not suitable for the problem at hand—it may be worthwhile considering a different process model for the problem.

4. Applying the Model

Effective use of the timeboxing model, as in any other process model, will require many practical issues to be addressed. In this section we discuss some other issues relating to deploying the model on projects.

4.1 Scope of Applicability

Like any other process model, the timeboxing model will be suitable only for some types of projects and some business contexts. The first clear requirement is that the business context should be such that there is a strong need for delivering a large number of features within a relatively short span of time. In other words, time to deliver is very important and is sought even if it implies that the team size will be large and there may be some wastage of manpower (due to slack times that may come in different situations).

As for any iterative development approach, the model should be applied for projects where the requirements are such that some initial wish list is known to the users/clients, but there are many aspects that are dynamic and change with the competitive and business landscape. (If all requirements are clearly known in the start then the waterfall model will be most suitable and economic.)

Timeboxing is well suited for projects that require a large number of features to be developed in a short time around a stable architecture using stable technologies. These features should be such that there is some flexibility in grouping them for building a meaningful system that provides value to the users. Such a situation is frequently present in many commercial projects where a system already exists and the purpose of the project is to augment the existing system with new features for it. Another example of projects that satisfy this are many web-site development projects—generally some architecture is fixed early, and then the set of features to be added iteratively is decided depending on what the competition is providing and the perceived needs of the customer (which change with time).

To apply timeboxing, there should be a good feature-based estimation method, such as the bottom-up estimation technique described in [14]. With a good feature-based estimation model, the set of features that can be built in an iteration can be decided. As technology churn and unstable architecture make it harder to do feature-based estimation, projects where technology and architecture changes are frequent and likely are not suitable candidates for this process model.

The team size and composition is another critical parameter for a project using timeboxing. Clearly the overall project team should be large enough that it can be divided into sub-teams that are dedicated for performing the tasks of the different stages. However, to keep the management complexity under control, it is desirable that the team be not so large that coordination between different sub-teams and different time boxes become too hard to manage.

There is a side benefit of having separate teams for different stages. As the teams are separate, they need not be collocated. This means that the different stages of an iteration need not be done in one location—something that must happen if the same team is to work on all stages. Having different stages being executed by different teams permits outsourcing of different stages to different teams in different locations, thereby allowing the possibility of leveraging the global delivery models of modern multinational enterprises.

The model is not suitable for projects where it is difficult to partition the overall development into multiple iterations of approximately equal duration. It is also not suitable for projects where different iterations may require different stages, and for projects whose features are such that there is no flexibility to combine them into meaningful deliveries. Such a situation may arise, for example, if only a few features are to be built, one (or a couple) in each iteration, each tied to some business need. In this case, as there is only one feature to be built in an iteration, that feature will determine the duration of the iteration.

4.2   Project Planning

One of the key activities in planning each time box will be selecting requirements that should be built in a time box. Remember, one dimension of planning does not exist anymore—the project manager does not have to do scheduling of the iteration or its stages as they are given to him. Also, in general, the effort and team sizes are also fixed. The quality requirement also remain the same. This means, that out of the four variables in a project, namely time, cost, quality, and scope [4], the only variable that is free for a time box is scope. Hence, the key planning activity for a time box is what requirements to build.

As discussed above, this can be achieved if there is a good feature-based estimation model, and there is some flexibility in grouping the features to be delivered. This assumes that the processes being used for each iteration are stable and repeatable and that the effort distribution of each iteration among the different stages is approximately the same. With a stable and repeatable process, if we have a feature based estimation, we can estimate the impact of each feature on the effort needed and the schedule. If we have some flexibility in grouping the features to be built in an iteration, we can select the set that can together be built in a time box, as we know the total effort available in a time box.

In the project commencement stage, the key planning activity with this model is the design of the time box to be used. That is, the duration of the time box, the number and definition of the stages, and the teams for the different stages. Having a large duration of the time box will minimize the benefits of iterative development. And having too small a time box may imply too little functionality getting developed to the customer. Hence, the size of the time box is likely to be of the order of a few weeks to a few months. Frequently, the exact duration will be determined by business considerations.

The next obvious issue is how many stages should be there in a time box. The answer to this will clearly depend on the nature of the project. However, as too many parallel executions can make it difficult to manage the project, it is most likely that the model will be used with a few stages, perhaps between two and four. It may be pointed out that substantial benefit accrues even with two stages—the delivery time (after the first delivery) is reduced by half. At Infosys, we suggest a 3-stage time box, as discussed in the example above.

The team sizes for the different stages need to be carefully selected so that the resource utilization is high. We know that effort distribution among different stages is not uniform and that number of resources that can be utilized effectively is also not uniform [2,3]. Generally, in a project, few resources are required in the start and the end and maximum resources are required in the middle. Within a time box, the same pattern should be expected. This means, that the team size for the first and the last stage should be small, while the size of the team for the middle stages should be the largest. The actual number, of course, will depend on the nature of the project and the delivery commitments. However, the team sizes should be such that the effort distribution among the different stages is reasonable.

A heuristic that can be used for selecting the team sizes for the different stages, once the time box duration and the stages are fixed, is given below. This heuristic tries to keep the resource utilization high, while preserving the timeboxing process model property of having approximately equal stages. It assumes that in the start, the project manger has a good idea of the effort estimate of each of the stages for a typical iteration.

(1) Select the stage that is likely to take the longest in an iteration. Often, this may be the build phase. Estimate the effort needed to complete the work for this stage in a typical iteration.

(2) Fix a stage duration from the time box duration and the number of iterations.

(3) Using the effort estimate and the stage duration, determine the team size needed to complete this stage. Check that the team size and the duration are feasible. If not, adjust the time box duration and/or the team size.

(4) From the finally selected time box duration and the finally selected team size for the stage, determine the total effort for that stage. Using the expected distribution of effort among different stages, determine the effort estimates for other stages.

(5) For the remaining stages, use the effort estimate of a stage and the stage duration to estimate the size of the team needed for that stage.

This heuristic is essentially trying to ensure that the different stages are of equal length and that the team size and duration of the key-stage is manageable. Note also, as we first fix the critical stage which potentially takes the longest time, it means that for the other stages, we are basically elongating the stage length to make it equal to the longest stage, and then suitably allocating the resources so the resource utilization is high. Note also that increasing the duration of a task by reducing the number of resources is possible even though the reverse (that is, reducing the time by increasing the resources) is not always possible. With this heuristic, the duration of the stage is determined by the "slowest" stage, which becomes the "rate determining step." Resources are then adjusted accordingly.

A challenge that project managers could face is determining the relationship between the effort estimates as determined from the estimation model and the cost model of the project. This problem is more acute in timeboxing as the different teams may not be collocated and hence may have different cost-basis. Such an issue can slow down negotiation and may result in features for an iteration not being finalized in time. One possible solution to this is to ensure that there is agreement between the customer and the supplier before-hand about the estimation model and how a feature is considered to be of a particular cost. Tying the feature estimate to cost also provides the cost visibility of different requirements groupings.

4.3   Project Monitoring and Control

Monitoring and controlling a project which employs timeboxing is clearly going to be more complex than a serial iterative development. There are a few clear reasons for it. First, as discussed above, the team size has become larger and the division of resources stricter. This makes resource management within the project harder. There are other issues also relating to project resources—for example the HR impact of having one team performing the same type of activity continuously.

Second, monitoring is now more intense as multiple iterations are concurrently active, each having some internal milestones (at the very least, completion of each stage will be a milestone). Generally, milestones are important points for monitoring the health of a project (for some example of analysis at milestones, the user is referred to [14,15]). In a timeboxing project, the frequency of milestones is more and hence considerably more effort needs to be spent in these analysis. Furthermore, project management also requires more regular monitoring and making local corrections to plans depending on the situation in the project. Due to the tight synchronization among stages of different iterations, making these local corrections is much more challenging as it can have an impact that will go beyond this iteration to other time boxes as well.

The project will require tight configuration management as many teams are working concurrently. A basic CM challenge is to ensure that a common consistent source code is made available to the teams for the different stages. Daily Build and Smoke Test [24] is a technique that can be used for ensuring a common consistent source code. With this technique, a software product is completely built very frequently (every day or every few days) and then put through a series of tests. These tests typically include compiling all files, linking all files, ensuring that there are no show-stopper bugs, and that the code passes the smoke test. The smoke test are typically test scripts that exercise the key functionality of the entire system. The test should be thorough enough that if the build passes the smoke test, it should mean that it is sufficiently stable and that changes made did not affect the functionality of any other portion of the system.

Despite frequent synchronization, there will be situations where multiple simultaneous changes are done to the same file. This is quite likely to happen between the build and deployment stages as the bugs found during deployment are typically fixed by the deployment team (though in consultation with the build team.) To handle this situation, the reconciliation procedures (i.e., procedures that are used to reconcile two changes if they are done concurrently [14]) need to be solid and applied regularly.

Another CM requirement is the need to have multiple areas whose access is strictly controlled. Typically these areas can be:

- Test—the software that has been put through various tests and is ready for integration and system testing.
- Preproduction—a copy of the production system to be used for testing.
- Production—the actual area where the software is running when in use.

Typically only the executable version and not the source code is available in either Preproduction or production environments. With multiple time boxes occurring at the same point in time, there is a necessity to ensure that the test, preproduction, and production environments are "clean" and strictly controlled. A lack of discipline in access control, which may be acceptable in non-parallel development, would result in confusion and rework and because multiple timeboxes are involved.

Overall, with timeboxing, the project management needs to be very proactive and tight. This can sometimes lead to decisions being taken that can have adverse impact. For example, a project manager, in order to complete in a time box might compromise on the quality of the delivery. This also implies that a project using timeboxing requires an experienced project manager—an inexperienced project manager can throw the synchronization out of gear leading to loss in productivity and quality, and delayed deliveries.

4.4   Handling Changes

We know that requirements change and that such changes can be quite disruptive [5,17]. Changes can vary from being very minor, such as a change to an error message being displayed in the system, to a significant requirement, such as to change the architecture or design. Major change requests could have a detrimental impact on the project by making work that was done in the past redundant and add new work that requires significant effort. Thus changes tend to be one of the major risks for any project on a tight schedule. Hence, most development processes add a change management process for accepting a change request, analyzing it, and then implementing it, if approved. Such a process is necessary if the process is not intrinsically capable of allowing change, as is the case with the waterfall model. A change management process is needed to ensure that changes do not have a very detrimental impact on the project. One such process works as follows [14]. When a change request arrives, it is logged into a system. It is then analyzed for its impact, that is, what will be the impact on the project if the change is implemented. Such an impact analysis will typically detail out the scope of the change, what are the risks, and what is the impact on the cost and schedule for implementing the change. Based on the impact analysis, a decision is taken whether to incorporate the change or not.

With timeboxing, requirement change requests can be handled in a somewhat different manner—unless a request is extremely critical, the change request is passed on to the next possible time box. That is, the change request comes as a new requirement in a future time box. Since the time boxes are likely to be relatively short, deferring the requirement change request to the next time box does not cause inordinate delay.

The same can be done for the defects that are found after deployment. Such defects are viewed as change requests. If the defect is such that it is hurting the business of the organization and whose repair cannot be delayed, then it is fixed as soon as possible. Otherwise, its fixing is treated like a change request and is fixed in the next possible iteration.

There is thus a significant benefit that a timebox can be executed without having to invest time and effort in incorporating modifications that arise due to change requests.

However, with timeboxing ensuring that related documents like design and test cases are updated and maintained under the face of changes becomes even more critical than in other process models because with overlaps and multiple teams, things can get outdated very quickly resulting in incorrect specifications, design or test cases that will directly impact the quality. The rework because of the lack of maintenance of documentation can also have a much harder impact on the timelines of a stage or time box. It is therefore necessary to have tighter management and control of requirements, design and test documentation. Frequent baselining, supported by a traceability matrix that ensures that a requirement can be traced from the requirements document to a test document and vice versa, a change matrix in all documentation that clearly identifies the changes that were made and ties it to the specific change request are steps that can help.

4.5   Localized Adjustments in Time Boxes

We have been assuming that the team for each stage is fixed. However, the basic requirement for the model to operate smoothly is that each stage should finish in its allotted time. If the number of resources in the sub-team of a stage changes across time boxes, there is no problem as far as the model is concerned (though the resource management may become harder). Clearly then, for some time boxes, additional resources can be added in some stages, if desired. This type of adjustment might be considered when, for example, the system "core" is to be developed, or some large feature is to be developed that requires more work than what a time box can provide, etc. This adjustment can also be used to first start the project with fewer resources and then when the project picks up and there is experience with the model, the resources for the different stages are increased while preserving the time box structure.

Similarly, if some time box has less work to be done, some resources can be freed for that time box. However, in practice, if the work is less, the chances are that the team composition will not be changed for temporary changes in work (it is very hard to find temporary work in other projects), and the adjustment will be made by putting in more or less hours.

Local adjustment of stages is also possible. For example, in some time box, the team of a stage can finish its work in less time and "contribute" the remaining time towards the next stage, effectively shortening one stage and correspondingly lengthening the other one. This local adjustment also has no impact on the functioning of the model and may be used to handle special iterations where the work in some stages is lesser.

4.6   Refactoring

Any iterative development, due to the fact that design develops incrementally, can eventually lead to systems whose architecture and designs are more complex than necessary. This problem can be handled by techniques used for refactoring, wherein code from the previous iterations are redesigned without changing functionality, but paves the way for extensibility and better design for the future iterations. Martin Fowler defines refactoring as "Refactoring is a process of changing a software system in such a way that it does not alter the external behavior of the code, yet alters its internal structure" [12]. The goal of refactoring is therefore to pave the way for software to be extended and modified more easily without adding any new functionality. An iteratively developed system should undergo some refactoring otherwise it may become too complex to easily enhance in future. Some methodologies, like the XP, explicitly plan for refactoring. In XP, for example, refactoring can be done at any time.

Refactoring provides a catalog of techniques, such as using "wrapper classes," to reuse code previously written while still improving the design of the system. The refactoring process can be viewed like a development process except that the activity in the different stages is different—the analysis is largely a "discovery" of redesign opportunities in the existing code, the design is actually "re-design" of the code for the purpose of improved design to reduce complexity and enhance extensibility, the coding is mostly "code transformation," and the testing is really "re-testing" for the same functionality that was originally intended.

Though refactoring suggests that it is a process of evolution of the quality of the code and therefore a continuous process, in the timeboxing model the most natural way to perform refactoring will be to consider it as the goal of one of the time boxes. That is, in some time box, the basic objective is to do refactoring and not to add new features (or minimal features). In this time box, refactoring undergoes the same process as developing new features—i.e., through its stages, except, as discussed above, the activity within each stage will be performed differently. So, if the pipeline has the three stages given earlier, then in the time box in which refactoring is done, first the requirements for refactoring will be decided. The team for requirements will analyze the system to decide what part of the system can and should be refactored, their priorities, and what parts of the system will be refactored in this time box, etc. In the build stage, the refactoring will actually be done and tested, and in the last stage, the new system will be deployed. So, for all practical purposes, refactoring is just another iteration being done in a time box, except that at the end of this iteration no new (or very little) functionality is delivered—the system that is delivered has the same functionality but is simpler (and perhaps smaller).

5. An Example

In this section we discuss a real commercial project on which this process model was successfully applied. We first give the background about the project and the commercial and other constraints on it and then describe how these constraints were accommodated within this process model. We also discuss the metrics data collected.

5.1 Background

A US-based e-store (the customer), specializing in selling sporting good, approached Infosys, for further developing its site. They already had a desired list of about 100 features that they wanted their site to have in the next 6 months, and had another set of features that they felt that they would need about a year down the road. This list was constantly evolving with new features getting added and some getting dropped depending on what the competitors were doing and how the trends were changing.

As many of the features were small additions, and as the list of features was very dynamic, Infosys proposed to use the timeboxing model, with a 3-stage time box (of the type discussed above). To keep the costs low, it was decided that the offshore model for development will be used. In this model, the team in India will do the development, while analysis and deployment will be done by teams at the customer's site. Furthermore, to reduce costs further, it was decided that total effort of the first and the third stages would be minimized, while passing most of the work on to the build stage.

After studying the nature of the project and detailed processes for the three stages, the actual duration chosen for the stages was as follows: 2 weeks for requirements, 3 weeks for build, and 1 week for deployment. The initial team size for the three stages was selected as 2 persons, 6 persons, and 2 persons respectively. It was felt that these times and team sizes are sufficient for the tasks of the different stages. (With these durations and team sizes, the effort distribution between requirements, build, and deployment is 4 : 18 : 2, which is consistent with what Infosys has seen in many similar offshore based development projects.)

The work was also classified using the matrix shown in Fig. 6. As shown in the figure, features were classified on the dimensions of their complexity and business payoff, and for each dimension they were classified as "high" or "low." Features in the top left quadrant, which represent those that have the maximum business payoff with the least technology complexity were taken up for development in the earlier iterations. In subsequent iterations, the features in the other quadrants were chosen.

On at least one occasion, one feature was too big to be completed within one iteration. This feature was split into two sub-features and executed across two consec-

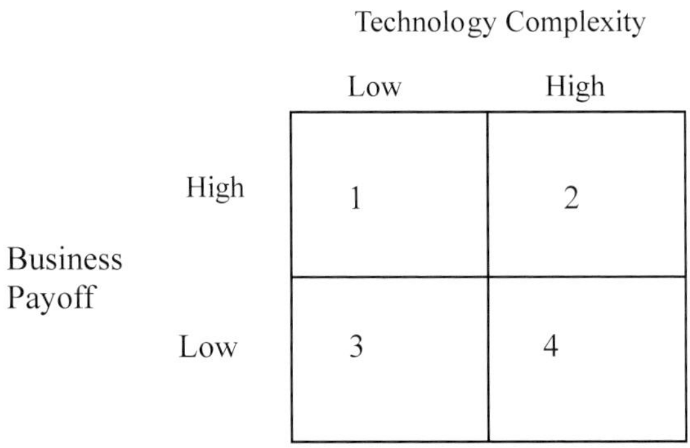

FIG. 6. Prioritizing the features.

utive iterations. However, the formal deployment of the two sub-features was done together.

5.2   Process Design

In this project, the size of the different stages is not equal. As discussed above, with unequal stages, the delivery frequency is determined by the longest stage. In other words, with these durations, by using the timeboxing model in this project, delivery will be done (except for the first one) after every 3 weeks, as this is the duration of the build stage which is the slowest stage in the time box. We have also seen that unequal stages result in slack times for the dedicated teams of the shorter stages. In this project, the slack times for the requirements team will be 1 week and the slack time for the deployment team will be 2 weeks. Obviously, this resource wastage has to be minimized.

So, we have a 3-stage pipeline, each stage effectively of 3-week duration. The execution of the different time boxes is shown in Fig. 7. The resource planning was done such that the requirements team executed its task in the 2nd and the 3rd weeks of its stage (with the 1st one as the slack), and the deployment team executed its task in the 1st week (with the 2nd and 3rd as the slack.)

Figure 7 shows four different time boxes—R refers to the requirements activity, B to the build activity, and D to the deployment activity. The boundaries of the different stages are shown, with each stage being of 3 weeks. The activity of each week is shown in the diagram. F is used to represent that the team is free—i.e., to show the slack time. The first delivery takes place 6 weeks after actually starting the iteration. (Note that this made possible by organizing the slack times of the first stage in the

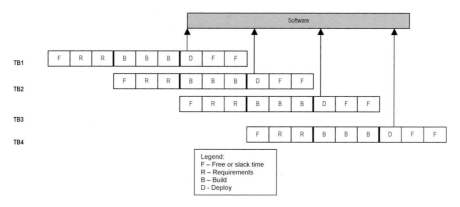

FIG. 7.   Time boxed execution of the project.

start and the last stage towards the end). All subsequent deliveries take 3 weeks, that is, deliveries are made after 6 weeks, after 9 weeks, after 12 weeks, and so on.

As mentioned above, this execution will lead to a slack time of 1 week in the first stage and 2 weeks in the third stage. This resource wastage was reduced in the project by properly organizing the resources in the teams. First we notice that the first and the last stage are both done on-site, that is, the same location (while the second stage is done in a different location). In this project as the slack time of the first stage is equal to the duration of the third stage, and the team size requirement of both stages is the same, a natural way to reduce waste is to have the same team perform both the stages. By doing this, the slack time is eliminated. It is towards this end that the slack time of the first stage was kept in the start and the slack time of the 3rd stage was kept at the end. With this organization, the slack time of the 1st stage matches exactly with the activity time of the third stage. Hence, it is possible to have the same team perform the activities of the two stages in a dedicated manner—for 1 week the team is dedicated for deployment and for 2 weeks it is dedicated for requirements.

With this, we now have two teams—on-site team that performs the requirements stage and the deployment stage, and the off-shore team that performs the build stage. The process worked as follows. The offshore team, in a 3-week period, would build the software for which the requirements would be given by the on-site team. In the same period, the on-site team would deploy the software built by the offshore team in an earlier time box in the 1st week, and then do the requirements analysis for this time box for the remaining 2 weeks. The activity of the two teams is shown in Fig. 8. As is shown, after the initial time boxes, there is no slack time.

We can also view this in another manner. We can say that the number of resources in the sub-team for the requirements stage is 4/3 and the number of resources in the sub-team for the deployment stage is 2/3 (or that two resources working 2/3rd of their time for requirements and 1/3rd for deployment.) With these team sizes, to perform the work of the stages which has been specified as $2 \times 2 = 4$ person-

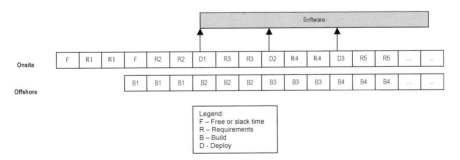

FIG. 8. Tasks of the on-site and offshore teams.

weeks for requirements and $2 \times 1 = 2$ person-weeks for deployment, full 3 weeks are required for these stages. In other words, with team sizes of 4/3, 6, and 2/3, respectively for the three stages, we now have a time box with three stages of 3 weeks each. That is, by dividing the on-site team into "dedicated" resources for the two stages, we have the ideal time box with each stage requiring 3 weeks.

It should be added that the team size was gradually ramped up while preserving the basic structure of the time boxes. Starting with a team size of 6 (in offshore) in Iteration 1, the team was ramped up to 8 persons in Iteration II and to 12 persons by Iteration V. Consequently the number of features handled per Iteration also increased from 3 to 12 between Iteration I and Iteration V.

5.3   Project Management

As discussed earlier, once the basic structure of the timeboxing process model is fixed, one of the key issues is to have a proper estimation procedure that can permit feature-to-cost mapping. In this project, the standard bottom-up effort estimation process of Infosys was used [14]. In this approach, estimation starts with identifying the main features to be built and classifying them as simple, medium, or complex based on some defined criteria. When the number of different types of features is known, using some baseline cost which is determined from data from past projects, the total effort for coding and unit testing is determined. Then from this effort, the effort for other phases is determined as a percentage of coding cost.

In this project there are only three major phases, unlike the standard process used at Infosys. Hence, the percentages were suitably combined to determine the distribution among these three stages. This distribution was then used to determine the effort for the other two stages from the build stage (the build stage is approximately the same as the coding and unit testing stage of the standard process).

For applying the estimation model, every feature was broken down in terms of the pages and components that needed to be created or changed. The simple, medium, and complex classification was clearly specified, using experience with similar projects in the past. The first few iterations were consciously underestimated to account for the learning-curve and to reduce the risks. However, a systematic adjustment was done for the subsequent iterations which corrected this bias. At the end of every iteration, effort consumed is compared with the estimates on the project, and the Adjustment Factor (AF) for an iteration computed as the ratio of the actual effort to the estimated effort. We arrive at the weighted adjustment factor for estimation for the Nth iteration by using the formula $0.5 * \text{AF}[N - 1] + 0.30\text{AF}[N - 2] + 0.20\text{AF}[N - 3]$. This adjustment factor was applied in the Nth iteration estimate. This ensured that errors in the estimation methodology were addressed in the subsequent Iterations. Interestingly, the value of Adjustment Factors for the later iterations was pretty close to 1.

The number of people offshore on the project varied between 8 to 15 for different iterations. This change was made on the basis of the estimate done for every iteration. However, the time box schedule remained the same. This ability to ramp up/down the amount of resources without compromising the delivery dates was very critical to the success of the project. As resource allocation cannot be arbitrarily expanded or shrunk without affecting the schedule, it was agreed with the client that a minimum offshore-team size of 6 would be maintained, and continuity of the key players will also be maintained across iterations. While increasing the team size so as to build more features, a sanity check was made whether the features that are being planned can be built within the build effort available for the stage.

For the project to proceed smoothly, since two different sites are involved, an on-site coordinator for the project was assigned. The main tasks for the coordinator were to coordinate with the users and other teams in the user organization and be the contact point for the project and the main communication channel between the teams in the two locations. He was also the point-person for reporting and escalation management. This position considerably helped in keeping the coordination smooth and keep the pipeline going.

Risk management and its planning is another key activity in a project. It is quite possible that a project using the timeboxing approach will experience different types of risks. The risk management approach followed in the project was also the standard organization approach (more details on this are given in [14,15]). In this approach, the risks to the project are first enumerated. They are then ranked for their probability of occurrence and the impact on a scale. The project generally focuses on high probability and high to medium impact risks for mitigation. The top few risks and their mitigation approach is shown in Table I.

As we can see, the top risk is changes in requirements as it can derail the process easily. The mitigation approach is to do an impact analysis for each change request with a special focus on its impact on the schedule. Then based on the impact analysis, a decision will be taken whether to include it in this iteration or include it in the next one(s). Notice that completing requirements within the time allocated for that stage is also a risk to the project. Interestingly, one of the risk mitigation strategies for this also leverages the iterative development approach with short delivery times—if some clarifications were holding up specification of some requirement, that requirement was shifted to the next time box. Code reconciliation is also a risk—handling of this we have discussed earlier in the chapter.

TABLE I
TOP RISKS AND THEIR RISK MITIGATION PLAN

Risk	Prob.	Impact	Mitigation
Changes in requirements	High	High	Impact analysis will be done based on impact on schedule. A decision will be taken to accommodate in the current or the next iteration.
New technology	Med	High	Training of team members in the technologies used. Identified integration issues as part of the requirements stage and work with product vendors to find a solution. Additionally specify the integration pattern early.
To complete requirements in time for build	Med	Med	Freeze requirements up-front; Have tight escalation rules for requirements clarifications; Keep a close interaction with the customer's representative; If answers not provided within specified timeslots, shift features to subsequent iterations.
Code reconciliation	Med	Med	Daily build and smoke test; strictly follow the CM procedures; frequent reconciliations.

5.4   Configuration Management

The primary purpose of configuration management (CM) in a project is to manage the evolving configuration of the various parts of the system like source files, documentation, plans, etc. A proper CM in a project will keep track of latest versions and state of different documents, allow for updates to be undone, prevent unauthorized changes, collect all sources related to a release, etc. Traditionally, the main mechanisms used to support CM are naming conventions, version control, and access control. In the project, as multiple iterations are simultaneously active, it was realized that the CM procedures will have to be enhanced and that versions and baselines will have to be handled carefully.

To allow the timeboxing model to work smoothly, at any given time the project supported a minimum of three baselines—production support baseline, acceptance test baseline, and the development baseline. The development baseline represents the state of the current development—it goes through a series of versions till it is ready for release, i.e., when the development team (i.e., the offshore team) is ready to release it for acceptance testing and deployment. The released version is taken as the starting baseline for acceptance testing. The acceptance test team (i.e., the onsite team) runs the acceptance tests and makes changes to the acceptance test baseline locally, creating a series of versions of this baseline. When all the defects are fixed and the software is ready for production release, the acceptance test baseline becomes the

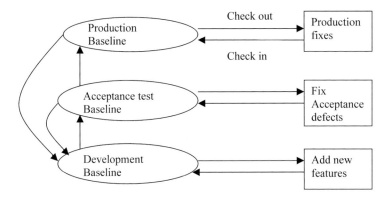

FIG. 9. Baselining process.

starting baseline for production. The deployment team (i.e., the onsite team) works with the production baseline and may make local changes to the production baseline, if needed, creating newer versions.

Besides the migration of baselines from development to acceptance testing to production, there is a reverse movement also—the starting baseline for any iteration is the latest production baseline. Due to the relationship between the three baselines, it is clear that the changes being done to a baseline will affect other baselines. To ensure that changes are not lost, changes made to the production baseline and the acceptance test baseline is regularly propagated to the development baseline. This process is shown in Fig. 9.

In the CM plan of the project, a clearly defined directory structure for managing the program assets was also planned. A baseline audit was done regularly, and before any release. A quality control check about the configuration procedures was performed once a month. At the start of every iteration, a synchronization of the complete development baseline was done with the production baseline. This synchronization is done to ensure that any changes made in other applications and modules (which may have been developed by a different team or a different vendor) on which this project depends are reflected in the sources used by the development team.

Requirement changes were handled as per the model—unless urgent, they were pushed to the next available time box. As the time boxes are small, there were no problems in doing this. For bug fixes also this was done. Unless the bug required immediate attention (in which case, it was corrected within 24 hours), the bug report was logged and scheduled as a part of the requirements for the next time box.

5.5   Data Collection and Analysis

As mentioned above, with the timeboxing process model, a project has to be very tightly monitored and controlled. For having an objective assessment of the health of a project, measurements are necessary. The basic measurements needed for monitoring a project are size, effort, schedule, and defects [25]. At Infosys, there are defined standards for collecting this data on projects. For effort, there is a weekly activity report system in which effort is logged in a project against different activities. For defects, there is a defect control system in which defects are logged along with their origin, severity, status and other properties. The reader is referred to [14,15] for further details on how these measurements are recorded in Infosys.

Even though this project used a different process model than was generally used, it followed the same measurements and analysis approach, and the standard tools were used. One main difference was that effort and defects were also tied to an iteration, not just to a project.

The data was analyzed at milestones using the standard milestone analysis template of the organization. In this analysis, an actual vs estimated analysis is done for effort and schedule, and customer complaints and change requests are examined. In this project, for an iteration there are only two milestones. In the project, the purpose of the milestone analysis is to properly control the execution of the iteration under progress. As the weekly status reporting mechanism was providing sufficient visibility and since the duration of an iteration was short, later on the milestone analysis was stopped.

At the end of each time box, an analysis of the time box was done, much in the same way a postmortem analysis is done for a project [3,9,11]. In general, a postmortem analysis is done to collect data and lessons learned that will benefit future projects and enhance the knowledge base of an organization. However, in an iterative development, the postmortem of one iteration can benefit the remaining iterations of the project itself. In this project, the standard postmortem analysis of the organization was followed [14]. The results were reviewed at the start of the next iteration. In this project, the analysis showed that the estimation approach being used was quite accurate and the process design was stable and the project was able to meet the commitments in each of the iterations.

6.   Conclusions

Iterative software development is now a necessity, given the velocity of business and the need for more effective ways to manage risks. The commonly used approach for iterative development is to decide the functionality of each iteration in the start of the iteration and then plan the effort and schedule for delivering the functionality in that iteration.

In the timeboxing model, the development is done in a series of fixed duration time boxes—the functionality to be developed in an iteration is selected in a manner that it can "fit" into the time box. Furthermore, each time box is divided into a sequence of approximately equal duration stages. There is a dedicated team for each stage, and as a team completes its task for a time box, it hands over the development of the iteration to the team for the next stage, and starts working on its task for the next time box (which is handed over to it by the team of the previous stage). The teams for the different stages all work concurrently, though each team works on a different iteration. And in a n-stage time box, n different iterations are simultaneously executing. The timeboxing model essentially emulates the pipelined execution of instructions in hardware which is now almost universally used.

Due to parallelism in the execution of different iterations, the turnaround time for each release is reduced substantially—for a n-stage time box, the average turnaround time for a time box of T time units duration will be T/n. That is, instead of each iteration completing after T time units, which is the case if the iterations are executed serially, with timeboxing, iterations complete, on an average, after every T/n time units. The execution speeds up by a factor of n, under ideal circumstances. The throughput, that is the amount of software delivered per unit time, also increases by a factor of n.

The total effort for each iteration, however, remains the same, and so does the productivity (total output per unit effort.) This compression of average delivery time without any increase in productivity comes as the total team size in the timeboxing model is larger. If the size of the team for each stage is the same, then the team size with a n-stage time box will be n times the team size needed if the same team is to execute all stages of an iteration, as is generally the case when iterations are performed serially. Hence, the timeboxing provides a structured approach of utilizing additional manpower in a project for reducing the software delivery times—something that is not generally possible.

We have discussed the impact of unequal stages and exceptions on the execution of this model, and have shown that even if the situation is not ideal with all stages fully balanced, a considerable speedup is still possible, but with a reduction in resource utilization. The model allows easy handling of change requests and in some ways simplifies the resource allocation issues by eliminating the need of resource ramp-up and ramp-down. Refactoring, which is needed in an iterative development, is treated as an iteration in its own right.

An example of applying the process model to a commercial project was also discussed. In the project, the duration of the three stages was set at 2 weeks, 3 weeks, and 1 week respectively. The initial size of the teams for these stages was 2 persons,

6 persons, and 2 persons. The first and the third stage were done at the customer's site while the second stage was done off-shore. With this time box, the first delivery was done after 6 weeks; subsequent deliveries were done after every 3 weeks. To minimize the slack time in the first and third stage, the same team performed the two stages—the resource requirements of these stages are such that it eliminated the slack times.

The timeboxing process model is applicable in situations where it is possible to construct approximately equal sized iterations, and where the nature of work in each iteration is quite repeatable. The development process for each iteration should also be such that it can be partitioned into clean stages with work of a stage requiring little interaction with people who perform the other stages. However, this process model makes the task of project monitoring and control more difficult and challenging. Consequently, it may not be well suited for projects with large teams.

So far the experience in using the model is very positive. However, further experience is needed to develop better guidelines for applying this model on real projects. There are many issues relating to project planning and project monitoring that need to be further studied. Experience is also needed to better understand the scope of applicability as well as the nature of exceptions that might occur, how to handle them, and the impact of such exceptions on the performance of this process model.

ACKNOWLEDGEMENTS

The authors greatly acknowledge the help provided by V.T. Peetamber, who was the project manager for the case study, and Shanmuganathan N., who was the project coordinator, for providing valuable inputs for improving this chapter.

REFERENCES

[1] Basili V.R., Turner A., "Iterative enhancement, a practical technique for software development", *IEEE Transactions on Software Engrg.* **1** (4) (1975) 390–396.
[2] Basili V.R. (Ed.), *Tutorial on Models and Metrics for Software Management and Engineering*, IEEE Press, 1980.
[3] Basili V.R., Rombach H.D., "The experience factory", *The Encyclopedia of Software Engineering*, John Wiley and Sons, 1994.
[4] Beck K., *Extreme Programming Explained*, Addison–Wesley, 2000.
[5] Boehm B.W., "Improving software productivity", *IEEE Computer* (1987) 43–57.
[6] Boehm B.W., "A spiral model of software development and enhancement", *IEEE Computer* (May 1988) 61–72.
[7] Boehm B.W., *Software Engineering Economics*, Prentice Hall, Englewood Cliffs, NJ, 1981.

[8] Brooks F.P., *The Mythical Man Month*, Addison–Wesley, Reading, MA, 1975.

[9] Chikofsky E.J., "Changing your endgame strategy", *IEEE Software* (1990) 87, 112.

[10] Cockburn A., *Agile Software Development*, Addison–Wesley, 2001.

[11] Collier B., DeMarco T., Fearey P., "*A* defined process for project postmortem review", *IEEE Software* (1996) 65–72.

[12] Fowler M., Beck K., Brant J., Opdyke W., Roberts D., *Refactoring: Improving the Design of Existing Code*, Addison–Wesley, Reading, MA, 1999.

[13] Hennessy J.L., Patterson D.A., *Computer Architecture—A Quantitative Approach*, second ed., Morgan Kaufmann, 1996.

[14] Jalote P., *CMM in Practice—Processes for Executing Software Projects at Infosys*, in: *SEI Series on Software Engineering*, Addison–Wesley, 2000.

[15] Jalote P., *Software Project Management in Practice*, Addison–Wesley, 2002.

[16] Jalote P., et al., "Timeboxing: A process model for iterative software development", *J. Systems and Software* **70** (1–2) (2004) 117–127.

[17] Jones C., "Strategies for managing requirements creep", *IEEE Computer* **29** (7) (1996) 92–94.

[18] Kerr J., Hunter R., *Inside RAD—How to Build Fully Functional Computer Systems in 90 Days or Less*, McGraw–Hill, 1994.

[19] Kruchten P., *The Rational Unified Process—An Introduction*, Addison–Wesley, 2000.

[20] Larman C., *Applying UML and Patterns*, second ed., Pearson Education, 2002.

[21] Larman C., Basili V.R., "Iterative and incremental development: A brief history", *IEEE Computer* (2003).

[22] Malotaux N., "Evolutionary project management methods", www.malotaux.nl/nrm/pdf/MxEvo.pdf.

[23] Martin J., *Rapid Application Development*, Macmillan Co., 1991.

[24] McConnell S., *Rapid Development: Taming Wild Software Schedules*, Microsoft Press, 1996.

[25] Putnam L.H., Myers W., *Industrial Strength Software—Effective Management Using Measurement*, IEEE Comput. Soc., 1997.

[26] Royce W.W., "Managing the development of large software systems", *IEEE Wescon*, Aug. 1970, reprinted in: *Proc. 9th Int. Conf. on Software Engineering (ICSE-9)*, IEEE/ACM, 1987, pp. 328–338.

[27] Stapleton J. (Ed.), *DSDM—Business Focused Development*, Addison–Wesley, 2003.

A Survey of Empirical Results
on Program Slicing

DAVID BINKLEY

Loyola College
Baltimore, MD 21210-2699
USA
binkley@cs.loyola.edu

MARK HARMAN

Brunel University
Uxbridge, Middlesex UB8 3PH
UK
Mark.Harman@brunel.ac.uk

Abstract

A program slice extracts a semantically meaningful portion of a program, based upon a user-selected slicing criterion. As the study of program slicing has matured, a growing body of empirical data has been gathered on the size of slices, slicing tools and techniques, the applications of slicing, and the beneficial psychological effects of slices on the programmers who use them. Empirical work on these topics is surveyed, highlighting trends and areas where additional empirical investigation is desirable, either because of contradictory findings or scarcity of results in the existing body of empirical knowledge.

1. Introduction

The utility and power of program slicing comes from its ability to assist in tedious and error-prone tasks such as program debugging, testing, parallelization, integration, software safety, understanding, software maintenance, and software metrics [15,83]. Slicing does this by extracting a computation that is potentially scattered throughout a program from intervening irrelevant statements. Consequently, it is easier for a programmer interested in a subset of the program's behavior to understand the slice.

Slicing has been proposed for use in many areas of software analysis such as debugging [69], comprehension [37,54,56,57], testing [12,16,44], and software maintenance, reverse engineering, and evolution [21,22,33,40,86]. For example, software maintenance includes refactoring, a realistic technique for managing rapid software development. Refactoring naturally suggests slicing, both as a means of identifying candidates for re-factoring and also in extracting the code to be refactored [51,53, 62]. Furthermore, new applications of slicing continue to be proposed. For example, it has been recently proposed that slicing and transformation could be used to assist in identification of metamorphic and polymorphic viruses [63]. These viruses are immune to simplistic signature-based anti-virus systems, and demand a more semantically based analysis approach. Slicing and transformation are ideal tools to attack this problem.

An important part of transferring proposed uses to actual practice is empirical evidence that demonstrates a technique's effectiveness. Empirical evidence from slicing tools supports the wider 'real world' use of slicing techniques. It has been argued [93] that such empirical evidence is an important prerequisite for facilitating of technology transfer. Empirical research also encourages and stimulates the research community to continue to develop less mature areas within slicing research. The recent development of industrial strength slicing tools has led to a notable increase in publication of empirical results concerning slicing over the past five years. There now exists sufficient empirical evidence, from over 30 publications concerning slicing, to make possible a detailed survey of empirical results.

This chapter presents a survey of empirical results related to program slicing. These include empirical investigations of slicing's impact on clone detection [52], semantic differences [14], semantic equivalence [32]. Empirical studies are also presented that investigate the impact of slicing on programmers. For example, studies have considered slice-based debugging tools [66], the effectiveness of slicers versus non-slicers [30,31], the fault localization ability of slice-aware programmers [30,31], and aiding programmers in the identification of unwanted ripple effects [14].

The remainder of this chapter is organized into eight sections. Section 2 provides background material to make the chapter self-contained, while Section 8 concludes with suggested directions for further empirical study. The middle five sections divide empirical work results on slicing into five broad categories:

- One of the most fundamental questions about slicing, is 'how big is a typical slice?' Section 3 summarizes results which attempt to answer this question.

- The size of a slice (and the speed at which it can be constructed) depend upon the quality of supporting analyses. Section 4 considers the impact of supporting analyses on slicing.

- Section 5 considers results concerning slicing tools and techniques.

- Section 6 presents experiments with applications of slicing.

- Section 7 presents results concerning the effect of slicing on human comprehension.

Finally, note that this chapter excludes work on slicing that does not include significant empirical data. As a result the chapter focuses on the more established forms of slicing, such as static and dynamic slicing, rather than newer variants such as conditioned slicing [20,28]. Existing surveys consider slicing techniques and applications [15,83], slicing tools [46] and forms of slicing [24,41] that lack empirical results.

2. Background

This section provides background information that makes the chapter self contained. It briefly reviews the variety of slicing formulations: static, dynamic, and amorphous, and then algorithms for constructing them. Finally, information useful in interpreting the statistical results that accompany many empirical studies and terminological definitions are provided.

2.1   Static Program Slicing

Weiser's original formulation of a slice was a static one [87,88,90]. A static slice is taken with respect to a *slicing criterion* that specifies a program location and a variable of interest. Weiser's slices are now referred to as *backward static* slices. *Backward* because of the direction edges are traversed when a slice is computed using a *dependence graph* and *static* because they are computed as the solution to a static analysis problem (i.e., without considering the program's input). For example, Fig. 1 shows a simple backward static slice, which captures the computation of variable i while excluding the computation of *sum*.

Weiser's original slicing algorithm was data-flow based [90]. An alternative algorithm first suggested by Ottenstein and Ottenstein et al. [27,76] computes backward static slices using the program dependence graph as an intermediate representation by traversing the dependence edges backwards (from target to source). This approach was pursued by Horwitz et al. [47,49,77,78], who introduced the notion of *forward* slicing. Informally, a forward slice answers the question "What statements are affected by the value of variable v at statement s?"

Original program	Slice on "**print** *i*"
| ```
int main()
{
``` | ```
int main()
{
``` |
| $sum = 0$
 $i = 1$
 while $i \leqslant 10$
 $sum = \mathrm{add}(sum, i)$
 $i = \mathrm{add}(i, 1)$
 print *sum*
 print *i*
 } | $i = 1$
 while $i \leqslant 10$

 $i = \mathrm{add}(i, 1)$

 print *i*
 } |
| ```
int add(a, b)
{
``` <br> **return** $a + b$ <br> } | ```
int add(a, b)
{
``` <br> **return** $a + b$ <br> } |

FIG. 1. A simple slice computed with respect to the value of i at the statement "**print** i."

2.2 Dynamic Program Slicing

Korel and Laski introduced the notion of *dynamic* slicing [55]: a slice computed for a particular fixed input. The availability of run-time information makes dynamic slices smaller than static slices, but limits their applicability to that particular input. As with Weiser's algorithm, Korel and Laski's algorithm was data-flow based. Agrawal and Horgan later presented a program dependence graph based dynamic slicing algorithm [3].

2.3 Amorphous Slicing

The definition of program slicing places a semantic constraint on the slice; it requires the slice to have a certain behavior. In his original definition, Weiser also placed a syntactic constraint on a slice: a slice is determined by deleting statements from a program [90]. If this syntactic requirement is relaxed, the result is an *amorphous program slice* [36,37], which allows arbitrary transformation to be combined with statement deletion to reduce the size of the slice.

For example, the amorphous slice of the program show in Fig. 1 is simply "**print** 11." A second example is given in Fig. 2, which compares the syntax-preserving slice and an amorphous slice of a short program.

Original program	Traditional slice	Amorphous slice

`base = 2;`
`count = 0;`
`for(i=0;i<N;i++)`
`{`
`  if (A[i] % base == 0)`
`  count++;`
`  R[N-i-1] = A[i];`
`}`
`b = (A[0]==R[0]);`
	`for(i=0;i<N;i++)`
	`{`
	
	`  R[N-i-1] = A[i];`
	`}`
	`b = (A[0]==R[0]);`
		
		`b = (A[0]==A[N-1]);`

FIG. 2. The traditional and amorphous slice taken with respect to b at the final statement.

2.4   Computing Static Slices

This section describes the computation of a slice first as the solution to a data-flow problem over the control-flow graph (CFG) [29] and then as a graph reachability problem over a dependence graph [48,76]. The data-flow algorithm presented herein applies to a simple block structured imperative language and is intended to convey the intuition only. Scaling up, for example to a C slicer, requires considerable machinery [5,67,68,88,89], but does not change the intuition behind the algorithm.

An intraprocedural slice can be computed by the **Function** IntraProceduralDataFlowSlice shown in Fig. 3. This function makes use of four data-flow

---

Function IntraProceduralDataFlowSlice (CFG G, criterion C)
Returns NodeSet
Let (node n and set of variables v) $= C$
Initialize all *relevant* sets to the empty set
relevant(n) $= \{v\}$
mark(n) $=$ **true**
while no changes
  foreach node m in G
   let $R = \bigcup_{n \in suce(m)} relevant(n)$
   if def(m) $\cap R \neq \emptyset$
    mark(m) $=$ **true**
    relevant(m) $= (R - def(m)) \cup ref(m)$
    foreach $u \in control(m)$
     call IntraProceduralDataFlowSlice $(G, u, ref(u))$
  return the set of all marked vertices

FIG. 3. **Function** IntraProceduralDataFlowSlice.

sets: def, ref, control, and relevant, defined as follows: The set def(n) includes all variables defined at node n [29]. The set ref(n) includes all variables referenced (used) at node n [29]. The set control(n) contains those statements that directly determine whether the node n executes. For a structured program, this is the single loop or predicate that directly controls the execution of n, or the empty set if n is a "top level" statement. For unstructured programs, the computation of this set is significantly more complex [2,7,23,38,60].

The set relevant(n) is computed as the solution to a backwards-flow problem [29]. It contains the variables whose values (transitively) affect the computation of v right before n. For the slice taken with respect to node n and variable v, relevant(n) is initialized to $\{v\}$. Other relevant sets are computed as slicing proceeds. As shown in Fig. 3 at CFG join points (where two nodes have the same predecessor), the relevant set contains the union of the relevant sets of the two nodes. For example, in Fig. 4, relevant(5) contains the union of relevant(6) and relevant(9). Slicing a program whose CFG contains loops involves iterating the propagation of relevant sets until a fixed-point is reached.

Example.   Figure 4 shows the data necessary to calculate the slice with respect to a at line 13. Working backwards from line 13, since def(12) $\cap$ relevant(13) $\neq \emptyset$, line 12 is included in the slice (mark(12) = **true**) and its relevant set is assigned $((\{a\} - \{a\}) \cup \{b, c\}) = \{b, c\}$. No change occurs at line 11, or 10. Line 9 is included in the slice because def(9) $\cap$ relevant(10) $\neq \emptyset$; Furthermore, as control(9) = $\{8\}$, the slice with respect to ref(8) = $\emptyset$ at line 8 is included. Line 8's control set includes

n	Statement	ref	def	control	relevant
1	$b = 1$		b		$\emptyset$
2	$c = 2$		c		b
3	$d = 3$		d		b, c
4	$a = d$	d	a		b, c, d
5	if (a) then	a			a, b, c, d
6	$\quad d = b + d$	b, d	d	5	b, d
7	$\quad c = b + d$	b, d	c	5	b, d
8	else				
9	$\quad b = b + 1$	b	b	8	b, c
10	$\quad d = b + 1$	b	d	8	b, c
11	endif				
12	$a = b + c$	b, c	a		b, c
13	print a	a			a

FIG. 4. Example data-flow slice computation for the slice taken with respect to a at line 13.

line 5; thus, the slice with respect to ref(5) = {a} at line 5 is also included. The algorithm continues in this manner until a fixed point is reached. At this point, only line 10 is not in the final slice.

Slicing across procedure boundaries complicates the situation due to the necessity of translating and passing slicing criteria into and out of procedures. To slice *down* into a procedure, Weiser defined the set of criteria $DOWN_0(C)$. This set is constructed by mapping the variables relevant at a call to the name space of the called procedure (primarily by replacing actual parameter names with formal parameter names). All slices are taken from the final node of the called procedure's CFG. The set $UP_0(C)$ performs the inverse mapping and is used to map criteria from the entry of a called procedure back to a call site. The sets $DOWN_0(C)$ and $UP_0(C)$ are mapped to functions from criteria to criteria:

$$DOWN(CC) = \bigcup_{C \in CC} DOWN_0(C)$$

$$UP(CC) = \bigcup_{C \in CC} UP_0(C)$$

Finally, the transitive closure $(DOWN \cup UP)^*(C)$ is used to identify the complete set of criteria required for an interprocedural slice. This closure is used in Fig. 5 by **Function** `InterProceduralDataFlowSlice`. Note that the use of transitive closure introduces an imprecision: the approach fails to account for calling context. That is, when a slice *descends* into a called procedure it does not record the call-site from which it descends. Upon completion of the slice of the called procedure, the slice ascends ("returns") to *all* call-sites rather than the specific call-site it originated from. Though safe, this imprecision has the potential to dramatically increase slice size. For example, this approach unnecessarily includes the computation of *sum* in the slice shown in Fig. 1.

The other method for computing slices that has been empirically studied uses a dependence graph to essentially cache the data-flow information gathered by Weiser's algorithm. Three dependence graphs are considered herein:

- A Procedure Dependence Graph (PDG) represents a single procedure [48,76].
- A System Dependence Graph (SDG) represents a program containing procedures and procedure calls and includes transitive dependence edges at call sites, called *summary edges* [49].
- A Interprocedural Procedure Dependence Graph (IPDG) is a simplification of the SDG that lacks summary edges [1,58].

Function `InterProceduralDataFlowSlice` (CFG G, criterion c_0)
Returns NodeSet
let *CallCriterion* be the set of all criterion for call nodes
    in `IntraProceduralDataFlowSlice`(G, c_0)
while *CallCriterion* is not empty
  c = RemoveElement(*CallCriterion*)
  $C' = (DOWN \cup UP)^*(c)$
  foreach criterion c' in C'
  add to *CallCriterion* all the criterion in
  `IntraProceduralDataFlowSlice`(G, c')
return all nodes marked by `IntraProceduralDataFlowSlice`

FIG. 5. **Function** `InterProceduralDataFlowSlice`.

The PDG for program P is a directed graph whose vertices represent the assignment statements and control predicates that occur in program P. The vertices are connected by several kinds of edge that represent *dependences* among program components. An edge represents either a *control dependence* or a *flow dependence*. A control dependence edge from vertex u to vertex v, means that during execution, the predicate represented by u controls the execution of v. For structured languages, control dependences reflect the program's nesting structure. A PDG contains a flow dependence edge from vertex u defining variable x to vertex v that uses x if control can reach v after u via an execution path along which there is no intervening definition of x.

An SDG is a collection of procedure dependence graphs connected at call-sites by interprocedural control- and flow-dependence edges. In an SDG, a call statement is represented using a *call* vertex; parameter passing is represented using four kinds of *parameter* vertices: on the calling side, parameter passing is represented by *actual-in* and *actual-out* vertices, which are control dependent on the call vertex; in the called procedure, parameter passing is represented by *formal-in* and *formal-out* vertices, which are control dependent on the called procedure's entry vertex.

The SDG contains four additional kinds of edges not found in the PDG: a *call* edge connects a call-site vertex to the corresponding procedure-entry vertex; a *parameter-in* edge connects an actual-in vertex to the corresponding formal-in vertex in the called procedure; and a *parameter-out* edge connects a formal-out vertex to the corresponding actual-out vertex at each call site [49]. To tackle the calling-context problem, the SDG contains transitive dependence edges called *summary edges*, which connect actual-in vertices to actual-out vertices [49,77]. A summary edge is added from an actual-in vertex to an actual-out vertex at a call-site if a path of control, flow, and summary edges exists in the called procedure from the corresponding formal-in vertex to the corresponding formal-out vertex provided that this path is a same-level realizable path as defined below.

In the IPDG, which lacks summary edges, calling-context must be explicitly tracked. This tracking can be achieved using call strings [58]. In essence, these strings are built by labeling the *call* and *return* for call-site c_i with unique terminal symbols (e.g., "$(_i$" and "$)_i$") and then ensuring that the string of symbols produced by a graph traversal belongs to a specified context-free language [77] (e.g., each "$(_i$" is matched with "$)_i$"). Reps et al. [77] formalize this notion in the definition of *same-level realizable path*:

Definition (same-level realizable path).
Let each call vertex in SDG G be given a unique index from 1 to k. For each call site c_i, label the outgoing parameter-in edges and the incoming parameter-out edges with the symbols "$(_i$" and "$)_i$", respectively; label the outgoing call edge with "$(_i$". A path in G is a *same-level realizable path* iff the sequence of symbols labeling the parameter-in, parameter out, and call edges in the path is a string in the language of balanced parentheses generated from nonterminal *matched* by the following context-free grammar:

$$\text{matched} \;\rightarrow\; \text{matched} \; (_i \; \text{matched} \;)_i \quad \text{for } 1 \leqslant i \leqslant k.$$
$$\mid \epsilon$$

Several algorithms for slicing dependence graphs are now considered. First, Fig. 6 shows an algorithm for computing intraprocedural slices using the PDG. To compute an intraprocedural slice, **Function** ContextInsensitiveSlice simply floods backwards across dependence edges marking the vertices encountered. The slice consists of the set of statements corresponding to marked vertices. Context *insensitive* interprocedural slices, which ignore calling context, can be computed with the algorithm from Fig. 6 and the SDG (or IPDG) by treating interprocedural edges as intraprocedural edges. The precision is equivalent to that of Weiser's interprocedural slicing algorithm.

More precise, context *sensitive*, interprocedural slices can be computed from the SDG using **Function** ContextSensitiveSlice shown in Fig. 7. The presence of summary edges allows a slice to be computed in linear time by first only ascending into calling procedures (here summary edges are used to "skip past" called procedures), and then only descending into called procedures [49]. The two passes can be performed "together" using two separate marks that represent ascending and descending (named Up and Down in Fig. 7). The two-mark version is conceptually more complex. It is used herein because it facilitates the comparison with later algorithms for dealing with calling context.

This same precision can be achieved in the IPDG, but requires explicit context tracking. **Function** ContextTrackingSlice shown in Fig. 8, which computes

---

Function `ContextInsensitiveSlice`(PDG $G = (V, E)$, Vertex v)
Returns VertexSet
  Worklist $W = \{v\}$
  mark(v) = **true**
  while W is not empty
    let w = RemoveElement(W)
    foreach edge $v \to w \in E$
      if not mark(v)
        $W = W \cup \{v\}$
        mark(v) = **true**
  return the set of all marked vertices

FIG. 6. **Function** `ContextInsensitiveSlice`.

Function `ContextSensitiveSlice`(SDG $G = (V, E)$, Vertex s)
  Returns VertexSet
  Worklist $W = \{s\}$
  mark(s) = Up
  while W is not empty do
    w = RemoveElement(W)
    foreach edge $v \to w \in E$ do
      if mark(v) $\neq$ Up
        switch EdgeKind($v \to w$)
          case parameter-in edge:
          case call edge:
            if mark(w) $\neq$ Down
              $W = W \cup \{v\}$
              mark(v) = Up
          case parameter-out edge:
            if mark(v) $\neq$ Down
              $W = W \cup \{v\}$
              mark(v) = Down
          default:
            if mark(w) $\neq$ mark(v)
              $W = W \cup \{v\}$
              mark(v) = mark(w)
  return the set of all marked (Up or Down) vertices

FIG. 7. **Function** `ContextSensitiveSlice`.

Function `ContextTrackingSlice` (SDG $G = (V, E)$, Vertex s)
Returns VertexSet
Worklist $W = \{(s, \epsilon)\}$
while W is not empty **do**
  Let $(w, c) =$ RemoveElement(W)
  foreach edge $v \to w \in E$ **do**
    if mark(v) does not include a context c' for which match(c, c') holds
    switch EdgeKind($v \to w$)
      case parameter-in edge:
      case call-edge:
        Let s_v be the call site associated with v
        if $c = \epsilon \vee$ head(c) $= s_v$
          $c' = $ up(c)
          $W = W \cup \{(v, c')\}$
          mark(v) $=$ mark(v) $\cup c'$
      case parameter-out edge:
        Let s_w be the call site associated with w
        $c' = $ down(c, s_w)
        $W = W \cup \{(v, c')\}$
        mark(v) $=$ mark(v) $\cup c'$
      default:
        $W = W \cup \{(v, c)\}$
        mark(v) $=$ mark(v) $\cup c$
return the set of all vertices marked with a calling context

FIG. 8. **Function** `ContextTrackingSlice`.

such slices, is parameterized by three functions: down, up, and match:

$$
\begin{aligned}
\text{down}(c, s) \quad &\to \text{cons}(s, c) \\
\text{up}(c) \quad &\to \text{tail}(c) \quad \text{if } c \neq \epsilon, \\
&\quad\; \epsilon \qquad\quad \text{if } c = \epsilon, \\
\text{match}(c1, c2) &\to c1 = c2
\end{aligned}
$$

Function `ContextTrackingSlice` replaces the two simple marks Up and Down of **Function** `ContextSensitiveSlice` with "marks" that represent context (made up of call strings). One implication of this is that each vertex may be processed multiple times (once for each unique context). **Functions** `Context-TrackingSlice` and `ContextSensitiveSlice` are equivalent in terms of slice precision with one caveat: in the presence of recursion, neither the set of call strings nor the call strings themselves are finite. Thus, the naïve implementation of `ContextTrackingSlice` will not terminate in the presence of recursion.

Agrawal and Guo propose a method for limiting the infinite number and length of call strings by removing cycles [1]. To do so, they replace down with the following

$$
\text{down}(c, s) \rightarrow \begin{cases} \text{cons}(c, s) & \text{if } c = s_1 s_2 \cdots s_k \wedge \forall s_i \mid s \neq s_i, \\ s_i \cdots s_k & \text{if } c = s_1 s_2 \cdots s_k \wedge s = s_i. \end{cases}
$$

Unfortunately, as shown by Krinke [58] this new definition removes too much information and the algorithm can fail to include vertices that rightly belong in a slice.

Krinke solved this problem by first identifying strongly connected components (SCCs) in the call graph. All (mutually) recursive functions are part of the same SCC. When entering a (mutually) recursive function, two entries are added to the main worklist. The first leads the algorithm to capture the program components when "leaving" the SCC, while the second leads the algorithm to capture the program components from within the SCC. Post SCC formation, **Function** `FoldedContextSensitiveSlice` (Fig. 9) uses the original definitions of up, down, and match.

2.5 Computing Amorphous Slices

Function `AmorphousSlice` (Fig. 10) computes static amorphous slices using **Function** `ContextSensitiveSlice` and the function `Transform`, which applies transformations to the graph. Many transformations are essentially graph based compiler optimizations such as constant propagation, procedure in-lining, and procedure specialization [26,27]. Other transformation are domain specific [13,42,43].

Example.   The amorphous slice of the program show in Fig. 1 is simply "**print** 11." Transformations such as loop unrolling, a version of strength reduction, and constant propagation were used to obtain this slice.

2.6 Statistics

Many of the results summarized in the following sections provide some measure of statistical significance. For example, a common test is a (one or two sided) t-test involving the difference of two means. Here the *null* hypothesis is $\mu_1 - \mu_2 = 0$ and the alternative hypothesis, for a one sided test, is $\mu_1 - \mu_2 < 0$ (i.e., the experimental group has a better mean score). For a two sided t-test the alternative hypothesis is $\mu_1 \neq \mu_2$.

When available, the p-value, the common standard deviation and the degrees of freedom $(d.f.)$ are included in the summaries of papers surveyed. The p-value can

---

Function `FoldedContextSensitiveSlice` (SDG $G = (V, E)$, Vertex s)
Returns VertexSet
  $W = \{(s, \epsilon)\}$
  while W is not empty
    let $(w, c) = \text{RemoveElement}(W)$
    foreach $v \rightarrow w \in E$
      if mark(v) does not include a context c' for which match(c, c') holds
        switch EdgeKind($v \rightarrow w$)
          case parameter-in edge:
          case call-edge:
            Let s_v be the call site of v
            if $c = \epsilon \vee \text{head}(c) = s_v$
              if s_v is marked as recursive and v has not been marked with a context c'
              for which match(c, c') holds
              $W = W \cup \{(v, c)\}$
              mark(v) = mark(v) $\cup \{c\}$
              $c'' = \text{up}(c)$
              $W = W \cup \{(v, c'')\}$
              mark(v) = mark(v) $\cup \{c''\}$
          case parameter-out edge:
            Let s_w be the call site of w
            if s_w is marked as recursive
            and car(c) = s_w
            $W = W \cup \{(v, c)\}$
            mark(v) = mark(v) $\cup \{c\}$
          else
            $c' = \text{down}(c, s_w)$
            $W = W \cup \{(v, c')\}$
            mark(v) = mark(v) $\cup \{c'\}$
        default:
        $W = W \cup \{(v, c)\}$
        mark(v) = mark(v) $\cup \{c\}$
  return the set of all nodes marked with a calling context

FIG. 9. **Function** `FoldedContextSensitiveSlice`.

be loosely interpreted as follows: values less than 0.01 are highly significant, values less than 0.05 are significant, and values less than 0.10 are weakly significant. In the sequel, p-values associated with a result are stated parenthetically.

Function AmorphousSlice(SDG G, VertexSet V) **Returns** SDG
  SDG G_{sliced} = ContextSensitiveSlice(G, V)
  SDG $G_{\text{transformed}}$ = Transform(G_{sliced})
  if ($G = G_{\text{transformed}}$)
    return G_{sliced} — guaranteed to be the smallest of G, G_{sliced}, and $G_{\text{transformed}}$
  else
    return smaller(AmorphousSlice($G_{\text{transformed}}, V$), G_{sliced})

FIG. 10. **Function** AmorphousSlice.

There is some concern in the empirical software engineering community about the statistical power of the techniques applied. For example, there has been criticism of the application of techniques and quoted p-values where there is no accompanying assessment of the impact of the size on the effect being measured [70]. However, these methodological issues are beyond the scope of the present survey.

2.7 Terminology

The following terminology is used throughout this chapter:

- When unqualified, the term "node" is used to refer to the nodes of a CFG.
- The term "vertex" is used to refer to the vertices of a dependence graph (PDG, IPDG, SDG).
- LOC abbreviates Lines Of Code.
- NC-LOC abbreviates Non-Comment Lines Of Code.
- NB-LOC abbreviates Non-Blank Lines Of Code.
- The term "*slice*" when unqualified refers to a static backward program slice [15].
- An "*executable*" slice is an executable program that behaves identically to the original program with respect to the slicing criterion [11].
- A "*closure*" slice includes all the components that might affect a given computation, but is not, itself, necessarily an executable program [11].
- *HRB* stands for the Horwitz, Reps, and Binkley interprocedural slicing algorithm [49].

The next five sections divide results on program slicing into five principal areas: The size of slices, the impact of supporting analysis, slicing tools and algorithms, applications of slicing, and finally, the impact of slicing on programmer comprehension.

3. Slice Size

All applications of slicing depend crucially upon the size of the slices constructed, because all applications rely upon the way in which slicing removes parts of the program which have nothing to do with the slicing criterion. The more that can be (safely) removed the better. This section considers the fundamental question "How big is a slice?" Four different kinds of slices are considered; thus, this question is considered four times. The first deals with static slice size, which is following by dynamic slice size, and then two static-dynamic hybrids: call-mark slice size, and finally union slice size.

3.1   Static Slice Size

Three studies of static slice size are reported in chronological order. They are followed by studies that have considered the impact of calling-context sensitivity on static slice size. The first study is the Unravel report [68], which considered a commercial sample of safety-related code and the Unravel source itself. Table I presents the sizes of these two programs in lines of code (LOC) as reported by wc -1, LOC post CPP (this is the actual input Unravel sees), and finally NB-NC-LOC post CPP (perhaps the most reasonable measure of input size). The objective of this evaluation is to determine whether "program slices are sufficiently smaller than the original program to be useful to a software reviewer [68]."

To evaluate Unravel, slicing criteria were automatically generated to slice on the last statement of the main procedure for each global variable and on the last statement of each procedure for each local variable declared in the procedure. Table II presents a breakdown of slice sizes for the commercial code. The sizes are clustered in terms of number of statements in a slice relative to the total program size. Slices of the source code for the Unravel program itself were similar.

TABLE I
UNRAVEL TEST PROGRAMS

File	LOC	CPP LOC	NB-NC-LOC
Commercial code	4,032	9,006	3,709
Unravel	19,656	112,191	55,095

In the second study, Krinke analyzed the 14 programs shown in Table III, which includes LOC (measured using `wc -1`) and the number of procedures, vertices and edges in each SDG [58]. The column labeled "slice count" shows the number of slices taken (following Agrawal and Guo [1], Krinke sliced on every formal-in vertex in the graph in Table III). The final two columns include average slice size and the percentage of the original graph that this average represents. The average slice size ranges from 7.3% (for `bison`) to 46.4% (for `gnugo`) with an overall average of 26.9%.

TABLE II
UNRAVEL SLICE SIZE ANALYSIS

Cluster	Slices in cluster	Percent of total slices
Size $\leqslant$ 1%	155	37%
1% < Size $\leqslant$ 25%	135	32%
25% < Size $\leqslant$ 50%	129	31%
50% < Size	0	0%
Sum	419	100%

TABLE III
DETAILS OF KRINKE'S TEST PROGRAMS

Program	LOC	Procedure count	Vertex count	Slice count	Edge count	Average slice size (Vertices)	Percent
gnugo	3,305	38	3,875	281	10,657	1,798	46.4%
ansitape	1,744	76	6,733	1,082	18,083	1,645	24.4%
assembler	3,178	685	13,393	2,401	97,908	4,286	32.0%
cdecl	3,879	53	5,992	697	17,322	880	14.7%
ctags	2,933	101	10,042	1,621	24,854	2,010	20.0%
simulator	4,476	283	9,143	1,019	22,138	3,212	35.1%
rolo	5,717	170	37,839	6,540	264,922	7,766	20.5%
compiler	2,402	49	15,195	1,017	45,631	6,731	44.3%
football	2,261	73	8,850	818	30,474	2,593	29.3%
agrep	3,968	90	11,922	1,403	35,713	3,183	26.7%
bison	8,313	161	25,485	3,744	84,794	1,859	7.3%
patch	7,998	166	20,484	3,099	104,266	7,965	38.9%
diff	13,188	181	46,990	10,130	471,395	6,172	13.1%
flex	7,640	121	38,508	5,191	235,687	9,179	23.8%
Sum	71,002	2,247	254,451	39,043	1,463,844	59,279	
Average	5,072	161	18,175	2,789	104,560	4,234	26.9%

The third study by Binkley and Harman [17] was a large-scale study of the 43 C programs shown in Table IV. This study constructed the forward and backward slice for every executable statement. In total 2,353,598 slices were constructed. As seen in the results shown at the bottom of columns 4 and 6 in Table V, the average backward slice size was 30.2% of the program, while the average forward slice size was 28.0% of the program. The range of the average slice size is striking. For example, the smallest average size for backward slices is 7.5% (for `acct-6.3`) and the largest is 62.2% (for `go`). It is reasonable to conclude that the nature of the program itself has a crucial impact upon the size of typical slices constructed from it. This may suggest the possibility of using slicing to 'characterize' a program. (The final four columns of Table V summarize slices computed from SDGs built with structure files expanded. This option is explored in Section 4.1.)

Finally, it is interesting to note that the programs `wpst` and `csurf-pkgs`, which are part of the `CodeSurfer` tool itself [34] (and thus written by "slicing aware" programmers) have comparatively small slices (although they were not written with slice-ability in mind). Program `wpst`, which performs the pointer analysis, has an average slice size of about 11%, while `csurf-pkgs`, which is an ADT repository for `CodeSurfer`, has an average slice size of about 15%. It is difficult to evaluate whether these averages, which are half the average across all programs, are influenced by programmer familiarity with program slicing.

This section concludes with the presentation of several studies dealing with the impact of context sensitivity. Slice computation cost is largely impacted by the approach to slicing (data flow or graph reachability). The impact is considerably higher for data-flow techniques. The reason for this is that tracking context without summary edges is expensive. Thus, techniques that do not use summary edges normally run faster when ignoring context than when tracking calling context, because simple vertex-marks are sufficient. In contrast, when using summary edges, context-insensitive slices often take longer to compute because they are larger and simply require traversing more of the program. Simply put, summary edges remove the overhead from tracking calling-context.

Three studies have focused on calling context as a simple "yes" or "no" question. A discussion of these is followed by Krinke's consideration of the depth of context sensitivity. To begin with, Agrawal and Guo evaluated the additional costs associated with computing context-sensitive slices as compared to computing context-insensitive slices and measured the relative precision achieved by the two slicing techniques [6]. Unlike the other studies in this section (which concerned C programs), Agrawal and Guo slice Java byte code as they were studying maintenance of programs in byte-code form. While program source sizes are not given for the 10 program studied, based on the graph sizes, it can be estimated that the input programs ranged up to about 3,000 LOC.

TABLE IV
BINKLEY AND HARMAN SUBJECT PROGRAMS (SORTED BY NUMBER OF VERTICES)

		Binkley and Harman subject programs				
Program	Size (LOC)	Vertices	Edges	Slices taken	Time (s)	Slicing pace (KLOC/s)
replace	563	1,097	3,500	867	0.02	9,417
time-1.7	6,033	4,583	14,092	1,049	0.03	14,922
which	4,880	4,666	13,327	1,156	0.06	16,337
compress	1,234	5,211	14,749	1,085	0.06	2,805
wdiff.0.5	5,958	7,213	21,793	2,421	0.12	12,916
termutils	6,697	8,869	27,442	3,096	0.40	12,424
barcode	5,562	10,916	35,796	3,824	1.47	5,315
bc	14,609	14,903	49,523	5,105	7.29	6,169
acct-6.3	9,536	18,531	80,584	7,222	0.97	6,783
gcc.cpp	4,079	19,095	89,513	7,354	12.47	1,272
space	9,126	20,018	64,537	10,311	13.63	2,240
prepro	14,328	20,578	65,353	10,779	13.50	3,471
oracolo2	14,326	20,654	65,734	10,846	14.38	3,329
EPWIC-1	8,631	22,217	79,026	12,447	2.45	5,267
gnubg-0.0	7,229	25,138	80,922	9,447	20.88	1,239
indent-1.10.0	6,100	25,737	582,728	6,602	14.64	1,511
findutils	16,891	30,322	170,697	14,320	25.21	3,215
byacc	6,337	34,019	114,377	10,150	16.75	1,098
diffutils	18,374	36,079	195,348	16,622	28.63	2,802
flex2-4-7	15,143	39,037	186,523	11,104	30.69	1,756
cadp	11,068	42,212	122,478	15,672	13.42	1,451
copia	1,170	43,513	126,943	4,680	22.08	74
ed	12,493	44,387	222,858	16,368	85.59	1,662
gnuchess	16,659	44,957	163,465	15,069	73.50	1,701
wpst	17,321	54,658	209,465	20,667	50.52	1,316
flex2-5-4	20,252	55,019	386,413	14,114	46.76	1,108
ftpd	15,914	56,981	366,095	24,820	157.22	1,225
tile-forth-2.1	3,717	59,247	215,288	11,940	142.44	157
ijpeg	24,822	62,698	265,650	23,954	193.84	1,390
userv-0.95.0	7,150	70,796	272,726	12,511	141.41	270
espresso	22,050	93,326	467,165	29,044	351.29	793
go	28,547	111,246	416,404	35,594	785.72	1,071
ctags	16,946	120,014	422,034	20,313	360.34	581
ntpd	45,647	204,420	804,652	39,573	1,452.69	600
gnugo	15,217	278,766	1,044,525	58,373	3,145.85	147
csurf-pkgs	36,593	295,220	973,703	42,777	1,363.73	261
a2ps	53,900	417,513	6,303,686	58,009	3,835.59	463
empire	53,895	496,033	2,022,295	105,918	7,664.52	505
li	6,916	889,260	3,762,858	13,521	5,181.00	14
sendmail	75,156	1,111,054	37,774,280	46,889	53,917.14	48

(*continued to next page*)

TABLE IV — *(Continued from previous page)*

	Size			Slices	Time	Slicing pace
Program	(LOC)	Vertices	Edges	taken	(s)	(KLOC/s)
named	103,670	1,326,070	21,824,057	104,567	100,196.17	81
spice	149,050	1,774,846	31,308,396	213,625	425,938.17	36
cvs	93,309	6,219,909	28,981,757	102,353	280,298.17	27
Sum	1,007,098	14,241,028	140,412,757	1,176,158	885,620.81	
Average	23,421	331,187	3,265,413	27,353	20,595.83	3,006

(Binkley and Harman subject programs — table heading)

For the context-insensitive algorithm they used **Function** ContextInsensitiveSlice (Fig. 6). For the context-sensitive algorithm they did not use the SDG (with its summary edges), but, instead tackled the calling context problem by explicitly propagating calling-contexts as in **Function** ContextTrackingSlice (Fig. 8).

In summary, Agrawal and Guo found that ignoring context caused an 86% increase in slice size and a 42% *reduction* in slice time (context-insensitive slices take less time to compute in their approach as they adopt an expensive approach to handling context). They report mixed results related to precision. For 53% of the 2,464 slices, the context-insensitive technique was just as precise as the context-sensitive technique. However, in one case, it led to a slice with 35 times more vertices. On average, context-insensitive slices were twice as large as their context-sensitive counterparts.

Unfortunately, as later shown by Krinke [58], the context sensitive algorithm implemented by Agrawal and Guo contains an error that caused it to omit vertices that should have been included in context-sensitive slices. Correcting for this would reduce the 86% figure for the increase in slice size by an unknown amount.

Similar studies have since been performed by Krinke [58] and Binkley and Harman [17]. Krinke compared the slices computed by **Function** ContextInsensitiveSlice and **Function** ContextSensitiveSlice. Following Agrawal and Guo, Krinke sliced on every formal-in vertex in the graph. Unlike Agrawal and Guo, he used the SDG, and therefore took advantage of the summary edges. The final four columns of Table VI compare context-sensitive and context-insensitive slice size. In summary, ignoring context caused a 68% increase in slice size and a 40% *increase* in slice time. However, there is a high degree of variance: the average context-insensitive slice is between 3 and 300% larger than the average context-sensitive slice.

TABLE V
BACKWARD AND FORWARD SLICES SIZES WITH BOTH COLLAPSED AND EXPANDED STRUCTURE FIELDS

| Program | Program size | Structure fields collapsed | | | | Structure fields expanded | | | |
| | | Ave backward slice size | | Ave forward slice size | | Ave backward slice size | | Ave forward slice size | |
	(LOC)	(LOC)	Percent	(LOC)	Percent	(LOC)	Percent	(LOC)	Percent
replace	563	122	21.6%	122	21.7%	122	21.6%	122	21.7%
copia	1,170	266	22.7%	192	16.4%	266	22.7%	192	16.4%
compress	1,234	307	24.9%	279	22.6%	307	24.9%	279	22.6%
tile-forth-2	3,717	1,959	52.7%	1,795	48.3%	1,929	51.9%	1,773	47.7%
gcc.cpp	4,079	1,938	47.5%	1,787	43.8%	1,868	45.8%	1,713	42.0%
which	4,880	1,464	30.0%	1,337	27.4%	1,449	29.7%	1,322	27.1%
barcode	5,562	1,763	31.7%	1,652	29.7%	1,696	30.5%	1,596	28.7%
wdiff.0.5	5,958	608	10.2%	572	9.6%	608	10.2%	572	9.6%
time-1.7	6,033	519	8.6%	392	6.5%	501	8.3%	386	6.4%
indent-1.10.	6,100	2,830	46.4%	2,580	42.3%	2,672	43.8%	2,446	40.1%
byacc	6,337	1,147	18.1%	1,039	16.4%	1,147	18.1%	1,039	16.4%
termutils	6,697	1,694	25.3%	1,560	23.3%	1,681	25.1%	1,547	23.1%
li	6,916	2,690	38.9%	2,607	37.7%	2,649	38.3%	2,580	37.3%
userv-0.95.0	7,150	1,480	20.7%	1,337	18.7%	1,387	19.4%	1,258	17.6%
gnubg-0.0	7,229	2,082	28.8%	1,981	27.4%	1,612	22.3%	1,482	20.5%
epwic-1	8,631	1,010	11.7%	967	11.2%	975	11.3%	932	10.8%
space	9,126	1,935	21.2%	1,944	21.3%	1,177	12.9%	1,205	13.2%
acct-6.3	9,536	715	7.5%	687	7.2%	706	7.4%	687	7.2%
cadp	11,068	919	8.3%	797	7.2%	863	7.8%	742	6.7%
ed	12,493	6,759	54.1%	6,059	48.5%	6,659	53.3%	5,984	47.9%
oracolo2	14,326	2,822	19.7%	2,822	19.7%	1,690	11.8%	1,748	12.2%
prepro	14,328	2,780	19.4%	2,765	19.3%	1,662	11.6%	1,719	12.0%
bc	14,609	7,173	49.1%	6,793	46.5%	7,129	48.8%	6,764	46.3%
flex2-4-7	15,143	3,755	24.8%	3,377	22.3%	3,755	24.8%	3,362	22.2%
gnugo	15,217	5,995	39.4%	5,402	35.5%	5,296	34.8%	4,306	28.3%

(continued to next page)

TABLE V — *(Continued from previous page)*

Program	Program size (LOC)	Structure fields collapsed				Structure fields expanded			
		Ave backward slice size (LOC)	Percent	Ave forward slice size (LOC)	Percent	Ave backward slice size (LOC)	Percent	Ave forward slice size (LOC)	Percent
ftpd	15,914	5,634	35.4%	5,061	31.8%	5,554	34.9%	4,981	31.3%
gnuchess	16,659	7,230	43.4%	6,780	40.7%	7,163	43.0%	6,714	40.3%
findutils	16,891	4,763	28.2%	4,307	25.5%	4,645	27.5%	4,206	24.9%
ctags	16,946	7,405	43.7%	6,982	41.2%	7,050	41.6%	6,660	39.3%
wpst	17,321	1,923	11.1%	1,836	10.6%	1,905	11.0%	1,836	10.6%
diffutils	18,374	4,355	23.7%	4,024	21.9%	4,153	22.6%	3,859	21.0%
flex2-5-4	20,252	4,759	23.5%	4,354	21.5%	4,233	20.9%	3,706	18.3%
espresso	22,050	7,012	31.8%	6,813	30.9%	6,791	30.8%	6,593	29.9%
ijpeg	24,822	7,769	31.3%	7,521	30.3%	7,695	31.0%	7,447	30.0%
go	28,547	17,756	62.2%	17,157	60.1%	17,613	61.7%	16,957	59.4%
csurf-pkgs	36,593	5,745	15.7%	5,489	15.0%	5,709	15.6%	5,452	14.9%
ntpd	45,647	11,777	25.8%	10,316	22.6%	12,279	26.9%	10,773	23.6%
empire	53,895	22,528	41.8%	18,971	35.2%	17,785	33.0%	15,198	28.2%
a2ps	53,900	17,140	31.8%	16,008	29.7%	16,547	30.7%	15,577	28.9%
sendmail	75,156	25,328	33.7%	23,073	30.7%	25,027	33.3%	22,772	30.3%
cvs	93,309	43,295	46.4%	40,869	43.8%	43,202	46.3%	41,149	44.1%
named	103,670	40,120	38.7%	36,907	35.6%	38,876	37.5%	35,973	34.7%
spice	149,050	41,287	27.7%	39,051	26.2%	32,493	21.8%	31,748	21.3%
Sum	1,007,098	339,140		314,673		308,527		295,574	
Minimum			7.5%		6.5%		7.4%		6.4%
Maximum			62.2%		60.1%		61.7%		59.4%
Average	23,421	7,877	30.2%	7,318	28.0%	7,715	28.1%	6,874	26.3%

TABLE VI
KRINKE'S CONTEXT SENSITIVITY EXPERIMENT

Program		Summary edge		Average slice size (vertices)			
	LOC	Count	Time (s)	Context-insensitive		Context-sensitive	
gnugo	3,305	2,064	0.03	1,861	48.0%	1,798	46.4%
ansitape	1,744	12,746	0.15	2,909	43.2%	1,645	24.4%
assembler	3,178	114,629	3.58	6,458	48.2%	4,286	32.0%
cdecl	3,879	9,089	0.08	1,039	17.3%	880	14.7%
ctags	2,933	20,483	0.24	3,207	31.9%	2,010	20.0%
simulator	4,476	5,022	0.06	5,455	59.7%	3,212	35.1%
rolo	5,717	170,108	5.53	12,819	33.9%	7,766	20.5%
compiler	2,402	58,240	0.80	7,474	49.2%	6,731	44.3%
football	2,261	17,605	0.35	3,081	34.8%	2,593	29.3%
agrep	3,968	12,343	0.19	3,521	29.5%	3,183	26.7%
bison	8,313	29,739	0.72	7,215	28.3%	1,859	7.3%
patch	7,998	83,597	4.39	9,680	47.3%	7,965	38.9%
diff	13,188	612,484	28.20	14,558	31.0%	6,172	13.1%
flex	7,640	144,496	4.19	19,641	51.0%	9,179	23.8%
Sum	71,002	1,292,645	48.51	98,918		59,279	
Average	7,640	92,331	3.47	7,065	39.5%	4,234	26.9%

Finally, Table VII shows Binkley and Harman's comparison of context-sensitive and context-insensitive slicing using the 43 programs shown in Table IV. Overall, the average slice-size increase is 50% and ranges from 0.17% for copia (rounded to 0% in the figure) to 330% for acct. Slicing time increases an average 77%. One cause for the difference when compared with Krinke's results may be the particular subset using criteria from which slices were taken.

Binkley and Harman note that for most programs, the size increase when ignoring calling context has the dominant effect on slice time. The most dramatic example of this is acct, whose backward slicing time more than quintuples and whose average slice size more than quadruples. However, with seven of the programs, the overhead of tracking calling context dominates and the slicing time decreases, even though the resulting slices are larger (these examples show negative 'increases' in Table VII). Program li had the largest: a 29% *reduction* in computation time.

Thus far, context sensitivity has been treated as a "yes" or "no" question. Krinke took a more refined approach, summarized in the remainder of this section. Krinke's study includes the effects of k-limiting call strings (context information is only kept to depth k) [58]. Thus, it provides a series of more precise (i.e., more context sensitive) slices.

TABLE VII
THE EFFECT OF CALLING CONTEXT ON
SLICE SIZE AND COMPUTATION TIME

| | Percent increase in | | |
Program	average slice size	backward slicing time	forward slicing time
a2ps	29%	69%	51%
acct	330%	418%	301%
barcode	36%	21%	19%
bc	1%	8%	−4%
byacc	60%	132%	160%
cadp	152%	248%	231%
compress	6%	−25%	0%
copia	0%	−5%	6%
csurf-pkgs	58%	76%	59%
ctags	21%	116%	85%
cvs	11%	23%	−13%
diffutils	113%	194%	141%
ed	1%	19%	15%
empire	17%	101%	52%
EPWIC-1	193%	258%	242%
espresso	56%	124%	103%
findutils	87%	169%	118%
flex2-4-7	34%	98%	68%
flex2-5-4	39%	81%	53%
ftpd	10%	59%	42%
gcc.cpp	11%	6%	−1%
gnubg-0.0	38%	76%	58%
gnuchess	13%	56%	49%
gnugo	9%	56%	55%
go	0%	40%	37%
ijpeg	16%	14%	−6%
indent-1.10	21%	−7%	35%
li	0%	−29%	−29%
named	6%	−12%	−7%
ntpd	18%	60%	49%
oracolo2	74%	120%	152%
prepro	75%	123%	156%
replace	19%	0%	−50%
sendmail	6%	−28%	−24%
space	76%	120%	160%
spice	16%	4%	−9%
termutils	82%	73%	38%
tile-forth	1%	−1%	3%

(*continued on next page*)

TABLE VII — *(Continued from previous page)*

Program	Percent increase in		
	average slice size	backward slicing time	forward slicing time
time-1.7	15%	0%	−67%
userv-0.95.	63%	99%	96%
wdiff.0.5	146%	100%	113%
which	40%	0%	−20%
wpst	139%	274%	304%
Average	50%	77%	66%

TABLE VIII
PRECISION OF kCTS AND kFCS

	1CTS	2CTS	3CTS	4CTS	5CTS	1FCS	2FCS	3FCS	4FCS	5FCS
gnugo	100	100	100	100	100	100	100	100	100	100
ansitape	7	74	74	74	74	7	74	74	74	74
assembler	48	48	48	100	100	48	48	48	100	100
cdecl	99	99	100	100	100	99	99	100	100	100
ctags	100	100	100	100	100	100	100	100	100	100
simulator	83	83	100	100	100	83	83	100	100	100
rolo	46	57	84	92	92	46	57	84	92	92
compiler	22	26	26	26	26	22	30	32	46	73
football	100	100	100	100	100	100	100	100	100	100
agrep	41	49	59	100	100	41	49	59	100	100
bison	74	96	96	97	97	74	96	96	98	100
patch	92	99	99	100	100	92	99	99	100	100
diff	29	29	29	29	29	29	30	30	32	98
flex	88	98	98	98	98	88	98	99	99	100
Average	64	74	78	86	86	64	74	79	88	95

Table VIII compares the precision of **Function** `ContextTrackingSlice` (labeled CTS) and **Function** `FoldedContextSensitiveSlice` (labeled FCS) for various depths (values of k shown preceding the labels). Precision is measured with context-insensitive slicing as 0% precision and slicing with summary edges as 100% precision. Many programs show high precision for small values of k.

Krinke concludes that, when computable, the use of summary information is the best solution. It is both precise and fast. If summary edges cannot be used, the k-limited version of **Function** `FoldedContextSensitiveSlice` is the function of choice, because it does not suffer from combinatorial explosion due to recursion. In some cases, the k-limited version of **Function** `ContextTrackingSlice` is also more precise, but it may lead to higher run times.

3.2 Dynamic Slice Size

Venkatesh was one of the first to construct a large scale study of slicing that involved slicing programs at every possible slicing criterion and the results remain interesting today [85]. The study considered executable and closure backward and forward dynamic slices. Its primary goal was to determine the size and computation time for dynamic slices (only the results relating to slice size are presented herein).

Venkatesh constructed slices for nine programs, ranging from 49 to 7,500 LOC (see Table IX). The smaller programs were publicly available utilities, while the larger programs were used in-house at Bellcore. Because the study was of dynamic slicing, it was important to have good quality test data. For each slicing criterion, at least three test cases (which gave reasonable coverage) were used. Inputs which led to unusually large repetitions of sections of code were ignored in order to keep the size of traces to a manageable size. The study of slice sizes found, *inter alia*, the following interesting results:

(1) Slice size is not correlated to program size.
(2) Forward slices tend to be larger than backward slices. (Binkley and Harman find the opposite for static slicing—see Table V).

TABLE IX
VENKATESH'S NINE PROGRAMS

Program	LOC	Description
		Public programs
sum	49	arithmetic
uniq	143	find adjacent duplicates
comm	167	find lines in common
cal	201	calendar program
join	215	relational database operator
		Bellcore programs
flex93	800	medical insurance cost estimation
spiff	4,700	smart file comparison utility
dq	2,700	database query client program
atac	7,500	testing and coverage measurement tool

(3) The average backward slice is 50% of the executed nodes (less than 20% of the program).

(4) The average forward slice was 65% of the executed nodes (less than 25% of the program).

(5) An executable slice is typically much larger than its corresponding closure slice. The scaling factor was 2–3 for backward slices and 5–10 for forward slices.

A subsidiary study, which concerned the distribution of slices, revealed a bi-modal distribution, with the smaller slices corresponding to trivial slicing criteria—those which identified a superfluous variable that played little part in the main computation(s) of the program. The larger slices, as one would expect, tended to capture variables which participated in the principal computations of the program. For some programs, several peaks were noticed, and these indicated programs which had several distinct computations. This suggests that slicing may be used to measure cohesiveness in the manner first suggested by Bieman and Ott [10] and could be used to isolate and identify portions of the program which perform relatively self-contained computations.

3.3 Hybrid Static–Dynamic Slice Size

This section summarizes two results concerning the size of slices that are static–dynamic hybrids. First, Nishimatsu et al. study *call-mark slicing*, a compromise between static and dynamic slicing that computes a slice using both static and dynamic information [73]. The motivation for this approach is that dynamic slice computation has a large time and space overhead from the size of the execution trace and the time taken to traverse large numbers of dynamic dependencies. On the other hand, conservative static data-flow analysis leads to imprecision.

The compromise collects dynamic information concerning whether a procedure is called (these are "marked" as called). This addresses the space issue. Dynamic data dependencies are not collected. Rather static dependencies are used. This addresses the space and time to handle the large quantity of dynamic dependencies. The approach leads to the computation of a dynamic slice which is less precise than a traditional dynamic slice, but which potentially can be computed with reduced time and space.

The principal focus of this work is the concept of call-mark slicing, its definition, algorithms and implementation in the Osaka program slicing system. The included study is small, consisting of three programs: a calendar program (88 LOC) and two different versions of a inventory control system (387 and 941 LOC). The three programs were sliced once each using a single slicing criterion derived from the authors' experience of 'typical criteria.'

TABLE X
CALL-MARK SLICE COMPARISONS (IN THE COLUMN HEADINGS, SS = STATIC SLICE,
DS = DYNAMIC SLICE, AND CM = CALL-MARK SLICE)

Program	Program size (LOC)	LOC in			Slice sizes vs. original program			Comparative reductions (from → to)		
		SS	DS	CM	SS	DS	CM	SS→DS	SS→CM	CM→DS
cal	88	27	14	22	31%	16%	25%	48%	19%	36%
inv1	387	175	139	156	45%	36%	40%	21%	11%	11%
inv2	941	324	50	166	34%	5%	18%	85%	49%	70%
Average	472	175	68	115	37%	19%	28%	51%	26%	39%

Table X summarizes the results. The sizes follow the expected trend from static slices being the largest, then the call-mark slices, and finally the dynamic slices being the smallest. The figure also includes the comparative reductions showing, for example, that with program inv2 the call-mark slice was 49% smaller than the corresponding static slice.

The second hybrid is the 'union slice' introduced by Beszédes et al. [9]. Reminiscent of Hall's work [35], a union slice is the union of dynamic slices, each constructed for the same criteria, but a different input. As more and more inputs are considered, the size of the union slice approaches that of the static slice. Indeed, since the static slice will inevitably include statements because of unrealisable dependences (e.g., due to infeasible paths), the union of dynamic slices, is never larger than the corresponding static slice. It may however, provide a better approximation to the (undecidable) minimal slice. Of course, care is required in reading too much into union slicing as a technique for constructing precise static slices. As Hall [35] and De Lucia et al. [25] showed, unions of dynamic slices may not be valid (executable) slices. Indeed, in some cases, unions of static slices are not slices [25].

Beszédes et al. [9] implemented a union slicing tool and used it to compare the sizes of union slices with the static slices of CodeSurfer. The study consisted of three programs ranging in size from 4,495 to 21,489 LOC (see Table XI). For each program, the authors selected a set of slicing criteria that they considered to be interesting and a set of test data (the size of the test-data sets, and the coverage they provide, is given in Table XI). Though the coverage (45% to 68%) is not high, it was not possible to achieve higher coverage without resorting to the use of a test-data generation tool.

The results showed that for bzip, the union slices constructed were about half the size of the static slices. For the other two programs, the size of their static slices is often very large (even as large as the entire program) making the result of union

TABLE XI
UNION SLICING RESULTS

Program	LOC	Executable LOC	Criteria	Executions	Statement coverage
bzip	4,495	1,595	154	18	68%
bc	11,555	3,220	57	49	63%
less	21,489	5,400	50	14	45%
Sum	37,539	10,215	261	81	
Average	12,513	3,405	87	27	59%

slicing proportionately much smaller. For these two programs, the union slices are typically 20–30% of the program.

4. The Impact of Supporting Analyses

The previous section concerned the question of slice size. Slice size is dependent, among other things, on the precision of supporting analyses used to compute the dependences from which slices are constructed. Three supporting analyses are considered in this section. By far the most important and the most studied concerns pointer analysis. Here empirically data has been both contradictory and surprising. The other two analyses considered are the handling of structure fields and the way in which data dependences are computed. Of key importance in these techniques is their "down stream" impact on slice size. Present studies indicate that large improvements in supporting analyses do not *necessarily* translate into large reductions in slice size.

4.1   The Impact of Pointer Analysis

The first supporting analysis considered is pointer analysis. A slice that includes the dereference of pointer p must also include all statements that potentially define the variables that p points to. Thus, the precision of points-to information is crucial. Unfortunately, computing precise points-to sets is hard [45,74,92] and tradeoffs between time, space, and precision must be made.

In practice, pointer analysis algorithms fall into one of four categories, depending on whether the analysis is flow-sensitive or flow-insensitive, and context-sensitive or context-insensitive. With increased sensitivity comes increased cost. All but the flow-sensitive, context-insensitive option have been experimented with. Furthermore, within the most common category of context- and flow-insensitive pointer analyses, there is a spectrum of precision ranging from Steensgaard's technique to Andersen's [79]. Three experiments on the "down stream" effect on slices of pointer analyses are now considered.

First, Liang and Harrold compare slice size using four points-to analyses: Steensgaard's, Andersen's, Landi and Ryder's (a flow- and context- sensitive analysis), and one developed by Liang and Harrold themselves [65]. The results are shown in Table XII. For all but `lharc` the difference in slice size is less than 2%. For `lharc` slice size varies from 488 to 562 LOC (a 14% difference). Note that for the three larger programs, `larn`, `bison` and `mpegplay`, it was impossible to run Landi and Ryder's points-to analysis, due to time constraints.

Liang and Harrold later consider a flow-insensitive, context-sensitive points-to analysis (hereafter referred to as LH-FICS) [64]. Their aim is to provide a compromise between Andersen's and Steensgaard's algorithms which are both flow- and context-insensitive and the flow- and context-sensitive approach of Landi and Ryder. As might be expected, the flow- and context-sensitive Landi and Ryder algorithm is more precise than any of the others. Interesting, for program `loader` (see Table XIII), Landi and Ryder's algorithm gives a slightly larger result [65].

In this experiment, slices are taken of the programs in Table XIII, which range in size from 1,132 to 17,263 LOC. For the seven smaller programs (less than 4,075 LOC), slices were constructed for every executable statement, while for the 6 larger programs only a single slice was constructed. The size of the resulting SDG was found to be reduced when using the LH-FICS, Landi and Ryder, and Andersen algorithms when compared to the least precise (Steensgaard) algorithm. This reduction in SDG size manifests itself primarily as a reduction in number of summary edges. The LH-FICS and Andersen algorithms have similar precision.

Interestingly, the reductions (primarily in numbers of summary edges) do not feed through to slice size. That is, though the more precise points-to analysis algorithms tended to produce fewer summary edges, the reduction in slice size was not dramatic. For the six programs where it was possible to slice on every statement and use all four pointer-analyses, the average slice size ranged from 86.5% to 100% of the size produced using Steensgaard's points-to analysis.

The second pointer analysis experiment was considered by Mock et al. [71]. They attempted to discover what kinds of program features combine with points-to analysis to yield an increase in program slice size when points-to information is imprecise. The slices concerned are computed by the data-flow slicer `Sprite` and are (for the most part) context insensitive.

The points-to information considered comes from both static and dynamic sources. The static source is Steensgaard's fast but imprecise algorithm. The dynamic points-to data is collected using the *Tumi* instrumentation tool [72] to record the sets of objects actually pointed to by particular pointer.

TABLE XII
EFFECT OF IMPROVED RECURSION HANDLING AND
POINTER ANALYSIS

Program	Aliasing algorithm	Slice size
loader	Steensgaard	237
	Liang–Harrold	196
	Andersen	196
	Landi–Ryder	197
ansi-tape	Steensgaard	290
	Liang–Harrold	284
	Andersen	277
	Landi–Ryder	300
dixie	Steensgaard	633
	Liang–Harrold	632
	Andersen	632
	Landi–Ryder	628
unzip	Steensgaard	807
	Liang–Harrold	806
	Andersen	805
	Landi–Ryder	803
lharc	Steensgaard	562
	Liang–Harrold	489
	Andersen	488
	Landi–Ryder	587
flex	Steensgaard	1871
	Liang–Harrold	1865
	Andersen	1863
	Landi–Ryder	1864
bison	Steensgaard	2362
	Liang–Harrold	2362
	Andersen	2306
larn	Steensgaard	4484
	Liang–Harrold	4427
	Andersen	4383
mpegplay	Steensgaard	5708
	Liang–Harrold	3935
	Andersen	3935

Based on previous work (summarized at the end of this section), structure fields were not expanded. In addition, based on the prior work of Horwitz et al. [50] and Liang and Harrold [64], Mock et al. claim that context sensitivity in slice construc-

TABLE XIII

COMPARISON OF LH-FICS POINTS-TO PRECISION EFFECT ON SLICE SIZE (S—STEENSGAARD,
A—ANDERSEN, LR—LANDI AND RYDER)

Program	Slice sizes				Percent of Steensgaard		
	S	LH-FICS	A	LR	LH-FICS	A	LR
loader	207	192	192	194	93.0%	93.0%	93.8%
ansitape	290	284	277	300	98.1%	95.7%	103.5%
dixie	705	704	704	699	99.9%	99.9%	99.2%
learn	442	442	442	440	100.0%	99.9%	99.3%
unzip	808	807	807	805	99.9%	99.8%	99.6%
smail	739	637	635	–	86.3%	86.1%	–
simulator	1258	1087	1087	1151	86.4%	86.4%	91.5%
flex	2025	2019	2019	2002	99.7%	99.7%	98.9%
space	2234	1936	1936	2086	86.7%	86.7%	93.4%
bison	2394	2394	2338	–	100.0%	97.7%	–
larn	6626	6602	6592	–	99.6%	99.5%	–
mpegplay	5708	3935	3935	–	68.9%	68.9%	–
espresso	6298	6291	6264	–	99.9%	99.5%	–

tion is unimportant with regard to slice size. That is, ignoring the procedure calling context problem has little impact upon the size of slices constructed. Caution is required here, because several, recent, large-scale studies (summarized in Section 3.1), have shown that context sensitivity has a dramatic effect on slice size.

The study concerns 18 programs (see Table XIV) ranging in size from 1,270 to 59,482 LOC. The programs were collected from the SPEC 2000 benchmark suite and from free software (principally GNU application programs and utilities). Importantly, five of the largest programs made heavy use of function pointers (these are the last five programs listed in Table XIV).

Dynamic points-to analysis, which reduced points-to sets size from 1.4 to 700 times, was used to experiment with the impact of points-to sets precision on slice size. Interestingly, as shown by the results in Table XV, the impact was bi-modal depending upon whether or not a subject program made heavy use of function pointers. The programs that use function pointers showed a marked improvement, while the 'non function pointer' programs showed little, if any, improvement. In summary, improved pointer analysis reduces the number of functions considered via function pointers but, otherwise, has little effect on slice size. As this result was produced using dynamic information it, in effect, places a bound on any static analysis.

Two related experiments are worth summarizing. First, one possible explanation for why certain programs did not increase in precision, was context sensitivity. Perhaps the slices remain imprecise when points-to information is more precise be-

TABLE XIV
PROGRAMS STUDIED IN TABLE XV

Program	Source lines	Executable functions	Reachable functions	Executed	Slicing criteria	Description
art	1,270	545	22	18	837	ANN for image recognition
equake	1,513	670	24	19	1,111	seismic simulator
mcf	1,909	635	24	21	880	combinatorial optimization
bzip2	4,639	1,246	63	21	1,579	compression
gzip	7,757	1,864	62	26	1,546	compression
ispell	8,020	2,742	107	33	1,617	spell checking
parser	10,924	4,414	297	230	6,223	word processing
diff	11,755	3,285	110	27	2,110	file comparison
ammp	13,263	5,614	161	46	5,146	molecular dynamics
vpr	16,973	5,954	255	163	7,993	placement and routing
less	18,305	4,371	328	117	1,879	text file viewing
twolf	19,748	11,304	167	104	3,816	placement and routing
vortex	52,633	23,245	643	518	1,324	object-oriented database
grep	13,084	3,674	108	39	3,520	pattern matching
find	13,122	3,004	96	37	740	file system searching
mesa	49,701	21,069	770	130	7,270	graphics
burlap	49,845	16,608	189	123	5,293	finite element solver
gap	59,482	19,998	826	356	5,245	group theory interpreter
Sum	353,943	130,242	4252	2028	58,126	
Average	19,664	7,236	236	113	3,229	

cause of the imprecision in calling context? To answer this question, the authors increased calling context where possible. However, they were, for most programs, only able to increase calling-context sensitivity up to a depth of 2 (for smaller programs greater increases were possible). The authors report that slices based on static points-to analysis and those based on dynamic points-to analysis decreased in size in a similar manner when calling context was enabled. Given the limited context depth, this result is inconclusive at best. An experiment with (fully) context-sensitive slices is called for.

An interesting possibility, suggested by Mock et al., is that the smaller reduction in slice size was due to the fact that the statements in a typical slice were 'in there' simply due to direct data dependence. That is, data dependence that is not induced through a pointer. Therefore, the addition of more precise points to information could not 'take these statements out.' For non-function pointers, this suspicion was borne out by the data. The authors cite here a modification of Amdahl's law:

TABLE XV
POINT-TO ALGORITHM'S EFFECT ON AVERAGE SLICE SIZE

Program	static	dynamic flow insensitive		dynamic flow sensitive	
art	59.6	57.1	4.2%	57.1	4.2%
equake	168.4	164.8	2.1%	164.8	2.1%
mcf	56.8	45.3	20.2%	45.3	20.2%
bzip2	73.0	58.5	19.9%	58.5	19.9%
gzip	54.0	42.0	22.2%	42.0	22.2%
ispell	242.2	185.5	23.4%	185.5	23.4%
parser	195.9	186.9	4.6%	186.7	4.7%
diff	228.3	171.2	25.0%	171.2	25.0%
ammp	339.0	247.0	27.1%	247.0	27.1%
vpr	117.0	100.5	14.1%	100.3	14.3%
less	536.9	394.3	26.6%	393.8	26.7%
twolf	335.6	237.9	29.1%	237.9	29.1%
vortex	3449.3	3240.3	6.1%	3240.3	6.1%
grep	527.8	183.2	65.3%	183.2	65.3%
find	460.8	47.4	89.7%	45.7	90.1%
mesa	3267.3	288.3	91.2%	288.3	91.2%
burlap	5291.6	369.6	93.0%	369.4	93.0%
gap	7758.1	3133.5	59.6%	3006.7	61.2%
Sum	23161.8	9153.3		9023.7	
Average	1286.8	508.5	34.6%	501.3	34.8%

If only the faction f of the slice is due to pointer induced data dependence, then the size of the slice can only be improved by a factor of up to $1/(1 - f)$ when the points-to information is improved.

The second related experiment considered if it *really was* the presence of function pointers that accounted for the improved size of slices for those that contained function pointers. For a single program, points-to data was computed in two formats. In the first, dynamic points-to data was used for function pointers, while static points-to information was used for non-function pointers. The second format reversed the use of static and dynamic points-to data. The first format was found to account for between 48% and 91% of the improvement using dynamic points to information for all pointers. By contrast, the second format led to little improvement.

Empirical data appears to support the notion that, in general, as long as points-to sets are of at least a certain 'basic' precision, additional precision in pointer analysis does not lead to much knock-on reduction is slice size. Steensgaard's algorithm seems to be the low end of the necessary quality with some data suggesting that more precise approaches are of little help and others suggesting that a little more precision is necessary. Improvement in the precision of function pointers appears to be particularly significant.

The previous study with dynamic points-to sets illustrates that better points-to sets are useful in reducing slice size when they reduce the number of functions potentially called at an indirect call site. Unfortunately, the use of dynamic information makes these results specific to a particular execution of the program. Atkinson and Griswold [6] performed a followup study that looked at purely static methods to reducing point-to set sizes. The impact of the four techniques they studied reinforces the belief that function pointers are the dominant issue. Starting with the points-to sets computed by Steensgaard's algorithm, the following four techniques were considered (the names are those used in Table XVI).

prototypes. Function prototyping uses the signature of the function (its prototype) to determine its type. This allows certain potential function points-to members

TABLE XVI

ATKINSON AND GRISWOLD'S RESULTS FOR EFFECTS OF POINTS-TO PRECISION IMPROVEMENTS ON SLICE SIZE

Program (slicing criterion)	Points-to option	Time (min)	Slice size	Statements examined
gcc (c-decl.c:2298,{b})	basic	49.44	236,366	282,192
	arrays	39.11	230,306	282,192
	prototypes	43.66	235,037	235,037
gcc (unroll.c:3085,{const0_rtx})	basic	42.32	236,354	282,192
	mallocs	48.20	236,351	282,192
	arrays	32.41	230,305	282,192
	prototypes	0.46	9,702	13,281
	combined	0.42	9,702	13,281
burlap (arith.c:145,{type_error})	basic	1.29	40,135	51,863
	arrays	1.04	40,204	51,863
	structs	1.72	40,883	53,535
	prototypes	0.20	8,849	12,195
	combined	0.23	8,661	12,319
burlap (matrixfunc.c:767,{status})	basic	1.29	40,135	51,863
	arrays	1.07	40,204	51,863
	structs	1.62	40,858	53,535
	prototypes	0.22	9,332	12,764
	combined	0.25	9,144	12,890

to be eliminated from points-to sets because they are not the right type. This is safe for ANSI C style function declarations, but unsafe for other versions of C, in which function prototypes are un-enforced.

mallocs. The private memory allocator distinction allows a user to tell the tool that certain functions are used as 'private' (that is, user-defined) memory allocation functions. Calls to these functions should be treated like calls to the standard memory allocator `malloc`. Private de-allocators are treated in a similar fashion.

structs. Many analysis techniques treat all members of a structure as a single entity. Distinguishing member fields of structures represents each field by a unique entity. This may improve points-to precision, but it may not be worth the additional cost in space and time in all cases. (Based on the data presented at the beginning of Section 4.2, this option is expected to have little impact.)

arrays. This option, determines whether arrays are treated as a single entity, or as separate independent elements.

The authors present two studies. The second is slicing related. It concerns the impact of points-to precision upon slice size. Slicing criteria were chosen to be 'typical' by the authors and results were recorded for the largest slices that resulted. The three programs studied were `emacs` (99,439 LOC), `burlap` (49,601 LOC) and `gcc` (217,675 LOC).

Table XVI shows two slices for each of the programs `gcc` and `burlap`. For `emacs` there was no combination of techniques that caused any substantial improvement in slice size. As is clear from the data in Table XVI, the improvements from `arrays`, `structs` and `mallocs` were small (at most 3%). In contrast, the prototype technique had a dramatic impact on slice size. This is because it reduces the collection of functions potentially called at an indirect call site.

Finally, Orso et al. [74,75] consider the way pointer assignments give rise to different forms of the def-use associations (DUA). They studied the effect of these different kinds of DUA on slice size. Twenty-four types of DUA are identified as follows. First, observe that, in the presence of pointers, a variable may be *definitely defined* (there is only a single lvalue in the points-to set of the left-hand side of the assignment) as well as *possibly defined* (there is more than one lvalue in the points-to set of the left-hand side of the assignment). Similarly, a variable may be *definitely used* as well as *possibly used*. This gives four "path end point" combinations.

Next, consider the set of paths from *def*, a definition of v, to *use*, a use of v. Each path from this set must contain either a killing definition of v, a possible definition of v, or no definition of v. These three options yield eight possibilities for each set, two of which are uninteresting:

A All paths from *def* to *use* contain killing definitions. In this case *def* does not reach *ref*.

B The absence of a killing definition, a possible definition, and no definition produces a contradiction: It implies that there is no path from *def* to *ref*, which
contradicts the assumption that the definition at *def* reaches the use at *use*.

The remaining six possible path set kinds are

C At least one path is definite def-clear, no path is possible def-clear, and no path
is definite-killing.

D At least one path is definite def-clear, no path is possible def-clear, and at least
one path is definite-killing.

E At least one path is definite def-clear, at least one path is possible def-clear, and
no path is definite-killing.

F At least one path is definite def-clear, at least one path is possible def-clear, and
at least one path is definite-killing.

G No path is definite def-clear, at least one path is possible def-clear, and no path
is definite-killing.

H No path is definite def-clear, at least one path is possible def-clear, and at least
one path is definite-killing.

The product of the six path types and the four path end point combinations yields 24
possible kinds of DUA.

Sinha et al. analyzed the frequency of the 24 def-use association types and their
effect slice size. The study used seven C programs, ranging from 477 to 11,320
LOC. The distribution of def-use association is sparse. Four association types did
not occur at all and 19 association types accounted for only 0.6% of the total number
of associations. The top four forms of association in descending order of occurrence
are

(1) Definite definition and definite use connected by path set Kind D. Here the
choice of path followed determines whether *def* reaches *use*.

(2) Definite definition and definite use connected by path set Kind C. Here *def* is
guaranteed to reach *use*.

(3) Possible definition and possible use connected by path set Kind C. Here if *def*
and *use* refer to the same variable, then *def* is guaranteed to reach *use*.

(4) Possible definition and possible use connected by path set Kind E. Here if *def*
and *use* refer to the same variable then *def* might reach *use* via a definition-
clear path or it might be killed, but only when the possible definition defines
the same variable as *def*.

Two experiments are of interest. The first considers 1,861 slices of the 2,906 line
program unzip [74]. (The authors do not say how the slicing criteria were chosen.)
"Slices" were computed in three incremental steps. The first increment included only
DUA Type 1 (the second most common type). In the second increment, DUA Types 2

and 3 were added, this principally adds the most common type (Type 3). In the third increment, all other types of DUA are added. Note that only the third increment computes safe slices. The other two fail to include statements reachable by DUA types not considered.

For the first increment each slice contains fewer than 20% of the program statements. For the second increment, 45% of the slices contains between 20% and 40% of the program's statements, and in the final increment, over 73% of the slices contained between 40% and 60% of the program statements. These results suggest that the size of the slice is sensitive to the type of define-use association considered. However, the results only concern a single program and so more work will be needed to see if these results generalize to other systems.

In the second experiment, slices were taken at every executable statement in each of the seven programs [75]. Four or five sets of slices using increasingly larger sets of define-use associations, were computed from each program. The first set is always a singleton consisting only of DUA Type 1, while the last is always inclusive of all DUA types and is thus computes 'normal' (correct) slices. The results show that slice sizes increased by between 1% and 19%.

4.2   Impact of Structure Fields

The potential effect of structure-field expansion on slice size [91] is best understood by way of example. Consider the following C code:

```
struct file_ops
{
    int (*write_fn)();
    int (*read_fn)();
} file1;
```

Assume `write_fn` potentially points to the functions `write_ext2` and `write_nfs`, and `read_fn` potentially points to the functions `read_ext2` and `read_nfs`. With structure fields expanded, the function call (`*file1.readfn`) (...) potentially calls `read_ext2` and `read_nfs`. With structure fields collapsed, all structure fields are treated as a single variable and the call (`*file1.readfn`)(...) potentially calls `write_ext2` and `write_nfs` in addition to `read_ext2` and `read_nfs`. For programs with structures that contain pointers, and especially function pointers, this collapse can significantly increase slice size.

Experiments with both the SDG-based `CodeSurfer` and the data-flow based `Sprite` have considered the impact of expanding and collapsing structure fields.

Both conclude that expanding structure fields yields little reduction in slice size. However, one important difficulty in studying supporting analyses is that benefits which accrue from improvement in one analysis may be *masked* by other poor quality analyses. In other words, it is possible for imprecise points-to analysis to mask gains from expanding structure fields.

First, consider the results presented in Table V, which compare slice sizes computed from SDGs built with structure fields collapsed and then expanded. In terms of the SDG, the total number of vertices and edges in all graphs when structure fields are collapsed are 14 and 140 million, respectively. The corresponding totals when structure fields are expanded are 16 and 68 million. Here, a mild increase in vertex count accompanies a dramatic reduction in edge count. Summing edges and vertices, this represents a 45% reduction in total SDG size. For backward slicing, expanding structure fields reduced total slicing time by 41%.

As can be seen in Table V, expanding structure fields reduces the overall average backward slice size from 30.2% of the program to 28.1% and the average forward slice from 28.0% to 26.3%. This is a 7% reduction for backwards slicing and a 6% reduction for forward slicing. This pattern is not atypical in this section: a dramatic improvement in a supporting analysis does not "show through" to similar reductions in slice size. In this case, a 45% reduction in SDG size and a 41% reduction in computation time led to only a 6% to 7% reduction is slice size.

Bent et al. [8] conduct a similar experiment with the data-flow slicer `Sprite` and found that expanding structure fields had essentially no effect on slice sizes. They speculate that this is due to the low quality of the points-to information. Note the `Sprite` uses Steensgaard's rather imprecise pointer analysis and computes context-insensitive slices. On the other hand, the similar results for `CodeSurfer` are perhaps more interesting (and surprising) as `CodeSurfer` uses Andersen's pointer analysis and computes context-sensitive slices.

4.3   Flow Sensitivity of Data Dependence

Krinke [59] reports on an experiment designed to evaluate the effect of replacing the flow-sensitive data dependence analysis, used to build the SDG, with a flow-insensitive analysis. The experiment took 1,000 slices from 1,000 evenly distributed vertices in the SDG for each program shown in Table XVII. The results show that flow-sensitivity in data-dependence construction has a dramatic impact on the precision of slices.

TABLE XVII
EFFECT OF FLOW-SENSITIVE AND FLOW-INSENSITIVE
DATA DEPENDENCE

| Program | Average slice size when data flow edge computation is | | Percent increase |
	flow-sensitive	flow-insensitive	
agrep	47%	56%	19%
ansitape	24%	45%	88%
assembler	34%	43%	26%
bison	11%	17%	55%
cdecl	32%	34%	6%
compiler	44%	48%	9%
ctags	24%	25%	4%
diff	33%	50%	52%
flex	31%	52%	68%
football	25%	26%	4%
gnugo	59%	70%	19%
lex315	26%	47%	81%
loader	22%	26%	18%
patch	47%	49%	4%
plot2fig	23%	24%	4%
rolo	25%	30%	20%
simulator	47%	54%	15%
Average	33%	41%	29%

5. Slicing Tools and Techniques

This section presents research on the refinement and extension of slicing algorithms. Typically, the improvements are aimed at reducing slice size, or the time and space required to compute slices. Such work accompanied by significant empirical data is presented.

5.1 Better switch Slicing

Kumar and Horwitz introduce a refined definition for control dependence and a refined slicing algorithm for programs that contain C-style switch statements [60]. The algorithm has essentially the same complexity as the HRB algorithm and is more precise.

Slice sizes of the C programs shown in Table XVIII were used to compare the new algorithm with HRB. Slices were taken from all of the vertices that could be reached by following one control-dependence edge forward from a switch case,

TABLE XVIII
BETTER SWITCH HANDLING AFFECTS SLICE SIZE

Program	LOC	Modified SDG size	Number of slices	Average slice size Old alg	New alg
gcc.cpp	4,079	16,784	1,932	11,693	11,670
byacc	6,626	21,239	468	2,119	2,110
CADP	12,930	35,965	499	7,921	7,905
flex	16,236	31,354	1,716	8,150	8,082
Sum	39,871	105,342	4,615	29,883	29,767
Average	9,968	26,335	1,154	7,471	7,441

and then following five data-dependence edges forward. This ensured that every slice would include a switch, but avoided, for example, slices that would include only switch cases and breaks.

Experimental results show that, while in most cases, slice sizes are reduced by no more than 5%, there are examples of reductions of up to 35%. In more detail, for 99.6% of the slices, the new algorithm produced smaller slices than its predecessor. Although 96% of these were only 5% reductions, there were some cases (2.4%) where the new algorithm provided reductions of more than 15%, and some cases (1.6%) where it provided reductions of more than 30%.

5.2   Better Interprocedural Control Flow Slicing

Sinha et al. [80] consider potentially non-returning call sites; a problem where control flow is not only unstructured, but also interprocedural. The particular statement of concern in this work was the C exit() statement, which causes control to drop out of the procedure without returning to the call site. They report finding such statements in 65% of a set of 70 C programs and try-throw statements in 31% of a set of 1,650 Java programs.

The experiment compares the standard SDG [49] with a slightly modified version that takes into account arbitrary interprocedural control flow. Five C programs (armenu, dejavu1, dejavu2, mpegplayer and space), ranging in size from 4,385 to 11,474 LOC were sliced at every executable statement, producing a total of 68,272 slices. Sinha et al. use Landi and Ryder's flow-sensitive and context-sensitive points-to analysis.

Three of the programs studied contained exit statements at the beginning of their entry procedures and therefore, perhaps unsurprisingly, more than 90% of the slices of these three programs differed between the two versions of the slicer. For the other two programs, the results indicated that approximately 60% of the slices differed. These programs were versions of the same system and so produced similar results. Detailed results concerning the size of the differences in slices are not presented, but the Sinha et al. do note that for the two programs with fewest differing slices, the slices constructed without accounting for arbitrary interprocedural control flow failed to identify up to 20% of the statements which rightly belonged in the slices.

5.3   Improved Summary Edge Computation

Reps et al. [49] present an improved algorithm for slicing the SDG [77] that is asymptotically faster than the original HRB algorithm. In particular, the new algorithm includes an improved approach for computing summary edges. The basic idea is to find, for every procedure P, all same-level realizable paths (as defined in Section 2.4) connecting one of P's formal-in vertices to one of its formal-out vertices. Such paths induce summary edges between the corresponding actual-in and actual-out vertices at all call sites on P.

The improved algorithm accomplishes this by first "asserting" that there is a same-level realizable path (hereafter simply a "path") from every formal-out vertex to itself; these paths are placed on the worklist. Then, the algorithm extends paths by repeatedly choosing a path from the worklist and extending it (backwards) by one edge, placing new paths on the worklist. When an edge is processed whose source is a formal-in vertex, corresponding summary edges are added. These new summary edges may, in turn, induce new paths: if there is a summary edge $x \rightarrow y$, then there is a same-level realizable path $x \rightarrow^+ a$ for every formal-out vertex a such that there is a same-level realizable path $y \rightarrow^+ a$.

A preliminary performance study was carried out to measure how much faster interprocedural slicing is when summary edges are computed using the new algorithm. The slicing algorithms were implemented in C and tested on a Sun SPARCstation 10 Model 30 with 32 MB of RAM. Tests were carried out for three example programs (written in a small research language): recdes is a recursive-descent parser for lists of assignment statements; calculator is a simple arithmetic calculator; and format is a text-formatting program. Table XIX gives some statistics about the SDGs of the three test programs. The experiment actually implemented three different slicing algorithms:

(A) The HRB slicing algorithm.

(B) The slicing algorithm with the improved method for computing summary edges.

(C) The "dual" of Algorithm B. (Algorithm C is just like Algorithm B, except that the computation of summary edges involves finding all same-level realizable

TABLE XIX
EFFECT OF IMPROVED SUMMARY EDGE COMPUTATION

Program	LOC	Vertices	Edges	Slice size		Times (s) for			Speedup	
				Vertices	%	A	B	C	A→B	A→C
recdes	348	838	1465	413	49%	2.08	0.35	0.39	5.4	4.8
calculator	433	841	1443	484	58%	3.06	0.46	0.45	6.3	6.5
format	757	1844	3276	1327	72%	6.64	0.98	1.09	6.1	5.4
Sum	1538	3523	6184	2224		11.78	1.79	1.93		
Average	513	1174	2961	741	60%	3.92	0.60	0.64	5.93	5.67

paths from formal-in vertices (rather than to formal-out vertices), and paths are extended forwards rather than backwards.)

Table XIX compares the performance of the three algorithms for a representative slice of each program. The time for the final step of computing slices is not shown separately. This step takes 3% or less of the total runtime. As shown in final two columns, Algorithms B and C are clearly superior to Algorithm A, exhibiting 4.8 to 6.5-fold speedup. Algorithm B appears to be marginally better than Algorithm C. The authors believe that this is because procedures have fewer formal-out vertices than formal-in vertices.

5.4   Dynamic Data Dependence

Zhang et al. [94] study the trade-offs between space and time in the computation of dynamic data dependence. There are two possible extremes to computing dynamic data dependence, which parallel exhaustive data-flow analysis and demand-driven data-flow analysis respectively: complete pre-processing and no pre-processing. Complete pre-processing, once done, yields fast tools, but requires a great deal of space. In contrast, no pre-processing is space-efficient, but may require a great deal of slicing time.

The study used five programs from the Specint92 and Specint95 suite, ranging in size from, 7,741 to 207,483 LOC. The experiments, based on the Trimaran system for C programs, were conducted on a 2.2 GHz Pentium 4 Linux workstation with 1 Gb RAM and 1 Gb swap. Execution traces were collected for three different executions of each program. For each execution trace, 25 slices were computed from the end of the program and 25 from the mid-point of the program.

Four dynamic slicing algorithms are studied: FP (Full Pre-processing), LP (Limited Pre-processing), which does no caching, NPwoC (No Pre-processing *without* caching of previously computed data dependencies), and NPwC (No Pre-processing *with* caching of previously computed data dependencies). The first finding was that the FP algorithm is impractical because it runs out of space on many of the slices considered.

The LP algorithm was found to grow more slowly in slice computation time, compared to the no pre-processing versions of the algorithm. The execution times for LP are typically 1 to 3 times lower than those of the no pre-processing versions. In addition, LP performed well compared to the Agrawal and Horgan's second (imprecise) dynamic slicing algorithm [3]. The effect of caching on the speed of slice computation for the two versions of the 'no pre-processing' appeared to be rather mixed. For some programs the number of cache hits was found to be low and therefore the overhead of maintaining the cache dominated, making the version with a cache slower than the version with no caching.

5.5   Graph Reachability Optimizations

Binkley and Harman [18] present a study of techniques to improve graph-based program analysis. Interprocedural program slicing is used to illustrate the impact of these techniques. Data collected from five different slicers, when applied to the programs shown in Table IV, is used to quantify the improvement of the following four optimization techniques:

std   The standard implementation, which computes slices using the HRB algorithm [49].

SCC   The second version adds SCC formation. The two key insights here are that all vertices in an SCC will have the same slice, and any slice that includes a vertex from an SCC must, by definition, include all the vertices of the SCC. Thus, SCCs can be collapsed into a single representative node.

+Pack   The third version incorporates data structure changes that reduce the size of a vertex and reorder structure fields to exploit cache behavior.

+TS   The fourth version sorts the vertices of each procedure into topological order to improve memory access patterns.

+Tran   The final version removes transitive edges. For slicing, transitive edges in the SDG have no exploitable pattern; therefore, they represent only extra work for the slicer.

Combined, these techniques increase the size of the problem that can be effectively handled by more than a factor of three. To avoid any slice-selection bias, the slice on every executable statement was taken. The results are shown in Table XX, where times are scaled so that std's run-time is 1.00 for each program. This was done

TABLE XX
GRAPH REACHABILITY OPTIMIZATIONS EFFECT ON SLICING (SCALED TO STD = 1.00)

Program	Std	SCC	+Pack	+TS	+Tran
			Version		
a2ps	1.00	3.33	4.59	6.64	7.13
acct-6.3	1.00	1.54	2.74	4.35	5.70
barcode	1.00	0.99	2.15	3.62	5.51
bc	1.00	1.06	1.84	3.10	3.88
byacc	1.00	1.38	2.08	3.28	3.58
cadp	1.00	1.14	1.63	2.94	3.28
compress	1.00	1.25	1.67	1.67	1.67
copia	1.00	0.88	1.18	1.43	1.50
csurf-pkgs	1.00	0.82	1.11	1.39	1.47
ctags	1.00	1.17	1.60	2.36	2.57
cvs	1.00	0.86	1.07	1.56	1.73
diffutils	1.00	1.80	2.68	3.93	4.43
ed	1.00	1.83	2.62	3.72	4.20
empire	1.00	1.32	1.82	2.57	2.79
epwic-1	1.00	1.14	2.32	5.32	7.36
espresso	1.00	1.18	1.59	2.25	2.48
findutils	1.00	1.56	2.48	3.94	4.56
flex2-4-7	1.00	1.63	2.29	3.16	3.37
flex2-5-4	1.00	2.34	3.23	4.66	5.29
ftpd	1.00	1.79	2.44	3.24	3.44
gcc.cpp	1.00	1.48	2.37	3.89	4.62
gnubg-0.0	1.00	1.00	1.52	2.31	2.64
gnuchess	1.00	1.34	1.91	2.79	3.25
gnugo	1.00	0.93	1.32	1.73	1.84
go	1.00	1.13	1.87	2.37	2.63
ijpeg	1.00	1.18	1.79	2.22	2.57
indent	1.00	5.40	7.85	11.59	14.01
li	1.00	0.90	1.20	1.62	1.77
named	1.00	1.35	1.66	2.16	2.25
ntpd	1.00	1.10	1.49	1.90	2.13
oracolo2	1.00	0.87	1.43	2.19	2.51
prepro	1.00	0.89	1.43	2.44	2.65
replace	1.00	1.67	2.50	2.50	2.50
sendmail	1.00	1.67	1.82	2.33	2.36
space	1.00	0.89	1.50	2.38	2.69
spice	1.00	1.02	1.52	1.80	1.80
termutils	1.00	1.09	3.15	4.31	5.28
tile-forth	1.00	1.00	1.41	1.80	1.97
time-1.7	1.00	1.25	2.50	1.67	1.67
userv-0.95.0	1.00	1.02	1.44	1.91	2.06
wdiff.0.5	1.00	1.56	1.87	1.87	2.33

(continued to next page)

TABLE XX — *(Continued from previous page)*

Program	Std	SCC	+Pack	+TS	+Tran
			Version		
which	1.00	1.33	1.50	1.71	2.00
wpst	1.00	1.19	1.72	2.45	2.75
Sum	43.00	60.28	89.91	127.07	146.24
Average	1.00	1.40	2.09	2.96	3.40
Cumulative reduction		29%	52%	66%	71%

because the raw times range from 0.05 seconds to 768,391 seconds, which makes summary statistics such as averages meaningless. The last three rows of Table XX, show the sum, average, and the cumulative run-time reduction. Combining all four techniques produces an average 71% time reduction (and a 64% reduction in memory usage).

Some details on individual versions prove interesting. To begin with, a total of 2,651,991 vertices in 73,292 SCCs gives an average of 36 vertices per SCC. The naïve implementation in the SCC version increases the vertex size. The true effect of SCC formation can be seen using a constant vertex size. Doing so, the average speedup is 1.92 (versus 1.40 in the SCC column of Table XX). Finally, +Tran removes an average of 25% of the intraprocedural edges, an led to a 15% run-time improvement.

5.6 Three Data-Flow Slice Enabling Techniques

Atkinson and Griswold implemented techniques to reduce the time and space required to compute dataflow information [5]. This information is useful in many static analyses, one of which is program slicing. The primary motivations for their work is to scale dataflow based slicing to large size programs. Their tool, Sprite is able to slice programs of the order of a hundred thousand lines.

However, the results focus on context-insensitive slices (see Section 4.1). Clearly, for programs where context sensitivity makes a large difference to slice size, this may not be appropriate and it remains unclear whether the data flow approach can be scaled to large programs when calling context must be correctly accounted for.

Atkinson and Griswold considered three approaches to reducing Sprite's space or time requirements: factorization of dataflow information, data flow set reclamation, and improving block visitation order. Factoring of data-flow sets can greatly improve set operation performance. For instance, a temporary is seldom the target of a pointer, so a special class is used to factor out temporaries. Similarly, the set of non-local, automatic variables does not change throughout the slice construction for a given function. Fixing these values allows a very compact factored bit sets representation of dataflow information. For example, factorization reduces the space required for the points-to sets of gcc from 10 Gb to 60 Mb.

The second technique saves space by selective dataflow set reclamation. The observation behind optimization is that, once the neighbors of a node have been processed, the dataflow set of the node is no longer needed. This works because the analysis is monotonic; thus, all that is required is the size of the old set (to test for changes (i.e., growth)).

Finally, a hybrid approach to visitation order is shown to reduce computation time. Here, every block is visited at most once per iteration (retaining the global 'fairness' of an iterative approach), but a block is only processed if data flow information of its neighbors has been updated (retaining the selective update of a worklist approach).

The study was based on an implementation of the three data flow optimization techniques to determine the effect on slice computation time and space requirements for the Sprite dataflow slicer. Seven programs were used in the study, ranging in size from 437 to 57,004 LOC. For each program a 'typical' slice was constructed. The authors chose the slicing criterion using their own expert knowledge to determine what constituted a 'typical' slice.

Results of this study are summarized in Table XXI. Timing data comes from the execution on a 440 MHz Sun UltraSparc 10 running Solaris 2.8 with 256 MB of physical memory and 1.6 GB swap space. Slices were computed using dataflow set factorization, with strong prototype filtering (see Section 4.1) enabled.

The authors note that the average reduction in space due to reclamation is 40%. However, this average is very much dependent upon the algorithm for node visitation order. For the hybrid algorithm, the reduction was only 17% on average, whereas for the worklist approach, the reduction was 40% of the iterative search approach it was 60%.

The hybrid approach to node visitation order results in about a 20% reduction in block visits compared to the traditional iterative algorithm, but large slices have fewer reclaimable blocks, reducing the impact of reclaimable blocks. The worklist algorithm performs too slowly to be practical for large slices.

When context sensitivity is disabled, the iterative search outperforms the worklist approach significantly. This points to the importance of the interplay between the question of whether context sensitivity is important for precise slice computation and the question of how slicing can be efficiently computed.

Finally, an interesting artifact of the slicer's calling context insensitivity is that, for some examples, the worklist algorithm produces smaller slices. The average difference is small, about a 1%, but it is interesting because, at first glance, one would expect all three visitation orders to produce identical slices. The difference is attributed

TABLE XXI

ATKINSON AND GRISWOLD'S RESULTS FOR EFFECTS OF SPACE AND TIME SAVING TECHNIQUES FOR DATA-FLOW BASED SLICING

Program (Slicing criterion)	Slice size (LOC)	Reclaim sets?	Iterative search		Hybrid search		Worklist	
			Time	Space	Time	Space	Time	Space
wc (wc.c:364: totallines)	437	no	0.22	0.34	0.19	0.34	0.21	0.31
		yes	0.27	0.25	0.22	0.30	0.33	0.29
diff (diff.c:1071: val)	1,976	no	2.17	2.54	1.82	2.54	3.46	2.45
		yes	2.68	1.55	2.09	2.29	4.93	1.92
gcc (unroll.c:3085: const_rtx)	2,617	no	11.13	8.33	10.36	8.33	17.76	8.12
		yes	11.18	2.88	10.40	6.87	19.33	5.31
BURLAP (matrixfunc.c: 767:status)	2,709	no	6.48	6.04	5.58	6.02	18.33	5.92
		yes	6.70	2.94	6.13	5.11	23.93	4.40
BURLAP (apply.c:243: result)	12,336	no	34.83	23.78	32.47	23.78	67.96	22.80
		yes	30.71	10.40	36.75	18.85	90.12	14.73
emacs (alloc.c:1936: gc_cons_threshold)	34,386	no	1793.68	208.42	1703.42	208.42	2596.02	188.71
		yes	347.39	64.69	815.66	163.37	1886.61	115.89
gcc (sched.c:4964: reg_n_calls_crossed)	57,004	no	10103.60	316.04	6657.77	316.04	10625.77	299.40
		yes	622.50	84.70	8679.52	253.68	14933.10	181.25

to the worklist algorithm being more localized during data-flow computation; thus, allowing it to be more precise.

5.7   The Slices of `Sprite` and `CodeSurfer`

There has been one direct comparison of the dataflow based slicing approach and the dependence graph-based slicing approach [8]. Of course, such a comparison, at best, compares two tools, rather than the two approaches. The study is also highly sensitive to the other issues of pointer analysis and context sensitivity which are handled differently in the two tools considered.

This study considers the slices of the tools `CodeSurfer` and `Sprite`. The two primary differences between the slicing tools are the treatment of context and the precision of the points-to sets. `Sprite` was configured to favor performance: It uses Steensgaard's almost linear points-to analysis [82] and performed context insensitivity slices (`Sprite`'s context-sensitivity is provided by k-limiting). `CodeSurfer` was configured to favor precision: It used Andersen's cubic time pointer analysis [4], which is more precise than Steensgaard's, and provides infinite context sensitivity through the use of summary edges.

Three slices, each of six benchmark programs were taken. An attempt was made to select slicing criteria such that both are dissimilar from each other and might be chosen by programmers in practice. One goal for this selection is to increase the external validity of the study. Of course, this collection of slicing criteria does not represent a typical, average, or complete profile, which must be considered when drawing conclusions from the data. All slices were computed on a 440 MHz UltraSparc 10 with 640 MB of real memory and 1.1 GB of virtual memory running Solaris.

For the purposes of comparison, the study used the intersection of corresponding slices returned by `Sprite` and `CodeSurfer`, called the intersected slice. The relative precision margin (PM) of a slice is the size of the slice divided by the size of the intersected slice. The precision margin provides a measure of the relative quality of a tool's slice. The results for all 18 slices are presented in Table XXII. Neither slicer's results are consistently contained within the other. However, on average `Sprite` was less precise.

Given `CodeSurfer`'s more precise data dependence and points-to algorithms, it is expected to produce more precise slices. This turned out to be the case; the average `Sprite` slice is 4,200% larger than the average `CodeSurfer` slice. Omitting three outliers, the average `Sprite` slice is 53% larger than the average `CodeSurfer` slice. There are three factors that account for this difference (note that they are not additive): first, `Sprite` uses the less precise Steensgaard points-to sets, which, at least for function pointers, can have a significant impact. Second, `Sprite`'s slices

TABLE XXII
SPRITE AND CODESURFER SLICE SIZE COMPARISON

Program	NB-NC LOC	Sizes					
		Intersection		Sprite		CodeSurfer	
		Lines	%	Lines	PM	Lines	PM
compress	842	13	0.02	13	1.00	13	1.00
	842	122	0.14	123	1.01	123	1.01
	842	261	0.31	287	1.10	261	1.00
wally	1,519	173	0.11	241	1.39	208	1.20
	1,519	492	0.32	492	1.00	502	1.02
	1,519	77	0.05	197	2.56	78	1.01
ispell	5,794	9	0.00	1,595	177.22	9	1.00
	5,794	334	0.06	492	1.47	341	1.02
	5,794	79	0.01	464	5.87	79	1.00
ed	7,084	127	0.02	142	1.12	129	1.02
	7,084	2,500	0.35	2,539	1.02	2,538	1.02
	7,084	168	0.02	180	1.07	2,214	13.18
diff	8,584	1,065	0.12	1,191	1.12	1,071	1.01
	8,584	5	0.00	2,859	571.80	5	1.00
	8,584	1,837	0.21	1,911	1.04	1,844	1.00
enscript	14,554	3,269	0.22	3,410	1.04	3,274	1.00
	14,554	327	0.02	504	1.54	338	1.03
	14,554	2,045	0.14	2,142	1.05	2,047	1.00
Sum	115,131	12,903		18,782		15,074	
Average	6,396	717	11.78	1,043	42.97	837	1.70

are context insensitive. Krinke, and Binkley and Harman report that ignoring context sensitivity in CodeSurfer increases slice size by 50–68% [18,58]. Third, it was discovered that CodeSurfer's libraries (that model libc.c) produce more precise slices.

Bent et al. [8] experiment with two of these factors. Using CodeSurfer's libraries and infinite context sensitivity brought all Sprite slices to within a precision margin of 1.50. The remaining difference might be accounted for by the difference in pointer analysis or slicing approach. The paper provides details for the impact of these two factors on three example slices is shown in Table XXIII.

Two remarks are relevant. First, two causes for concern with this study are the average slice size of 11.78% and the maximum slice size of 35%. These values are considerably smaller than those reported by other static slice size studies appearing in this chapter. The likely cause for this is the small number of slices used, which introduces significant selection bias into the results. Unfortunately, Sprite's slicing speed makes a large-scale study, including all slices on executable statements,

TABLE XXIII

Slice	Original	w/ Infinite Context	w/ CodeSurfer libraries	Combined
wally 1	241	241	180	174
ispell 2	492	467	489	419
ispell 3	464	271	261	80
Sum	1197	979	930	673
Average	399	326	310	224

presently impractical. The particular implication of this bias is that the reported results need to be taken "with a pinch of salt." On the other hand, as the 18 slices were chosen by experienced programmers as representative, the smaller average slice size may be an encouraging sign.

Second, in comparison, CodeSurfer's slice time is incredibly small (often 0.00). It pays for this during the pre-computation of dependence edges. It is possible to compute the "break-even" point at which the pre-computation pays for itself in faster slice times and thus all future slices are essentially "free." Using the average slice time of the three slices time for each program shown in Table XXII, the break-even point ranges from 2 to 34 (for compress and enscript, respectively), and has an average of 7.6. Two important caveats in this computation require mentioning. First, slice times, which are proportional to slice size, were inflated by a factor of 3 to account for the uncharacteristically small average slice size of 11% versus 30% [18,58]. Second, Sprite's times are for are context-insensitive slices; full context sensitivity is expensive as implemented in Sprite (i.e., without pre-computing summary edges); thus, the break-even point would be lower if comparable slices were computed.

6. Applications of Slices

Traditionally slicing has been applied to program comprehension activities (like supporting code understanding, fault localization, and debugging). This section considers four empirical studies of these applications. The next section considers the empirical studies into the way slicing supports human comprehension.

6.1 Clone Detection

In the first application, Komondoor and Horwitz apply program slicing to clone detection [52]. The major benefit of a slicing-based approach is the ability to find possibly non-contiguous, reordered, and intertwined clones that involve possible variable renaming. Such clones are missed by other approaches. Their technique has three steps:

Step 1: Find pairs of clones (two isomorphic PDG subgraphs) as follows. PDG vertices are first partitioned into equivalence classes based on the syntactic structure of the code represented by the vertex. Two vertices in the same class are called *matching* vertices. For each pair of matching vertices $(v1, v2)$, a "lock-step" backward slice starting from $v1$ and $v2$ is used to identify two isomorphic PDG subgraphs. Lock-step slicing includes a predecessor vertex in one slice iff there is a corresponding, matching predecessor in the other PDG. Furthermore, whenever a pair of matching loop or predicate vertices is added, one step of the forward slice from these vertices is used to add matching control-dependent successors to the two slices.

Step 2: Remove subsumed clone pairs. The pair $(S1, S2)$ is subsumed if there exists a clone pair $(S1', S2')$ such that $S1 \subset S1'$ and $S2 \subset S2'$.

Step 3: Combine clone pairs into clone groups using a kind of transitive closure. For example, clone pairs $(S1, S2)$, $(S1, S3)$, and $(S2, S3)$ would be combined into the clone group $(S1, S2, S3)$.

Komondoor and Horwitz implemented a tool based on CodeSurfer for finding clones in C programs. The tool was then run on three Unix utilities, bison, sort, and tail, and four files from a graph-layout program used in-house by IBM. Table XXIV presents the program sizes and running times for the three steps of the algorithm. Table XXV presents the sizes of the discovered clones which are divided into eight size ranges. Clones with fewer than five PDG vertices were deemed too

TABLE XXIV
PROGRAM SEARCHED FOR CLONES AND THE TOOLS RUNNING TIME

	Program size		Running times (elapsed time)		
		PDG	Find clone	Eliminate subsumed	Create clone
Program	LOC	vertices	pairs	clone pairs	clone
bison	11,540	28,548	1 : 33 h	15 s	50 s
sort	2,445	5,820	10 min	5 s	2 s
tail	1,569	2,580	40 s	1 s	2 s
IBM 1	1,677	2,235	1 : 02 min	For the IBM programs, total times were not broken	
IBM 2	2,621	4,006	7 : 49 min	down by step. Finding clone pairs was reported	
IBM 3	3,343	6,761	5 : 15 min	to take 90% of the time.	
IBM 4	3,419	4,845	13 : 00 min		

TABLE XXV
CLONES DETECTED

Program		Clone size ranges (PDG vertices)							
		5–9	10–19	20–29	30–39	40–49	50–59	60–69	70+
bison	clone groups identified	513	164	34	16	9	9	6	49
	max clones in a group	61	26	11	2	2	2	2	4
	mean clones in a group	3.7	2.8	3.3	2	2	2	2	2.1
sort	clone groups identified	105	57	30	9	14			
	max clones in a group	17	8	6	3	2			
	mean clones in a group	3.0	2.8	2.4	2.1	2			
tail	clone groups identified	21	4	0	0	4	1	0	2
	max clones in a group	12	8			3	2		2
	mean clones in a group	3.2	3.5			2.3	2		2

small to be good candidates for extraction and were ignored. This work includes several examples of the interesting clones including intertwined clones.

To further evaluate the tool, several studies are described that relate tool-discovered clones with clones extracted by hand. For example, lex.c (from bison) was examined by hand and found to contain four ideal clone groups. The tool identified 43 clone groups. Nineteen of these were variants of one of the ideal clone groups, while the other 24 were uninteresting (13 of the 24 contained clones with fewer than 7 vertices). Another example study examined all 25 clone groups found in bison in the size range 30-49 (an intermediate clone size). All but one were variants of the 9 ideal clone groups (i.e., only one of them was uninteresting).

Finally, from the IBM code, 250 larger clones found by the tool were examined. They were used to manually identify 77 ideal clones (17 of which were non-contiguous). The 77 clones belonged to 30 clone groups, which included 2 that involved reordering of matching statements and 2 that involved intertwined clones. Most of these clones involved renamed variables. Identified clone groups were manually extracted and replaced with C pre-processor macros. The reduction in code size ranged, on a per program basis, from 1.9% to 4.9% and, on a per function bases, from 4.4% to 12.4% of a function that included at least one clone.

6.2   Semantic Differences

Binkley et al. [14] studied the *semantic* differences between two versions of a program. Their implementation takes, as input, two C programs: old and new, and outputs a third program differences that captures the semantic (rather then syntactic) changes from old to new. Program differences is computed by first building the SDGs of old and new. The algorithm then gathers a series of slices of new's SDG starting with a set of points called the *directly affected points*, which are points known to have different behavior in old and new [12].

At a low level this study investigates the time taken to compute differences and, more importantly, the size of differences relative to the size of new. At a high level, the study seeks to illustrate the value of semantic differencing, which is useful in a variety of tasks. For example, the authors discuss the application of semantic differencing to testing and impact analysis.

The experiment considers two groups of programs. The first group includes multiple versions of 7 programs ranging in size from 145 to 514 LOC. Consecutive versions were used as old and new. SDG build time ranged from 0.24 to 0.80 seconds and the computation of differences took no measurable time. Thus, the entire computation of differences took less than one second for each run. The size of differences ranged from 9% to 95% of new with an average reduction of 26%.

The second group of programs consists of ten larger programs (ranging in size from 3000 to 22,000 lines of code). The second experiment was exhaustive. For each program, differences was computed for each executable statement in the program.

The results, summarized in Table XXVI, include the "pace" in LOC processed per second on a 450 MHz Pentium II with 256 Mb of memory. On average this is about 250 lines per second, or 25% to 50% of the speed of gcc with full optimization. The most important information presented in Table XXVI relates to the size of differences as shown in the final three columns. This includes its mean and median size and the mean percentage reduction. Over all programs, the average reduction was 37.70%. Weighting the reduction of each program by its size produces a weighted average of 36.58%. It is interesting to note that this is an improvement over the 26% average reduction obtained with smaller programs.

Binkley et al. observe that the ten subject programs exhibit five distinct patterns. These range from programs where most of the time differences include essentially all of the input program to those that include a wide variety of sizes. A further breakdown of two of the largest programs shows that they represent two extremes in the effectiveness of computing differences.

For the program acct, about 75% of the executions of differences include less than half of the program. In contrast, for the program ed over 70% of the executions of differences include over 90% of the program. It is clear from these numbers that ed is a tightly knit program while acct is not. These sorts of observation led to Bieman an Ott suggesting slicing as a means of assessing the level of functional cohesion in a program [10].

TABLE XXVI

SEMANTIC DIFFERENCING DATA AND THE SIZE OF DIFFERENCES

Program	LOC	SDG size (vertices)	Vertices per LOC	SDG build		differences time (s)		differences size (vertices)		Mean percent reduction
				time (s)	pace (LOC/s)	average	max	mean	median	
a2s	22,068	57,922	2.62	106	208	0.94	2.26	30,161	31,873	47.93%
acct	10,182	110,860	10.89	99	103	0.89	5.07	29,830	28,298	73.09%
barcode	5,848	19,562	3.35	17	344	0.16	0.26	13,209	15,646	32.48%
bc	8,364	70,502	8.43	64	131	2.34	3.59	64,909	67,990	7.93%
copia	3,488	46,130	13.23	9	388	0.72	1.87	29,404	22,295	36.26%
ed	13,578	98,479	7.25	243	56	4.29	7.76	79,823	90,721	18.94%
flex	21,543	53,418	2.48	120	180	0.72	2.24	29,660	37,875	44.48%
oracolo2	14,382	92,200	6.41	44	327	1.17	3.54	65,918	82,028	28.51%
prepro	14,330	95,757	6.68	44	326	1.22	3.60	68,321	85,225	28.65%
termutils	7,006	10,161	1.45	15	467	0.05	0.11	4,192	5,120	58.74%
Average	12,079	65,499	6.28	76	253	1.25	3.00	41,543	46,707	37.70%

6.3 Semantic Equivalence

Gallagher and O'Brien [32] examine the impact of *decomposition* slice equivalence. A decomposition slice [33] is the union of the slices on a particular variable. It captures the relevant computations involving a variable without regard for location (i.e., starting statement).

Table XXVII summarizes the data collected, which includes the size of the programs in LOC (as reported by wc -l) and the initial number of decomposition slices computed. This reflects the number of variables and enumeration values declared in the program. The value includes *all* variables declared in header files including struct fields. Many of these variables (in particular those from header files) go unused in the program. Columns 4 and 5 show the number of decomposition slices when empty slices are ignored along with the percent reduction. Finally, the last 3 columns show the reduction obtained by forming equivalence classes based upon decomposition slice equivalence. This includes the percent reduction from both the original graph and the graph without empty slices.

Gallagher and O'Brien consider two applications of this reduction. First, it can simplify other operations. For example, the reduction has an impact on testing. In the case of P1 and P2, some 200 variables include the same computation, any testing criterion that tests one of these tests them all.

The second application forms a *decomposition slice graph* using the partial order induced by proper subset inclusion on sets of equivalent decomposition slices. These graphs provide a visualization of the complexity of a piece of software. Viewing the graph after collapsing equivalent slices provides insights into how many variables share the same core computation and thus the complexity of analyzing the program.

TABLE XXVII

REDUCTION FROM EQUIVALENT DECOMPOSITION SLICES

| Program | LOC | Initial decomp. slices | w/o empty slices | | Decomp. slice equiv. partitions | Reduction | |
			decomp. slices	Reduction		from original	from w/o empty
dif	767	95	66	31%	34	62%	48%
lattice	1,625	168	104	38%	83	51%	20%
unravel	803	482	281	42%	129	73%	54%
analyzer	1,287	817	327	59%	198	76%	39%
parser	6,314	788	470	40%	201	75%	57%
P1	2,678	344	267	22%	76	78%	72%
P2	4,539	315	279	11%	61	81%	78%
Sum	18,013	3,009	1,794		782		
Average	2,573	430	256	35%	112	71%	53%

6.4   Concept Lattice of Decomposition Slices

Tonella [84] considered using the theory of formal concept assignment [81] to organize decomposition slices. This led to the formulation the concept lattice of decomposition slices, which differs from the decomposition slice graph in that it is a complete lattice, and, perhaps more importantly, it contains additional 'interference' nodes not found in the decomposition slice graph. The concept lattice is formed using standard set operations applied to the sets of statements in the decomposition slices.

Since the principal difference between the decomposition slice graph and the lattice of decomposition slices lies in the presence of interference nodes, it is important to ask how many additional nodes are present. If such nodes occur only occasionally, then perhaps the phenomenon is not worthy of study. On the other hand, if they are frequent, then they will make any analysis rather difficult and therefore, potentially, impractical.

TABLE XXVIII
FREQUENCY OF INTERFERENCE NODES

Program	Nodes in lattice	Interference nodes
cat	32	11
chgrp	16	3
chmod	16	5
cmp	37	20
cp	11	1
date	34	9
df	30	5
du	13	1
ln	11	3
mt	25	7
rm	12	1
strip	11	1
stty	50	18
su	22	4
tee	9	2
time	14	4
wall	21	2
who	16	4
whoami	7	0
write	25	7
Sum	412	108
Average	20.6	5.4

Tonella studied this problem looking to see if it occurred in practice. The study consisted of 20 BSD Unix programs consisting of 20 to 2,000 LOC, with the typical size of approximately 1,000 LOC. For each program, a lattice of decomposition slices was constructed and the number of nodes in the lattice and the number of interference nodes was recorded.

As seen in Table XXVIII, only `whoami` has no interference nodes and yet, for a few programs, interference nodes account for more than 50% of the total number of nodes. This indicates that interference nodes are sufficiently prevalent to warrant analysis and study, while they are not so numerous as to prohibit effective analysis by humans using the lattice of decomposition slices as a guide to impact analysis and other comprehension tasks.

7. Human Comprehension Studies

This section considers empirical studies that have investigated the psychological effects slices have on the programmers. This was the original motivation for slicing [87] and has remained a dominant application area for all forms of program slices.

This section describes eight experiments involving programmers and (some form of) program slicing. Each study seeks to ascertain the relationship between program slicing and some aspect of programmer comprehension. The first two were performed by Weiser, and Weiser and Lyle as they sought to formulate a basic understanding of slicing as used by programmers during debugging. Next, Francel and Rugaber conducted an experiment that compared the comprehension of slicers and non-slicers. The same two authors also experimented with the fault localization abilities of slice-aware programmers. The fifth experiment revisits fault localization. The sixth experiment explores the comprehension of programmers aided by an *amorphous slice* called a *safety slice*. The seventh experiment investigates the impact of semantic differencing on programmer comprehension, and the final experiment investigates the impact of semantic differencing on uncovering unwanted ripple effects.

7.1   Programmers Use Slicing While Debugging

Mark Weiser conjectured that experienced programmers compute slices when debugging code. Specifically, his research hypothesis was "debugging programmers, working backwards from the variable and statement of a bug's appearance, use that variable and statement as a slicing criterion to construct mentally the corresponding program slice [89]."

Weiser administered an experiment designed to test this hypothesis. The experiment involved 21 experienced programmers who each debugged three programs. After debugging (and a short break), each participant was asked to identify several code fragments. (Participants were not asked to reconstruct slices as this would have required an explanation of slicing and thus biased the results.) Five categories of code fragments were shown to each participant:

Relevant slice A set of statements necessary for understanding the bug taken from the slice on the variable and the print statement whose execution first caused an error to appear in the output.

Relevant contiguous A region of contiguous code overlapping the relevant slice fragment.

Irrelevant contiguous A region of contiguous code not overlapping the relevant contiguous or relevant slice fragments.

Irrelevant slice A set of statements near the faulty statement taken from a slice on a variable not directly related to the bug.

Jumble Every third of fourth statement in the program, minimally modified to display reasonable syntax.

Participants were shown the fragments and asked to rate their initial impression on the following scale:

(1) almost certainly used,
(2) probably used,
(3) probably not used, or
(4) almost certainly not used.

The ratings given to the relevant slice fragments were then compared to those of other fragments. The relevant slice was recognized 54% of the time, while the irrelevant slice and the jumble were recognized less often only 28% and 20% of the time, respectively ($p = 0.03$, and $p = 0.005$, respectively).

There are no significant differences between the participant's recognition of the relevant slice and the relevant contiguous fragments. Because each relevant slice overlaps with a relevant contiguous fragment, the experiment gives no absolute assurance that the relevant slices are not being recognized only because of that overlap. However, the irrelevant slice has almost the same percentage overlap with the relevant contiguous fragment as the relevant slice and its percentage recognition is far lower.

7.2 Slice-Based Debugging Tools

Lyle and Wiser consider program *dicing* as an aid to debuggers [66]. A dice is the intersection of two or more slices. The central hypothesis use in this study is that "programmers using the dicing information find faults faster than programmers using traditional methods."

Subjects consisted of 20 graduate students and System Center staff from the Computer Science Department at the University of Maryland. After answering background questions and undertaking a practice treatment, the control group was told that the experimenter was collecting data on how programmers debug and that the subject should explain what he was doing and thinking as he goes. The experimental group also received an explanation of slicing and dicing and had dices highlighted in the code they received. Lyle and Wiser found a significant difference between the time taken by the two groups ($p = 0.025$) on two of three seeded faults. Thus, they concluded that dicing provides assistance.

7.3 Slicers Versus Non-Slicers

Francel and Rugaber compared the comprehension of programmers who were natural slicers with those who were not [30,31]. Their research hypothesis was that "slicers have a better understanding of program code after debugging than non-slicers do." Seventeen fourth-year undergraduate computer science majors took part in this experiment, which involved debugging a 200 line Pascal program. Each subject went through three phases: instructions and practice, program debugging, and subprogram re-construction.

While debugging, participants marked each statement considered as they worked. Those who stayed mostly within the slice taken with respect to the incorrect output variable were considered slicers; everyone else was considered a non-slicer. Results indicate that on the average non-slicers examined a larger average number of statements (12 versus 0) from outside the slice ($p = 0.001$). Surprisingly, non-slicers also examined a larger average number of statements (14 versus 9) from within the slice ($p = 0.0025$). Finally, slicers took less time to debug the code (an average of 15 versus 33 minutes) than non-slicers ($p = 0.045$).

Post debugging, participants were asked to re-construct the minimal subprogram that produced the incorrect output. Using the accuracy of reconstruction as a measure of understanding, slicers had better understanding of the code after debugging ($p = 0.02$); thus, a relationship between slicing while debugging and program understanding exists. It is interesting to note that, while not statistically significant, on the average slicers took more time (24 versus 11 minutes) to construct the subprogram ($p = 0.16$). A potential explanation for this unexpected result is what Binkley et al. labeled "throwing in the towel" (discussed in Section 7.7); in other words, non-slicers took less time because they simply gave up.

The authors conclude that slicers have higher comprehension than non-slicers. However, this study does not demonstrate that slicing leads to or causes either improved debugging or understanding. Further experimentation is needed to determine if the relationship between slicing while debugging and program understanding is caused by slicing or by some other influence.

7.4 Fault Localization Ability of Slice-Aware Programmers

Francel and Rugaber compared the fault localization abilities of slice-aware programmers with those who were slice unaware [30,31]. Their research hypothesis is "debuggers are better able to localize [a] program fault area when using slicing while debugging than while debugging without slicing." Where "better able" was defined as "took less time." Twenty undergraduate students from a standard first programming course took part in this experiment.

Subjects were divided into two groups, a control group and an experimental group. Both groups were asked to debug two programs, recording the program statements they examined as they worked. Between debugging the first and second programs, the experimental group received training on how to use slicing in debugging.

Results from this experiment indicate that slicing improves the fault localization abilities of debuggers. While there was no difference ($p = 0.343$) in the average time taken (19 versus 31 minutes) for the first program, the experimental group is significantly faster ($p = 0.019$) in debugging the second program (taking only 30 versus 65 minutes for the control group).

Finally, it is interesting to note that participants had computer access during the experiment. The authors observed that some participants used program execution to obtain crude dynamic slices. This suggests a study on how much static versus dynamic slicing debuggers employ.

7.5 Slicing Assists in Fault Localization

Kusumoto et al. [61] studied the effect of slicing on human fault localization ability. The aim was to determine whether a debugger augmented with a slicing tool could lend practical assistance to the task of localizing a fault. Their research hypothesis was that access to slices would reduce the time taken to correctly localize fault.

The experiment used a debugger for a variant of Pascal that lacked pointers. This debugger provided standard features, such as single step execution, break points and variable look-up and a graphical front-end to a slicer. The study had two halves: first a few subjects were given a complex fault-localization task and second more subjects were given a less complex fault-localization task.

The first half used a cross-over design with two programs (of the order of hundreds of LOC). Program 1 contained eight seeded faults while Program 2 contained nine seeded faults. There were six subjects (students of Osaka University), split (at random) into two groups of three. The first group used the full debugging tool (including slicing ability) with Program 1 and then only the traditional debugging features with Program 2. The second group used only the traditional debugging features with Program 1 and then the slice-enabled version with Program 2. The authors report that the time taken to localize the faults was reduced when the students were using the slice-enabled debugger. However, no statistical confidence can be placed in these results, due to the small number of subjects involved.

In the second half of the study, 34 subjects (also students at Osaka University) considered six smaller programs, ranging in size from 25 to 51 LOC. In each program a single fault was seeded. Once again, the groups with the slice-enabled debugger took less time taken to localize faults. In this case a Welch test indicates that the results are statistically significant [61].

7.6   Safety Slices

Amorphous slicing relaxes the syntactic constraint of traditional slicing and can therefore produce considerably smaller slices [36]. This simplification power can be used to answer questions a software engineer might have about a program by first augmenting the program to make the question explicit and then slicing out an answer. One benefit of this technique is that the answer is in the form of a program and thus, in a language that the software engineer understands well [39].

Array safety is a problem to which this technique has been applied [19]. Experiments were conducted to determine whether the resulting *safety slice* was an effective aid to an engineer. In the simplest case, such a slice is one of the following

print **true**   // the original program has no array bounds errors
or
print **false**   // the original program always causes an array bounds error

In the more general case, the safety slice is a program that computes the safety of the original program. The experiment was designed to test the general hypothesis that a safety slice assists in program comprehension. Specifically, two hypotheses were under test:

Hypothesis I. Safety slices make human debugging of array safety more *accurate*.

Hypothesis II. Safety slices make human debugging of array safety more *efficient*.

Seventy nine subjects, all students half way through the first, second, or third years of study at Loyola College, took part in the study. Students from each year were divided into a control group and an experimental group. Both groups were given the definition of an array bounds violation, a worked example, and a brief 15 minute lecture on array bounds violations. In order to train the subjects in the use of safety slices, the lecture included an explanation of safety slicing and how to use the safety slice in searching for array bounds violations.

All groups were then given seven programs containing array subscript violations. In addition, experimental groups received the safety slice for each program. Following the seven programs was a questionnaire, which asked participants subjectively to rate their performance, confidence, and the difficulty of the problems. Each group was then given the remainder of the lecture period to find array subscript violations.

The data related to Hypothesis I for all six groups is summarized in Table XXIX. Note that mean scores increase with experience and with access to the safety slice.

Taking all subjects together, safety slicing improves the debugging of array access safety ($p = 0.016$, $s = 1.57$, $d.f. = 67$). Considering only the more advanced second and third year students safety slicing is quite effective ($p = 0.008$, $s = 1.04$, $d.f. = 37$).

The data related to Hypothesis II was only meaningful for the second-year students. For different reasons the first and third-year students didn't produce meaningful timing numbers [19]. Subjectively, the experimental groups finished faster or completed more of the problems in the time alloted. This result was not statistically significant.

TABLE XXIX

Hypothesis I—results summary			
Group	$\bar{x}$	s	n
First-year control	4.64	1.92	22
First-year experimental	5.00	1.85	8
Second-year control	5.27	1.35	11
Second-year experimental	6.33	0.87	9
Third-year control	6.00	0.89	11
Third-year experimental	6.50	0.93	8

7.7   Semantic Differencing

The sixth experiment investigates the impact of semantic differencing on comprehension [14]. The semantic difference between two programs is computed by taking a collection of backwards and forward slices. The resulting program captures all changed *computations* from an old version of the program to a new version of the same program. The experiment tests the general hypothesis that access to semantic differences aids in program comprehension. Specifically, two hypotheses are under test:

Hypothesis I. access to semantic differences makes programmers more *efficient* (faster) at tasks that require program comprehension, and

Hypothesis II. access to semantic differences makes programmers more *accurate* at tasks that require program comprehension.

Sixty-three subjects participated in two controlled experiments. The subjects included undergraduate students half-way through the second, third and fourth years of study at Loyola College. Each experiment was administered in a fifty minute class period. It began with ten minutes of instructions and practice. The remaining forty minutes were alloted to complete the problems. Subjects were divided into a control group and an experimental group. The only difference between the two groups was that the experimental group had semantic differences highlighted in the programs they were given.

Subjects were asked to debug two C programs: a small 50 line version of `word count`, and a 500 line version of the CP/M disk utility `wash`. Subjects were asked to identify the statements they considered during their initial study of the program and those relevant to the fault in the program after answering the questions (without looking back at the original marked code). Note that two factors potentially influence these hypotheses: the group (experiential vs. control) and the class (second year or underclassmen vs. third and fourth year, or upperclassmen).

For Program 1, `word count`, a two-way ANOVA (see Table XXX) indicates that there is no evidence of interaction between the two factors with regard to the times for Program 1 ($p = 0.39$). Thus, the two factors can be considered separately. In support of Hypothesis I, the experimental group is significantly faster ($p = 0.023$).

TABLE XXX
TWO-WAY ANOVA p VALUES

Time (minutes)	Interaction	Group	Class
Program 1	0.39	0.023	0.53
Program 2	0.041	0.013	0.28

Next consider the correctness data related to Hypothesis II. Over half (52%) of the statements considered by the experimental group were affected by the change. In contrast, over half (57%) of the statements considered by the control group were not part of the semantic difference at all. Overall, the experimental group gave a higher percentage of correct answers (85% versus 68%). However, this result is not statistically significant ($\chi^2 = 2.07$, $p = 0.15$—because the data is essentially binary, a χ^2 test was used). It is worth noting that additional questions show that the control group had higher comprehension of unrelated parts of the program. Thus, highlighting that semantic differences helped focus participants on the relevant parts of the code.

For Program 2, `wash`, the experimental subjects appear to take longer. This is the opposite of the expected result. The results of the two-way ANOVA related to Hypothesis I (Table XXX) show significant evidence of interaction between the group and class-year factors ($p = 0.041$); thus, it is impossible to consider the two factors independently. Instead, Tukey's pairwise comparison among means was applied. This test shows that the mean for the experimental upperclassmen is not statistically different from that of the experimental underclassman (Tukey simultaneous pairwise comparison adjusted p-score 0.14). Nor is it different from the upperclassmen control, but just barely (adjusted p-score 0.051). Finally, it is statistically different from the control underclassmen (adjusted p-score 0.0075). All other pairwise comparisons showed no significant difference. Thus, the experimental upperclassmen took significantly *longer* than the control underclassmen. It is impossible to isolate the cause of this effect.

The interaction between factors and the inversion from the expected completion time, are potentially explained by what might be called the "throwing in the towel" effect. For example, a number of control group subjects finished in three minutes or fewer, which is clearly insufficient time to understand 500 lines of code.

The results related to Hypothesis II follow the expected trend with experience and the treatment appearing to improve the percent correct. Of the 54 subjects, seven correctly identified the fault: one control group subject (an upperclassman) and six experimental group subjects (including one underclassman). Here the χ^2 test reports a p score of 0.033. However, since the sample size is small (violating an assumption of the χ^2 test), Fisher's exact test was also used. The result is statistically significant ($p = 0.047$). Given they binary nature of the data, this result indicates a strong pattern.

In summary, for Program 1, the experimental group is significantly faster, but not significantly more accurate, while, for Program 2, the experimental group is more accurate, but can not be shown to be faster. Combined there is evidence that the experimental group, which had access to semantic differences, performed significantly faster ($p = 0.023$) and more accurately ($p = 0.047$) than the control group.

The study thus provides empirical support to the assertion that semantic information assists in program comprehension.

7.8   Ripple Effects

The final experiment investigates the value of semantic differencing in uncovering unwanted ripple effects [14]. Nine subjects participated in this experiment. Each was given a 200 line C program that computes parking fees, and asked if a proposed modification correctly implemented a change in the program's specification. While not explicitly stated in the instructions, the problem was designed to test semantic differencing's ability to assist in the identification of unwanted ripple effects, which the proposed modification introduced.

With only four control subjects and five experimental subjects, there are no statistically significant results from this experiment. Informally, the following observations are of interest: first, one of the four control subjects and two of the five experimental subjects correctly discovered the (unwanted) ripple effect. Second, there was some evidence that the control group was again giving up (throwing in the towel) on the problem as their average time of 8:15 was less than the experimental group's average time of 10:24.

8.   Conclusion and Future Work

This survey has presented empirical work involving program slicing of relatively large scale programs (ranging from a few thousand lines of code to tens and even hundreds of thousands of lines of code). The results concern questions about the efficacy of slicing, its applications, the nature of the slices themselves, and the interplay between slicing and other source code analyses. Results from over thirty papers, that contain empirical results are included. Some general trends in the results reported are evident and also some directions for future work emerge:

(1) *Slice size*. In two separate studies with two different static slicing tools and two different ways of determining slicing criteria, it was reported that a typical static slice was approximately one third of the size of the program from which it was constructed. There has only been a single study of dynamic slice size and the results indicate that the typical slice size is approximately one fifth of the size of the program from which it is constructed. There also appears to be a small (perhaps not significant) difference in forward and backward slice size. Finally, there is disagreement in the empirical literature as to whether calling context makes a difference in slice size with some studies finding little impact

and others significant impact. More work is needed in this area to clear up this important issue.

(2) *The impact of supporting analyses.* It has been shown that a variety of supporting analyses and algorithms used for tuning slice construction have an impact upon slice size. However, one of the striking aspects of the empirical results on supporting analyses is the way in which a dramatic increase in precision of some supporting analyses do not lead to a commensurate decrease in slice size. Pointer analysis is a prime example. This phenomenon is worthy of further investigation.

(3) *Slicing tools and techniques.* This chapter has reported several areas of work which show how the standard approaches to slicing have been improved upon. The primary observation which emerges is that this continues to be a worthwhile area of research and where there are, as yet undiscovered, techniques for improving slicing. Therefore, the results for slice sizes should be regarded as upper bounds, rather than limits. Finally, more work is required to better understand the pros and cons of the essentially demand driven, data flow slicing techniques as compared to the caching graph reachability based slicing techniques.

(4) *Applications of slices.* The growing body of empirical evidence for applications of slices and in particular what might be termed the 'non-traditional' applications is encouraging. Though slicing was original deemed to be an end in itself, more recent work has used slicing as a part of an overall approach or as a way of solving problems for which it was not originally intended (such as clone detection). These results are encouraging, because they indicate that slicing has many applications beyond those originally envisaged.

(5) *Human comprehension studies.* The application of program slicing to aid human comprehension has shown that slicing does, indeed, assist programmers when performing comprehension-intensive activities such as debugging, fault localization, and impact analysis. Furthermore, there is evidence to suggest that slicing-aware programmers work differently than non-slicing aware programmers. In many ways the surface has only been scratched: the studies concern primarily static slicing. There are some indications that more recent forms of slicing, such as amorphous and conditioned slicing [20,28] may offer even greater benefits in programmer comprehension activities.

In conclusion, there is now a large body of evidence to suggest that slicing is practical and effective. New application areas and improvements to slice computation techniques are being regularly introduced, and results regarding the existing techniques and applications are encouraging.

ACKNOWLEDGEMENTS

The authors wish to thank GrammaTech Incorporated (http://www.grammatech. com) for providing CodeSurfer, and Erin Ptah for her editorial assistance. Mark Harman is supported, in part, by EPSRC Grants GR/R98938, GR/M58719, GR/M78083 and GR/R43150 and by two development grants from DaimlerChrysler. Dave Binkley is supported by National Science Foundation grant CCR-0305330.

REFERENCES

[1] Agrawal G., Guo L., "Evaluating explicitly context-sensitive program slicing", in: *Proceedings of the ACM SIGPLAN–SIGSOFT Workshop on Program Analysis for Software Tools and Engineering, Snowbird, Utah*, 2001, pp. 6–12.

[2] Agrawal H., "On slicing programs with jump statements", in: *ACM SIGPLAN Conference on Programming Language Design and Implementation, Orlando, FL*, June 20–24, 1994, pp. 302–312; *Proceedings in SIGPLAN Notices* **29** (6) (June 1994).

[3] Agrawal H., Horgan J.R., "Dynamic program slicing", in: *ACM SIGPLAN Conference on Programming Language Design and Implementation, New York*, June 1990, pp. 246–256.

[4] Andersen L.O., "Program analysis and specialization for the C programming language", PhD thesis, DIKU, University of Copenhagen, May 1994. (DIKU report 94/19).

[5] Atkinson D., Griswold W., "Implementation techniques for efficient data-flow analysis of large programs", in: *Proceedings of the IEEE International Conference on Software Maintenance (ICSM 2001)*, November 2001, pp. 52–61.

[6] Atkinson D.C., Griswold W.G., "Effective whole-program analysis in the presence of pointers", in: *Proceedings of the ACM SIGSOFT 6th International Symposium on the Foundations of Software Engineering (SIGSOFT '98/FSE-6), New York*, in: *Software Engineering Notes*, vol. 23, ACM, November 3–5, 1998, pp. 46–55.

[7] Ball T., Horwitz S., "Slicing programs with arbitrary control-flow", in: Fritzson P. (Ed.), *1st Conference on Automated Algorithmic Debugging, Linköping, Sweden*, Springer, 1993, pp. 206–222. Also available as University of Wisconsin–Madison Technical Report (in extended form) TR-1128, December, 1992.

[8] Bent L., Atkinson D., Griswold W., "A qualitative study of two whole-program slicers for C", Technical Report CS2000-0643, University of California, San Diego, CA, 2000. (A preliminary version, appeared at FSE 2000).

[9] Beszédes A., Faragó C., Szabó Z., Csirik J., Gyimóthy T., "Union slices for program maintenance", in: *IEEE International Conference on Software Maintenance (Montreal, Canada)*, IEEE Comput. Soc., Los Alamitos, California, USA, October 2002, pp. 12–21.

[10] Bieman J.M., Ott L.M., "Measuring functional cohesion", *IEEE Transactions on Software Engineering* **20** (8) (August 1994) 644–657.

[11] Binkley D.W., "Precise executable interprocedural slices", *ACM Letters on Programming Languages and Systems* **2** (1–4) (1993) 31–45.

[12] Binkley D.W., "Semantics guided regression test cost reduction", *IEEE Transactions on Software Engineering* **23** (8) (August 1997) 498–516.

[13] Binkley D.W., "Computing amorphous program slices using dependence graphs and a data-flow model", in: *ACM Symposium on Applied Computing, The Menger, San Antonio, Texas, USA*, ACM Press, New York, NY, USA, 1999, pp. 519–525.

[14] Binkley D.W., Capellini R., Raszewski L., Smith C., "An implementation of and experiment with semantic differencing", in: *Proceedings of the 2001 IEEE International Conference on Software Maintenance (Florence, Italy)*, November 2001, pp. 82–91.

[15] Binkley D.W., Gallagher K.B., "Program slicing", in: Zelkowitz M. (Ed.), in: *Advances in Computing*, vol. 43, Academic Press, 1996, pp. 1–50.

[16] Binkley D.W., Harman M., "An empirical study of predicate dependence levels and trends", in: *25th IEEE International Conference and Software Engineering (ICSE 2003), Portland, Oregon, USA*, IEEE Comput. Soc., Los Alamitos, California, USA, May 2003, pp. 330–339.

[17] Binkley D.W., Harman M., "Large-scale empirical study of forward and backward static slice size and context sensitivity", in: *Proceedings of the 2003 IEEE International Conference on Software Maintenance (Amsterdam, Netherlands)*, IEEE Comput. Soc., Los Alamitos, California, USA, 2003.

[18] Binkley D.W., Harman M., "Results from a large-scale study of performance optimization techniques for source code analyses based on graph reachability algorithms", in: *3rd IEEE International Workshop on Source Code Analysis and Manipulation, Amsterdam, Netherlands*, IEEE Comput. Soc., Los Alamitos, California, USA, 2003.

[19] Binkley D.W., Harman M., Raszewski L.R., Smith C., "An empirical study of amorphous slicing as a program comprehension support tool", in: *8th IEEE International Workshop on Program Comprehension (IWPC 2000), Limerick, Ireland*, IEEE Comput. Soc., Los Alamitos, California, USA, June 2000, pp. 161–170.

[20] Canfora G., Cimitile A., De Lucia A., "Conditioned program slicing", in: Harman M., Gallagher K. (Eds.), in: *Information and Software Technology Special Issue on Program Slicing*, vol. 40, Elsevier, 1998, pp. 595–607.

[21] Canfora G., Cimitile A., Munro M., "RE^2: Reverse engineering and reuse reengineering", *Journal of Software Maintenance: Research and Practice* **6** (2) (1994) 53–72.

[22] Canfora G., Lucia A.D., Munro M., "An integrated environment for reuse reengineering C code", *Journal of Systems and Software* **42** (1998) 153–164.

[23] Choi J., Ferrante J., "Static slicing in the presence of goto statements", *ACM Transactions on Programming Languages and Systems* **16** (4) (July 1994) 1097–1113.

[24] De Lucia A., "Program slicing: Methods and applications", in: *1st IEEE International Workshop on Source Code Analysis and Manipulation, Florence, Italy*, IEEE Comput. Soc., Los Alamitos, California, USA, 2001, pp. 142–149.

[25] De Lucia A., Harman M., Hierons R., Krinke J., "Unions of slices are not slices", in: *7th IEEE European Conference on Software Maintenance and Reengineering (CSMR 2003), Benevento, Italy*, IEEE Comput. Soc., Los Alamitos, California, USA, March 2003, pp. 363–367.

[26] Ernst M.D., "Practical fine-grained static slicing of optimised code", Technical Report MSR-TR-94-14, Microsoft research, Redmond, WA, July 1994.

[27] Ferrante J., Ottenstein K.J., Warren J.D., "The program dependence graph and its use in optimization", *ACM Transactions on Programming Languages and Systems* **9** (3) (July 1987) 319–349.

[28] Field J., Ramalingam G., Tip F., "Parametric program slicing", in: *22nd ACM Symposium on Principles of Programming Languages, San Francisco, CA*, 1995, pp. 379–392.

[29] Fischer C.N., LeBlanc R.J., *Crafting a Compiler*, in: *Benjamin–Cummings Series in Computer Science*, Benjamin–Cummings, Menlo Park, CA, 1988.

[30] Francel M., Rugaber S., "The relationship of slicing and debugging to program understanding", in: *Proceedings of the 7th International Workshop on Program Comprehension*, May 5–7, 1999, pp. 106–113.

[31] Francel M., Rugaber S., "The value of slicing while debugging", *Science of Computer Programming* **40** (2–3) (July 2001) 151–169.

[32] Gallagher K., O'Brien L., "Analyzing programs via decomposition slicing: Initial data and observations", in: *Proceedings of the 7th IEEE Workshop on Empirical Studies of Software Maintenance (Florence Italy)*, November 2001, pp. 188–198.

[33] Gallagher K.B., Lyle J.R., "Using program slicing in software maintenance", *IEEE Transactions on Software Engineering* **17** (8) (August 1991) 751–761.

[34] Grammatech Inc., *The Codesurfer Slicing System*, 2002.

[35] Hall R., "Automatic extraction of executable program sub-sets by simultaneous dynamic program slicing", *Journal of Automated Software Engineering* **2** (1) (March 1995) 33–53.

[36] Harman M., Binkley D.W., Danicic S., "Amorphous program slicing", *Journal of Systems and Software* **68** (1) (October 2003) 45–64.

[37] Harman M., Danicic S., "Amorphous program slicing", in: *5th IEEE International Workshop on Program Comprenhesion (IWPC'97), Dearborn, Michigan, USA*, IEEE Comput. Soc., Los Alamitos, California, USA, May 1997, pp. 70–79.

[38] Harman M., Danicic S., "A new algorithm for slicing unstructured programs", *Journal of Software Maintenance and Evolution* **10** (6) (1998) 415–441.

[39] Harman M., Fox C., Hierons R.M., Binkley D.W., Danicic S., "Program simplification as a means of approximating undecidable propositions", in: *7th IEEE International Workshop on Program Comprenhesion (IWPC'99), Pittsburgh, Pennsylvania, USA*, IEEE Comput. Soc., Los Alamitos, California, USA, May1999, pp. 208–217.

[40] Harman M., Gold N., Hierons R.M., Binkley D.W., "Code extraction algorithms which unify slicing and concept assignment", in: *IEEE Working Conference on Reverse Engineering (WCRE 2002), Richmond, Virginia, USA*, IEEE Comput. Soc., Los Alamitos, California, USA, October 2002, pp. 11–21.

[41] Harman M., Hierons R.M., "An overview of program slicing", *Software Focus* **2** (3) (2001) 85–92.

[42] Harman M., Hu L., Munro M., Zhang X., Binkley D.W., Danicic S., Daoudi M., Ouarbya L., "Syntax-directed amorphous slicing", *Journal of Automated Software Engineering* (2004), in press.

[43] Harman M., Hu L., Zhang X., Munro M., Danicic S., Daoudi M., Ouarbya L., "An interprocedural amorphous slicer for WSL", in: *IEEE International Workshop on Source
Code Analysis and Manipulation (SCAM 2002), Montreal, Canada*, IEEE Comput. Soc.,
Los Alamitos, California, USA, October 2002, pp. 105–114. Selected for consideration
for the special issue of the Journal of Automated Software Engineering.

[44] Hierons R.M., Harman M., Danicic S., "Using program slicing to assist in the detection
of equivalent mutants", *Software Testing, Verification and Reliability* **9** (4) (1999) 233–
262.

[45] Hind M., "Pointer analysis—haven't we solved this problem yet?", in: *Program Analysis for Software Tools and Engineering (PASTE'01), Snowbird, Utah, USA*, ACM, June
2001.

[46] Hoffner T., Kamkar M., Fritzson P., "Evaluation of program slicing tools", in:
Ducassé M. (Ed.), *AADEBUG, 2nd International Workshop on Automated and Algorithmic Debugging, Saint Malo, France*, IRISA-CNRS, May 1995, pp. 51–69.

[47] Horwitz S., Pfeiffer P., Reps T., "Dependence analysis for pointer variables", in: *Pro-
ceedings of the ACM SIGPLAN 89 Conference on Programming Language Design and
Implementation, Portland, OR*, June 21–23, 1989, pp. 28–40; *ACM SIGPLAN Notices* **24**
(July 1989).

[48] Horwitz S., Reps T., "The use of program dependence graphs in software engineering",
in: *14th International Conference on Software Engineering, Melbourne, Australia*, 1992,
pp. 392–411.

[49] Horwitz S., Reps T., Binkley D.W., "Interprocedural slicing using dependence graphs",
ACM Transactions on Programming Languages and Systems **12** (1) (1990) 26–61.

[50] Horwitz S., Reps T., Sagiv M., "Demand Interprocedural Dataflow Analysis", in: *Proceedings of SIGSOFT'95 3rd ACM SIGSOFT Symposium on the Foundations of Software
Engineering (FSE 95)*, October 1995, pp. 104–115.

[51] Komondoor R., Horwitz S., "Semantics-preserving procedure extraction", in: *Proceedings of the 27th ACM SIGPLAN–SIGACT Symposium on Principles of Programming
Languages (POLP-00), New York*, ACM, January 19–21, 2000, pp. 155–169.

[52] Komondoor R., Horwitz S., "Using slicing to identify duplication in source code", in:
Proceedings of the 8th International Symposium on Static Analysis (Paris, France), July
16–18, 2001.

[53] Komondoor R., Horwitz S., "Effective automatic procedure extraction", in: *11th IEEE
International Workshop on Program Comprehension, Portland, Oregon, USA*, IEEE
Comput. Soc., Los Alamitos, California, USA, May 2003.

[54] Korel B., "Black-box understanding of COTS components", in: *7th IEEE International Workshop on Program Comprenhesion (IWPC'99), Pittsburgh, Pennsylvania,
USA*, IEEE Comput. Soc., Los Alamitos, California, USA, May 1999, pp. 92–99.

[55] Korel B., Laski J., "Dynamic program slicing", *Information Processing Letters* **29** (3)
(October 1988) 155–163.

[56] Korel B., Rilling J., "Dynamic program slicing in understanding of program execution",
in: *5th IEEE International Workshop on Program Comprenhesion (IWPC'97), Dearborn, Michigan, USA*, IEEE Comput. Soc., Los Alamitos, California, USA, May 1997,
pp. 80–89.

[57] Korel B., Rilling J., "Program slicing in understanding of large programs", in: *6th IEEE International Workshop on Program Comprenhesion (IWPC'98), Ischia, Italy*, IEEE Comput. Soc., Los Alamitos, California, USA, 1998, pp. 145–152.

[58] Krinke J., "Evaluating context-sensitive slicing and chopping", in: *IEEE International Conference on Software Maintenance (ICSM 2002), Montreal, Canada*, IEEE Comput. Soc., Los Alamitos, California, USA, October 2002, pp. 22–31.

[59] Krinke J., "Advanced slicing of sequential and concurrent programs", PhD thesis, Universität Passau, July 2003.

[60] Kumar S., Horwitz S., "Better slicing of programs with jumps and switches", in: *Proceedings of the 5th International Conference on Fundamental Approaches to Software Engineering (FASE 2002)*, in: *Lecture Notes in Computer Science*, vol. 2306, Springer-Verlag, 2002, pp. 96–112.

[61] Kusumoto S., Nishimatsu A., Nishie K., Inoue K., "Experimental evaluation of program slicing for fault localization", *Empirical Software Engineering* **7** (2002) 49–76.

[62] Lakhotia A., Deprez J.-C., "Restructuring programs by tucking statements into functions", in: Harman M., Gallagher K. (Eds.), in: *Information and Software Technology Special Issue on Program Slicing*, vol. 40, Elsevier, 1998, pp. 677–689.

[63] Lakhotia A., Singh P., "Challenges in getting 'formal' with viruses", *Virus Bulletin* (2003).

[64] Liang D., Harrold M.J., "Efficient points-to analysis for whole-program analysis", in: Nierstrasz O., Lemoine M. (Eds.), *ESEC/FSE '99*, in: *Lecture Notes in Computer Science*, vol. 1687, Springer-Verlag/ACM, 1999, pp. 199–215.

[65] Liang D., Harrold M.J., "Reuse-driven interprocedural slicing in the presence of pointers and recursion", in: *IEEE International Conference of Software Maintenance, Oxford, UK*, IEEE Comput. Soc., Los Alamitos, California, USA, August 1999, pp. 410–430.

[66] Lyle J.R., Weiser M., *Experiments on Slicing-Based Debugging Tools*, Ablex, 1986.

[67] Lyle J.R., Binkley D.W., "Program slicing in the presence of pointers", in: *Foundations of Software Engineering, Orlando, FL, USA*, November 1993, pp. 255–260.

[68] Lyle J.R., Wallace D.R., Graham J.R., Gallagher K.B., Poole J.P., Binkley D.W., "Unravel: A CASE tool to assist evaluation of high integrity software, vol. 1: Requirements and design", Technical Report NISTIR 5691, US Department of Commerce, Technology Administration, National Institute of Standards and Technology, Computer Systems Laboratory, Gaithersburg, MD 20899, 1995.

[69] Lyle J.R., Weiser M., "Automatic program bug location by program slicing", in: *2nd International Conference on Computers and Applications, Peking*, IEEE Comput. Soc., Los Alamitos, California, USA, 1987, pp. 877–882.

[70] Miller J., Daly J., Wood M., Brooks A., Roper M., "Statistical power and its subcomponents—missing and misunderstood concepts in software engineering research", *Journal of Information and Software Technology* **39** (4) (1997) 285–295.

[71] Mock M., Atkinson D.C., Chambers C., Eggers S.J., "Improving program slicing with dynamic points-to data", in: Griswold W.G. (Ed.), *Proceedings of the 10th ACM SIGSOFT Symposium on the Foundations of Software Engineering (FSE-02), New York*, ACM, November 2002, pp. 71–80.

[72] Mock M., Das M., Chambers C., Eggers S.J., "Dynamic points-to sets: A comparison with static analyses and potential applications in program understanding and optimization", in: *Proceedings of the 2001 ACM SIGPLAN–SIGSOFT Workshop on Program Analysis for Software Tools and Engineering (Snowbird, UT)*, June 2001, pp. 66–72.

[73] Nishimatsu A., Jihira M., Kusumoto S., Inoue K., "Call-mark slicing: An efficient and economical way of reducing slices", in: *Proceedings of the 21st International Conference on Software Engineering*, ACM, May 1999, pp. 422–431.

[74] Orso A., Sinha S., Harrold M.J., "Effects of pointers on data dependences", in: *9th IEEE International Workshop on Program Comprehension (IWPC'01), Toronto, Canada*, IEEE Comput. Soc., Los Alamitos, California, USA, May 2001, pp. 39–49.

[75] Orso A., Sinha S., Harrold M.J., "Incremental slicing based on data-dependences types", in: *Proceedings of the IEEE International Conference on Software Maintenance (ICSM 2001), Florence, Italy*, IEEE Comput. Soc., Los Alamitos, California, USA, November 2001, pp. 158–167.

[76] Ottenstein K.J., Ottenstein L.M., "The program dependence graph in software development environments", *SIGPLAN Notices* **19** (5) (1984) 177–184.

[77] Reps T., Horwitz S., Sagiv M., Rosay G., "Speeding up slicing", in: *ACM Foundations of Software Engineering (FSE'94), New Orleans, LA*, December 1994, pp. 11–20; *ACM SIGSOFT Software Engineering Notes* **19** (5) (December 1994).

[78] Reps T., Yang W., "The semantics of program slicing", Technical Report 777, University of Wisconsin, 1988.

[79] Shapiro M., Horwitz S., "The effects of the precision of pointer analysis", in: *Lecture Notes in Computer Science*, vol. 1302, 1997, pp. 16–34.

[80] Sinha S., Harrold M.J., Rothermel G., "System-dependence-graph-based slicing of programs with arbitrary interprocedural control-flow", in: *Proceedings of the 21st International Conference on Software Engineering*, ACM, May 1999, pp. 432–441.

[81] Snelting G., "Concept analysis—a new framework for program understanding", in: *ACM SIGPLAN–SIGSOFT Workshop on Program Analysis for Software Tools and Engineering (PASTE'98), Montreal, Canada*, June 1998, pp. 1–10; *SIGPLAN Notices* **33** (7) (1998) 1–10.

[82] Steensgaard B., "Points-to analysis in almost linear time", in: *Conference Record of the 23rd ACM SIGPLAN–SIGACT Symposium on Principles of Programming Languages (POPL'96), St. Petersburg, Florida*, ACM, January 1996, pp. 32–41.

[83] Tip F., "A survey of program slicing techniques", *Journal of Programming Languages* **3** (3) (September 1995) 121–189.

[84] Tonella P., "Using a concept lattice of decomposition slices for program understanding and impact analysis", *IEEE Transactions on Software Engineering* **29** (6) (2003) 495–509.

[85] Venkatesh G.A., "Experimental results from dynamic slicing of C programs", *ACM Transactions on Programming Languages and Systems* **17** (2) (March 1995) 197–216.

[86] Ward M., Calliss F.W., Munro M., "The maintainer's assistant", in: *Proceedings of the International Conference on Software Maintenance 1989*, IEEE Comput. Soc., Los Alamitos, California, USA, 1989, p. 307.

[87] Weiser M., "Program slices: Formal, psychological, and practical investigations of an automatic program abstraction method", PhD thesis, University of Michigan, Ann Arbor, MI, 1979.

[88] Weiser M., "Program slicing", in: *5th International Conference on Software Engineering, San Diego, CA*, March 1981, pp. 439–449.

[89] Weiser M., "Programmers use slicing when debugging", *Communications of the ACM* **25** (7) (July 1982) 446–452.

[90] Weiser M., "Program slicing", *IEEE Transactions on Software Engineering* **10** (4) (1984) 352–357.

[91] Yong S., Horwitz S., Reps T., "Pointer analysis for programs with structures and casting", in: *Proceedings of the SIGPLAN 99 Conference on Programming Language Design and Implementation (Atlanta, GA)*, May 1999.

[92] Yur J., Ryder B.G., Landi W.A., "An incremental flow-and context-sensitive pointer aliasing analysis", in: *Proceedings of the 21st International Conference on Software Engineering*, IEEE Comput. Soc., Los Alamitos, California, USA, May 1999, pp. 442–452.

[93] Zelkowitz M., Wallace D., Binkley D., "Experimental validation of new software technology", in: Juristo N., Moreno A. (Eds.), *SE Empirical Validation*, Molex, 2003, Chapter 12.

[94] Zhang X., Gupta R., Zhang Y., "Precise dynamic slicing algorithms", in: *Proceedings of the 25th International Conference on Software Engineering, Portland, Oregon, USA, May 3–10, 2003*, IEEE Comput. Soc., 2003, pp. 319–329.

Challenges in Design and Software Infrastructure for Ubiquitous Computing Applications[1]

GURUDUTH BANAVAR

IBM TJ Watson Research Center
Hawthorne, NY
USA
banavar@us.ibm.com

ABRAHAM BERNSTEIN

University of Zurich
Zurich
Switzerland
avi@acm.org

Abstract

In traditional computing environments, users actively choose to interact with computers. Ubiquitous computing applications are likely to be different—they will be embedded in the users' physical environment and integrate seamlessly with their everyday tasks. This vision leads to a set of defining characteristics, requirements, and research challenges for ubiquitous applications. This chapter identifies some of the key characteristics via a scenario and derives the important application design and software infrastructure challenges that need to be addressed by the computing research community.

[1] This work is based on an earlier work: "Software Infrastructure and Design Challenges for Ubiquitous Computing Applications", in Communications of the ACM {Vol. 45, Issue 12, (Dec 2002)} © ACM, 2002. http://doi.acm.org/10.1145/585597.585622

179

1. Scenario: A Day in the Life of a CIO

Jane is the Chief Information Officer (CIO) of an organization that relies heavily on computer services. She is attending an important meeting in her organization's headquarters in New York City. She is in a conference room with three co-workers and two remote participants who have joined via a computer-based video conferencing system. The system allows her team to see and hear the remote participants as well as use a shared white-board space to jointly edit documents and explore data. As the meeting progresses, Jane's friend calls about their weekend social—the system routes the call to her voice mail, noting that she cannot be interrupted from this important meeting.

Unfortunately, Jane has to leave the meeting early, as she has to catch a plane to visit a supplier in Paris. Luckily, she can continue participating in the meeting, via her smart Personal Digital Assistant (PDA). As soon as her PDA detects that she left the conference room, it routes the audio-part of the meeting to her mobile smart phone. As she enters the Limousine that is taking her to the airport, the car detects who she is and adjusts the seat, the screen and keyboard, and customizes the voice recognition software to her voice settings. The screen built into the back of the driver seat displays the video stream of the meeting, including both the people as well as the shared white-board space. Furthermore, the audio portion of the meeting is transferred to the in-car speakerphone system. As the car starts to move the video is adapted automatically to changing network quality by changing its resolution. When one of the meeting participants starts showing a PowerPoint slide, which is marked as confidential, the car's sound is automatically muted and a pop-up window appears pointing out to Jane that the following part of the meeting seems to be confidential and might be overheard by the driver. The car's built in system then offers her to either continue the remote meeting using headphones or by having the Limousine's divider windows raised in order to ensure the needed privacy. Given the car's security certification Jane can be at ease about spying software in the car's security system that might record the conversation for later analysis.

As the meeting progresses, an instant message pops up on the screen alerting her of a fire accident in her organization's data center in Colorado Springs. She taps the message on the touch-sensitive screen in order to dial the sender's phone-number. Her personal software agent, noticing that Jane is going into crisis handling mode, notifies the meeting attendees that Jane is in a situation that urgently needs her attention, and that she has to excuse herself from the meeting. The sender of the instant message, the data center manager, reports to Jane that the fire in the data center severely damaged some important servers. He was alerted to the fire and its location by the building management system, which had sensed a fall in pressure in the sprinkler system. The building management system deduced that there might be a fire (or a breach in one of the pipes) and decided to close all fire doors in the facility. It had then localized the source of the fire by tapping into the heating/air-conditioning thermostats which were reporting high temperatures in the server room before going off-line. Thanks to the automated fire-management system, much of the data center had been saved. For those servers that were damaged, the backups were luckily safe off-site.

Jane decides to change her plans and fly to Colorado Springs immediately to help with the repairs. She asks the data center manager to send her a detailed damage report in order to plan the repair. She activates her software personal agent using the in-car keyboard and tells it to change her flight reservations from Paris to Colorado Springs. She also requests that all the files regarding the data center configuration be transferred to her PDA as soon as the required network bandwidth is available. The agent rebooks the flights. In addition, it infers that she will not be able to fulfill her appointments in Paris. So it cancels the hotel room reservation using the hotel's on-line services and the meetings with the supplier and sends the appropriate emails. As Jane leaves the limo, the personal agent "hops" from the car's computer to the PDA and scans the area for a better network connection. As she enters the airport terminal, the agent detects a high-capacity wireless LAN to which it authenticates itself and starts downloading the requested data about the data center.

While waiting at the terminal, Jane calls the data center manager to get the latest update. Meanwhile her Smart phone-agent registers her nervousness as expressed by the resistance of her skin and her increased heart rate (as sensed through the sensors on the phone's earpiece that touches her skin). Therefore, the agent reroutes all non-essential phone calls to her voice mail. Her plane is delayed a bit, and as she continues waiting, she spots a business associate, Mark, who happens to be flying on the same plane. She explains the situation to Mark and shares from her PDA the photos, videos, and the data sheets related to the warehouse fire. Mark views the information on his larger screen tablet computer, and suggests that he can help by contacting an insurance evaluator for a field inspection. Jane is relieved to accept the help, and the two of them decide to share all their information and computing tasks related to the fire as they travel together to Colorado Springs. They set up their computing devices so that each of them is able to see the progress the other has made in resolving the issues they're collaborating on.

Once she boards the plane, her PDA again scans for possible services in her environment and detects that it can connect to the screen and keyboard built into the plane's seat using an in-airplane wireless network. It displays Jane's desktop environment on the screen and highlights the data center information. After the plane takes off, Jane carefully plans the necessary repairs, and shares this information with Mark who concurrently sets up the insurance evaluation. Jane puts in express orders for the needed parts, and enters requests for freelancers with the appropriate skills to relieve her own employees who are working around the clock. The PDA's personal agent automatically prioritizes her requests and transfers some files over the slower airplane network. As she lands in Colorado Springs, it can transfer the remaining files using the terminal's wireless LAN. By the time she arrives at the data center, the first bids by freelancers have already arrived, and the computer equipment providers have received the orders for the replacement parts.

2. Ubiquitous Computing Characteristics

The above scenario illustrates many aspects of ubiquitous computing, of which we highlight three major characteristics below—social factors, task factors, and technology factors.

2.1 Computing in a Social Environment

Privacy

One major characteristic of ubiquitous computing technology is that it has a significant impact on the social environments in which it is used. Any introduction of a ubiquitous computing environment implies the introduction of sensors, which irrevocably causes an impact on the social structure no matter how unobtrusive it seems to be. Imagine, for example, that your apartment is outfitted with all kinds of sensors to feed a ubiquitous computing system. As described in the scenario these sensors could help you to manage life threatening situations, such as fires. They could also help to improve general quality of life issues by adjusting temperatures and lighting to people's preferences, etc. However, a big concern would be about how the collected data is used: Would you want your neighborhood police station to be able to monitor in which room you are currently residing (as indicated by the alarm system's motion detectors) and how much alcohol you are consuming (as inferred from your food inventory system)? How about your thermometer: Would you like it to share information about your temperature with your employer? What about your physician?

Gathering data of any kind irrevocably leads to privacy concerns. Where should the data be stored and what boundaries shouldn't it cross? Who should have access to it and who doesn't? These questions aren't new to ubiquitous computing. But the pervasiveness of these sensors adds a new layer of complexity to understanding and managing all the possible data streams. Can one subpoena the data collected by ubiquitous computing systems? As the answer is probably yes, there might be a demand for ubiquitous computing systems where the raw sensor data cannot be accessed at all, but only processed inferences from the data, like "burglar entry," can.

Perpetual, Pervasive Observation

Apart from the legal/privacy implications the ubiquity of sensors may also lead to psychological unease on the part of users. As Zuboff [28] describes it, people don't like to be observed all the time. In Zuboff's book, a manager in a computerized plant says: "... this computer is like X-Ray vision. It makes the people who operate the process very unfriendly ..." (p. 316). Or in the words of an employee in that same plant (p. 343): "... we don't want them to second-guess our minute-to-minute decisions. ... our concern is that they will be on our backs and we will all end up with ulcers." For that reason, Zuboff compares such environments where people feel constantly observed to a jailhouse design by the moral philosopher Jeremy Bentham, which he calls the Panopticon, that (as cited by Zuboff [28, p. 321]) "... induces on the inmate a state of conscious and permanent visibility that assures the automatic functioning of power ..." and thus perfect control of the inmates. The constant feeling of observability, as it can be generated by the perpetual presence of certain sensors can, hence, lead to undesirable psychological feelings and unease about the sensor-laden environment.

As Grudin [9] mentions, even sensors that are highly desirable by all participants may have socially unacceptable implications. He points out the example of a meeting, where one participant is late. In the physical world, it is not uncommon to joke at the latecomer's expense in order to diffuse frustration. Having the same meeting in a phone teleconference situation might, however, make the jokes look rather awkward, since the late arriver might check the prerecorded bits in order to catch up on things already discussed. Unfortunately, sensors typically record only one aspect of an occurrence and, thus, decontextualize the sensory data. Social interpretability, however, requires exactly this contextual information leading to undesirable effects and misinterpretations.

These social issues are going to become a major non-technical issue when developing ubiquitous computing applications. They are going to shape their acceptance, which will in turn decide their success. It is going to be a major challenge to convince privacy advocates who already argue that ubiquitous computing will lead to "small, usually invisibly sensors that will be everywhere, including food and clothing, to gather data about people that can be used [for marketing purposes]" (paraphrased from [12]).

HCI, CSCW, and Ubiquitous Devices

Jane's smooth use of the ubiquitous technology as pictured in the scenario is rather optimistic, in that it assumes that Jane knows how to use all the different user interfaces she is confronted with. For most of us, it is complicated enough to navigate one user interface environment like MS Windows or Apple's Aqua. Only stringent user interface guidelines ensuring consistency will allow us to use programs that we haven't seen before. But imagine what would happen when those programs have a variety of different interfaces due to the different capabilities of the devices on which they are used? When the video-conferencing application that Jane was using hopped from her Laptop to her cell-phone to the car, it had to adapt not only to changing technological capabilities like bandwidth, but also to different input/output modalities, and hence, human computer interaction models. This opens a plethora of questions—e.g., what does it mean to have a consistent interface across platforms?

One approach, taken by Microsoft, is to make all user interfaces from the PC to the PDA and cell phone look (seemingly) the same. Unfortunately, this approach isn't necessarily successful, because this seeming sameness suggests similar capabilities, which cannot be assumed for devices with various limitations. This leads to, for example, serious confusions by the users of PDA versions of Word, Excel, and PowerPoint, which seemingly look like their big brother but sometimes behaved annoyingly differently.

Another approach would be to accept the different look and feel of the user interfaces (after all it is difficult to type on the back of a car seat), but adhere to the same interaction logic (i.e., sequence of user actions) across devices. Nokia has been employing this approach in their phones with great success. If you have gotten used to one of the Nokia phone models, then you can use other models in more or less the same manner. This approach ensures logical consistency, but does not allow user interfaces to take advantage of unique options available on certain devices, like gesture recognition or touch sensitiveness.

The above discussion is intended to point out that the problem of writing cross-platform adaptive and intuitive user interfaces is a major challenge for user interface research. It gets aggravated by the problem that ubiquitous devices are often used in social environments where multiple people may either be present or even collaborate. When Jane walks into the airport terminal, it might not be socially acceptable for her to issue hand gesture commands (as some of the people in the terminal might think that she has behavioral problems). On the other hand, social acceptability may change as we see with cell phones, where we consider it (somewhat) acceptable for people to walk alone on the street and have a conversation in public with others using a hands-free mobile phone (an activity which might have earned one an admission to a psychiatric ward just half a century ago).

2.2   Task Dynamism

Dimensions of Dynamism

The history of work is full of attempts to optimize our work processes and take out all traces of exceptions. This process-oriented approach was formally started by Frederick Winslow Taylor [23] in industrial environments and was passed on to the office floor at Citibank [19]. Consequently, most computer systems so far have been introduced in environments that have been made as static as possible in order to ensure efficiency. Ubiquitous computing applications, by virtue of being available everywhere at all times, will have to adapt to conditions that have not been engineered to be constant and predictable. People have to cope with *dynamic* environments that change in sometimes unpredictable ways, and the applications supporting them will have to help them do so. In our scenario, for example, the fire in the data-center is clearly an unpredictable event. Jane's PDA helped her to cope with the newly arising situation by changing her hotel reservations and re-routing her calls.

A second characteristic of such uncontrolled environments is that they are at least partially *inaccessible* to sensory monitoring. A vast amount of occurrences happen outside the perceptual range of any application. Therefore, applications have to be written bearing in mind that they act in an open environment [13], where any type of closed world assumption is wrong. In our scenario the building management system had to infer that there was probably a fire given that the water-pressure in the sprinkler system had gone down, and it did not have direct access to fire-sensors (or smoke detectors).

A third characteristic of such environments is their *non-deterministic* behavior. It is not always the case that actions will have the same results each time, since their outcome may be dependent on the action of others and unforeseeably changing constraints. Jane's plan to relieve her workers with free-lancers will only work if there are actually free-lancers available to help out. While this is a fair assumption if the fire is limited to Jane's facility, it would seem highly unlikely in the case of a large scale bush-fire in Colorado, when all free-lancers would be booked.

We can, hence, infer that people using ubiquitous devices will act in environments that are dynamic, at least partially inaccessible, and non-deterministic. Such environments are not amenable to traditional planning of tasks and their subsequent execution, as the basic assumptions and constraints on which the plan is based might change during execution requiring a different course of action. Looking at the social science literature (as excellently summarized and extended in [22]) we find that people in such environments don't really rely on plans as fixed instructions, but use them as a resource for action just as much as any other resource. They may *serendipitously change their goals* or *adapt their actions to a changing environment* [22]. Consider for, example, arriving in Boston Logan airport and getting instructions on how to drive to MIT. These instructions would probably include where to turn and what bridges/tunnels/roads to take. However, when a road is closed due to construction (and this has happened rather often in Boston during the last few years), those instructions would be problematic. They could serve as a resource up until the point where they would become just another input on finding MIT. One could, for example, show the instructions to a by-passer and ask her what other path there would be to MIT, leading to change in the plan of *how* to get to MIT. Our scenario illustrates a second type of change. When new information about the data center fire arrived unexpectedly, Jane changed the destination she wanted to go to: rather than changing the combination of tasks to lead to a goal, the scenario shows a situation where changing circumstances warrant changing the goal itself.

Task Dynamism and Task Support

Bernstein [3] extends this understanding of people acting in dynamic environments to find the support types that might be needed. He finds that it is useful to focus on the specificity of the task as a guideline for how much a system can rely on existing plans to guide the user. For highly specific tasks, plans might be used to inform a workflow management like system. For highly unspecific tasks plans serve just as yet another input for a human actor to decide what to do next. The system might just be able to extract possible constraints for the plan and make the user aware of them. During execution, tasks might become more or less specific depending on occurrences beyond the reach of the system such as exceptions occurring (as the fire in the scenario) or new information arriving that further specifies the task.

To succeed in such fluid environments, one will thus have to leverage the human ability to act and reason with incomplete information based on hunches and vast experience as well as the ubiquitous computing system's ability to meticulously execute and observe large amounts of well structured tasks and data. Sometimes the user might actively reconfigure the system to adapt to the new task settings (relying on information that might be inaccessible to the system); at other times the system might have to infer from its sensory input that the user changed his or her mind (such as when the agent cancels Jane's hotel reservation based on the flight changes). In order to allow the user to follow any reasoning the system might have made, applications will have to be able to explain why they inferred those task-changes and learn from their right and wrong inferences. In summary, human and machine actors will have to cooperate, each bringing its strengths to bear in truly mixed-initiative collaborations [7,26,6,3].

2.3   Devices and Their Characteristics

Devices That Users Interact With

A primary goal of ubiquitous computing is to ensure that users have access to their applications and data anywhere and on any device. The conventional way of achieving this is to directly install applications on devices that users can carry around with them. Devices such as PDAs, mobile phones, smart watches, flash-memory devices, etc. typically provide some storage for a user's personal data and applications, some computational power to perform essential functions, as well as some level of network connectivity for interacting with other devices. These are a critical part of the ubiquitous computing vision, since they provide an easy way for users to carry personal data and applications in a manner that is secure and available at all times.

However, this is not practical for all applications—you probably do not want to do your email on your watch's GUI. Nor is it necessarily desirable, since you may want to, for example, share the data on your calendar with others. In many cases, it is more effective to think of devices as "portals" into a personal application and data space [1]. With this perspective, users can use devices that they may carry with them (for ease of use, familiarity), or they can use devices that are installed in the environment. In our scenario, Jane was using her smart phone and smart PDA as well as the devices available in the car and the airplane. In either case, the user should be able to access the applications and data they need. This, of course, is only possible when there is a suitable networking environment and a secure way to communicate with other devices. (When this is not possible, we fall back on the conventional computing environment of the previous paragraph.)

One consequence of this perspective is that applications have to adapt to *changing technological capabilities in their environment*. If the *device itself is mobile* (following the user or being carried around by him/her) then it usually has some constraints in terms of physical dimensions. These physical constraints limit resources such as battery power, screen size, networking bandwidth, etc. A PDA, for example, has relatively little screen real estate and limited battery power, a cell-phone has an even smaller screen size but typically a longer battery life and is at least connected to a network, etc. These limitations impose various requirements on application adaptability. Screen real estate, and more generally, the input and output interface modalities of a device have a major impact on the design of applications, which in turn has a major impact on the usability and satisfaction of a user on that device. As a result, an application should be fine-tuned for, or at least satisfactorily usable, for each device it is intended to execute on. Battery power is a precious resource for mobile devices, since the growth in mobile power levels is far slower than the growth in other aspects of computing such as processor power, memory, etc. Applications should be aware of and adapt to the available power on a device. It is also necessary for the device to orchestrate the suite of applications being run, based on the power availability and application need based on user's priorities.

Furthermore, applications might also experience *variability in the availability of resources*, as demonstrated in our scenario. There may be varying levels of connectivity from a given device, ranging from full network availability to intermittent connectivity, to lower bandwidth connections, to no connections at all. An application should be able to gracefully provide useful and usable functions in all of these environments. In fact, it is important to note that application adaptability is necessary not only for supporting user mobility but also for supporting failure and recovery of pieces of the ubiquitous computing infrastructure. Lack of networking availability is equivalent to the failure of the networking subsystem; lack of a large screen is equivalent to the failure of an existing large screen, and so forth.

Another aspect of mobility is having the *application following the user* and *moving seamlessly* between devices. Applications will thus have to *adapt to changing hardware capabilities* (mice, pens, jog-dials, keyboards, network types, etc.) and variability in the available software services. In our scenario, Jane moved from the office (with a rich multimedia environment for a conferencing application) to the street (where the only available modality was a voice device) to the car (with a more limited handheld and in-car computer and speakers), with different user interface and networking capabilities in these two locations. Some resources might even become completely unavailable, as the limo might not have any printer. The meeting software will have to dynamically adapt to changing technological capabilities by adapting the compression rate and size of transmitted pictures or determining an alternative output to a printout. Obviously these considerations also influence the development of applications and their capabilities.

Devices Embedded in the Environment

A second category of devices—sensors and actuators—are critical in enabling ubiquitous computing applications. There are many examples of sensors in our scenario: The PDA subsystem that tracks and discovers other devices, the car interior that recognizes that a specific person entered the car, the smart phone that recognizes that Jane is stressed, the fire sensors in the warehouse, etc. These devices collect data about the real world and pass it on to the computing infrastructure for enabling decision-making. On the other hand, the isolation device in the warehouse in our scenario is an example of an actuator. Actuators are devices that allow a computing environment to affect changes in the real world.

Sensors and actuators come in a wide variety of capabilities. The size of sensors can vary from "smart dust" [15] to cell phones to even larger devices. Sensors may track using electromagnetic, chemical, or other means. Some sensors need power, whereas others do not. Due to their limited capability, sensors will need to network with other devices to become an effective part of a computing system. In some scenarios, sensors can communicate with centralized aggregators of information via a fixed network infrastructure. In other scenarios (e.g., deep sea or military applications), it may be necessary for sensors to network among themselves to realize an effective application.

A major implication of using large number of sensors in the environment is that there will be a tremendous amount of data that will be generated. Data generated by sensors is often dynamic and not "persistent"—for example, the fact that my car is currently at a particular location may not necessarily be useful after a few minutes. Furthermore, it should be possible to derive useful information from "raw" sensor data. The fact that the light was off, the computer was off, and my office door locked is not useful information by themselves, but the combination of these which implies that I was not in my office at that time is perhaps useful to an application.

3. Research Challenges

Given the above characteristics, we identify a number of challenges for the computing research community, organized into four broad categories—semantic modeling, developing and configuring applications, building the software infrastructure, and validating the user experience.

3.1 Semantic Modeling

A fundamental necessity for an adaptable and composable computing environment is the ability to describe the preferences of users and the relevant characteristics of computing components using a high-level semantic model. For example, if we have information that a user prefers aisle seats on an airplane and that the user's device can support voice interaction, then a travel application can ask the user whether they would like to have an aisle seat as usual. *Ontologies* [8] can be used to describe the user's task-environments as well as their goals, to enable reasoning about the user's need and therefore to dynamically adapt to changes.

Modeling Device and Service Capabilities

The effort around the semantic web [2] is partially aiming at developing languages to specify, in a logically sound manner, the capability of devices and the requirements of services for their execution. Furthermore, descriptions of the device capabilities and their appropriate use will allow applications to reason about how to best support users in any given context. For example, the system could down-sample pictures when network bandwidth decreases on a device. The changing bandwidth availabilities that Jane encounters when going from the facility (with presumably a wired giga-bit Ethernet and 54 MBit WLAN) to the car (with a hopefully roughly 100 KBit 3G connection) to the airport terminal (with presumably 10 MBit WLAN), and finally to the plane (with a low bandwidth wireless connection through satellites) require her software agent to constantly adapt to changing capabilities. One way to deal with this problem is to model each network in the form of an instance in an ontology describing all attributes of the service (such as bandwidth, latency, etc.). When an application, such as the video-conferencing tool that Jane is using at the beginning of the scenario is looking for a service such as a network, it could provide a description of the required network capabilities, again in the form of an instance of an ontology describing the desired properties of such a connection. The agent will now be able to take the required capabilities as well as the available services and match using the ontologies that define the two. When the bandwidth changes (for example, when Jane exits the building and enters the car) the agent will try to re-match the required capabilities and, when a match is found, inform the application of the changed circumstances (i.e., reduced bandwidth) which will result in the video-conferencing software requesting a different (i.e., lower bandwidth) video-stream.

Modeling the User's Task Environment

A good ubiquitous computing application should determine how to most appropriately interact with users given a social context by, for example, deciding not to ring on the arrival of a new message during an opera but only vibrate. Again, imagine a semantic description of the user's context with its appropriate interruption methods (such as vibrating, just flashing the message on the screen of the phone or watch, vibrating, or ringing) and the importance of a message will help an agent to determine what method to use given the specific context. Jane's agent, for example, was able to determine that the message about the fire was important enough to interrupt the videoconference she was engaged in. A call from a colleague about a possible lunch-meeting in a few weeks, however, could have been deemed less important and been routed to her voice-mail for later attention. Such message filtering approaches could be extended with machine learning methods for determining interruptibility and importance of the message (as used in Mozilla mail for SPAM filtering), which may include approaches such as relevance feedback to improve their performance.

Extending Existing Semantic Modeling Techniques for Knowledge Interchange and Reasoning

The research challenges in semantic modeling include developing a modeling language to express the rich and complex nature of ontologies, developing and validating ontologies for various domains of user activity, and finally, agreeing on shared ontology parts or translations for each application domain (see also [2]). While the semantic web-effort has resulted in a standard language for expressing ontologies called OWL (Ontology Web Language) [25], this language "only" enables the syntactical exchange but not the translation between ontologies. OWL's XML descendant mark-up language allows different tools to exchange ontologies using a common format. Different applications (and organizations) are still highly likely to develop different ontologies. Just imagine the network ontology for end users (typically only encountering a small selection of protocols and physical connectors) compared to the ontology a network engineer at a large telecom might encounter (encompassing a large variety of standards). One would, therefore, have to use some translation procedure when reasoning about items specified in different ontologies. For open systems, where the mapping might not be straightforward, this is still an open problem.

Another issue is the inherent limitation of the OWL language due to its basis in description logic. This limited logic is incapable of describing certain kinds of relationships [10] and in return benefits from reduced computational complexity. One example is OWL's inability to describe non-monotonic knowledge, i.e., features that are "un-inherited" from a more general concept. This could be particularly important as end users (as opposed to software developers) oftentimes prefer non-monotonic systems [16].

Validating Semantics

Finally, there is the issue of validating the semantic markup. Almost any semantic specification of items existing in the socially accessible world is bound to cause disagreement. Semantic markup attempts to capture *meaning*, which is philosophically difficult to track. Depending on the research tradition the meaning of items is either well defined (as for example words are in the French language by a committee) or by its use (as Habermas [11] asserts). Obviously, computer scientists developing applications in the ubiquitous computing domain do not want to get entangled in such philosophical issues. Nevertheless they will have to understand that any specification of meaning will eventually entangle them in such problems [18]. It is, therefore, imperative to validate any ontology with which users will have contact with representatives of that same user community.

3.2   Developing and Configuring Applications

There are three stages in the lifecycle of applications: At *design-time*, a developer creates, maintains and enhances an application. At *load-time*, that is when the user invokes the application, the system adapts the application to the user's context and delivers it. *Run-time* is when the user actually uses an application for its intended purpose. This subsection discusses the issues at design-time, and the following section discusses the research issues at delivery-time and runtime.

To understand the issues involved in developing applications, it is necessary to first understand a model of applications. An application is structured into two parts: interaction logic and application logic. Interaction logic defines the interchange between a user and the system, regardless of the "context" of the user, including the device being used and the user's particular preferences. The application logic is organized into reusable software modules, which encapsulate a packaging of computation and data, perhaps to expose the information interface of physical artifacts. The current trend in the software industry is for providers to encapsulate these reusable functions via application components called *services*.

Within this application model, building applications involves specifying the right composition of services, building the interaction logic, and orchestrating the data flow among the various components. For example, an application to book a hotel room consists of composing a hotel search service, a hotel reservation service, the user's credit card service, and the user's calendar service, and creating the right user interface to provide the necessary information for these services to collaborate and complete the task.

Building the Application Logic

Building the application logic as reusable services in a ubiquitous computing environment has several challenges. First, these services need to be described using standard ontologies as described in the previous subsection. Such semantic descriptions are needed to enable automatic composition of services, which in turn enables an infrastructure that dynamically adapts to tasks.

Second, not only will services encapsulate business logic and data, but also "information interfaces" to physical artifacts such as sensors and actuators. Due to the extensive heterogeneity of these devices, it is important that the service interaction interface is standardized. However, the implementation of these services will be intimately tied to the underlying functionality of the device. For example, a temperature sensor will provide a programmable function for reading the temperature, and the function could be exposed as a method of a web service.

Third, configuring services so that they can be easily and reliably reused by other developers and composed into applications will be a major challenge. In addition to describing the interface of the service, it is necessary to register them in the right registries which are available to service discovery services. The service discovery algorithms, which in turn depend on the ontologies, should be complete enough to reliably discover the most appropriate services. Furthermore, the registry and the discovery infrastructure should be scalable to support massive numbers of services.

Building the Interaction Logic

The requirements of ubiquitous computing impose a significant shift in the developer's mindset while building the interaction logic of applications [1]. Applications are not pieces of software targeted to a particular device or a particular environment, but rather, they are high-level descriptions of the task that a user needs to perform. The goal is to be able to specify the interaction logic at an "intent-level," and the application's requirements on data and computation. An intent-level specification describes the user's task at a logical level, e.g., this task gathers a customer's contact information (as defined by a schema), rather than at a concrete presentation level, e.g., this screen requires the customer to enter their street address, city, and phone number using input fields of length 20. This kind of abstract, intent-level, specification allows the infrastructure to adapt the application to heterogeneous devices with constrained resources. This leads to several research challenges:

First, the interaction logic specified at the intent level, or at a generic level, has to be transformed to concrete device-specific applications. If this transformation is completely automated, the risk is that the generated user interface code may fall short of hand-written interface code, making the application not very usable and aesthetic. As a result, one approach is to make the transformation semi-automatic, meaning that the application developer provides some extra information to help the transformation engine make the right choices. Furthermore, the developer should be able to modify the generated code to add style elements to increase the aesthetics and UI uniformity of the generated code. This kind of intermixing of manual input with automated transformation raises several challenges in the development methodology.

Second, it may be desirable to convert existing, concrete, device-specific applications into intent-level applications so that they can be re-targeted to other devices. In addition, user-interface designers may prefer to build the UI in concrete device-specific terms rather than an abstract intent-level. There are many technical challenges in addressing this problem, for which guidance can be obtained from the area of programming by demonstration.

Incorporating Context into Applications

Ubiquitous applications of the future will be context-aware, in the sense that they will have information about the environment and activities of the user (thanks to sensors), and they can choose to adapt their behavior based on the user's circumstances. As a simple example, a message notification application may choose to deliver a message by email or by voice (telephone) depending on the current state of the user (Is the user in a meeting? Handling a crisis? Etc.). Consider the issues that an application developer faces in writing an application of this nature.

Writing context aware applications can be extremely complex. At a minimum, the application developer should have an easy way to specify the actions an application should take under specific conditions. This requires a high-level programming model, preferably a declarative programming model that is easy to specify and debug.

As the number of context sources increase, however, this poses an enormous problem. The developer cannot possibly hand-code the way in which an application should react to each possible user circumstance, since there can be an unbounded number of complex situations. In these situations, it becomes important for the system to support additional automation in determining the most useful combination of context data that can be relevant to particular applications. A more sophisticated approach would be to support some level of automated learning based on patterns of past context [20,21]. For example, the learning system can recognize that when Jane's calendar has a meeting, and her current position is outside of her office, and her PDA has sufficient bandwidth and power, the meeting stream should be re-directed to her PDA. Learning algorithms, however, are complex to develop, and require a significant amount of fine-tuning to make them friendly to end-users.

3.3   Building the Software Infrastructure

The software infrastructure needed to support the kinds of applications envisioned in our scenario is extensive and complex. Such an infrastructure must be able to support task dynamism as well as heterogeneous and resource constrained devices.

The *hardware* infrastructure consists of end-user devices, sensors and actuators, interconnecting networks (both wired and wireless), as well as the server computers that are used to collect data from, analyze, and control the devices. For the purposes of this chapter, we assume that these devices already contain the low-level operating systems and the drivers needed to interconnect with other devices, and to allow other software applications access to their functions. Thus, we think of the software infrastructure necessary for ubiquitous computing as the pre-existing software that is embedded within the devices and the network (servers) to enable the ubiquitous computing applications. In this section, we cover the various aspects of software infrastructure in turn.

Composing and Instantiating Applications

An effective software infrastructure for running ubiquitous applications must be capable of dynamically creating a customized application by composing the right components based on the user's context. The infrastructure must be able to (1) determine, (2) synthesize, and (3) deliver the application to the user's computing environment, i.e., the collection of devices that the user prefers to work with. Semantic models for users, applications, tasks, and computing environments will be used for this purpose. Let us consider each of these steps in turn.

The first step is to determine which user tasks are most relevant to a user in a particular context. For example, in our scenario, when Jane hears about the warehouse fire and switches into crisis mode, her software personal agent infers that she needs to pay attention to the crisis as opposed to the meeting, and helps with the social protocol to end her meeting attendance (e.g., notifying others that Jane needs to handle a crisis). These tasks may be determined based on history, on preferences, or other knowledge of the user's behavior and the environmental conditions. In general, this problem is also heavily based on the semantic models and the context-enablement discussed earlier.

The second step, once the user has selected the task, is to create an application to suit the user's task by finding and composing the appropriate components and services. For example, in our scenario, consider the application that cancels Jane's trip to Paris. This application consists of a flight reservation service, a hotel reservation service, Jane's financial accounting service, the calendar services of multiple people (for canceling the meetings), an email service (for notifying participants of Jane's status), and finally, a user interface to inform Jane and to get confirmation from her for the different steps. In our envisioned future world, such applications cannot be composed a priori, since not every combination of services can be foreseen in advance. As a result, there is a need to translate the user's intent (e.g., to cancel a trip) to an application that performs the necessary sub-steps. The challenge here is to determine which aspects of the application are pre-defined, and which aspects are built and composed on the fly.

The third step, once the application is created, is to deliver the application by potentially partitioning the application among various devices to take advantage of the relative strengths. For example, in our scenario, the meeting application may be partitioned in one way in Jane's office, e.g., with an audio/video decoder, and renderer on the room's computer, and a mixer and demultiplexer on the backend server. The application may be partitioned very differently in the case when she is walking to the Limo with her SmartPDA, e.g., only audio components such as a decompressor, decoder, decrypter (for security purposes), and renderer may be on the device. The challenge here is for the software infrastructure to understand the user's computing environment, i.e., the devices, networks, UI modalities, etc., as well as the user's preferences, to appropriately partition and deploy the application components onto different devices. Note that the partitioning may be dynamically changed, that is, the software infrastructure must be capable of monitoring the user's computing environment and dynamically modify the application partitioning based on changes in the environment.

In the last step above, it is clear that the software infrastructure spans the devices as well as the network server infrastructure. The device software infrastructure helps determine the device capabilities, negotiate with the server infrastructure, provide an execution environment for the application, and helps monitor and adapt the application as necessary. The network server infrastructure, on the other hand, may typically be responsible for the other steps above, such as the context collection, application determination, application composition and delivery. However, in general, these functions can occur either in the network server infrastructure or the device software infrastructure.

Seamless Migration Among Devices

Once instantiated, applications may have to move seamlessly from one device to another and from one environment to another, based on the user's activity. In our scenario, the meeting application moved from the office environment, to Jane's personal computing environment, to the car. Later in the scenario, the task analysis application Jane uses moves from the car to the airport to the airplane, etc. In each of these cases, there is a need for dynamic monitoring of the user and task context, and the ability to migrate the application as the usage context changes. This entails suspending the application, refactoring the application based on the new target environment, and restoring the application in the new environment. These are all non-trivial technical challenges for which there are no widely accepted solutions.

Applications must provide reasonable function even when network connectivity is intermittent or unavailable, and must recover graciously from failures. The above discussion assumed constant and full network connectivity, but in general, connectivity can be anywhere from unavailable, to intermittent, to available at various bandwidth levels. Even in a future world where the network infrastructure is ubiquitous, factors such as cost, security, and responsiveness, may require that the software infrastructure be aware of the network connectivity level and adapt itself accordingly. In our scenario, when Jane asked her PDA to download the schematics of the data center, the PDA deferred the request until a higher-capacity network could be found. When

Jane puts in requests for bids during her airplane trip, the infrastructure, recognizing that network connectivity is low capacity, queues up the transfer of larger data files, but still allows her to continue her work in the weakly connected environment.

Aggregation and Analysis of Data

As alluded to in the discussion above, one of the key challenges in ubiquitous computing is the computing machinery required to collect and analyze data from a large number of data sources like sensors, databases, web services, etc. There are two main challenges here—dynamic binding to data sources and rich composition of heterogeneous data. Dynamic binding is the notion that an application should not be rigidly bound to a data resource, but instead capable of re-binding to the most appropriate resource based on the current conditions of the application execution. For example, in our scenario, Jane's meeting application should not be rigidly bound to a particular audio receiver (microphone) on a PC, but rather should be able to rebind itself to the audio receiver in the office, or on the PDA, or in the car, etc. The application requires audio data from Jane—regardless of where Jane is and which device she is using. Application developers should be able to easily specify this type of dynamic composition, rather than having to explicitly specify the manner in which an application should bind to each type of audio receiver in each environment. Multiple research projects are ongoing to address this issue (e.g., UDDI [24], Jini (see Table I accompanying Section 4 of this article), and iQueue [4]).

The other challenge is that of rich composition of heterogeneous data. Information coming from data sources is typically low-level, in the sense that information from each source may only give a low degree of confidence of an event meaningful to applications. For example, in our scenario, the fact that a meeting is going on in Jane's boardroom is determined by sensors that detect that there are multiple people in the room, and there are voices being heard, and there are devices and programs that are active, and so forth. Similarly, when Jane is waiting at the airport, her PDA detects that she is nervous by sensing her skin resistance (due to sweating) and her elevated heart rate, and perhaps also taking into account that she is reacting to a crisis (based on semantic information about her activity). The software infrastructure should enable rich and flexible composition of data from multiple sources such as in these examples. The programming model for specifying these compositions is non-trivial, and is currently being developed in ongoing research projects [5].

In many cases, it is very difficult, if not impossible, for a human application developer to explicitly specify the particular combination of low-level context data that should be composed into a high-level event. For example, in our scenario, the fact that Jane is "handling a crisis" is a piece of high-level context information, based on which several kinds of useful applications can be built—to help end non-essential activities, to re-route non-essential phone calls to her voice mail, to re-schedule non-essential events on her calendar, etc. However, an application developer will find it very difficult to enumerate *a priori* which combination of events should result in the state "in a crisis." It may be more feasible for the user to help the infrastructure to "learn" what constitutes a crisis, perhaps by initially providing explicit manual input, but also to let the infrastructure learn that a combination of a particular history of events and the current state of the environment should result in a state of crisis. If the infrastructure is able to reliably come to these kinds of conclusions, the application developer can then provide the computational logic that reacts to these states and takes actions to assist the user.

Scalability

Finally, the software infrastructure must be scalable to support the huge numbers of devices and applications that ubiquitous applications will enable. The world of the future is likely to consist of trillions of devices, most of which will be sensors and actuators of various kinds, and some of which will be end-user devices. Data from these devices must be collected and processed in useful ways to enable the kinds of applications discussed above. On the other hand, the world of the future will also consist of millions of application software components that will need to be composed and coordinated for creating the applications discussed above. Furthermore, both the devices and the application components need to be managed through their lifecycle, e.g., for installing, configuring, upgrading, fixing, and replacing.

3.4   Validating the User Experience

As argued earlier, ubiquitous computing has the potential to fundamentally change the way in which people use computing devices to perform their tasks. The utility of some computing advancements cannot be evaluated without performing significant user studies and in some cases, widely deploying it. For example, the meeting application in our scenario is rife with usability issues—Will it be possible and reasonable for users to be able to continue meeting with a group of people while moving from one environ to another? How effective can they be? How will the other meeting participants react? How will the other people around them (e.g., if Jane was taking a train ride) react? As a second example, Jane is performing tasks that are quite complex—how can the user interface for such complex tasks be built to perform well on a variety of device form factors? On different modalities, e.g., voice, GUI, handwriting, etc.? What kinds of complex tasks will she be able to perform while on the move and while within public environments with distractions? What are the privacy and the security considerations for these applications in these environments (a separate paper can be written on this subject)?

Consequently, the development of effective methods of testing and evaluating the usage scenarios enabled by ubiquitous applications is an important area that needs more attention from researchers. The dynamic nature of some of these usage situations, the device heterogeneity with its varying resource availability, and the widely varying social environments in which mobile computing solutions are being used are, however, complicating the development of such evaluation methods (see the article on "Beyond Prototypes" in [14]). Traditional laboratory experiments might not work in many cases, as they don't capture the rich essence of the usage environments. This will force researchers to use more complicated approaches such as field-based quasi-experiments or ethnographies.

4. Ongoing Projects

There are several ongoing projects that deal with various challenges mentioned above. A sampling of projects is given in Table I.

TABLE I

Project	Vision/Goals	Challenges addressed
Aware home (Georgia Tech.) http://www.cc.gatech.edu/fce/ahri	To develop the requisite technologies to create a home environment that can both perceive and assist its occupants.	User experience enhancement and validation
Aura (CMU) http://www.cs.cmu.edu/~aura/	To fundamentally rethink system design to address the problem of reduced user effectiveness due to explicit and implicit distraction from computers. To provide each user with an invisible halo of computing and information services that persists regardless of location.	Software infrastructure; Service construction and composition; and User experience validation
Cooltown (HP) http://www.cooltown.hp.com	Cooltown's vision is of a technology future where people, places, and things are first class citizens of the connected world, wired and wireless—a place where e-services meet the physical world, where humans are mobile, devices and services are federated and context-aware, and everything has a web presence.	Service construction and composition; User experience enhancement and validation

(*continued on next page*)

TABLE I — *(Continued from previous page)*

Project	Vision/Goals	Challenges addressed
Jini™ (Sun) http://www.sun.com/jini	Jini network technology is an open architecture that enables developers to create network-centric services—whether implemented in hardware or software—that are highly adaptive to change.	Context-based adaptation
Oxygen (MIT) http://oxygen.lcs.mit.edu/	The Oxygen system aims to bring an abundance of computation and communication to users through natural spoken and visual interfaces, making it easy for them to collaborate, access knowledge, and automate repetitive tasks.	User experience enhancement and validation
Pervasive Computing at IBM Research http://www.research.ibm.com/compsci/mobile/	A collection of projects that aim to build the software infrastructure and tools for building pervasive computing applications, as well as to validate this infrastructure in concrete usage environments.	Software infrastructure; Application development tools; Context-aware computing; User interaction
Portolano (University of Washington) http://portolano.cs.washington.edu/	The Portolano project seeks to create a testbed for investigation into ubiquitous task-specific computing devices, which are so highly optimized to particular tasks that they blend into the world and require little technical knowledge on the part of their users.	Software infrastructure; Service construction and composition; User experience enhancement and validation
Semantic Web (W3C) http://www.semanticweb.org/	The Semantic Web is an extension of the current web in which information is given well-defined meaning, better enabling computers and people to work in cooperation.	Semantic modeling

5. Conclusion

As Mark Weiser described in his seminal article [27], ubiquitous computing is about interconnected hardware and software that are so ubiquitous that no one will notice their presence. This will enable people to focus on their tasks and on interacting with other people. This far-reaching vision is still far from our reach [14,17], and will require fundamental advances in semantic modeling, context-aware software infrastructure, application modeling and tools, and user experience validation. Going back to our scenario, in order to help Jane manage the fire, we need major advances in each of the challenge areas we identified (as well as in others we have not mentioned). Most importantly, all these advances will have to be integrated in a seamless manner into Jane's life so that she can use it without worrying about either its mechanics or its social appropriateness.

REFERENCES

[1] Banavar G., Beck J., Gluzberg E., Munson J., Sussman J., Zukowski D., "Challenges: An application model for pervasive computing", in: *Proceedings of the ACM Conference on Mobile Computing and Communications (Mobicom), Boston*, August 2000.

[2] Berners-Lee T., Hendler J., Lassila O., "The Semantic Web", *Scientific American* (May 2001).

[3] Bernstein A., "How can cooperative work tools support dynamic group processes? Bridging the specificity frontier", in: *Proceedings of the Computer Supported Cooperative Work*, ACM Press, Philadelphia, PA, December 2000.

[4] Cohen N.H., Purakayastha A., Wong L., Yeh D.L., "iQueue: A pervasive data-composition framework", in: *3rd International Conference on Data Management, Singapore*, January 8–11, 2002, pp. 146–153.

[5] Cohen N.H., Lei H., Castro P., Davis J.S. II, Purakayastha A., "Composing Pervasive Data Using iQL", in: *Proceedings of 4th IEEE Workshop on Mobile Computing Systems and Applications (WMCSA 2002), Callicoon, New York*, June 20–21, 2002, pp. 94–104.

[6] Cox M.T., Veloso M.M., "Supporting combined human and machine planning: an interface for planning by analogical reasoning", in: *Second International Conference on Case Based Reasoning, ICCBR*, Springer-Verlag, 1997, pp. 531–540.

[7] Ferguson G., Allen J., Miller B., "TRAINS-95: Towards a mixed-initiatve planning assistant", in: *3rd International Conference on Artificial Intelligence Planning Systems*, AAAI Press, 1996, pp. 70–77.

[8] Gruber T.R., "A translation approach to portable ontologies", *Knowledge Acquisition* **5** (2) (1993) 199–220.

[9] Grudin J., "Groupware and social dynamics: Eight challenges for developers", *Communication of the ACM* **45** (2002) 72–78.

[10] Grosof B., Horrocks I., Volz R., Decker S., "Description logic programs: Combining logic programs with description logic", in: *Proceedings of World Wide Web (WWW-2003), Budapest, Hungary*, 2003.

[11] Habermas J., *On the Pragmatics of Communication*, MIT Press, Cambridge, MA, 1998, p. 454.

[12] Heise, "Schweizer Datenschutzbeauftragter übt harte Kritik an den USA", Heise onLine http://www.heise.de/newsticker/data/anm-01.07.03-000/, 2003.

[13] Hewitt C., "Office are open systems", *ACM Transactions on Information Systems* **4** (3) (1986) 271–287.

[14] IEEE Pervasive Computing, "Reaching for Weiser's vision", *IEEE Pervasive Computing Magazine* **1** (1) (January–March 2002).

[15] Kahn J.M., Katz R.H., Pister K.S.J., "Next Century Challenges: Mobile networking for "smart dust" ", in: *Proceedings of ACM Mobicom 1999, Seattle, Washington*, August 1999, pp. 271–278.

[16] MacLean A., Carter K., Lövstrand L., Moran T., "User-tailorable systems: Pressing the issues with buttons", in: *Proceedings of Human Factors in Computing Systems, ACM-SIGCHI, Seattle, Washington*, 1990.

[17] "Mobicom Challenges", Challenges papers in *Proceedings of the ACM Conference on Mobile Computing and Communications (Mobicom)*, 1999, 2000, 2001.

[18] Orlikowski W.J., "The duality of technology: Rethinking the concept of technology in organizations", *Organization Science* **3** (3) (1992) 398–427.

[19] Seeger J.A., Lorsch J.W., Gibson C.F., *First National City Bank Operating Group (A)*, 474-165, Case, Harvard Business School, Boston, MA, 1975, p. 11.

[20] Sow D.M., Olshefski D.P., Beigi M., Banavar G.S., "Prefetching based on web usage mining", in: *IFIP/ACM/USENIX Middleware Conference 2003*, 2003, pp. 262–281.

[21] Ranganathan A., Campbell R.H., "A middleware for context-aware agents in ubiquitous computing environments", in: *IFIP/ACM/USENIX Middleware Conference 2003*, 2003, pp. 143–161.

[22] Suchman L.A., *Plans and Situated Actions: The Problem of Human–Machine Communication*, Cambridge Univ. Press, Cambridge, UK, 1987.

[23] Taylor F.W., *The Principles of Scientific Management*, Harper & brothers, New York, London, 1911, p. 144.

[24] UDDI.org., "UDDI Technical White Paper", 2000, pp. 12, http://www.uddi.org.

[25] Van Harmelen F., Hendler J., Horrocks I., McGuinness D., Patel-Schneider P., Stein L.A., "OWL web ontology language reference", WD-owl-ref-20030331, W3C working draft, World Wide Web Consortium, Cambridge, MA, 2003.

[26] Veloso M.M., "Toward mixed-initiative rationale-supported planning", in: A. Tate (Ed.), *Advanced Planning Technology: Technological Achievements of the ARPA/Rome Laboratory Planning Initiative*, AAAI Press, Menlo Park, CA, 1996, pp. 277–282.

[27] Weiser M., "The computer for the twenty-first century", *Scientific American* (September 1991).

[28] Zuboff S., *In the Age of the Smart Machine: The Future of Work and Power*, Basic Books, New York, NY, 1998, 468.

Introduction to MBASE (Model-Based (System) Architecting and Software Engineering)

DAVID KLAPPHOLZ

Department of Computer Science
Stevens Institute of Technology
USA
d.klappholz@worldnet.att.net

DANIEL PORT

Information Technology Management
University of Hawaii, Manoa
USA
dport@hawaii.edu

Abstract

Even when sophisticated software development process is used, e.g., the Stakeholder Win Win Risk-Driven Spiral Process, software development projects often fail. A prime reason for this failure is unresolved, often undetected, differences among stakeholders' sets of assumptions—their "models"—of various aspects of the project. MBASE is an approach to identifying "model clashes" so that their risks can be dealt with. Although it was originally developed as an extension to plan-driven development processes like the Stakeholder Win Win Risk-Driven Spiral Process, it can be adapted for use with any type of development process from Agile to Plan-driven. We discuss the notion of a "model," the various types of "model clashes" and their consequences, and the MBASE approach to dealing with them.

ADVANCES IN COMPUTERS, VOL. 62
ISSN: 0065-2458/DOI 10.1016/S0065-2458(03)62005-X

1. Introduction

MBASE [8,9] is a framework that can be used with any type of software development process, from Agile to Plan-driven [10], to deal with "model clashes," a type of problem that has sabotaged many development projects and that had not, to the authors' knowledge, been dealt with systematically before MBASE's introduction in 1998 [8].

In Section 1.1 we discuss the notion of models in software development, and, in Section 1.2 model clashes, and their potentially severe consequences. In Section 2, we discuss retrospective methods for dealing with model clashes, show that their use is infeasible, except in the case of very small projects, and introduce the notion of dealing with model clashes during model construction—the foundation of MBASE. In Section 3 we define and elaborate the MBASE approach and in Section 4 we discuss MBASE and experiences in its application.

1.1   Software Engineering Models

Stakeholders in a software development project typically include customers, end users, developers, and maintainers. Additional stakeholders may include marketers, venture capitalists, proprietors of collaboratively-developed interoperating products, and others, specific ones depending upon the project's specific circumstances. In the case of safety-critical systems such as automobiles and medical systems, the general public are also stakeholders.

When an individual becomes a stakeholder in a new or ongoing software development project, s/he usually approaches it with some assumptions about how it will/should proceed and what its outcome will/should be. Even a customer who has never before participated in a software development project comes to it with assumptions:

- at the very least, assumptions about the organizational objective for engaging in the project, and the benefits to be realized;
- possibly, assumptions about the cost of developing the software;
- possibly, some idea—perhaps incorrect—about the way customers and developers interact during a development project;
- perhaps, assumptions—often erroneous—concerning what developers know about the way organizations involved in the customer's line of business operate.

The naive customer is also likely to be lacking assumptions that might avoid later disappointment, e.g., assumptions about the need for maintenance and its cost, or, to put it differently, the naive customer is likely to tacitly assume that the only cost will be that of developing the software product.

Developers coming to a new project are likely to have assumptions about: which software development process will be used, say Waterfall, because their computer science education emphasized it; their demands on customer and end-user time during the course of the project; the amount of cost and schedule slippage that the customer should be willing to tolerate; etc.

Different stakeholders may have assumptions on related issues; some of their assumptions on a given issue may be consistent with one another, and some may not. Different types of stakeholder are also likely to have assumptions on different sets of issues. In what follows we will term a set of assumptions on a specific issue a "model."

While stakeholders often come to a development project with some general models, most of the detailed models involved in a project are developed as the project progresses. The developer's models include representations that s/he has created of various aspects of the ultimate product and of the process whereby it will be developed. These models typically include such artifacts as UML diagrams, Entity-Relationship Diagrams, etc. They also include such artifacts as Gantt charts, Pert charts, and cost/effort/schedule estimates. The ultimate representation/model is the software itself.

An important property of those models is that they are likely to change, some only slightly, but some drastically, as a project progresses, for example, as prototypes cause end users and/or customers to realize that developers aren't envisioning details of operation in the "right" way, as business cases clarify the relative importance of different features, etc.

In a project that uses a Plan-driven development process, developers document models, not just their own, but, also those of other stakeholders, in writing. In large development organizations or in organizations subject to industry or government standards, the precise titles and the nature of the content of each of the mandated documents is strictly specified, either by company policy or by the relevant industry or government standards. In an agile project, models are, naturally, developed, and are discussed by relevant stakeholders, but far less emphasis is placed on writing them down, or on preserving those that are; rather, a document is produced and preserved only when its continuing value to the project or users can be demonstrated.

Regardless of the process used in a development project and regardless of whether that process requires that models be discussed only verbally or written down to either loose or tight specifications, it is clear that the developers must create models in the following product- and process-related areas:

- Operational Concept: product's objectives and relation to organization objectives; product's scope; people and other software with which the product will interact; operational scenarios; perhaps, the direction in which the objectives are likely to evolve over time.

- Requirements: product's detailed functions, perhaps prioritized; details of product's interfaces; necessary quality attribute (reliability, availability, maintainability, etc.) levels.

- Architecture/Design: logical and physical elements/components that will constitute the product, and their relationships.

- Development Plan: the development process to be used; schedules and milestones; individual developers' responsibilities.

- Business Case: project rationale, including costs, value-added and return on investment estimates; process rationale, requirements satisfaction; project risk assessment.

It is easy to see that a project runs most smoothly when the following is true of all stakeholders' models:

- Each model is internally consistent. That is, in no model is there a set of assumptions that contradict one another, nor is there a set of assumptions, whose logical consequences contradict one another;

- An individual stakeholder's models—on different issues—are consistent with one another;

- Different stakeholders' models on the same aspect of the product/project are consistent with one another.

Plan-driven software development processes [10,16] typically require inter-document (traceability) references that can be viewed as a small first step toward verifying certain aspects of consistency; some [18,17] require that a document, with

els other than success models. As a project proceeds, most stakeholders mentally create and populate models of the other three types—product, project, and property. Some of a stakeholder's original success model assumptions may gain (additional) membership in one or more of that stakeholder's other models. An assumption can, thus, be a member of multiple different models. For example, as is suggested above, a nine-month delivery constraint or a $2,000,000 budget constraint might start as assumptions in a customer's success model, and may later be incorporated into developers' property models. Elaborations on success model assumptions and/or on ways of achieving them also often become parts of other-than-success models.

In a software development project, some stakeholders' initial models are revealed during early project meetings. Particular assumptions or entire models are often revealed to their holder, who didn't previously realize that s/he had assumptions on various topics, at the same time as they are revealed to other stakeholders. Often, inconsistencies, or "clashes," between or among stakeholder models, are uncovered and are discussed at project meetings; some are resolved and some may be temporarily tabled, to be revisited later. As a project proceeds, dropped assumptions, changed assumptions, and new assumptions are often recognized and discussed, and new inconsistencies are often revealed, and either resolved or tabled.

Product-product model clashes, being the most obvious, have been recognized and discussed [13] in the past; with few exceptions, however, most other types of clash (product-process, product-property, process-property, process-process, etc.) received little or no attention before the introduction of MBASE [8].

1.1.2   Common Models

The following table illustrates common clusters of generic success model assumptions of the four major types of stakeholder:

- Users:

- The product shall include a sizeable number of features.

- I want to be free to require additional features as I think of them over the course of the project.

- Requirements shall remain changeable for as long as possible into the project.

- The product shall be compatible with as many as possible, preferably all, of the products that I currently use.

- I want to be involved in the decision as to whether the new software product is needed, in who should be engaged to do the development, and, should there be go/no-go decisions along the way, in those decisions as well.

- The development contract shall be flexible so that changes to aspects of both the project and the product that affect me can be made as late as I want.
- The product shall be ready at a very early date.

- Maintainers:

- Transition of the product into production use shall require a minimum amount of my, and my staff's, time.
- Maintenance of the product shall require a minimum amount of my, and my staff's, time—by being developed using languages and COTS products with which I am familiar.
- The product shall be compatible with most or all of the products that I already maintain.
- I want to be involved in the decision as to whether a new software product is needed, in who should be engaged to do the development, and, should there be go/no-go decisions along the way, in those decisions as well.

- Acquirers (Customers):

- The product shall produce a significant return on investment and/or other significant benefits related to my organization's business objectives (and my own personal objectives).
- The product shall be built at a low cost and shall be ready at an early date.
- The product shall comply with all potentially relevant government standards.
- The product's GUI shall not be perceived to be offensive to people of either gender or to members of any ethnic group.
- I shall get credit within my organization for initiating the project and shall have ultimate control over its course.
- The development contract shall tie down the developers to the greatest extent possible (and shall tie me down to the least extent possible).

- Developers:

- The development contract should tie me down to the least extent possible.
- The budget and schedule should have sufficient slack for me to be able to finish the job regardless of what problems I run into; furthermore both budget and schedule should always remain negotiable as the project proceeds.
- The requirements should be fixed as early as possible, and should change as little as possible.

– The development team should be free to choose any development process we like, and should be free to program in the language(s) that we prefer.
– The development team will be formed by common agreement of potential members—and its members will decide on later additions, should any become necessary.
– The development team should be free to choose which COTS products will be incorporated into the product.

Less obvious models used by software developers, but ones that can have critical effects on software development projects, are the sets of assumptions—and their consequences—underlying:

– each software development process, e.g., RUP, XP, SCRUM, other agile, RAD, JAD, Risk-Driven Spiral, etc.;
– each complexity/cost/schedule estimation method, e.g., function points, feature points, COCOMOII [4], etc.;
– software analysis, design and implementation methods such as OO;
– analysis and design notations such as the various types of UML diagram; etc.;
– choices of equipment, infrastructure software, programming languages, etc.

As an example, the following constitute a simple version of the key assumptions underlying the Waterfall model:

(1) Participants can determine all requirements in advance of implementation.
(2) Requirements have no unresolved, high-risk implications such as

– risks associated with commercial-off-the shelf software choices;
– consequences of cost, schedule, performance, security, user interface, and organizational issues.

(3) Participants understand the right architecture for implementing the requirements.
(4) Stated requirements match the expectations of all the system's key stakeholders.
(5) The requirements' nature will change little during development and evolution.
(6) Deadlines allow enough calendar time to proceed sequentially through design, implementation, testing, and deployment.

Knowing what model assumptions are being made is often a vital element in managing or avoiding potentially risky situations. For example, assumption (1) stipulates that participants can determine requirements in advance of implementation. Project staff that believes this or that collect progress payments by delivering a complete requirements specification under a Waterfall-Process contract may formalize user-interface formats and behaviors as ironclad requirements specifications, and then build the system to those specifications. This can easily result in a delivered system with a GUI that fails the user's IKIWISI[1] success model test. Inevitably, the client either rejects the system or demands a major rework effort that is both expensive and time-consuming. Assumptions (2), (3), and (4) frequently conflict with property-model assumptions if a software acquisition hastily locks the project into unrealizable property-level contract requirements. We now take a closer look at how model assumptions may conflict and their potential consequences.

1.2   Model Clashes

A model clash is an inconsistency between/among different models of a single stakeholder or between/among same or different models of different stakeholders. If one model belonging to a single stakeholder contains inconsistent assumptions, then, formally speaking, that model is "unsound," i.e., it can't properly be called "a model." In the present discussion we will ignore this fine point and will use the term "model clash" to include the situation in which a single "model" is unsound as well as the case in which two different models are inconsistent with one another.

The simplest type of model-clash creating inconsistency is between an assumption and its negation, e.g., between one developer's process model assumption of "a waterfall process will be used to develop the product" and another developer's process model assumption of "a waterfall process will not be used to develop the product." Some model clashes result from assumptions whose contradiction is slightly less immediate, but which any literate person would catch, e.g., between a customer's property model assumption that "the product will be delivered in six months" and a developer's property model assumption that "the product will be delivered in twelve months."

Many model clashes, though, exist between assumptions that only an experienced software developer, or software development customer, would understand to have contradictory consequences, e.g.,

- between a customer's success model assumption that "requirements will have to remain somewhat flexible until well into the product's development" and a developer's process model assumption that "a Waterfall Process will be used to develop the product,"

[1]In modern software development projects, the customer and users often don't know precisely what precise functionality and precise interface they want/need until they see it in a prototype that is developed iteratively with their participation; hence the term IKIWISI: I'll Know It When I See It.

- between a developer's process model assumption that "Extreme Programming will be used to develop the project" and a customer's success model assumption that "we are so understaffed, that we will meet with developers during the project's first week, and will not meet with developers again until the product is ready to be installed."
- between:
  - a development manager's process model assumption of "the product has to be ready by Comdex or we'll lose too much market share to stay afloat, so we'll work on all the product's features and I'll move additional developers from some other project into this one in the last two weeks if it doesn't look like we'll make it,"
  - and the customer's success model assumption of "better a reduced set of end-to-end core capabilities by Comdex than a complete product delivered the day after Comdex."

How do model clashes occur? There are many situations that lead to model clashes. Many of them are completely "innocent" in that stakeholders involved are following accepted (or perhaps even mandated) practice. Some common model clash situations that may lead to serious project risk happen when:

- An inexperienced stakeholder doesn't realize that two of his/her assumptions are inconsistent, e.g., the process model assumption that a Waterfall Process will be used and the success model or product model assumption that product will be largely or completely constructed from COTS products.
- One or more stakeholders change their assumptions on a particular issue over time so that previously consistent assumptions become inconsistent; e.g., stakeholders agree that requirements should be fixed, and, subsequently, one realizes that there are critical requirements that must be changed.
- An apparently reasonable assumption turns out to be false, e.g., a developer's property model contains an assumption that a particular COTS product will perform at a given level, and testing proves him/her wrong.
- A stakeholder accidentally forgets to articulate a critical assumption; e.g., the customer forgets to indicate that the product's financial success depends on its availability on multiple platforms, and the developer assumes that the product need run on only one—the most popular—platform.
- A stakeholder doesn't bother to articulate a critical assumption because "everyone knows that …;" e.g., a customer neglects to describe a project- or product-critical aspect of the way his/her business operates, and the developers, having no previous experience in the customer's field, aren't among the "everyone" who knows that the customer's business operates that way.

1.2.1 Model Clash Patterns

Figure 1 shows common model clashes that occur between product, process, and property models of the common clusters of generic success model assumptions for the four major types of stakeholder as described previously in Section 1.1.2.

Although it may not be entirely obvious, clashes can occur between models of every pair of the four types, as is exemplified in Table I.

1.2.2 Consequences of Model Clashes

Consequences of model clashes can be:

- insignificant in the case of clashes whose negative effects on the project or product are easily reversed. An example would be two (different stakeholders') product models that include different ways of approaching the graphical design of web pages;
- time- and resource-consuming in the case of a clash resulting from:
    - a developer's (success model) desire to be free to start a more interesting project in a month, and, as a consequence, a product model incorporating a quick-to-implement but inflexible architecture;
    - a customer's (success model) need for the product to be extensible;
- catastrophic in the case of:
    - an inexperienced development manager's process model in which the development team will proceed apace on all the product's features, with the idea of doubling the team's size if progress hasn't been sufficient a month before the scheduled delivery date;
    - a marketing manager's success model requiring that the product be shown at Comdex two days after the scheduled delivery date;

The MasterNet project, described in [14] is one of many important software development projects that turned into catastrophes because of undetected model clashes and/or detected but unresolved model clashes, and/or detected but badly resolved model clashes. The MasterNet project was to develop a system that would update and automate the online generation of monthly statements for Bank of America's trust accounts. The project began in the early 1980s with a $22 million budget and a two-year completion schedule.

Project contractor/developer Premier Systems tried to build MasterNet by scaling up a small existing trust system. Their misguided effort took five years, cost $80 million, and delivered a system that Bank of America rejected. Worse yet, the project tarnished Bank of America's reputation, causing some of its major customers to lose confidence in the bank. The total number of institutional accounts dropped from 800

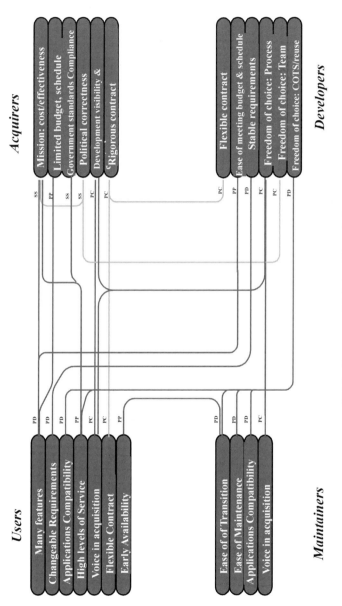

Fig. 1. Common model clashes (MasterNet).

TABLE I
MODEL CLASHES

	Product model	Process model	Property model	Success model
Product model	• Structure clash[a] • Traceability clash[b] • Architecture style clash[c]	• COTS-driven product vs. Waterfall (requirements-driven) process	• Interdependent multiprocessor product vs. linear performance scalability model	• 4GL-based product vs. low development cost and performance scalability
Process model		• Multi-increment development process vs. single-increment support tools	• Evolutionary development process vs. Rayleigh-curve cost model	• Waterfall process model vs. "I'll know it when I see it" (IKIWISI) prototyping success model
Property model			Minimize cost and schedule vs. maximize quality ("Quality is free")	Fixed-price contract vs. easy-to-change, volatile requirements
Success model				Golden Rule vs. stakeholder win-win

[a] Structure clashes between a project's input and output structures [15].

[b] Traceability clashes among a product's requirements, design and code [17]; and architectural style.

[c] Clashes in integrating commercial off-the-shelf (COTS) or other reusable software components [13].

to 700, while managed assets shrank from $38 billion to $34 billion. The MasterNet project suffered from the following model clashes:

- *Product-Property.* The MasterNet users' (product model) desire of many features resulted in 3.5 million lines of code, which conflicted with Bank of America's, i.e., the customers' (property model of) limited budget and schedule. This conflict led to a large overrun in budget and schedule.

- *Property-Product.* The customer's budget and schedule (property) models assumed stable requirements, but the users' and developer's (product) model of frequent feature changes also contributed to the large overrun.

- *Product-Product.* The developer's (product) model of users' needs provided features, such as full customer access, that matched poorly with real users' (product model) needs such as accurate and timely reports.

– *Product-Property.* The developer's (product) model of server to be used—one manufactured by Prime, Inc.—offered inadequate performance and reliability to meet users' desired level of service (property) models. Even after several upgrades, the Prime system suffered repeated performance overloads and crashes.

– *Product-Success.* The developer's (product) model of server to be used also conflicted with the users' and maintainers' applications- compatibility (success) model, as Bank of America had relied exclusively on IBM hardware and software up to that point.

– *Process-Property.* The maintainers' tightly scheduled transition (process) model conflicted with the testing delays brought on by the customer's limited development budget and schedule (property) model.

The clashes shown with solid lines in Fig. 1 are among those that occurred in the MasterNet project.

2. Dealing With Model Clashes

The first step in dealing with model clashes is identifying them. In the present section, we discuss two retrospective approaches to model-clash identification, i.e., two approaches to identifying model clashes after models have been constructed. In Section 3 we discuss MBASE's prospective approach to dealing with model clashes, i.e., an approach in which clashes are identified and resolved as models are constructed.

2.1 Retrospective Approaches

The most obvious way to identify model clashes is to write down all assumptions in all stakeholders' models, and to perform pair-wise consistency analysis. If each individual stakeholder's model is already known to be sound, a bit of organizational help can be had by first sorting assumptions by stakeholder and organizing them as in the "spider web" diagram of the sort shown in Fig. 1. This seat-of-the-pants approach is extremely time consuming for a project of more than minimal size, and relies entirely on the developer's experience and talent.

A second retrospective method based on [1], one that provides the developer with substantive aid in finding clashes, starts with:

(1) a list/table of areas for which models must exist in any software development project;
(2) for each model area, a list/table of critical issues that a model must address;

(3) for each major software development method/process, a list/table of that method's/process' assumptions on each major issue on which it makes assumptions (see below and [1] for examples);

(4) An "inverted" version of the lists/tables in item (3) that can be used to determine if a method/process chosen by the development team is consistent with stakeholder assumptions regarding the project at hand.

Examples of instances of the various lists are, respectively:

(1) The model areas shown in the middle column of the "Model Assumptions Identification Taxonomy" of Fig. 2. (The model areas are: Requirements; Architecture & Design; Coding–Testing–Integration–Transition; Maintenance; Environment; Developer(s); and Customer(s).)

(2) For each model area, the critical issues, shown in the right-most column of Fig. 2, that must be addressed by the model(s) in that area. For example, a requirements model for a project must address the issues of:

  – when requirements are likely to be complete, i.e., whether they are complete at the project's start or must evolve over time;

  – the stability of requirements, i.e., the likelihood that requirements already agreed upon will have to be changed during the course of the project;

  – whether it is a foregone conclusion that requirements can be met, or whether meeting the requirements is a challenge (risk issue);

  – how clearly requirements must be specified, i.e., how much leeway developers have in deciding their fine points;

  – the detail with which requirements are/must be documented.

(3) The waterfall process model assumptions and the COTS development model assumptions (see [1] for details on this).

(4) The model clash tables of [1], a small excerpt from which is shown in Table II.

3. MBASE

MBASE is founded upon pro-active, rather than retrospective, model "integration." In a retrospective approach, models are first created and then checked for model clashes. In MBASE's prospective approach, model clashes are identified and dealt with during the construction of models. But attempting to integrate every model, during its construction, with every other, partially-developed or completed, model would be implausibly time consuming if there were no further aid/direction.

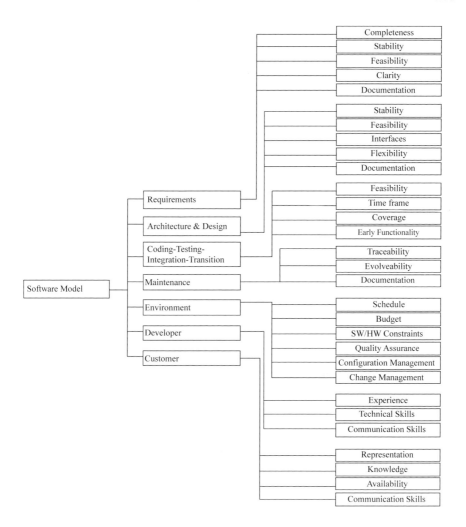

FIG. 2. Model assumptions identification taxonomy.

An approach to this is to boil-down to the essentials what is required in order to enact effective model-clash identification and avoidance through model integration. Through years of refinement and empirical study a set of essentials has been established that if incorporated into a development process, will substantially reduce the risk of model-clashes [1]. These essentials define MBASE and any approach that in-

TABLE II
EXAMPLE OF MODEL-CLASH IDENTIFICATION

Model	Assumption	Completeness before design	Clash
Waterfall	Developer defines and documents a complete set of requirements for each system capability before starting the system detail design	Yes	
COTS	System requirements and architectures are often driven by the capabilities and structures of the final set of COTS components selected for integration	No	

corporates them is deemed an MBASE approach. These essentials will be introduced and subsequently elaborated.

3.1 MBASE Model Integration Framework

The first essential comes from extensive empirical studies of model usage in large numbers of projects and analysis of their model-clash patterns. These studies reveal that the highest-risk model clashes are those that violate one or more of the relationships, shown in Fig. 3, among the four model types: success, product, process, and property.

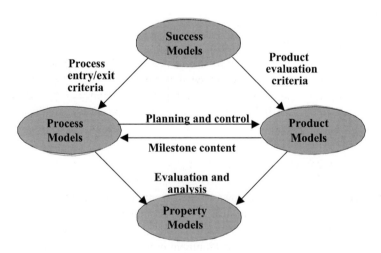

FIG. 3. Element integration.

The five relationships shown in Fig. 3, with examples, are as follows:

Success → *Product*: A product must satisfy the success criteria agreed upon among critical stakeholders. Another way of looking at this is that the agreed upon success models imply evaluation criteria for the product. Looked at this way, product models must represent a product that satisfies the evaluation criteria established by the success models. For example:

- An organization is developing a new hardware/software system; the organization has a strategic partnership with a specific hardware vendor; one element of the organization's success model will, therefore be the continued use of the vendor's products. Use of the vendor's products thus becomes an evaluation criterion for the product; it is violated by a developer's product model in which the new system incorporates COTS products that do not run on the vendor's platforms.

- A university service department is having an outside team develop an enhancement of its web site; the budget is reasonably low. One desired, but not absolutely required, feature is the ability to receive payment for services by credit card, as opposed to just by mail. The development team designs and implements a system that uses Paypal. Because of the low budget, the designers decide to use mySQL as the database engine. Because of the development team's technology preferences, and the members' backgrounds, they decide to use PHP as the scripting language. The developers do an excellent job of eliciting the client's functional requirements, but fail to elicit the client's success model elements to the effect that:
  - the head of the department is not willing to take on personal financial liability for departmental activities;
  - the web site must be hosted by the university's IT department.

  The university doesn't have a Paypal account, so the department head would have to open one and assume personal liability. The university's IT department does not support mySQL or PHP. As a result, the product fails to meet critical success criteria and, though implemented and tested extremely well, cannot be made operational.

- A research department of a high-tech company is having a team develop a system for posting of papers and research results for use by its members. A product model includes universal posting rights as well as universal access. The customer's success model naturally includes avoiding legal liability. The product model violates the implied evaluation criterion of allowing only legal postings by not vetting posts and, thereby, allowing users to post copyrighted material without appropriate compensation to copyright holders.

- A software company is developing a product, on speculation, with the intention of demonstrating it at Comdex in nine months. The project staff consists of two developers and there is no budget for hiring additional staff. The product models include full maintenance and user documentation, an impossibility given the time to Comdex.

Success → *Process*: A software development process is defined by a set of activities and conditions, or criteria, for beginning and finishing—entering and exiting—each activity. (In this context, "process" refers not just to the overall process to be used to execute the project—XP, waterfall, spiral, etc.—but, rather, includes the result of applying the high-level process's approach to the details of a particular software development project. It thus includes individual activities, dependencies among them, etc.) Success models must provide or, at least, be consistent with, entry and exit criteria for process.—Each milestone review in the process needs to use the agreed-on success models as pass/fail criteria. For example:

- A client's IKIWISI success model is consistent with an overall process consisting of the construction of a prototype followed by evolutionary development.
- A project with a success model of extending a successful family of software products to meet developing market trends is consistent with a waterfall development process. In fact, the success model likely dictates a waterfall process as the least costly so long as the market trends are not changing too fast.
- A marketing manager's success model of presenting a product at the next Comdex is inconsistent with a developer's process model of performing beta testing before product release or of proving correctness before release.
- The stakeholders of a project that is developing a system on which lives may depend has the, extremely obvious, success model of no loss of life after the system goes operational. This success model is consistent with—probably dictates—that a testing method such as "clean room" be used or that formal techniques be used to prove correctness (exit criteria for testing).

Process ↔ *Product*: Process models must provide plans and control for product model development (and product models must supply milestone content for process models). For example:

- In general, the schedule (process model) of any project must include tasks/activities covering all the architectural (product model), class diagram (product model), etc. elements; it must also address the question of which elements will be developed by which developer(s), and when; it must also conform to product element dependencies.

- In general, the process model of any development project must include (control) details for the validation and verification of developed product (model) components, for the review of product (model) components, for the pace (control) and adjustment of pace of development of product (model) components.
- A very short schedule requires a product architecture (model) architected for ease of shedding lower-priority features.

Property → *Process* & *Property* → *Product*: Cost and schedule (property) models are used to evaluate and analyze the consistency of product, process, and success (not shown in diagram) models. In general:

- In any software development project, a cost-schedule (property model) estimate would determine whether implementation of the proposed (product model) design/architecture following the proposed (process model) schedule would result in software with the required (product model) capabilities and levels of service in the proposed (success model) time and within the proposed (success model) budget.

3.2   MBASE Process Integration Framework

The Model Integration Framework shows a static picture of inter-model consistencies that must be achieved for project success. Moreover, as indicated earlier, these are the very consistency patterns that are most frequently violated in actual projects, and, in fact, whose violations are among those most frequently responsible for project failure. Because it shows only a static picture, the Model Integration Framework doesn't completely describe the MBASE notion of integrating models, to eliminate risky clashes, during the construction of models. This latter, dynamic, function is served by the Process Integration framework shown in Fig. 4. This dynamic integration framework dictates how particular model-integration activities must relate to each other. In contrast to model-element integration which deals chiefly with the relationships between values contained within models as discussed in Section 3.1, process integration indicates what model development and stakeholder activities must be present between the models focus on high-risk model identification and avoidance. As to be expected, these integration activities are highly dependent on the model-element integrations, but are not equivalent to them. A concrete example of how the two integration frameworks collaborate is illustrated in detail within the extend example of Section 3.5.

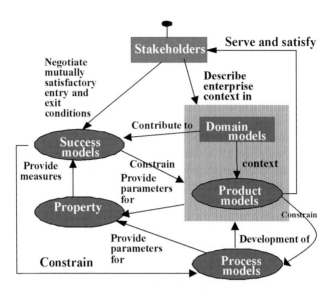

FIG. 4. MBASE process integration.

3.3 MBASE Anchor Points

The idea of standardized milestones, or "anchor points," that divide software development projects into phases is at least as old as the Waterfall Process, whose anchor points are: completion of system requirements, completion of software requirements, completion of preliminary design, completion of detailed design, completion of implementation (coding), completion of unit testing, completion of software acceptance testing, and completion of system acceptance testing.

Where Waterfall is not used, developers still need well-defined anchor points to plan, organize, monitor, and control a project. A critical reason for using anchor points is to allow critical stakeholders to periodically—at important phase change points—determine if a project is proceeding satisfactorily and whether it pays to continue its execution. In [2], Boehm suggests three anchor points for use with any software development process, spiral or other. The three anchor points are called Life Cycle Objectives (LCO), Life Cycle Architecture (LCA), and Initial Operational Capability (IOC). In very simple terms, a project reaches LCO when developers have produced a first cut at: objectives to be achieved for the sponsoring organization; a design/architecture; a project plan; and a demonstration of the feasibility of achieving the objectives through implementation of the design/architecture using the project plan.

TABLE III
LCO, LCA, IOC SUCCESS CRITERIA

LCO	LCA	IOC
For at least one architecture, a system built to that architecture will:	For a specific detailed architecture, a system built to that architecture will:	An implemented architecture, an operational system that has:
– Support the core Operational Concept.	– Support the elaborated Operational Concept.	– Realized the Operational Concept.
– Satisfy the core Requirements.	– Satisfy the elaborated Requirements.	– Implemented the initial Operational Requirements.
– Be faithful to the Prototype(s).	– Be faithful to the Prototype(s).	– Prepared a system operation and support plan.
– Be buildable within the budgets and schedules in the plan.	– Be buildable within the budgets and schedules in the plan.	– Prepared the initial site(s) in which the system will be deployed for transition.
– Show a viable business case.	– Have all major risks resolved or covered by a risk management plan.	– Prepared the users, operators, and maintainers to assume their operational roles.
– Have its key stakeholders committed to support the Elaboration Phase (to LCA).	– Have its key stakeholders committed to support the full life cycle.	

In similarly simple terms, a project reaches LCA when developers have produced a detailed/mature version: of objectives to be achieved for the sponsoring organization; of a design/architecture; of a project plan; and of a demonstration of the feasibility of achieving the objectives through implementation of the design/architecture using the project plan.

A slightly more detailed description of the definitions of LCO, LCA, and IOC may be found in Table III.

The precise definition of each of the three milestones is in terms of a specific set of models, the degree of development that each must have attained, and the types of consistency that must be demonstrated between/among them in order for a project to attain that milestone. These naturally vary depending upon the specific development process being used.

3.4 MBASE Risk Management and Stakeholder (Win-Win) Involvement

For the first few decades of software development, the Waterfall process— requirements definition, followed by analysis and design, followed by implementation, testing, and deployment in that order—was the most commonly used development process. Developers working in later phases of a Waterfall project regularly recognized that errors had been made in earlier phases, and performed the rework necessary to correct them, though doing so violated the strict definition of Waterfall Process. Unfortunately, neither commercial nor governmental contracting practices caught up with these realities quickly enough and, as a result, many Waterfall projects ran into devastating technical and legal problems.

The worst problem with Waterfall Process is that early fixing of requirements doesn't allow the developer the flexibility to deal reasonably with a project's high-risk aspects if there are any.[2] For example, it is often difficult to know in advance how expensive it might be for a proposed new system to achieve a specified response time—or even if current technology can support the response time. The Waterfall Process, however, dictates that some response time must be fixed in the requirements phase. A more prudent approach, but one inconsistent with strict Waterfall Process would be to:

- recognize that demanding the proposed response time is risky;
- buy information about the risk by doing a partial design and implementation of the response-time-related parts of the proposed system and measuring response times attainable using one or more available technologies;
- finalize an attainable response time requirement based upon tests performed— or cancel the system's development because the response time initially proposed is critical to the system's success, but is not attainable, at an acceptable cost, using current technology.

These days an equally important reason for doing risk-driven software development is that much software development is COTS-based [6]. Among the risks that arise from the incorporation of COTS products into a new software product are that:

- a COTS product may not have precisely the functionality promised in vendor literature;
- a COTS product may not live up to quality attribute levels promised in vendor literature;
- a new release of a COTS product may not support the same interfaces as previous versions; i.e., it may not integrate with other components of the new product as did earlier versions;

---

[2]Waterfall Process works perfectly well in many types of highly-precedented project, for example: in the re-implementation, for a new platform, of a software product that has been successful on an older platform; in an implementation of the next member of a successful family of software products, where the new product's extensions of the old one have been gleaned from years of experience with the old product.

- a new release of a COTS product may not have precisely the same functionality and/or may not support the same quality attribute levels as did earlier versions;
- a COTS vendor may go bankrupt and no longer support periodically required increases in quality attribute levels.

It was for reasons like these that Boehm proposed [2] the Risk-Driven Spiral process for software development. While MBASE doesn't, by any means, require that the basic development process be the Spiral Process, every process can be viewed as having phases of some sort; the notion of being risk-driven in MBASE simply means:

- Establishing, for each phase:
  - product and project objectives;
  - constraints affecting both the product and the project;
  - alternative courses of action that can be taken to meet the objectives and satisfy the constraints;
- Evaluating the relative merits of the various alternatives, and their associated risks.
- Deciding upon the specific course of action (from among the possible alternatives) to be followed during the next phase.
- Validating the chosen course of action.
- Reviewing the validated choice and commencing the next phase.

MBASE's borrowing is, thus, not the notion of spirals/iterations, but, rather, the notion of:

- recognizing those aspects of a software development project that present high risks;
- buying information needed to resolve, mitigate or live with the risks, by whatever means is reasonable, e.g., various types of prototyping;
- committing to a course of action based upon the results of the above.

A recurring theme is the need to reconcile the key stakeholders' success models. Thus, a stakeholder win-win negotiation process becomes a key step in each spiral cycle of the MBASE approach, as shown in Fig. 5.

In the COMDEX application discussed previously (Section 3.1), for example, the initial spiral cycle would focus on evaluating COTS products and scoping the overall system to be buildable in nine months. In a subsequent spiral cycle, the next-level stakeholders would include representative users of the e-commerce system, and the reconciliation of their win conditions would include prototyping of the user interface

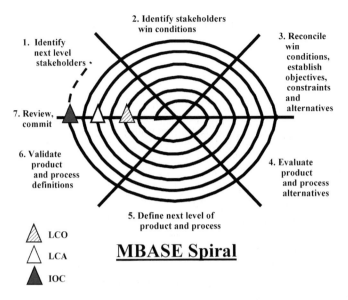

FIG. 5. The WinWin spiral with MBASE milestones.

to eliminate the risk of showing up at COMDEX with an unfriendly user interface. The MBASE tool support includes a groupware system called Easy WinWin, which enables distributed stakeholders to enter their win conditions and to negotiate mutually satisfactory (win-win) agreements with other stakeholders [7].

The WinWin spiral model in Fig. 5 provides another view of how risk considerations are used to reconcile stakeholder success conditions in terms of product, process, and property models. A complementary view was shown in Fig. 4 (see Section 3.2), which also identifies the win-win spiral model's role in guiding the early feedback cycles involved in defining and reconciling the system's domain, product, process, and property models.

3.5   MBASE Integration Example

The elements described above all work in concert to help identify and avoid potentially high-risk model clashes. The particular integration elements and activities are driven by the MBASE spiral (which incorporates the risk-driven stakeholder win-win approach) to deliver a comprehensive integrated model. To illustrate the synergistic application of MBASE elements, we consider the following example taken from an actual project. A USC Librarian presented the following problem statement for a multi-media information system:

I am interested in the problem of scanning medieval manuscripts in such a way that a researcher would be able to both read the content, but also study the scribe's hand, special markings, etc. A related issue is that of transmitting such images over the network.

We now describe how the model-integration steps within MBASE elements might be performed within the Medieval Manuscript (MM) project throughout one full MBASE spiral cycle. The initial goal here is to develop models that will satisfy the LCO success criteria (i.e., identify at least one feasible architecture). That is, pass the first anchor point milestone (as described in Section 3.3).

Spiral step 1: Identify initial stakeholders. The primary stakeholders for the MM are the librarian Mrs. W. who is an authority on the archival of medieval manuscripts and will serve as domain expert in addition to customer, and Mr. Z. a graduate student in Software Engineering who is leading the development team. Hence the initial stakeholder set for this step is Mrs. W. and Mr. Z. The Process Integration framework dictates that these stakeholder must work together to "describe the enterprise context" for the domain of the MM project. In this case, the enterprise context is "Multimedia Library Services" and the domain is "Multimedia Information Services." A Domain model was developed by making use of a domain description from a previous Multimedia Archive Library project. This step is illustrated graphically for this instance in Fig. 6.

Spiral step 2: Identify stakeholder win conditions. This step dictates that Mrs. W. and Mr. Z. converge on an initial set of mutually satisfactory win-conditions for the MM project. Aside from the functionally elements (e.g., main application functions,

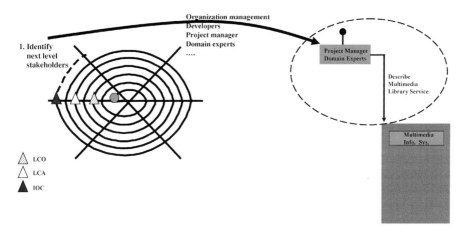

FIG. 6. MM project spiral step 1.

Humanized I/O, etc.), Mrs. W. wanted to ensure that development and operational costs did not outweigh the value MM could provide in a short amount of time (high return on her investment). As this project originated within a 2-semester software engineering course project, the project must be completed within 12 months. The win-conditions establish the initial Success and the Basic and Main capabilities that were negotiated to provide the candidate Product models (whose context was obtained from the Domain model created previously). (See Fig. 7.)

Spiral step 3: Reconcile win-conditions; establish objective, constraints, and alternatives. This is a major step in the model-integration process. Here the process integration framework dictates that Mrs. W. and Mr. Z. need to agree on what constitutes a mutually satisfactory starting and ending point for the project. In this case, "success" has been defined so that the MM product will have a high return on investment and be completed within 12 months. It was agreed that a high return on investment was likely to be achieved if enough "valuable" features were implemented. Here "enough" meant that there was a high-value for relatively little effort (i.e., "high-payoff"). The features were ordered according to development dependencies and value to the Librarians (in terms of time saved, lower staffing requirements, customer satisfaction, etc.). The "exit" point for the development was now defined as "build enough valuable features in order to obtain at least 80% of the overall expected value of the MM system." This is what is meant by the "high payoff" range. The model-integration framework dictates that this must be used to evaluate the Basic and Main features described in the Product models. In addition, Mr. W. had to choose a Process model that would likely develop the product into the high-payoff range and satisfy

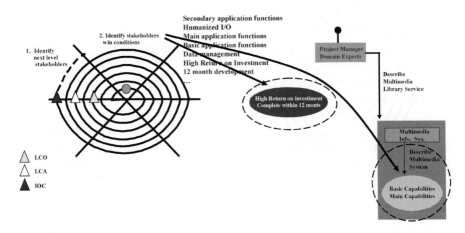

FIG. 7. MM project spiral step 2.

the 12-month schedule constraint. A Design to Schedule model was chosen to be compatible with this. (See Fig. 8.)

Spiral step 4: Evaluate product and process alternatives. In this step, the integration and process frameworks dictate that the Product models be evaluated with respect to their possible size and used to estimate the overall effort. A Function Point (FP) estimate was made for the Basic capabilities and used as the size input for a COCOMO II effort estimate. Again, as dictated by the MBASE integration framework, this effort estimate must reconcile with the 12-month development constraint within a design to schedule to deliver the high-payoff features. If it does not reconcile, then the development parameters must be adjusted (more staff, extra tools, buy COTS, etc.) or a different Process model must be considered. As a last resort, the high-payoff feature set can be re-negotiated. In the case of MM, some re-negotiation of the Basic Capabilities was needed. Specifically, it was agreed that a COTS package would be used to enable the user to navigate a manuscript image (zoom, move to a location, etc.) within a web browser. This increased the project cost and modified the specifics of some of the Basic Capability requirements. It will have to be verified that these changes do not reduce the value outside the high-payoff range. (See Fig. 9.)

Spiral step 5: Define next Product and Process elements and activities. At this point the Product models are refined into basic designs. The integration framework dictates that these designs must be used as input ("milestone content") to the Design to Schedule process. This must result in an explicit plan within the Design to Schedule process to implement the Basic Capabilities (however, the Design to Schedule process can and likely will include other plans). The high-risk potential due to the use of an unknown COTS package indicate that the development plan should include some prototyping of the COTS package under consideration and draft web-page implementations. (See Fig. 10.)

Spiral step 6: Validate product and process definitions. As per the process integration framework, Mr. Z. now verifies that the new effort estimate satisfies the 12-month development constraint and can be used as an explicit measure (preliminary) of likely success of the project. A problem occurred in that the COCOMO II effort estimate cannot adequately account for use of the COTS package now under consideration. This Property model now clashes with the new Product model (COTS). With this model clash identified, Mr. Z. chose to undertake some initial prototyping with the COTS package to determine what the COTS effort might be. After this, Mr. Z, was able to make a confident COTS integration effort estimate and add it to the COCOMO II effort predicted for implementing the Basic Capabilities outside of what the COTS package handles. (See Fig. 11.)

Spiral step 7: Review commitments. Now with slightly re-negotiated Basic Capabilities, verify that they still are compatible with the Success, Process, and Property

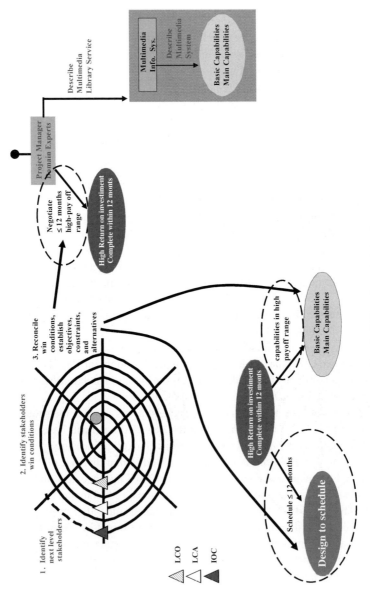

FIG. 8. MM project spiral step 3.

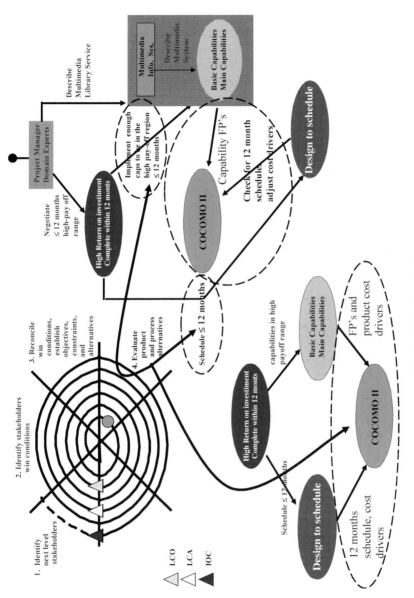

FIG. 9. MM project spiral step 4.

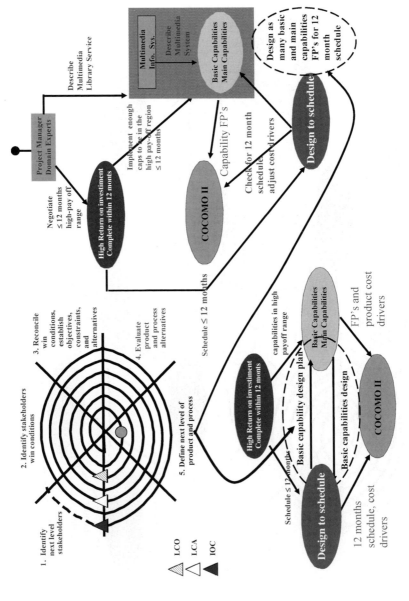

FIG. 10. MM project spiral step 5.

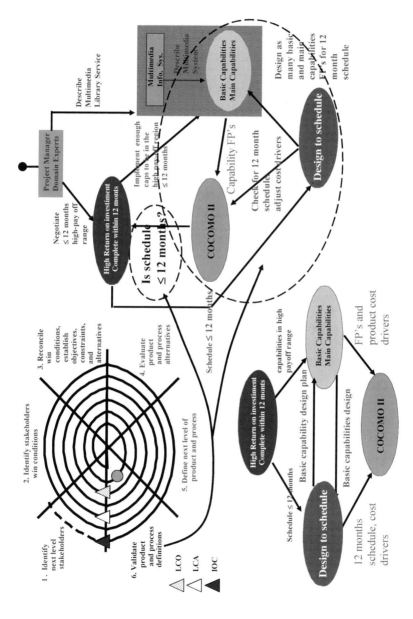

FIG. 11. MM project spiral step 6.

models. That is, buy the COTS package to implement the image navigation capabilities and custom build the remainder of the Basic Capabilities. (See Fig. 12.)

Our tour through one MBASE cycle has illustrated how the integration frameworks work together to drive a project towards the LCO anchor point while either avoiding model clashes as a matter of course (though judicious model choice or explicit sharing of information) or identifying potentially risky model clashes by explicitly verifying model element compatibility. While we did not explicit describe what particular activities evolved the project towards LCO, these are somewhat self evident given the definition of the integration frameworks. For example, developing the Success models and Product models contribute to the Operational Concept elements of the LCO.

3.6   MBASE Invariants

MBASE is intentionally very broad in order to encompass a broad spectrum of projects both large and small. Within the MBASE superset, there are five elements, the model integration guidelines, that are universal for all MBASE projects. These elements are called *invariants*. Additionally, there are elements of MBASE and of the process and method guidelines, which are categorized as *variants,* and can be adjusted according to particular project parameters (team size, application scope, etc.). Through use of the invariants and particular choices of these variants MBASE becomes a development process add-on framework/adjunct that can be used with any software development process, from agile to Plan-driven, for identifying and dealing with model clashes. For example, MBASE model integration, MBASE process integration, and the three other attributes that define MBASE can be attached/adjoined to XP, or SCRUM, or Waterfall, or Risk-Driven Spiral to form MBASE-XP, MBASE-SCRUM, MBASE-Waterfall, or MBASE-Risk-Driven Spiral.

There are five "MBASE invariants" based on the essentials described in Sections 3.1–3.4 that define MBASE. If X is a software development model, then X-BASE is the extended version of X in which:

(i) the model integration framework (discussed in Section 3.1) and
(ii) the process integration framework (discussed in Section 3.2) have been added to X;
(iii) the developers use the Life Cycle Objectives (LCO), Life Cycle Architecture (LCA), and Initial Operational Capability (IOC) milestones/anchor points (defined in Section 3.3) as stakeholder commitment points for proceeding from stage to stage of the project. (Note that [18] LCO is the milestone at the end of the Inception phase of a project, LCA is the milestone at the end of the Elaboration Phase, and IOC is the milestone at the end of the Construction phase.)

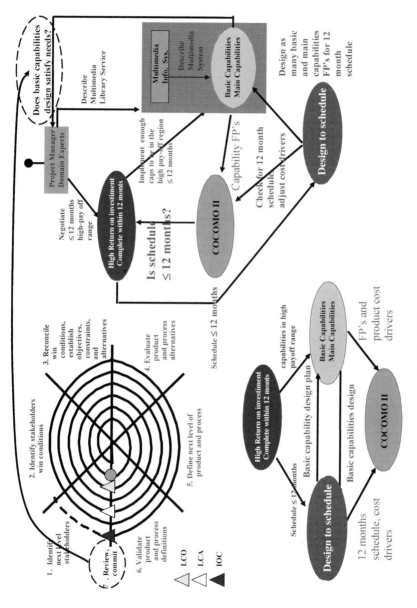

FIG. 12. MM project spiral step 7.

(iv) a stakeholder win-win relationship (defined in Section 3.4) is defined and sustained, in a fashion compatible with X, for the purpose of dealing with model clashes, throughout the project's life-cycle. This means that periodically:

- success-critical stakeholders are identified;
- each stakeholder participates in the integration of models relevant to him/her;
- models are modified, as required;
- all critical stakeholders come to an agreement on the latest, updated models to be used to further pursue the project.

(v) model integration activities are risk-driven as are contents of all artifacts produced during model integration (discussed further in Section 3.4). That is, such details as:

- the number of times that stakeholders meet between anchor points
- the specific issues/models dealt with in developing project artifacts other than LCO-, LCA-, and IOC-mandated issues/models (see below)
- the detail with which each issue/model is addressed
- and the total amount of time spent on model integration

be decided through an evaluation of their risk-reduction value.

The invariants impose a significant amount of structure on a process used to integrate models, yet they leave room to accommodate a number of important project-related choices. In fact, the invariants imply that certain choices must be "tailor" made per project. These are called MBASE "variants," i.e., choices of project details that are not dictated. Some of these include:

- The development process used to execute the project—XP, Scrum, RAD, waterfall, spiral, RUP, incremental, etc.
- The methods used to construct, or notations used to represent, specific models.
- The amount of development effort between anchor points.
- The staffing levels of the various, MBASE and non-MBASE project activities.

Table IV summarizes the MBASE invariants and variants which will be further elaborated in the subsequent sections.

3.7   Plan-Driven MBASE

As indicated previously, MBASE is intended for use with any software development process. Up to this point it has been used mainly with more "Plan-

TABLE IV
MBASE INVARIANTS AND VARIANTS

Invariants	Variants
(1) Defining and sustaining a stakeholder win-win relationship through the system's lifecycle. (2) Using the MBASE Model Integration Framework. (3) Using the MBASE Process Integration Framework. (4) Using the LCO and LCA Anchor Point milestones. (5) Ensuring that the content of MBASE artifacts and activities is risk-driven.	(1) Use of particular success, process, product, or property models. (2) Choice of process or product representation. (3) Degree of detail of process, product, property, or success modeling. (4) Number of spiral cycles or builds between anchor points. (5) Mapping of activities onto Inception–Elaboration–Construction–Transition phases. (6) Mapping of staff levels onto activities.

driven" or "heavier weight" development processes—variants of Stakeholder Win-Win Spiral Process. One such variant of MBASE has been used by over 1000 developers, on about 200 projects, in Barry Boehm's USC CS577, a two-semester graduate-level Introduction to Software Engineering. Other variants have been used by XEROX and the U.S. Army. Agile variants of MBASE are currently under development.

Few of the over-1000 MBASE developers were, however, sufficiently skilled and sufficiently experienced to be able to use MBASE given no more than its definition in Sections 3.1–3.5 above. The intended use of MBASE is, thus, via incorporation into software development guidelines, different ones for different types of project. That is, each set of MBASE guidelines specifies particular models to be constructed as well as methods for constructing them in such way that the five MBASE invariants are followed in their construction.

For example, in CS577 students execute real software development projects for real clients, mostly USC faculty and staff, but occasionally for outsiders—non-profit organizations and, less frequently, small businesses. Development teams typically consist of five people, and projects run for two semesters. As a result, the development process used is usually Schedule As Independent Variable [5], a process in which the inception and elaboration phases are run as Stakeholder Win-Win, Risk-Driven Spiral projects, and the Implementation phase is run either as a Waterfall project or as one type or another of Incremental project—depending upon the project's circumstances, and decided upon, with guidance, by the teams themselves.

The purpose of CS577 is, however, two-fold. One purpose is to guide students through an actual project in which five people work, part time, over a period of approximately 24 weeks, with product delivery and transition required by the end of the twenty-fourth week. A second purpose is to educate students in developing larger scale software products. The CS577 MBASE guidelines [12] are therefore, designed to elicit somewhat more documentation than is actually required for the execution of the project. Industry/government MBASE guidelines have been developed for specific types of larger projects. We are currently developing a set of minimal MBASE—referred to as minBASE—guidelines that can be tailored upward for use with any development process from agile to "Plan-Driven."

In the CS577 version of the MBASE guidelines, the models to be created are organized under artifacts named Operational Concept Definition (OCD), System and Software Requirements Definition (SSRD), System and Software Architecture Definition (SSAD), Life Cycle Plan (LCP), and Feasibility Rationale Description (FRD). As an example, Table V below shows the components of the LCO (Life Cycle Objectives) version of the OCD. Appendix A shows the components of all LCO, LCA (Life Cycle Architecture) and IOC (Initial Operational Capability) versions of CS577 MBASE artifacts.

TABLE V

LCO Milestone Elements	
Operational Concept Definition (OCD)	• Top level system objectives and scope
	– system boundary (i.e., what are the developers responsible for developing and what in the system's environment may they assume is either being developed by someone else or already exists);
	– environment parameters and assumptions (i.e., key parameters and assumptions about the nature of the system's users, data volume and consistency, workload levels, interoperating systems, etc., both at initial operating levels and in terms of likely evolution);
	– evolution parameters.
	• Operational Concept
	– operations and maintenance scenarios and parameters. (These many involve prototypes, screen layouts, UML diagrams, and other relevant representations. They should include scenarios for off-nominal situations if important and for system maintenance, including which organizations are responsible for funding and performing the various functions.)
	– organizational (stakeholders') life-cycle responsibilities.

The guidelines specify traceability and consistency requirements, as well as required FRD (Feasibility Rationale Description) arguments which, together, guarantee, to the extent possible, the consistency of all project models.

Table VI shows some of these consistency traces.

Given the relatively Plan-Driven nature of the MBASE guidelines variant described above, it might be unclear what a more agile version of MBASE might look like. The first point to note in this regard is that the following proviso is included in every section of more Plan-Driven MBASE guidelines:

> If it's risky to document something, because doing so expends stakeholder time and other resources, but doesn't likely contribute significantly to the success of the project, then it should not be documented; if its risky not to document something, because the risk exposure arising from not documenting it exceeds the cost, in time and other resources, of documenting it, then it should be documented.

Agile methods take this one step further [11] by starting from a baseline of producing an artifact to be archived only when stakeholders agree that the cost of doing so is outweighed by the long-term value of the artifact, or, in other words, if the risk exposure of not producing the document is greater than the cost of producing it. In terms of other agile-process details, MBASE, by virtue of its variants (see Section 3.6 above) holds no brief for or against such practices as pair programming,

TABLE VI
COVERAGE/TRACEABILITY OF MBASE PRODUCT MODELS*

Domain Description	System Analysis	System Design	Implementation
Organization Background	Statement of Purpose	System Definition	Release Description
Organization Goals	Project Goals	Project Requirements	Reqs. Satisfaction
	Levels of Service Goals	LOS Requirements	LOS Tests
Organization Activities	System Capabilities	Capability Requirements	Capability Tests
	Behavior Model	Operations Model	Methods/functions
Organization Entities	Component Model	Object Model	
			Data Structures
Interaction Model	Enterprise model	Class Model	

Operational Concept Description (OCD)   Construction,Transition,Support (CTS)
System and Software Requirements Definition (SSRD)   External to MBASE
System and Software Architecture Description (SSAD)   * Does not include all MBASE models

XP-style low-detail-upfront architecture, user stories vs. UML use cases, short, e.g., weekly, incremental cycles, or, for that matter, most other aspects of XP, SCRUM, and other agile processes.

A project is perfectly in consonance with the definition of MBASE if, in the most extreme case, stakeholders can, in face-to-face conversations, however short or long in duration:

- agree on a set of models to construct;
- sketch out those models without preserving any written documentation of them;
- refine the models, using informal versions of the MBASE model and process integration guidelines;
- agree on the consistency of all models, except, possibly, those whose clashes present low risk to the project;
- at suitable points in time, agree that LCO, LCA, and IOC milestone requirements have been met.

It is with this in mind that we are developing a minimal, upwardly-tailorable, set of MBASE guidelines.

As important as is model-clash elimination to the success of software development projects, not all projects are candidates for the use of MBASE—at least not full-scale MBASE. For one thing, MBASE comes with a certain amount of overhead that is justified only when it is outweighed by a sufficiently large reduction in risk exposure. As an example, consider a project whose goal is to port a successful product to a new platform or one whose goal is to implement relatively small incremental extensions to a successful product family. In both these cases, the small reduction in risk exposure provided by the use of MBASE is not likely to be justified by the added overhead.

Finally, some of the work dictated by MBASE to be done during one project phase, say elaboration, is for use in a later phase, say implementation. For example, the LCA (end-of-elaboration phase) LCP (Life Cycle Plan) in the CS577 MBASE guidelines must contain a detailed schedule for the implementation phase. A project whose goal is the production of a prototype to possibly be implemented at a later date, is therefore not a candidate to be an MBASE project.

4.   MBASE Usage Experience

For the past seven years, USC has used and refined MBASE extensively within its two-semester graduate software-engineering course. The students work on a Web-based electronic services project for a real USC client (frequently a digital library application for the university information services division) from initial system definition through transition, utilizing a specialized form of MBASE. This specialization includes particular tools and models such as Easy WinWin, Rational Rose, MSProject, and elements of the Rational Unified Process. More than 200 real-client projects have used MBASE, and over 90 percent have delivered highly satisfactory products on very short fixed schedules. The annual lessons learned have been organized into an extensive set of usage guidelines and an Electronic Process Guide [12], all accessible at http://sunset.usc.edu/research/MBASE. In the spring of 1999, MBASE was used in both the undergraduate and graduate software engineering courses at Columbia University. Although these are single semester courses, MBASE was successfully adapted to help student teams complete a full project life cycle for real clients.

Within industry, Xerox has adopted many elements of MBASE to form its time-to-market process, including the use of the LCO and LCA anchor points as synchronization points for the hardware and software portions of their printer product definitions.

Rational has adopted the LCO, LCA, and IOC anchor points within their Rational Unified Process while MBASE adopted Rational's Inception–Elaboration–Construction–Transition phase definitions.

C-Bridge has mapped their define, design, develop, deploy rapid development methodology for e-commerce systems to the MBASE spiral model.

The Internet startup company Media Connex adopted MBASE and used Easy WinWin to establish win-win relationships among their key stakeholders. Each of these companies converged on different balances of discipline and flexibility to satisfy their stakeholders' success models.

Additionally, there are numerous companies and organizations directly making use of MBASE elements within their project development efforts. For example, the U.S. Army Tank and Automotive Command has used Easy WinWin and other MBASE elements to reconcile its software technology organizations' process and product strategies.

ACKNOWLEDGEMENTS

The majority of the material presented here was developed by, or in heavy collaboration with Barry Boehm, Director of the University of Southern California's Center for Software Engineering. We thank him for his many contributions and editing of this presentation. Several of the extensions and refinements of MBASE presented here were developed by Mohammad Al-Said as part of his doctoral dissertation. We would like to acknowledge the support of the Defense Advanced Research Projects Agency and the National Science Foundation in establishing and refining MBASE, the DoD Software Intensive Systems Directorate in supporting its application to DoD projects and organizations, and the affiliates of the USC Center for Software Engineering for their contributions to MBASE.

Appendix A: LCO, LCA, and IOC Artifacts

Tables A.1–A.5 show detail of the models, and their degrees of completion that define attainment of the LCO milestone.

Table A.6 shows detail of the models, and their degrees of completion that define attainment of the LCA milestone.

TABLE A.1

	LCO Milestone Elements

Operational Concept Definition (OCD)	• Top level system objectives and scope
	
	   – system boundary (i.e., what are the developers responsible for developing and what in the system's environment may they assume is either being developed by someone else or already exists);
	
	   – environment parameters and assumptions (i.e., key parameters and assumptions about the nature of the system's users, data volume and consistency, workload levels, interoperating systems, etc., both at initial operating levels and in terms of likely evolution);
	
	   – evolution parameters.
	
	• Operational Concept
	
	   – operations and maintenance scenarios and parameters. (These many involve prototypes, screen layouts, UML diagrams, and other relevant representations. They should include scenarios for off-nominal situations if important and for system maintenance, including which organizations are responsible for funding and performing the various functions);
	
	   – organizational (stakeholders') life-cycle responsibilities.

TABLE A.2

	LCO Milestone Elements

System & Software Requirements Definition (SSRD)	• Top level functions, interfaces, and quality attribute levels, including
	
	   – priorities;
	
	   – growth vectors.

TABLE A.3

LCO Milestone Elements	

System & Software Architecture Definition (SSAD)	• Top level definition of at least one feasible architecture, including:
	
	   – logical and physical elements and their relationships;
	   – choices of COTS products and other reusable software components.
	
	Note that:
	
	   – At this (LCO) stage, it is acceptable to still be considering multiple feasible architectures, e.g., two feasible alternative COTS choices—with different architectural implications—for one or more critical components.
	   – If no feasible architecture can be developed, then the project should be canceled or its requirements, scope, and objectives should be changed.
	
	• Identification of infeasible architecture options (in order to prevent wasted time resulting from later re-consideration of alternatives already ruled out).

TABLE A.4

LCO Milestone Elements	

Life Cycle Plan (LCP)	• Identification of life-cycle stakeholders, e.g., customers, users, developers, maintainers, inter-operators, general public, etc.
	• Identification of life-cycle process model.
	• Top level WWWWWHH (Why, What, When, Who, Where, How, and How Much) by stage. The WWWWWHH principle organizes the plan into:
	
	   – Objectives: Why is the system being developed?
	   – Milestones and Schedules: What will be done by When?
	   – Responsibilities: Who is responsible for a function? Where are they organizationally located?
	   – Approach: How will the job be done, technically and managerially?
	   – Resources: How much of each resource is necessary?

The key elements of the IOC anchor point are:

– Software preparation, including both operational and support software with appropriate commentary and documentation; data preparation or conversion; the necessary licenses and rights for COTS and reused software, and appropriate operational readiness testing.

TABLE A.5

LCO Milestone Elements	
Feasibility Rationale Definition (FRD)	• Assurance of consistency among above-listed milestone elements
	– via analysis, measurement, prototyping, simulation, etc. (with the purpose of demonstrating that adherence to the LCP in the implementation of the design in the SSAD will result in a product that satisfies the requirements in the SSRD);
	– via business case analysis for requirements and feasible architectures (with the purpose of showing that implementing the requirements in the SSRD will accomplish the objectives in the OCD and will create enough value to justify the investment).

TABLE A.6

LCA Milestone Elements	
Operational Concept Definition	• Elaboration of system objectives and scope. • Elaboration of operational concept.
System & Software Requirements Definition	• Elaboration of functions, interfaces, and quality attribute levels including identifications of TBD's (items To Be Determined). • Prioritization of Concerns.
System & Software Architecture Definition	• Choice of architecture and elaboration of:
	– logical and physical components, connectors, configurations, and constraints;
	– COTS and other software reuse choices;
	– Domain architecture and architectural style choices;
	• Architecture evolution parameters.
Life Cycle Plan	• Elaboration of WWWWWHH for Initial Operational Capability (IOC), including partial identification And elaboration of key TBD's.
Feasibility Rationale Definition	• Assurance of consistency among all (OCD, SSRD SSAD, and LCP) LCA milestone elements. • Resolution or coverage, by risk management plan, of all major risks.

- Site preparation, including facilities, equipment, supplies, and COTS vendor support arrangements.
- User, operator and maintainer preparation, including selection, team building, training and other qualification for familiarization usage, operations, and maintenance.

REFERENCES

[1] Al-Said M., Ph.D. Thesis, University of Southern California, Department of Computer Science, 2003.
[2] Boehm B., "Anchoring the software process", *IEEE Software* (July 1996) 73–82.
[3] Boehm B., Egyed A., Kwan J., Port D., Shah A., Madachy R., "Using the WinWin spiral model: A case study", July 1999.
[4] Boehm B., et al., *Software Cost Estimation with Cocomo II*, Prentice Hall PTR, 2000.
[5] Boehm B., Port D., Huang L., Brown W., "Using the spiral model and MBASE to generate new acquisition process models: SAIV, CAIV, and SCQAIV", *Crosstalk* (January 2002).
[6] Boehm B., Abts C., "COTS integration: Plug and pray?", *Computer Magazine* (January 1999).
[7] Boehm B., Gruenbacher P., Briggs R. (Eds.), "Developing groupware for requirements negotiation: Lessons learned", *IEEE Software* (May/June 2001) 46–55.
[8] Boehm B., Port D., "Conceptual modeling challenges for model-based architecting and software engineering (MBASE)", in: *Proceedings, Conceptual Modeling Symposium*, 1998.
[9] Boehm B., Port D., "Escaping the software tar pit: Model clashes and how to avoid them", in: *Software Engineering Notes*, Association for Computing Machinery, New York, January 1999, pp. 36–48.
[10] Boehm B., *Balancing Agility and Discipline. A Guide for the Perplexed*, Addison–Wesley, Reading, MA, 2003.
[11] Cockburn A., *Agile Software Development*, Addison–Wesley, Reading, MA, 2001.
[12] USC-CSE, "MBASE Guidelines and MBASE Electronic Process Guide", http://sunset.usc.edu/research/MBASE.
[13] Garlan D., Allen R., Ockerbloom J., "Architectural mismatch: Why reuse is so hard", *IEEE Software* (November 1995) 17–26.
[14] Glass R., *Software Runaways*, Prentice Hall, Upper Saddle River, NJ, 1998.
[15] Jackson M.A., *Principles of Program Design*, Academic Press, San Diego, 1975.
[16] "Rational objectory process, version 4.1", Rational Software Corp., Santa Clara, CA, 1997.
[17] Rosove P.E., *Developing Computer-Based Information Systems*, John Wiley and Sons, Inc., 1967.
[18] Royce W.E., *Unified Software Management*, Addison–Wesley, 1998, John Wiley and Sons, Inc., 1967.

FURTHER READING

[19] Babcock C., "New Jersey motorists in software jam", *ComputerWorld* (September 30, 1985) 1, 6.
[20] Boehm B., *Software Risk Management*, IEEE Comput. Soc., Los Alamitos, CA, 1989.

[21] Boehm B., Egyed A., Kwan J., Madachy R., "Developing multimedia applications with the WinWin spiral model", in: *Proceedings, ESEC/FSE 97*, Springer-Verlag, Berlin/New York, 1997.

[22] Boehm B., "Software risk management: Principles and practices", *IEEE Software* (January 1991) 32–41.

[23] Boehm B., Bose P., "A collaborative spiral process model based on theory *W*", in: *Proceedings, ICSP3*, IEEE, 1994.

[24] Boehm B., In H., "Identifying quality-requirement conflicts", *IEEE Software* (March 1996) 25–35.

[25] Jacobson I., Griss M., Jonsson P., *Software Reuse*, Addison–Wesley, Reading, MA, 1997.

[26] Kazman R., Bass L., Abowd G., Webb M., "SAAM: A method for analyzing the properties of software architectures", in: *Proceedings, ICSE 16, ACM/IEEE*, 1994, pp. 81–90.

[27] Lee M.J., "Formal modeling of the WinWin requirements negotiation system", Ph.D. Thesis, USC Computer Sciences Department, 1996.

[28] Madachy R., "Knowledge-based risk assessment using cost factors", *Automated Software Engineering* **2** (1995).

[29] Marenzano J., "System architecture validation review findings", in: Garlan D. (Ed.), *ICSE17 Architecture Workshop Proceedings*, CMU, Pittsburgh, PA, 1995.

[30] Ross D.T., Schoman K.E., "Structured analysis for requirements definition", *IEEE Trans. SW Engr.* (January 1977) 41–48.

Software Quality Estimation
with Case-Based Reasoning

TAGHI M. KHOSHGOFTAAR[1] AND NAEEM SELIYA

Florida Atlantic University
Boca Raton, FL
USA
taghi@cse.fau.edu

Abstract

The software quality team of a software project often strives to predict the operational quality of software modules prior to software deployment. A timely software quality prediction can be used for enacting any preventive actions so as to reduce software faults from occurring during system operations. This is especially important for high-assurance systems where software reliability is very critical. The two most commonly used models for software quality estimation are, software fault prediction and software quality classification. Generally, such models use software metrics as predictors of a software module's quality, which is either represented by the expected number of faults or a class membership to quality-based groups. This study presents a comprehensive methodology for building software quality estimation models with case-based reasoning (CBR), a computational intelligence technique that is suited for experience-based analysis. A CBR system is a practical option for software quality modeling, because it uses an organization's previous experience with its software development process to estimate the quality of a currently under-development software project. In the context of software metrics and quality data collected from a high-assurance software system, software fault prediction and software quality classification models are built. The former predicts the number of faults in software modules, while the latter predicts the class membership of the modules into the fault-prone and not fault-prone groups. This study presents in-depth details for the CBR models so as to facilitate a comprehensive understanding of the CBR technology as applied to software quality estimation.

---

[1] Readers may contact the authors through Taghi M. Khoshgoftaar, Empirical Software Engineering Laboratory, Department of Computer Science and Engineering, Florida Atlantic University, Boca Raton, FL 33431, USA. Phone: (561)297-3994, Fax: (561)297-2800.

ADVANCES IN COMPUTERS, VOL. 62
ISSN: 0065-2458/DOI 10.1016/S0065-2458(03)62006-1

249

1.   Introduction

In software engineering practice, software quality enhancement activities may involve additional software design and code reviews, automated test case generation for extensive software testing, verification and validation, and re-engineering of low-quality software modules. However, generally the resources allocated for software quality enhancements are usually only a small fraction of the total budget allocated for the software project. Therefore, it is of practical importance that the software quality team utilize the limited resources allocated for software quality improvement in the best possible way. An effective way to do so is to identify (prior to system operations) software modules that are likely to have more faults, and subsequently, expend the limited software quality improvement resources toward those modules. A software module is the lowest level of software for which we have data.

Software measurements [5,12,51] have been shown to be good indicators of software quality, which for a software module is usually represented by a quality factor, such as the expected number of faults in the module, or a class membership into quality-based groups. Software metrics which represent the software product and its process can be collected relatively earlier than the software quality factor. Hence, for a currently under-development project the software metrics data may be known, but its software quality data is not known. The aim of a software quality estimation model is to predict the software quality factor based on the known software metrics. Generally, a software quality estimation model is built using a previously developed project for which the software metrics and software quality data is known. The software metrics are the independent variables that are used to predict the software quality factor, which is the dependent variable. Subsequently, the software quality model can be applied to estimate the software quality of the modules in the currently under-development software project.

Generally speaking, two types of metric-based software quality estimation models are used for a targeted software quality improvement. They are software fault prediction and software quality classification models. The former is a quantitative estimation model which is used to predict the number of faults (or any other quantitative software quality factor) a software module is likely to have [13,62], whereas, the latter is a qualitative estimation model that is used to predict the class-membership of a module into quality-based groups such as fault-prone (*fp*) and not fault-prone (*nfp*) [9,40,41]. In related literature, various techniques have been explored for building software quality estimation models, such as decision trees [14,29,30,57], discriminant analysis [42], logistic regression [20,50], fuzzy logic [48,55,61], artificial neural networks [27,43,45], and genetic programming [10,37]. The aim of this study is to present a comprehensive understanding of building software quality estimation models with the case-based reasoning (CBR) technique, which is part of the computational intelligence field.

Software fault prediction models are desired by the software quality team when they are interested in quantifying the quality of a software module. Such a model is of importance from a practical software quality improvement point of view, because based on such a prediction the software quality team can simply prioritize their enhancement efforts starting with the most faulty modules. Consequently, according to the allocated software quality improvement resources, a set of the most faulty modules can be subjected to enhancements. In contrast, a software quality classification model that classifies modules as *fp* and *nfp*, may be desired when the software quality team is only interested in knowing (according to the quality improvement goals of the project) which modules need to be targeted for quality inspections and enhancements. Hence, based on a software quality classification model all the modules predicted as *fp* will be subjected to quality improvements, regardless of their relative quality. The choice between the two types of software quality models is dependent on the discretion of the project management team and their specific needs.

A case-based reasoning system can be viewed as an automated reasoning approach which obtains (in the specified problem domain) a solution for a current case based on the knowledge of instances of past cases. The known knowledge of the past cases is stored in a case library, and represents the experience of the organization within the problem domain. For example, in the context of software quality estimation, the known software metrics and software quality information (of a previously developed project) that will be used for analysis is stored in the case library. In addition, a current case represents a software module whose software measurement data is known, but its quality factor is unknown. The CBR methodology has been explored for various prediction problems in the software engineering field, including software cost estimation [6,16,17,19,53], software reuse [47], software design [2,3,54], software quality [13,18,31], and software help desk [35]. In addition to the software engineering domain, the CBR methodology has also been applied to other fields, such as weather prediction [1] and path prediction for autonomous underwater vehicles [58]. A CBR prediction system has noticeable practical advantages, such as:

- It can be designed to alert users when a new case is outside the bounds of current experience. A solution of "I don't know" is more practical than a guess. In contrast, a typical prediction model always provides some kind of decisive solution.

- As new information becomes available, cases can be added to, or deleted from, the case library of the CBR system without the hassle of building a new model to track the new information.

- It is scalable to very large case libraries with fast retrieval, even as the case library scales up.

- Users of CBR systems can be easily convinced that the solution was derived in a reasonable way, i.e., they are not "black boxes", and hence, the CBR system lends itself to user acceptance.

- They are attractive because they are modeled with the premise of human intuition in mind in that we use our past experiences to analyze and resolve current problems.

A CBR system is typically built with a working hypothesis of how the past cases are to be used for the prediction problem. For example, CBR systems developed for the software cost/effort estimation problem are based on the hypothesis that the cost of developing a new software project (with known cost drivers) will be similar to that of previously developed software projects with similar cost drivers [16,17]. In the case of the CBR models presented in this study for software quality estimation, the working hypothesis is that a software module currently under-development will be as faulty as the previously developed (in the case library) software modules with similar software metrics. The similarity or distance between the current and previously developed modules is evaluated by a *similarity function*. Subsequently, a *solution algorithm* is used to predict the software quality factor of the current module. There are different types of similarity functions and solution algorithms, as shown in Section 2.

In our previous studies [13,26,56], we have performed extensive empirical investigations of building the two types of software quality estimation models based on CBR. However, each study focussed either on software fault prediction or software quality classification. The aim of this study is to present the complete methodology in one place as a guidance to practitioners in developing CBR models for software quality estimation. In addition, since the two types of models share some commonality in their modeling processes, this study is useful from a pedagogical point of view. We review our empirical results obtained from our recent studies [31,56]. In the context of software metrics and fault data collected from a large-scale legacy telecommunications system, the two types of software quality models are built and evaluated. In the case of the software fault prediction models, three types of similarity functions and two types of solution algorithms were considered. In the case of the software quality classification models, three types (same as the software fault prediction) of similarity functions and two types of solution algorithms were considered.

The rest of this study is structured as follows: Section 2 discusses the theoretical details of the two CBR models; Section 3 presents a detailed stepwise procedure of our CBR modeling methodology; Section 4 presents the case study description of the legacy telecommunications system; Section 5 discusses the empirical results; and Section 6 summarizes our work and provides directions for future research.

2. Software Quality Estimation with CBR

Case-based reasoning is an analysis and reasoning approach that allows problem solving based on previous experiences with the same or similar situation [34]. The applicability of CBR principles is largely beneficial to problem situations that are likely to recur with some or no variation. This is because intuitively speaking, the more similar a new *case* is to a previously encountered case, the more precisely can we determine its solution. The problem of understanding a new problem in terms of old experiences generally consists of two parts: (1) retrieving old experiences and (2) analyzing the new situation in terms of the retrieved experiences.

The old cases and their solutions are collectively known as a case library, because they serve as a reference to the CBR system when it needs to obtain a solution for a new case. The problem of retrieving the specific old cases that are "*similar*" to the new case is often called as the *indexing problem*. The case retrieval problem is resolved by incorporating similarity functions to determine which of the old cases are the closest match. However, since no (usually) old case is precisely the same as the new case, it is necessary for a CBR system to "adapt an old solution to fit a new situation" [34], i.e., *case-adaptation*. Thus, CBR can be viewed as meeting the requirements of new demands by adapting from old solutions. The case adaptation feature of CBR refers to the second part mentioned in the previous paragraph. In summary, a CBR prediction system generally consists of a case library (with the cases of previous experiences), a solution algorithm (for case-adaptation), and a similarity function (for case retrieval) [34,36].

We now present a very simple (hypothetical) example of how the basic CBR principles can be used for reasoning in a prediction system. Consider two previously developed software projects A and B, each expressed in terms of their total lines of code. Assume that for the lines of code, Project A has 15 000 and Project B has 12 000. In addition, assume Project A was completed in 12 months and Project B was completed in 9 months. Thus, a software project is a case in the case library, lines of code is the project attribute (independent variable) that will be used to estimate the project completion time (dependent variable). The values of the independent and dependent variables are known for the cases in the case library. Now consider a new software project (Project C, similar to Projects A and B) that is under development and is estimated to have 14 000 lines of code. Intuitively speaking, in order to estimate the completion time for the new project a CBR system will evaluate the proximity of its lines of code with those of Projects A and B. Thus, we reason by analogy that since Project A is closer (than Project B) to Project C, the completion time of Project C will be closer to 12 months (of Project A) than 9 months (of Project B). Thus, a prediction of 11 months for Project C is a likely solution. The hypothetical example presented above is a very simple (by no means a practical scenario) example, and was meant to illustrate the intuitive nature of a CBR system. In a real-world CBR application, such as the one presented in this chapter, a case is usually represented by multiple attributes, and the case library can generally have several cases.

In the context of software quality estimation, the case library consists of well-known project data from previously developed system release or similar projects, and contains all relevant information pertaining to each case (software module). In the context of software metrics-based quality prediction, such cases are composed of a set of software metrics or independent variables ($\mathbf{x}_i$), and a response or dependent variable (y_i). In the case of software fault prediction modeling, y_i represents the number of faults in module i. In the case of software quality classification modeling, y_i represents the quality class, i.e., *fp* or *nfp*, of module i. The cases in the case library can be added, deleted, or updated by the analyst according to the needs of the estimation problem. The software metrics collected during the software development process are often measured in varying ways and could contain a variety of ranges and scales. Therefore, before using the data for modeling purposes, it should be *standardized* (or *normalized*) [4].

A solution algorithm uses a similarity function to estimate the relationship or distance between the target case (whose dependent variable is to be estimated) and each case in the case library. Subsequently, the algorithm retrieves relevant cases and determines a solution to the new problem, i.e., it predicts the y_i value of the target case. In the case of the two types of software quality estimation models, the same similarity function can be used because it only computes the distances between the target case and those in the case library. However, a different solution algorithm is needed for the two types of models. This is because for a fault prediction model we are interested in a quantitative estimation, whereas for a software classification model we are interested in a qualitative estimation. In our study, we considered three types of similarity functions for computing the respective distances. Moreover, for each of the two types of models, we considered two solution algorithms. We now discuss the different similarity functions and solution algorithms used in our study.

A *similarity function* determines, for a given case, the most similar cases from the case library (*fit* or *training* data). The function computes the distance d_{ij}, between the current (or target) case $\mathbf{x}_i$, and every case $\mathbf{c}_j$ in the case library. The three types of similarity functions considered in this study are: *City Block distance, Euclidean distance*, and *Mahalanobis distance*. The cases with the smallest possible distances are of primary interest, and the set of similar cases forms the set of *nearest neighbors*, N. The CBR model parameter n_N, represents the number of the best (most similar to current or target case) cases selected from N for further analysis. The parameter n_N can be varied during model calibration to obtain different models. Once n_N is selected, a solution algorithm (quantitative or qualitative) is used to predict the dependent variable. In the case of software fault prediction modeling, we used the *unweighted average* and *inverse distance weighted average* solution algorithms. In the case of software quality classification modeling, we used the *majority voting* and *data clustering* solution algorithms.

2.1   Similarity Functions

2.1.1   City Block Distance

This similarity function is also known as *Absolute distance* or *Manhattan distance*. It is computed by taking the weighted sum of the absolute value of the difference in independent variables between the current case and a past case. The weight associated with each independent variable is provided by the user or the analyst. This distance function is primarily used for numeric attributes, and is given by:

$$d_{ij} = \sum_{k=1}^{m} w_k |x_{ik} - c_{jk}| \tag{1}$$

where, m is the number of independent variables, and w_k is the weight of the kth independent variable. In our study, $w_k = 1$ for the City Block distance and the Euclidean distance similarity measures.

2.1.2   Euclidean Distance

This similarity function views the independent variables as dimensions within an m-dimensional space, with m being the number of independent variables. A current case is represented as a point within this space. The distance is calculated by taking the weighted distance between the current case and a past case within this space. This distance function is also commonly used when the data set contains quantitative attributes, and is given by:

$$d_{ij} = \sqrt{\sum_{k=1}^{m} \left(w_k (x_{ik} - c_{jk}) \right)^2}. \tag{2}$$

2.1.3   Mahalanobis Distance

This distance measure is an alternative to the Euclidean distance. It is used when the independent variables are *highly correlated*. The Mahalanobis distance is a very attractive similarity function to implement because it can explicitly account for the correlation among the attributes [25], and the independent variables do not need to be standardized or normalized. It is given by [8]:

$$d_{ij} = (\mathbf{c}_j - \mathbf{x}_i)' S^{-1} (\mathbf{c}_j - \mathbf{x}_i) \tag{3}$$

where, $(')$ implies transpose, S is the variance-covariance matrix of the independent variables over the entire case library, while S^{-1} is its inverse.

2.2   Quantitative Solution Algorithms

In the context of the software fault prediction problem, a CBR system estimates the number of faults in a program module based on attributes of similar modules that were previously developed. The two solution algorithms that are used in our study to estimate the number of faults in a module are described in the next two subsections.

2.2.1   Unweighted Average

This algorithm estimates the dependent variable, $\hat{y}_i$, by calculating the average of the number of faults of the most similar modules, i.e., n_N, from the case library. The predicted value is therefore given by:

$$\hat{y}_i = \frac{1}{n_N} \sum_{j \in N} y_j. \tag{4}$$

2.2.2   *Inverse Distance Weighted Average*

The dependent variable is estimated using the distance measures for the n_N closest cases as weights in a weighted average. Since smaller distances indicate a closer match, each case is weighted by a normalized inverse distance. The case most similar to the target module has the largest weight, thus playing a major role in the obtained fault prediction.

$$\delta_{ij} = \frac{1/d_{ij}}{\sum_{j \in N} 1/d_{ij}},$$
(5)

$$\hat{y}_i = \sum_{j \in N} \delta_{ij} y_j.$$
(6)

2.3   Qualitative Solution Algorithms

In the case of software quality classification, a good solution algorithm is the one that provides (during pre-operations) a module class assignment which turns out to be correct after (during operations) all the fault data is known. The definition of whether a module is *fp* or *nfp* depends on the pre-set threshold value of the quality factor, which, in our studies, is the number of faults. If each case in the library has known attributes and class membership, then given a target case with an unknown class, we predict its class to be the same as the class of the most similar case(s) in the case library.

The characteristics of software quality metrics and fault data can make accurate software quality classification difficult. In the case of high-assurance software systems, the number of *fp* modules is a small fraction ($< 10\%$) of all the modules. Common classification methods are often unsuited to model such a small percentage of faulty modules, and are vulnerable to producing high misclassification rates for the fault-prone group. This negates the purpose of the classification models, because many *fp* modules may remain undetected. Furthermore, practically speaking the cost of a Type II error (when a *fp* module is misclassified as *nfp*, indicating a missed opportunity to detect a faulty module) is much greater than that of a Type I error (when a *nfp* module is misclassified as *fp*). Type II errors are more expensive and involve severe consequences, such as repairs at remote sites and damaging an organization's reputation. On the other hand, Type I errors are relatively less expensive, and may involve in-effective reviews and testing.

A classification model may be sensitive to the ratio of the costs of the Type I and Type II misclassifications. This is because, in practice, actual costs of the two misclassifications (C_I and C_{II}) are not known during the modeling period. And because the two costs are not similar, the use of equal costs for C_I and C_{II} during model calibration is not realistic. Moreover, other factors besides cost ratio may determine the best balance between the Type I and Type II error rates. For example, when the proportion of *fp* modules (as compared to *nfp* modules) is very small, and Type II misclassifications have relatively higher consequences, one may prefer equal misclassification rates, with Type II being as low as possible. The preferred balance between the two error rates depends on the domain of the software system and the project management team. For example, a safety-critical or medical software system may desire a very low Type II error rates, because missing a faulty module may lead to compromising the safety of the system users.

In many software projects, costs of misclassifications are very difficult to estimate, and similarly, prior probabilities of membership to the *fp* and *nfp* classes might be unknown or difficult to estimate. In such cases, the classification rule that minimizes the expected cost of misclassification, presented in [21] may be impractical. Thus, in the context of CBR, a generalized classification rule that does not require the knowledge of the misclassification costs and prior probabilities is needed. In our recent study [31], we introduced (in the context of software quality classification with CBR) generalized software quality classification rules that address the above mentioned issues related to the characteristics of software quality data and the unbalanced costs of the two misclassification error rates. The two generalized classification techniques, shown in the next subsections, facilitate customizing the preferred balance between the two misclassification error rates.

2.3.1   Majority Voting Classification Rule

The cases from the nearest neighbor set, N, are *polled* to determine the classification of the current case. The probability of a module being classified as either *fp* or *nfp*, depends on the percentage of cases within n_N that are *fp* and *nfp*, respectively. However, as pointed out earlier a generalized classification rule is needed to obtain the desired balance between the two misclassification error rates. The generalized majority voting classification rule in the context of CBR is given by:

$$\text{Class}(\mathbf{x}_i) = \begin{cases} nfp, & \text{if } \frac{P_{fp}}{P_{nfp}} < \zeta, \\ fp, & \text{otherwise,} \end{cases} \tag{7}$$

where, $\text{Class}(\mathbf{x}_i)$ is the predicted risk class for module i, P_{nfp} and P_{fp} are the probabilities of the target case being *nfp* and *fp*, respectively, and ζ is a variable modeling parameter. The value of 'ζ' can be chosen empirically (as shown in Sections 3 and 5) to suit the needs of a given case study or project. Therefore, the classification of the current case would then depend on whether the chosen value of ζ, exceeds the ratio $\frac{P_{fp}}{P_{nfp}}$.

2.3.2 Data Clustering Classification Rule

In this classification method, the case library is partitioned into two clusters, *fp* and *nfp*, according to the class of each case in the fit data set (case library). For a currently unclassified case $\mathbf{x}_i$, $d_{nfp}(\mathbf{x}_i)$ is the average distance (based on a similarity function) to the nearest *nfp* neighbor cases, and $d_{fp}(\mathbf{x}_i)$ is the average distance to the nearest *fp* neighbor cases. The number of nearest neighbor cases, i.e., n_N, to be used for analysis, can be varied as a model calibration parameter.

Once the average distances to the nearest neighbor cases are computed, the generalized data clustering classification rule is then used to estimate the class, Class($\mathbf{x}_i$), of the unclassified case. The classification rule is given by:

$$
\text{Class}(\mathbf{x}_i) = \begin{cases} nfp, & \text{if } \frac{d_{nfp}(\mathbf{x}_i)}{d_{fp}(\mathbf{x}_i)} < c, \\ fp, & \text{otherwise.} \end{cases} \tag{8}
$$

The right hand side of the inequality, c, is the modeling cost ratio parameter, $\frac{C_I}{C_{II}}$, where C_I is the cost of a Type I misclassification, and C_{II} is the cost of a Type II misclassification. It should be noted that c does not represent (for a given software project) the actual cost ratio, which is unknown at the time of modeling. The actual misclassification costs are not known until very late in the software life cycle. The parameter, c, can be empirically varied as per the needs of the given case study or project. Therefore, the classification of the current case or module would then depend on whether the ratio, $\frac{d_{nfp}(\mathbf{x}_i)}{d_{fp}(\mathbf{x}_i)}$, is lower than the chosen value of c.

3. Modeling Methodology

The complete CBR modeling process for building software fault prediction and software quality classification models has been implemented and automated in an empirical software quality modeling tool, the Software Measurement Analysis and Reliability Toolkit (SMART) [24,46]. The tool, developed by our research team at the Empirical Software Engineering Laboratory, Florida Atlantic University, is a Windows©-based application implemented in Visual C++© and has a user-friendly graphical interface. The modeling capability of the current version of SMART includes building and evaluating CBR models for software fault prediction and software quality classification. The latter includes both two-group [31] and three-group [32] software quality classification models. In addition, the tool also supports building module-order models, a software quality modeling approach that predicts and evaluates the relative ranking of the software modules [23].

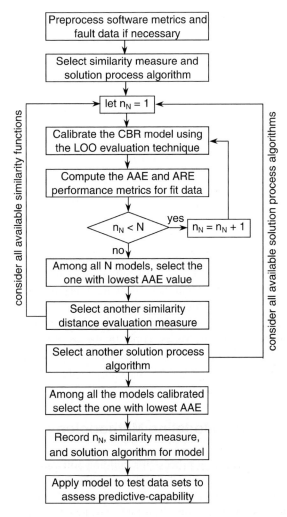

FIG. 1. Modeling procedure for software fault prediction.

The model building, selection, and evaluation procedure for the CBR-based software fault prediction and software quality classification models are respectively summarized in Figs. 1 and 2. The aim of including the figures is to facilitate analysts and practitioners who wish to repeat our empirical efforts for their respective use. The modeling methodology for the two CBR-based software quality models is discussed

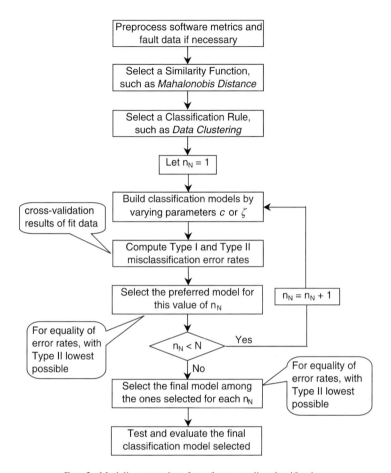

FIG. 2. Modeling procedure for software quality classification.

below. In addition, the performance metrics used for model selection and evaluation of the respective software quality models are presented at the end of this section.

3.1   Case-Based Reasoning Modeling Process

(1) *Case Library*: A fit (or training) data set is selected as the case library. For the case study presented later (Section 4), Release 1 is used as the training data set. In the case of the software fault prediction study, the software metrics in the case library consists of the 24 product and 4 execution metrics of the

modules in Release 1. In the case of the software quality classification study, the software metrics in the case library consists of all 42 software metrics presented in Section 4.

(2) *Target Data*: A test (or target) data set is selected for evaluating the performance of the CBR models. The software modules of Releases 2, 3, and 4 are used as target data sets for the case study.

(3) *Similarity Function and Solution Algorithm*: The desired similarity function, i.e., City Block, Euclidean, or Mahalanobis, is selected for modeling. In the case of software fault prediction modeling, one of the two quantitative solution algorithms (i.e., unweighted average or inverse distance weighted average) is selected. In the case of software quality classification modeling, one of the two qualitative solution algorithms (i.e., generalized majority voting or generalized data clustering) is selected.

(4) *Parameter n_N*: The number of cases to be selected from the nearest neighbor set, N, for analysis is a model parameter that is varied (for both types of software quality models) to yield different models. A broad spectrum of values of n_N (a maximum of the number of modules in the case library) were considered during our empirical studies.

(5) *Parameter ζ or c*: This step only applies to the software quality classification modeling study. For the majority voting classification models, the parameter ζ was varied from 0.01 to 1.00. For the data clustering classification models, the parameter c was varied from 0.0001 to 5.0. Other values of c and ζ were considered at the time of modeling, but did not yield better empirical results. The variation of these parameters allows the selection of a classification model with the desired (preferred) misclassification error rates. This is an important feature of the generalized classification rules, because it facilitates the software quality team to select a classification model that best suits their software quality improvement goals.

(6) *Model Fitting*: The respective software quality models are built using the *leave-one-out* (LOO) cross-validation technique, which is described as follows. Assume a *fit* data set, i.e., case library, with p cases. During each iteration one case is removed and the model is trained using the $p-1$ cases. The trained model is then used to predict the dependent variable (number of faults or class membership) for the removed case, which acts as the test case. Hence, p iterations are performed such that the dependent variable estimation of a case, v, is based on a model that is trained using all the cases in the case library, except v.

In the case of software fault prediction modeling, at the end of p iterations of the LOO technique, a number of faults estimation for all the cases in the fit data set is obtained. The *average absolute error* (AAE) and *average relative error* (ARE) of the fault prediction models (see Section 3.2) for a given n_N are computed. Subsequently, the n_N is varied to obtain different fault prediction models.

In the case of software quality classification modeling, at the end of p iterations of the LOO technique, a class (*fp* or *nfp*) estimation for all the cases in the fit data set is obtained. The Type I and Type II misclassification error rates of the classification model for a given n_N and c (or ζ) are computed. Subsequently, the n_N and c (or ζ) are varied to obtain different classification models.

(7) *Model Selection*: In the case of software fault prediction modeling, our model selection strategy was such that among all (by varying n_N) the trained models, a model which had the lowest AAE was selected as the final fault prediction model. However, in order to relate to the works of other researchers, we also computed the ARE values of all the prediction models. The error values used for model selection are based on the LOO technique.

In the case of software quality classification modeling, for a given similarity function and generalized classification rules, our model selection strategy was such that among all (by varying n_N, and for each n_N varying c or ζ) the trained models, the preferred classification model had approximately equal misclassification error rates with the Type II error rate being as low as possible. This model selection strategy is reflective of our discussions with the project management team of the legacy system, as discussed in Section 3.3. Once again, the error values used for model selection are based on the LOO technique.

(8) *Model Validation*: The test data sets are used to validate the prediction accuracy of the models trained using the fit data set. The respective performance metrics for the two software quality models are computed for the test data sets. The obtained performance metrics are then compared with those of the fit data set. A stable software quality model should exhibit minimal variation in its performance across the training and test data sets.

3.2 Performance Evaluation for Software Fault Prediction

The prediction accuracy of the software fault prediction models is determined by computing the two commonly used performance measures, i.e., AAE (average absolute error) and ARE (average relative error). The AAE and ARE performance metrics are given by,

$$AAE = \frac{1}{n} \sum_{i=1}^{n} |y_i - \hat{y}_i|, \tag{9}$$

$$\text{ARE} = \frac{1}{n} \sum_{i=1}^{n} \left| \frac{y_i - \hat{y}_i}{y_i + 1} \right| \tag{10}$$

where, n is the number of modules in the given data set. The denominator in ARE has a '1' added to avoid division by zero. We have presented and utilized both measures, because the comparative study of AAE and ARE as performance metrics is out of scope for this chapter. Moreover, there is no consensus in the literature as to which of those two metrics is a better performance evaluator for a quantitative prediction model. Among the competing software fault prediction models, the one with the lowest AAE (or ARE) is selected as the final model.

3.3   Performance Evaluation for Software Quality Classification

The accuracy of a classification model is usually measured in terms of it's Type I and Type II misclassification error rates. A Type I error occurs when a *nfp* module is misclassified as *fp*, while a Type II error occurs when a *fp* module is misclassified as *nfp*. Thus, the accuracy of a software quality classification model is indicated by how well the class predictions for software modules are realized later in the life cycle, i.e., during testing or operations. The classification accuracy is especially important because the cost of misclassifying a *fp* module is invariably greater than the cost of misclassifying a *nfp* module. Furthermore, the obtained balance between the two error rates may affect the usefulness of a two-group software quality classification model. In the context of a two-group software quality classification model, for a given classification technique the Type I and Type II error rates are inversely proportional.

Recent research has indicated that published software quality classification modeling methods may not consistently produce a useful balance between the Type I and Type II error rates [22]. If either type of misclassification error rate is high, the model is generally not useful to guide software quality improvement efforts. In the case when the Type I error rate is high, then targeting of enhancement efforts will be inefficient because many of the modules classified as *fp* are actually *nfp*. On the other hand, if the Type II error rate is very high, then many faulty modules will not be detected for enhancements prior to system operations. Therefore, a *preferred* balance, as per the quality needs of the project, between the two types of misclassifications is desired. This is especially important for high-assurance systems in which the cost of correcting a Type II error is relatively much higher than that for a Type I error, and the proportion of the *fp* modules is a small fraction of the total number of modules. Therefore, a practical classification rule(s) that allows the analyst to obtain the desired balance between the error rates is more useful [21].

In our study, the model-selection strategy for the software quality classification models is such that the Type I and Type II error rates (for the fit data set) are approximately equal with the Type II error rate being as low as possible. The model selection strategy was determined based upon discussions with our industry partner, i.e., the management team of the legacy telecommunications system. According to their software quality improvement needs, such a strategy yielded useful classification models from a practical point of view. However, we note that another software project may consider a different model-selection strategy that is reflective of their software quality needs.

4. Case Study Description

The software metrics and fault data for this case study (denoted as LLTS) was collected over four historical releases from a very large legacy telecommunications system. The software system is written in a high-level language, using the procedural paradigm, and maintained by professional programmers in a large organization. The telecommunications system had significantly over ten million lines of code and included numerous finite-state machines and interfaces to various kinds of equipment. We labeled the four system releases, 1 through 4. These releases were the last four releases of the legacy system. The modules of Release 1 were used are as the *fit* data set for training the software quality estimation models. The respective modules of Releases 2, 3, and 4 are used as the three *test* data sets for evaluating the predictive performances of the models.

A software module was considered as a set of functionally related source-code files according to the system's architecture. Fault data, collected at the module-level by the problem reporting system, consisted of faults discovered during post unit testing phases, and were recorded before and after the product was released to customers. The software faults discovered by customers were recorded only when their discovery resulted in a change in the source code. Faults in deployed telecommunications systems are extremely expensive because, in addition to down-time due to failures, visits to remote sites are usually necessary to repair them.

The number of modules associated with faults discovered by customers were very few as compared to modules with no faults. This is reflective of the nature of the system being modeled, i.e., a high-assurance system. Two clusters of modules were identified: unchanged and updated. The updated modules consisted of those that were either new or had at least one update to their source code since the prior release. Configuration management data analysis identified software modules that were unchanged from the prior release. Among the unchanged modules, almost all of them had no faults. Consequently, in our studies we only considered modules that were new, or had at least one source code update since the prior release. The system had several million lines of code in a few thousand modules per release. Each release had approximately 3500 to 4000 updated or new software modules. The number of modules considered in Releases 1, 2, 3, and 4 were 3649, 3981, 3541, and 3978 respectively.

The set of available software metrics is usually determined by pragmatic considerations. A data mining approach is preferred in exploiting software metrics data [11], by which a broad set of metrics are analyzed rather than limiting data collection according to a predetermined set of research questions. Data collection for this case study involved extracting source code from the configuration management system. The available data collection tools determined the number and selection of the software metrics. Software measurements were recorded using the EMERALD (Enhanced Measurement for Early Risk Assessment of Latent Defects) software metrics analysis tool, which includes software-measurement facilities and software quality models [15].

Preliminary data analysis selected metrics (aggregated to the module level) that were appropriate for our modeling purposes. The software metrics considered in our studies included 24 product metrics, 14 process metrics, and 4 execution metrics. As we will see later in this section, that the 14 process metrics are not used while building the software fault prediction modeling. In contrast, while building the software quality classification models all 42 metrics are used. It should be noted that the sets of software metrics used for the legacy system may not be universally appropriate for all software systems. Another project might collect (depending on availability) and use a different set of software metrics [7,44,39].

The software product metrics in Table I are based on call graph, control flow graph, and statement metrics. A module's call graph depicts the calling relationships among procedures. A module's control flow graph consists of nodes and arcs depicting the flow of control of the program. Statement metrics are measurements of the program statements without expressing the meaning or logic of the statements. The process metrics in Table II may be associated with either the likelihood of inserting a fault during development, or the likelihood of discovering and fixing a fault prior to product release. The configuration management systems tracked each change to source code files, including identity of the designer and the reason of the change, e.g., a change to fix a problem or to implement a new requirement. The execution metrics listed in Table III are associated with the likelihood of executing a module, i.e., operational use. The proportion of installations that had a module, *USAGE*, was approximated by deployment data on a prior release. Execution times were measured in a laboratory setting with different simulated workloads.

In the case of software fault prediction with CBR, the models were built based upon 28 software metrics, which included the 24 product metrics and the 4 execution

TABLE I
SOFTWARE PRODUCT METRICS

Symbol	Description
Call graph metrics	
CALUNQ	Number of distinct procedure calls to others.
CAL2	Number of second and following calls to others.
	$CAL2 = CAL - CALUNQ$ where CAL is the total number of calls.
Control flow graph metrics	
CNDNOT	Number of arcs that are not conditional arcs.
IFTH	Number of non-loop conditional arcs, i.e., if–then constructs.
LOP	Number of loop constructs.
CNDSPNSM	Total span of branches of conditional arcs. The unit of measure is arcs.
CNDSPNMX	Maximum span of branches of conditional arcs.
CTRNSTMX	Maximum control structure nesting.
KNT	Number of knots. A "knot" in a control flow graph is where arcs cross due to a violation of structured programming principles.
NDSINT	Number of internal nodes (i.e., not an entry, exit, or pending node).
NDSENT	Number of entry nodes.
NDSEXT	Number of exit nodes.
NDSPND	Number of pending nodes, i.e., dead code segments.
LGPATH	Base 2 logarithm of the number of independent paths.
Statement metrics	
FILINCUQ	Number of distinct include files.
LOC	Number of lines of code.
STMCTL	Number of control statements.
STMDEC	Number of declarative statements.
STMEXE	Number of executable statements.
VARGLBUS	Number of global variables used.
VARSPNSM	Total span of variables.
VARSPNMX	Maximum span of variables.
VARUSDUQ	Number of distinct variables used.
VARUSD2	Number of second and following uses of variables.
	$VARUSD2 = VARUSD - VARUSDUQ$ where $VARUSD$ is the total number of variable uses.

metrics. Hence, those 28 metrics are used to predict the dependent variable of the prediction model, i.e., faults. The fault data used for fault prediction consisted of the software faults discovered during the post-unit testing phases, including those discovered by customers. In the case of software quality classification with CBR, the models were built based upon all 42 software metrics. Hence, the 42 metrics are used to predict the dependent variable of the classification model, i.e., class. The fault data

TABLE II
SOFTWARE PROCESS METRICS

Symbol	Description
DES_PR	Number of problems found by designers.
BETA_PR	Number of problems found during beta testing.
DES_FIX	Number of problems fixed that were found by designers.
BETA_FIX	Number of problems fixed that were found by beta testing in the prior release.
CUST_FIX	Number of problems fixed that were found by customers in the prior release.
REQ_UPD	Number of changes to the code due to new requirements.
TOT_UPD	Total number of changes to the code for any reason.
REQ	Number of distinct requirements that caused changes to the module.
SRC_GRO	Net increase in lines of code.
SRC_MOD	Net new and changed lines of code.
UNQ_DES	Number of different designers making changes.
VLO_UPD	Number of updates to this module by designers who had 10 or less total updates in entire company career.
LO_UPD	Number of updates to this module by designers who had between 11 and 20 total updates in entire company career.
UPD_CAR	Number of updates that designers had in their company careers.

TABLE III
SOFTWARE EXECUTION METRICS

Symbol	Description
USAGE	Deployment percentage of the module.
RESCPU	Execution time (microseconds) of an average transaction on a system serving consumers.
BUSCPU	Execution time (microseconds) of an average transaction on a system serving businesses.
TANCPU	Execution time (microseconds) of an average transaction on a tandem system.

used for classification modeling reflect the software faults discovered by customers during system operations. We note that the two software quality models are built to reflect software quality estimation at different stages in the software development life cycle. The software fault prediction models are built right after the coding (including unit testing) phase. The software quality classification models are built just prior to releasing the software system for operations.

A module was considered *fp* if any faults were discovered during operations, and *nfp* otherwise. Therefore, all the modules in the case library (for software quality classification) and the test data sets that had one or more customer-discovered faults were classified as *fp*, and *nfp* otherwise. This threshold value was determined as per the modeling requirements of the legacy telecommunications system. The distribution of the customer-discovered faults for the updated modules of the four system

TABLE IV
LLTS FAULT DISTRIBUTION

Faults	Percentage of updated modules			
	Release 1	Release 2	Release 3	Release 4
0	93.7%	95.3%	98.7%	97.7%
1	5.1%	3.9%	1.0%	2.1%
2	0.7%	0.7%	0.2%	0.2%
3	0.3%	0.1%	0.1%	0.1%
4	0.1%	a		
6	a			
9	a			

[a] One module.

releases is presented in Table IV. The numbers of fp and nfp modules for the four releases are as follows: Releases 1 through 4 have 229, 189, 47, and 92 fp modules, and 3420, 3792, 3494, and 3886 nfp modules, respectively. The proportion of modules with no customer-discovered faults among the updated modules of the first release (fit data set) was $\pi_{nfp} = 0.937$, and the proportion with at least one fault was $\pi_{fp} = 0.063$. Such a small set of faulty modules is often difficult for a software quality modeling technique to identify. Therefore, a need for the generalized (in the context of CBR) classification rules as presented earlier was highly desired.

5. Results and Analysis

5.1 Software Fault Prediction Results

In the case of software fault prediction modeling, we present the results of the models based on all combinations of the three similarity functions and the two quantitative solution algorithms. The number of nearest neighbor cases (n_N) used by the CBR system for obtaining the software fault prediction is a variable that can affect the prediction accuracy. Determining the optimum value of n_N is dependent on the characteristics of the fit data set, and hence, requires an empirical approach. Given a similarity function and a solution algorithm, the trained model whose n_N yields the minimum AAE or ARE using the LOO technique is selected as the preferred CBR fault prediction model. The software fault prediction models were built using the 24 product and 4 execution metrics described earlier.

The performances of the different prediction models (by varying n_N) based on the three similarity functions are shown in Tables V, VI, and VII. We note that the empirical results from all (odd and even) values of n_N we have considered are not

TABLE V
OPTIMUM n_N WITH EUCLIDEAN DISTANCE

	Unweighted		Weighted	
n_N	AAE	ARE	AAE	ARE
1	1.152	0.560	1.152	0.560
3	1.081	0.548	1.022	0.509
5	1.042	0.538	0.983	0.496
7	1.024	0.534	0.966	0.492
9	1.016	0.531	0.953	0.486
11	1.011	0.532	0.947	0.485
13	1.009	0.534	0.945	0.486
15	1.002	0.532	0.938	0.484
17	1.000	0.532	0.935	0.483
19	**0.995**	**0.530**	0.930	0.481
21	0.995	0.530	0.929	0.480
23	0.998	0.531	0.931	0.481
25	0.996	0.530	0.929	0.480
27	0.996	0.531	0.928	0.480
29	0.996	0.531	0.928	0.479
31	0.996	0.531	0.928	0.479
33	1.057	0.607	**0.927**	**0.479**
35	1.057	0.607	0.928	0.479
37	1.057	0.607	0.928	0.479
39	1.057	0.607	0.928	0.479
41	1.057	0.607	0.928	0.479
43	1.057	0.607	0.928	0.479
45	1.057	0.607	0.928	0.479
47	1.057	0.607	0.929	0.474

presented. The tables report only some of the odd values that were considered for n_N. However, we have presented a good spectrum (from either end) of values covering the selected n_N. The prediction models based on other values of n_N are not shown because their inclusion would not impart any additional empirical information.

Table V presents the AAE and ARE values when the unweighted average and inverse distance weighted average (abbreviated as "weighted" in the table) solution algorithms are used in combination with the Euclidean distance similarity function. Similarly, Tables VI and VII respectively present the AAE and ARE values when the City Block and Mahalanobis distance similarity functions are used. We observe a trend in the AAE values with respect to n_N. As n_N is increased, the AAE value decreases until a particular n_N is reached, after which it starts to increase. Consequently, the n_N corresponding to the minimum AAE is chosen as the optimum n_N. The respective selected models are highlighted in bold.

TABLE VI
OPTIMUM n_N WITH CITY BLOCK DISTANCE

n_N	Unweighted		Weighted	
	AAE	ARE	AAE	ARE
1	1.147	0.554	1.147	0.554
3	1.060	0.538	1.008	0.503
5	1.031	0.530	0.971	0.488
7	1.015	0.527	0.951	0.483
9	1.011	0.530	0.945	0.483
11	1.012	0.532	0.944	0.484
13	1.004	0.529	0.938	0.481
15	1.000	0.527	0.934	0.480
17	0.994	0.526	0.928	0.478
19	0.999	0.528	0.930	0.479
21	0.994	0.525	0.926	0.476
23	**0.991**	**0.523**	0.925	0.475
25	1.055	0.600	0.924	0.474
27	1.055	0.600	0.924	0.474
29	1.054	0.599	0.924	0.474
31	1.053	0.599	0.924	0.474
33	1.051	0.598	0.923	0.473
35	1.049	0.597	**0.922**	**0.473**
37	1.051	0.598	0.923	0.473
39	1.049	0.598	0.924	0.474
41	1.057	0.607	0.924	0.474
43	1.057	0.607	0.925	0.474
45	1.057	0.607	0.925	0.474
47	1.057	0.607	0.926	0.475

Table VIII summarizes the AAE and ARE values (and their standard deviations) of the CBR models across the different system releases. Among the models calibrated by using different similarity functions and solution algorithms, the ones with the lowest AAE values are shown in the table. The error values (AAE and ARE) for Release 1 are based on the LOO cross-validation technique. The selected model is then applied to the test data sets, i.e., Releases 2, 3, and 4, and the respective error statistics are computed. It is observed that for this case study, the Mahalanobis distance measure has the lowest AAE (with both solution algorithms). This suggests that it will yield a better fault prediction as compared to the Euclidean and City Block distance measures. Furthermore, for almost all (11 out of 12) the cases shown in Table VIII, the inverse distance weighted average solution algorithm yielded a lower AAE value.

Our empirical results demonstrated that among the fault prediction models built using the different similarity functions, those based on the Mahalanobis distance

TABLE VII

OPTIMUM n_N WITH MAHALANOBIS
DISTANCE

n_N	Unweighted		Weighted	
	AAE	ARE	AAE	ARE
1	1.010	0.455	1.010	.455
3	0.984	0.452	0.936	0.42
5	0.959	0.444	0.905	0.406
7	0.962	0.446	0.902	0.404
9	0.960	0.445	0.900	0.403
11	**0.958**	**0.446**	0.897	0.402
13	0.961	0.449	0.896	0.402
15	0.963	0.449	0.895	0.401
17	0.965	0.450	0.897	0.402
19	0.964	0.448	**0.896**	**0.400**
21	0.965	0.448	0.896	0.399
23	0.966	0.448	0.899	0.400
25	0.966	0.446	0.899	0.399
27	0.967	0.446	0.900	0.398
29	0.967	0.445	0.900	0.398
31	0.968	0.446	0.900	0.398
33	0.968	0.445	0.901	0.398
35	0.968	0.445	0.901	0.397

yielded better prediction accuracies than the models based on the City Block and Euclidean distances. In addition, it is also observed that the inverse distance weighted average technique when used as a solution algorithm yielded better results (with all similarity functions) than the models based on the unweighted average solution algorithm. However, evaluating the respective performances based solely on the AAE and ARE values does not provide statistical verification.

In order to investigate whether the difference observed between the respective similarity measures and the respective solution algorithms is of statistical significance, we performed two-way ANOVA tests [4] as described in Appendix A. The similarity function was considered as factor A, whereas the solution algorithm was considered as factor B. Prior to the ANOVA tests, a log transformation was performed on the performance metrics data, i.e., absolute error and relative error. This is because, the error values encompassed a wide range and the ratio of the maximum value to the minimum value of the errors was large. The results from these tests are tabulated, as shown in Tables IX–XVI. In these tables SS denotes the sum of squares, df represents the degree of freedom, MS denotes the mean square of factor, and MSE represents the mean square of error. In the above mentioned tables, AB indicates

TABLE VIII
FAULT PREDICTION MODEL

Data set	Similarity function	Unweighted average				Weighted average			
		AAE	SDAE[a]	ARE	SDRE[b]	AAE	SDAE	ARE	SDRE
Release 1[c]	Euclidean	0.995	1.618	0.530	0.537	0.927	1.635	0.479	0.513
Release 1	CityBlock	0.991	1.619	0.523	0.520	0.922	1.642	0.473	0.514
Release 1	Mahalanobis	0.958	1.745	0.446	0.394	0.896	1.762	0.399	0.345
Release 2	Euclidean	0.904	1.019	0.595	0.589	0.884	1.100	0.585	0.562
Release 2	CityBlock	0.898	1.020	0.590	0.580	0.885	0.994	0.584	0.556
Release 2	Mahalanobis	0.824	1.048	0.490	0.425	0.879	0.980	0.528	0.551
Release 3	Euclidean	0.955	1.142	0.598	0.633	0.926	1.100	0.581	0.572
Release 3	CityBlock	0.950	1.135	0.594	0.616	0.927	1.090	0.581	0.568
Release 3	Mahalanobis	0.869	1.153	0.495	0.418	0.861	1.119	0.499	0.456
Release 4	Euclidean	0.944	1.030	0.588	0.607	0.925	0.998	0.576	0.571
Release 4	CityBlock	0.943	1.037	0.588	0.620	0.925	1.091	0.581	0.568
Release 4	Mahalanobis	0.846	1.002	0.502	0.473	0.831	0.981	0.492	0.426

[a]SDAE denotes standard deviation of absolute error.
[b]SDRE denotes standard deviation of relative error.
[c]Release 1 was fit data set.

TABLE IX
ANOVA FOR RELEASE 1: ABSOLUTE ERROR

	SS	df	MS	MS/MSE
A	69.940	2	34.968	34.942
B	470.492	1	470.493	470.144
AB	15.551	3	7.776	7.770
Error	21904.266	21888	1.001	
Total	22460.249	21894		

TABLE X
ANOVA FOR RELEASE 1: RELATIVE ERROR

	SS	df	MS	MS/MSE
A	68.308	2	34.154	39.307
B	435.911	1	435.911	501.68
AB	14.805	3	7.402	8.519
Error	19018.35	21888	0.869	
Total	19537.374	21894		

TABLE XI
ANOVA FOR RELEASE 2: ABSOLUTE ERROR

	SS	df	MS	MS/MSE
A	96.863	2	48.431	150.050
B	14.201	1	14.201	43.999
AB	8.740	3	4.370	13.538
Error	7707.683	23880	0.323	
Total	7827.487	23886		

whether an interaction exists between the two factors, i.e., similarity function and solution algorithm.

The tables also indicate the significance of an F-test (for the absolute and relative errors) for each factor. We observe that a significant effect exists (large F values) due to factor A, i.e., similarity function. The observed difference among the similarity functions is at a 1% (or lower) significance level for all four releases. This suggests that for this case study, the Mahalanobis distance measure performs significantly better than the other two similarity measures. In addition, a significant effect also exists (very large F values) due to factor B, i.e., solution algorithm, sug-

TABLE XII
ANOVA FOR RELEASE 2: RELATIVE ERROR

	SS	df	MS	MS/MSE
A	95.559	2	47.780	160.478
B	12.865	1	12.865	43.208
AB	8.351	3	4.176	14.025
Error	7109.891	23880	0.298	
Total	7226.666	23886		

TABLE XIII
ANOVA FOR RELEASE 3: ABSOLUTE ERROR

	SS	df	MS	MS/MSE
A	19.049	2	9.525	28.746
B	17.064	1	17.064	51.501
AB	39.738	3	19.869	59.966
Error	7037.596	21246	0.331	
Total	7113.447	21252		

TABLE XIV
ANOVA FOR RELEASE 3: RELATIVE ERROR

	SS	df	MS	MS/MSE
A	49.870	2	24.935	82.268
B	14.164	1	14.164	46.731
AB	8.471	3	4.236	13.975
Error	6437.701	21246	0.303	
Total	6510.206	21252		

TABLE XV
ANOVA FOR RELEASE 4: ABSOLUTE ERROR

	SS	df	MS	MS/MSE
A	45.186	2	22.593	74.664
B	16.184	1	16.184	53.484
AB	6.857	3	3.429	11.331
Error	7220.605	23868	0.303	
Total	7288.832	23874		

TABLE XVI

ANOVA FOR RELEASE 4: RELATIVE ERROR

	SS	df	MS	MS/MSE
A	43.612	2	21.806	77.121
B	14.274	1	14.274	50.482
AB	6.253	3	3.126	11.057
Error	6746.984	23868	0.283	
Total	6811.123	23874		

gesting that the inverse distance weighted average algorithm provided significantly better results when compared to the unweighted average algorithm. Once again, for all four releases the observed improvement is at a 1% (or lower) significance level. Regarding the interaction between the two factors, we observe that in addition to the individual similarity functions and solution algorithms, their combination may also yield significantly different fault predictions.

5.2   Software Quality Classification Results

The three similarity functions, for each of the two generalized classification rules, were used to compute the set of nearest neighbor cases. However, for the case study presented, similar empirical results were obtained for all three similarity functions [49]. Consequently, we only present the results of classification models built using the Mahalanobis distance similarity function. It is not claimed that the Mahalanobis distance is better than the City Block and Euclidean distances for software quality classification modeling. However, it is more attractive since it explicitly accounts for the correlation among the software metrics, and requires no data pre-processing, i.e., normalization and standardization. In the next two subsections, we present and discuss our empirical results obtained by the software quality classification models built using CBR. The classification models are built using all 42 software metrics.

5.2.1   Majority Voting-Based Classification Model

The model parameters, n_N and ζ, are varied for fitting and evaluating different classification models using the majority voting generalized classification rule. Recall, the goal of varying the model parameters is to calibrate a classification model with the preferred balance (equality) between the Type I and Type II error rates, with the latter being as low as possible. Therefore, the final classification model selected would have the optimum values for n_N and ζ.

For a given value of n_N, the parameter ζ was varied. Subsequently, among the respective calibrated models for the given n_N, a model with the preferred balance is selected. A similar process was followed for different values of n_N. The best models for the different values of n_N are listed in Table XVII. Among these, the selected preferred classification model is illustrated in bold. The table shows only a few combinations of n_N and ζ from those that were considered, because the other combinations did not yield better results for the Type I and Type II errors. The misclassification error rates shown in Table XVII are those obtained from the LOO cross-validation technique. The values shown are for Release 1, which was used to fit different models. As shown in the table, the selected model has the best possible preferred balance between the two error rates. Thus, the preferred model based on the generalized majority voting classification rule using the Mahalanobis distance function, has $n_N = 16$ and $\zeta = 0.04$.

Table XVIII presents the effect of varying the parameter ζ (for $n_N = 16$) on the balance between the misclassification error rates for Release 1. As observed in the table, there is a tradeoff between the Type I and Type II misclassification error rates, with respect to ζ. For $\zeta = 1.00$ all software modules of the fit data set are classified

TABLE XVII
MAJORITY VOTING & MAHALANOBIS:
MODEL SELECTION

n_N	ζ	Type I	Type II
1	0.10	3.860%	85.590%
3	0.10	9.678%	69.869%
5	0.10	14.094%	58.952%
7	0.10	17.924%	48.908%
9	0.10	21.170%	44.978%
11	0.09	24.064%	40.611%
13	0.08	26.696%	35.808%
15	0.07	28.743%	31.878%
16	**0.04**	**29.854%**	**29.258%**
17	0.06	31.053%	28.384%
19	0.05	33.743%	24.454%
21	0.04	35.643%	24.107%
23	0.04	37.544%	22.271%
25	0.04	39.649%	19.651%
27	0.03	40.906%	17.467%
29	0.03	42.398%	16.157%
31	0.04	22.601%	41.048%
33	0.04	23.860%	39.301%
35	0.04	24.854%	37.991%

TABLE XVIII

MAJORITY VOTING & MAHALANOBIS:
ERROR RATES VS. ζ

	$n_N = 16$	
ζ	Type I	Type II
0.01	29.854%	29.258%
0.02	29.854%	29.258%
0.03	29.854%	29.258%
0.04	**29.854%**	**29.258%**
0.05	29.854%	29.258%
0.06	29.854%	29.258%
0.07	11.550%	57.642%
0.08	11.550%	57.642%
0.09	11.550%	57.642%
0.10	11.550%	57.642%
0.20	4.269%	79.039%
0.30	1.257%	89.083%
0.40	0.439%	93.886%
0.50	0.088%	97.380%
0.60	0.029%	99.127%
0.70	0.029%	99.127%
0.80	0.000%	99.563%
0.90	0.000%	99.563%
1.00	0.000%	99.563%

as *nfp*. Such a model is useless because it does not classify any of the modules as *fp*. However, as ζ decreases the Type II error rate decreases and the Type I error rates increases. It is observed that the absolute difference between the Type I and Type II errors reduces with the decrease in the ζ value. This difference between the two error rates does not change with the decrease in ζ below 0.06. Therefore, we selected our preferred classification model (for $n_N = 16$) that corresponds to a median value of ζ from 0.06 to 0.01. We can thus observe how the ζ value has a strong influence on the preferred balance between the misclassification rates. The generalized majority voting classification rule can therefore facilitate the selection of a classification model with the preferred error rates.

5.2.2   *Data Clustering-Based Classification Model*

Classification models using the data clustering generalized classification rule are identified by their model parameters, n_N and c. For a given n_N, different models are built by varying the parameter c, and among these, the model with the preferred balance between the error rates is selected. The best classification models for different

n_N values are presented in Table XIX, where the final classification model (based on data clustering) selected for the case study is illustrated in bold. The misclassification error rates shown (Release 1) in the table are those obtained from the LOO cross-validation technique. The error rate values shown in the table are those of the training data set. The table shows only a few combinations of n_N and c from those that were considered, because the other combinations did not yield better results for the Type I and Type II errors.

The variation of misclassification rates for a given n_N with respect to c, is demonstrated in Table XX which represents the case when $n_N = 7$. For a given n_N, as c is increased, the Type I error rate decreases, whereas the Type II error rate increases. Therefore, the preferred balance between the error rates can be obtained by selecting an appropriate value of c, for the given n_N. If we consider the model with $c = 0.1$, we note that though the model has a perfect classification for all the 229 fp modules of Release 1, it misclassifies 3084 out of the 3420 nfp modules as fp, i.e., over 90% of the nfp modules are misclassified. If such a model is selected, then the cost of inspection will be very high, primarily because most of predicted fp modules are

TABLE XIX
DATA CLUSTERING & MAHALANOBIS:
MODEL SELECTION

n_N	c	Type I	Type II
1	.960	26.491%	26.638%
3	.920	26.404%	25.328%
5	.940	24.064%	24.454%
6	.945	23.684%	23.144%
7	**.950**	**23.158%**	**23.144%**
8	.950	23.129%	23.581%
9	.950	23.041%	23.581%
11	.940	23.772%	23.581%
13	.930	24.035%	23.144%
15	.930	23.713%	23.581%
17	.920	24.240%	23.581%
19	.920	23.830%	24.017%
21	.910	24.327%	24.017%
23	.905	24.327%	24.017%
25	.905	24.211%	24.017%
27	.905	23.977%	24.017%
29	.905	23.830%	24.017%
31	.900	24.064%	24.017%
33	.900	23.772%	24.017%
35	.890	24.327%	23.581%

TABLE XX

DATA CLUSTERING &

MAHALONOBIS: ERROR RATES VS. c

$n_N = 7$		
c	Type I error	Type II error
0.10	90.175%	0.000%
0.20	81.287%	0.873%
0.30	73.655%	1.310%
0.40	66.257%	2.620%
0.50	58.041%	4.803%
0.60	50.760%	8.734%
0.70	42.310%	12.227%
0.80	34.181%	17.904%
0.90	26.754%	21.834%
0.91	26.053%	22.271%
0.92	25.322%	22.271%
0.93	24.561%	22.271%
0.94	23.860%	22.271%
0.95	**23.158%**	**23.144%**
0.96	22.427%	24.454%
0.97	21.988%	24.891%
0.98	21.579%	25.328%
0.99	20.936%	26.201%
1.00	20.526%	27.948%

actually *nfp*. Though such a classification model may be justifiable for safety-critical and medical software systems, it is not practical for most software systems.

In the case of the modeling cost ratio parameter, c, values other than those shown in Table XX were also considered. However, they did not yield better results and hence, are not presented. The case when $c = 0.95$ represents the value for the selected classification model for $n_N = 7$. The row highlighted in bold is the model with the preferred balance between the Type I and Type II errors. Let us consider the case of $c = 1.00$ in Table XX. This value of c implies equal modeling costs for the two types of misclassification errors. The balance between the Type I and Type II errors is not the best, as seen in the table. Upon comparing the error rates of the selected model and the model for $c = 1$, we observe that the Type II error of the latter is relatively higher while its Type I error is relatively lower. This suggests that the $c = 1$ model, as compared to the $c = 0.95$ model, will detect fewer (about 4%) faulty modules, and slightly more (about 3%) non-faulty modules. Since the actual costs of rectifying the two misclassification errors are not equal (Type II being more serious), the gain of detecting 4% of the *fp* modules clearly outweighs the loss of not detecting 3% of the *nfp* modules.

5.2.3 Majority Voting vs. Data Clustering

In this section we present a brief comparison of classification models based on the two generalized classification rules. The models are compared with respect to performance measures such as, classification accuracy, model over-fitting, stability, and robustness. Classification accuracy is measured with respect to the performance metrics, Type I and Type II errors rates. Over-fitting is observed when the model performs, relatively much better (error rates) for the training data set than for the test data sets [38]. Stability is observed when the classification model maintains a good balance between the Type I and Type II error rates across the different data sets, i.e., system releases. Robustness is observed when the classification model maintains a good classification accuracy (relative to the training data set) across the different data sets. A further detailed empirical and statistical comparison of these two analogy-based classification techniques (using different similarity functions) is part of our related future research work.

The selected classification models and their classification accuracies across the multiple releases of the telecommunications system are presented in Tables XXI and XXII, respectively. For ease in comparison, lets denote the model based on the data clustering generalized classification rule, as *Model A*. Along the same lines, the model based on the majority voting generalized classification rule is denoted as *Model B*. A quick look at the quality-of-fit (performance for the fit data set) of the two classification models, indicates that Model A has lower misclassification rates (over 6% improvement) as compared to those of Model B. For Release 1, the Type I error rate of Model A is 23.158% as compared to 29.854% for Model B. This implies that Model A misclassifies 792 out of the 3420 *nfp* modules of Release 1 as *fp*, while for the same release Model B misclassifies 1021 *nfp* modules as *fp*. Along the same

	TABLE XXI				TABLE XXII	
	MODEL BASED ON DATA CLUSTERING & MAHALANOBIS				MODEL BASED ON MAJORITY VOTING & MAHALANOBIS	
	$n_N = 7, c = 0.95$				$n_N = 16, \zeta = 0.04$	
Data set	Type I error	Type II error		Data set	Type I error	Type II error
Release 1	23.158%	23.144%		Release 1	29.854%	29.258%
Release 2	25.132%	26.984%		Release 2	31.276%	26.984%
Release 3	28.792%	27.660%		Release 3	32.799%	25.532%
Release 4	28.667%	25.000%		Release 4	30.957%	29.348%

lines, the Type II error for Model A is 23.144% (53 out of the 229 *fp* modules are misclassified) as compared to 29.258% (67 out of the 229 *fp* modules are misclassified) for Model B. Similarly, the misclassification numbers of the other releases can be obtained.

Recall that the error rates for Release 1 are computed using the cross validation technique discussed earlier. The tables also indicate that the predictive capability (performance for the test data sets) of Model A is generally better than that of Model B. All the Type I error rates of Model A are lower than those of Model B. Moreover, all (except for Release 3) the Type II error rates of Model A are lower than or similar to those of Model B. As compared to Model B, Model A is more practical for a cost effective usage of quality improvement resources. This is because considering the proximity of their Type II error rates, the Type I error rates of Model A are lower than those of Model B. This implies that among the (respective) modules predicted as *fp*, Model A will have fewer *nfp* modules than Model B. Since Model B would lead to a greater waste of the limited software quality improvement resources, it is not attractive from a software engineering point of view. The software quality assurance team would prefer to expend its allocated resources toward software modules that are actually *fp*.

The total numbers of predicted *fp* and *nfp* modules according to both Model A and Model B are summarized in Table XXIII. As compared to the actual *fp* and *nfp* modules for each release, both preferred models predict a surplus number of modules as *fp* and a deficit number of modules as *nfp*. We note that this is reflective of the adopted model selection strategy for the legacy telecommunications system being studied, i.e., balancing the two error rates with the Type II error rate being as low as possible.

When comparing the models based on their degree of over-fitting, both Model A and Model B show a *very low degree* of model over-fitting. However, a relative comparison between the two indicates that the latter has a slightly lower degree of over-fitting. Model A shows a maximum variation (for its error rates) across the sys-

TABLE XXIII
ACTUAL VS. PREDICTED NUMBERS OF MODULES

	Actual		Model A		Model B	
	fp	*nfp*	*fp*	*nfp*	*fp*	*nfp*
Release 1	229	3420	968	2681	1183	2466
Release 2	189	3792	1091	2890	1324	2657
Release 3	47	3494	1040	2501	1181	2360
Release 4	92	3886	1183	2795	1268	2710

tem releases, of about 5%, whereas Model B shows a maximum variation of about less than 4%. It is also observed from Tables XXI and XXII that Model A reflects good stability as compared to Model B. Stability is an important performance measure for classification models, because if the preferred balance, i.e., equality in our case, between the two error rates fluctuates considerably, it may affect the usefulness of the classification model [33].

The two CBR software quality classification models depict good robustness in their classification accuracy across different releases. This is because the maximum variation (across releases) of the misclassification error rates is only about 5%. However, relative to each other Model A shows poor robustness than Model B. Its Type I error varies (generally increases) from 23.158% (Release 1) to 28.792% (Release 3), i.e., 5.634%. Furthermore, its Type II error fluctuates, across the different system releases, from 23.144% to 27.660%, i.e., 4.516%. In contrast, the Type I error of Model B varies from 29.854% to 32.799%, i.e., 2.945%, whereas its Type II error varies from 25.532% to 29.348%, i.e., 3.726%.

The overall conclusion for the classification modeling study is that the classification model based on the data clustering classification rule are better than the model based on the majority voting classification rule. The observed classification accuracy and usefulness of software quality estimation models, based on the proposed generalized classification rules, have been explored by our empirical investigations with other case studies [28,49]. Empirical results and conclusions obtained from those case studies further validate the effectiveness and applicability of the classification methodologies presented in this chapter.

As mentioned earlier, the very low number of *fp* modules (as compared to *nfp*) for a software system such as LLTS make software quality modeling very difficult. We note that the misclassification rates obtained by the two generalized (for CBR) classification rules (Tables XXI and XXII) are very useful for the system being modeled. Furthermore, our empirical investigations (with CBR) with case studies of other software systems have reported the two misclassification rates lower than 10% [28]. A similar approach of model calibration and application, can be *universally adopted* for software engineering of other systems.

5.3   Threats to Validity

In an empirical software engineering task it is important to consider the threats to validity of the obtained results and conclusions [60]. We consider three types of threats to validity for the case study presented earlier. They include: threats to internal validity, threats to external validity, and threats to conclusion validity.

Threats to internal validity are unaccounted influences that may affect case study results. Internal validity is the ability to show that results obtained were due to the manipulation of the experimental treatment variables. In the context of this study, poor estimates (fault prediction or quality classification) can be caused by a wide variety of factors, including measurement errors while collecting and recording software metrics; modeling errors due to the unskilled use of software applications; errors in model-selection during the modeling process; and the presence of noise in the training data set. Measurement errors are inherent to the software data collection effort, which is usually specific to the system under consideration. In our study with CBR-based software quality estimation modeling, a common model-building and model-selection approach have been adopted for each combination of the similarity function and solution algorithm. Moreover, the modeling, experimental, and statistical analysis was performed by only one skilled person (one for each of the two types of software quality estimation models) in order to keep modeling errors to a minimum.

External validity is concerned with generalization of the obtained results outside the experimental setting. Therefore, threats to external validity are conditions that limit generalization of case study results. To be credible, the software engineering community demands that the subject of an empirical study be a system with the following characteristics [59]: (1) developed by a group, rather than an individual; (2) developed by professionals, rather than students; (3) developed in an industrial environment, rather than an artificial setting; and (4) large enough to be comparable to real industry projects. The software system investigated in this study meets all these requirements.

However, it is known in the software engineering field that a given software metrics-based prediction system is likely to be affected by (among other issues) the characteristics of the data and the application domain of the system under consideration [52]. The results and conclusion of this chapter are based on the case study presented, and cannot be generalized for another software system, because it may: have different software data characteristics; utilize different software metrics; and have different software quality improvement objectives. However, the respective CBR-based software quality estimation modeling procedures can certainly be applied to other systems.

Conclusion validity is concerned with the statistical relationship between the treatment and the outcome. It is sometimes also referred to as statistical conclusion validity, i.e., is the relationship between the treatment and the outcome satisfiable for a given significance level. Threats to conclusion validity are issues that affect the ability to draw the correct inferences. In this study the discussions related to performance comparisons of the software fault prediction models based on the different combinations of similarity functions and solution algorithms were based on the obtained two-way ANOVA modeling results.

6. Conclusion

In this study we have presented a comprehensive methodology for building software quality estimation models with case-based reasoning, which is part of the computational intelligence field. More specifically, the CBR modeling procedures for building software fault prediction and software quality classification models are presented. The aim of building such software quality estimation models is to allow a targeted software quality improvement effort. A targeted software improvement provides a better utilization of the limited resources allocated for software quality improvement.

The simplicity, ease in modeling, and user-acceptance of the CBR-based software quality estimation models demonstrates their practical and application attractiveness. Since the CBR-based software quality estimation models are based on past experience with similar instances, they are easier to understand and interpret as compared to black-box software quality models such as artificial neural networks. The CBR-based software fault prediction and software quality classification methodologies are demonstrated through a case study of software metrics and software fault data collected over four successive releases of a legacy telecommunications system. In other related studies we have also applied the respective CBR-based modeling procedures to case studies of other software systems [28]. In addition, various studies were performed (for the LLTS case study) to investigate the effect of building software quality models based on reduced set of software metrics [49,56]. However, in the context of CBR-based software quality modeling, the software metric selection is an open research issue.

In the case of the CBR-based software fault prediction models, we performed a statistical verification of the effects of using different similarity functions and solution process algorithms to obtain the final fault predictions. It was observed that among all the combinations of the different similarity functions and solution process algorithms, the software fault prediction models based on the Mahalanobis distance similarity measure and the inverse distance weighted average solution algorithm yielded the best models in terms of the AAE and ARE performance metrics. In the case of the CBR-based software quality classification models, we performed a relative comparison of the two qualitative solution process algorithms, i.e., majority voting and data clustering. It was observed that the classification models based on our previously proposed generalized data clustering classification rule yielded better classification accuracy.

Our future work related to CBR-based software quality estimation will include investigating the feature subset selection problem. We have initiated preliminary studies related to the software metrics selection problem. In addition, since CBR prediction systems are usually affected by the presence of data noise or outliers in the case library, our future studies will focus on the feature subset selection problem in the context of the CBR prediction systems.

ACKNOWLEDGEMENTS

We thank Nandini Sundaresh and Fletcher Ross for their assistance with data analysis and empirical studies. We also thank Kehan Gao for her assistance with patient reviews. We thank John P. Hudepohl, Wendell D. Jones and the EMERALD team for collecting the necessary case-study data. This work was supported in part by the Cooperative Agreement NCC 2-1141 from NASA Ames Research Center, Software Technology Division, and the NASA Grant NAG 5-12129 for the NASA software Independent Verification and Validation Facility at Fairmont, West Virginia.

Appendix A: Two-Way Analysis of Variance Models

In our empirical study of building CBR models for software fault prediction, we investigate whether the fault prediction models based on a particular similarity function or solution process algorithm yielded significantly better results than models based on the other similarity functions and solution process algorithm. The statistical analysis is done by building two-way analysis of variance (ANOVA) models. We recall that the similarity functions studied include the Euclidean, City Block, and Mahalanobis distance measures, whereas the solution process algorithm studied include the unweighted average and inverse distance weighted average algorithms. Hence, we have six unique combinations of a similarity function and a solution process algorithm. The two-way ANOVA models will assess if the difference in the predictions, i.e., AAE and ARE, obtained by each of the six combinations are of statistical significance. A two-way ANOVA model with replication is used [4], and the response variable for the statistical test is the error value: absolute error or relative error. The ANOVA test, models the response variable as,

$$y_{ijk} = \mu + A_j + B_i + AB_{ij} + e_{ijk} \tag{A.1}$$

where y_{ijk} is the response variable for the kth replication of the experiment with the jth level of the similarity function and ith solution process algorithm, μ is the mean response, A_j is the effect of the jth level of similarity function, B_i is the effect of the ith level of solution process algorithm, AB_{ij} is the effect of the interaction between similarity function and solution process algorithm and e_{ijk} is the experimental error.

The statistical test is performed with the null hypothesis that there is no significant difference between the performance of factors (as defined above). The ratios of mean squares of factors to mean squared error are distributed according to F-distributions. The null hypothesis is rejected if the computed ratio is greater than the selected value from the F-distribution, concluding that the factor is statistically significant at that level of significance.

REFERENCES

[1] Aha D.W., Bankert R.L., "Feature selection for case-based classification of cloud types: An empirical comparison", in: Aha D.W. (Ed.), *Workshop on Case-Based Reasoning (Technical Report WS-94-01)*, AAAI Press, Menlo Park, CA, August 1994.

[2] Bartsch-Spoerl B., "Toward the integration of case-based, schema-based, and model-based reasoning for supporting complex design tasks", in: *Proceedings of the 1st International Conference on Case-Based Reasoning*, Springer-Verlag, 1995, pp. 145–156.

[3] Bell B., Kedar S., Bareiss R., "Interactive model-driven case adaptation for instructional software design", in: *Proceedings of the 16th Annual Conference of the Cognitive Science Society*, Lawrence Erlbaum Publishers, 1994, pp. 33–38.

[4] Berenson M.L., Levine D.M., Goldstein M., *Intermediate Statistical Methods and Applications: A Computer Package Approach*, Prentice Hall, Englewood Cliffs, NJ, 1983.

[5] Briand L.C., Emam K.E., Morasca S., "On the application of measurement theory in software engineering", *Empirical Software Engineering Journal* **1** (1) (1996) 61–88.

[6] Briand L.C., Langley T., Wieczorek I., "A replicated assessment and comparison of common software cost modeling techniques", in: *Proceedings of the International Conference on Software Engineering, Limerick, Ireland*, Association for Computing Machinery, June 2000, pp. 377–386.

[7] Briand L.C., Melo W.L., Wust J., "Assessing the applicability of fault-proneness models across object-oriented software projects", *IEEE Transactions on Software Engineering* **28** (7) (July 2002) 706–720.

[8] Dillon W.R., Goldstein M., *Multivariate Analysis: Methods and Applications*, John Wiley & Sons, New York, 1984.

[9] Ebert C., "Classification techniques for metric-based software development", *Software Quality Journal* **5** (4) (December 1996) 255–272.

[10] Evett M.P., Khoshgoftaar T.M., Chien P.-D., Allen E.B., "GP-based software quality prediction", in: Koza J.R., Banzhaf W., Chellapilla K., Deb K., Dorigo M., Fogel D.B., Garzon M.H., Goldberg D.E., Iba H., Riolo R. (Eds.), *Proceedings of the 3rd Annual Conference on Genetic Programming, Madison, WI, USA*, Morgan Kaufmann, July 1998, pp. 60–65.

[11] Fayyad U.M., "Data mining and knowledge discovery: Making sense out of data", *IEEE Expert* **11** (4) (October 1996) 20–25.

[12] Fenton N.E., Pfleeger S.L., *Software Metrics: A Rigorous and Practical Approach*, second ed., PWS Publishing Company: ITP, Boston, MA, 1997.

[13] Ganesan K., Khoshgoftaar T.M., Allen E.B., "Case-based software quality prediction", *International Journal of Software Engineering and Knowledge Engineering* **10** (2) (April 2000) 139–152.

[14] Gokhale S.S., Lyu M.R., "Regression tree modeling for the prediction of software quality", in: Pham H. (Ed.), *Proceedings of the 3rd International Conference on Reliability and Quality in Design, Anaheim, California, USA*, International Society of Science and Applied Technologies, March 1997, pp. 31–36.

[15] Hudepohl J.P., Aud S.J., Khoshgoftaar T.M., Allen E.B., Mayrand J., "EMERALD: Software metrics and models on the desktop", *IEEE Software* **13** (5) (September 1996) 56–60.

[16] Idri A., Abran A., Khoshgoftaar T.M., "Estimating software project effort by analogy based on linguistic values", in: *Proceedings of the 8th International Software Metrics Symposium, Ottawa, Ontario, Canada*, IEEE Computer Society, June 2002, pp. 21–30.

[17] Idri A., Khoshgoftaar T.M., Abran A., "Fuzzy analogy: A new approach for software cost estimation", in: *Proceedings of the 11th International Workshop on Software Measurements, Montreal, Canada*, August 2001, pp. 93–101.

[18] Imam K.E., Benlarbi S., Goel N., Rai S.N., "Comparing case-based reasoning classifiers for predicting high-risk software components", *Journal of Systems and Software* **55** (3) (2001) 301–320.

[19] Kadoda G., Cartwright M., Chen L., Shepperd M., "Experiences using case-based reasoning to predict software project effort", in: *Proceedings of the 4th International Conference on Empirical Assessment in Software Engineering, Staffordshire, UK*, April 2000, pp. 23–33.

[20] Khoshgoftaar T.M., Allen E.B., "Logistic regression modeling of software quality", *International Journal of Reliability, Quality and Safety Engineering* **6** (4) (December 1999) 303–317.

[21] Khoshgoftaar T.M., Allen E.B., "A practical classification rule for software quality models", *IEEE Transactions on Reliability* **49** (2) (June 2000) 209–216.

[22] Khoshgoftaar T.M., Allen E.B., "Modeling software quality with classification trees", in: Pham H. (Ed.), *Recent Advances in Reliability and Quality Engineering*, World Scientific Publishing, Singapore, 2001, pp. 247–270, chapter 15.

[23] Khoshgoftaar T.M., Allen E.B., "Ordering fault-prone software modules", *Software Quality Journal* **11** (1) (May 2003) 19–37.

[24] Khoshgoftaar T.M., Allen E.B., Busboom J.C., "Modeling software quality: The software measurement analysis and reliability toolkit", in: *Proceedings of the 12th International Conference on Tools with Artificial Intelligence, Vancouver, BC, Canada*, IEEE Computer Society, November 2000, pp. 54–61.

[25] Khoshgoftaar T.M., Allen E.B., Shan R., "Improving tree-based models of software quality with principal components analysis", in: *Proceedings of the 11th International Symposium on Software Reliability Engineering, San Jose, California, USA*, IEEE Computer Society, October 2000, pp. 198–209.

[26] Khoshgoftaar T.M., Cukic B., Seliya N., "Predicting fault-prone modules in embedded systems using analogy-based classification models", *International Journal of Software Engineering and Knowledge Engineering* **12** (2) (April 2002) 201–221.

[27] Khoshgoftaar T.M., Lanning D.L., "A neural network approach for early detection of program modules having high risk in the maintenance phase", *Journal of Systems and Software* **29** (1) (April 1995) 85–91.

[28] Khoshgoftaar T.M., Lim L., Geleyn E., "Developing accurate software quality models using a faster, easier, and cheaper method", in: *Proceedings of the 7th International Conference on Reliability and Quality in Design, Washington, DC, USA*, International Society of Science and Applied Technologies, August 2001, pp. 31–35.

[29] Khoshgoftaar T.M., Seliya N., "Software quality classification modeling using the SPRINT decision tree algorithm", in: *Proceedings of the 14th International Conference on Tools with Artificial Intelligence, Washington, DC, USA*, IEEE Computer Society, November 2002, pp. 365–374.

[30] Khoshgoftaar T.M., Seliya N., "Tree-based software quality models for fault prediction", in: *Proceedings of the 8th International Software Metrics Symposium, Ottawa, Ontario, Canada*, IEEE Computer Society, June 2002, pp. 203–214.

[31] Khoshgoftaar T.M., Seliya N., "Analogy-based practical classification rules for software quality estimation", *Empirical Software Engineering Journal* **8** (4) (December 2003) 325–350.

[32] Khoshgoftaar T.M., Seliya N., "Three-group software quality classification modeling using an automated reasoning approach", in: Kandel A., Bunke H., Last M. (Eds.), *Artificial Intelligence Methods in Software Testing*, in: *Machine Perception and Artificial Intelligence Series*, World Scientific Publishing, 2003, pp. 139–182, chapter 5.

[33] Khoshgoftaar T.M., Yuan X., Allen E.B., "Balancing misclassification rates in classification tree models of software quality", *Empirical Software Engineering Journal* **5** (2000) 313–330.

[34] Kolodner J., *Case-Based Reasoning*, Morgan Kaufmann Publishers, Inc., San Mateo, CA, 1993.

[35] Kriegsman M., Barletta R., "Building a case-based help desk application", *IEEE Expert* **8** (6) (1993) 18–24.

[36] Leake D.B. (Ed.), *Case-Based Reasoning: Experience, Lessons, and Future Directions*, MIT Press, Cambridge, MA, 1996.

[37] Liu Y., Khoshgoftaar T.M., "Genetic programming model for software quality prediction", in: *Proceedings of the 6th International High Assurance Systems Engineering Symposium, Boca Raton, Florida, USA*, IEEE Computer Society, October 2001, pp. 127–136.

[38] Michalski R.S., Bratko I., Kubat M., *Machine Learning and Data Mining: Methods and Applications*, John Wiley & Sons, 1998.

[39] Ohlsson M.C., Runeson P., "Experience from replicating empirical studies on prediction models", in: *Proceedings of the 8th International Software Metrics Symposium, Ottawa, Ontario, Canada*, IEEE Computer Society, June 2002, pp. 217–226.

[40] Ohlsson N., Alberg H., "Predicting fault-prone software modules in telephone switches", *IEEE Transactions on Software Engineering* **22** (12) (1996) 886–894.

[41] Ohlsson N., Helander M., Wohlin C., "Quality improvement by identification of fault-prone modules using software design metrics", in: *Proceedings of the International Conference on Software Quality, Ottawa, Ontario, Canada*, 1996, pp. 1–13.

[42] Ohlsson N., Zhao M., Helander M., "Application of multivariate analysis for software fault prediction", *Software Quality Journal* **7** (1) (1998) 51–66.

[43] Paul R., "Metric-based neural network classification tool for analyzing large-scale software", in: *Proceedings of the International Conference on Tools with Artificial Intelligence, Arlington, Virginia, USA*, IEEE Computer Society, November 1992, pp. 108–113.

[44] Ping Y., Systa T., Muller H., "Predicting fault-proneness using OO metrics: An industrial case study", in: Gyimothy T., Abreu F.B. (Eds.), *Proceedings of the 6th European Conference on Software Maintenance and Reengineering, Budapest, Hungary*, March 2002, pp. 99–107.

[45] Pizzi N.J., Summers A.R., Pedrycz W., "Software quality prediction using median-adjusted class labels", in: *Proceedings of the International Joint Conference on Neural Networks, Honolulu, Hawaii, USA*, vol. 3, IEEE Computer Society, May 2002, pp. 2405–2409.

[46] Rajeevalochanam J.M., "A metrics-based software quality modeling tool", Master's thesis, Florida Atlantic University, Boca Raton, FL, USA, December 2002. Advised by Taghi M. Khoshgoftaar.

[47] Ramamoorthy C.V., Chandra C., Ishihara S., Ng Y., "Knowledge-based tools for risk assessment in software development and reuse", in: *Proceedings of the 5th International Conference on Tools with Artificial Intelligence, Boston, MA, USA*, IEEE Computer Society, November 1993, pp. 364–371.

[48] Reformat M., Pedrycz W., Pizzi N.J., "Software quality analysis with the use of computational intelligence", in: *Proceedings of the IEEE International Conference on Fuzzy Systems, Honolulu, HI, USA*, vol. 2, May 2002, pp. 1156–1161.

[49] Ross F.D., "An empirical study of analogy based software quality classification models", Master's thesis, Florida Atlantic University, Boca Raton, FL, USA, August 2001. Advised by T.M. Khoshgoftaar.

[50] Schneidewind N.F., "Investigation of logistic regression as a discriminant of software quality", in: *Proceedings of the 7th International Software Metrics Symposium, London, UK*, IEEE Computer Society, April 2001, pp. 328–337.

[51] Schneidewind N.F., "Body of knowledge for software quality measurement", *IEEE Computer* **35** (2) (February 2002) 77–83.

[52] Shepperd M., Kadoda G., "Comparing software prediction techniques using simulation", *IEEE Transactions on Software Engineering* **27** (11) (November 2001) 1014–1022.

[53] Shepperd M., Schofield C., "Estimating software project effort using analogies", *IEEE Transactions on Software Engineering* **23** (12) (November 1997) 736–743.

[54] Smith N.T., Ganesan K., "Software design using case-based reasoning", in: *Proceedings of the 4th Software Engineering Research Forum, Boca Raton, FL*, November 1995, pp. 193–200.

[55] Suarez A., Lutsko J.F., "Globally optimal fuzzy decision trees for classification and regression", *Pattern Analysis and Machine Intelligence* **21** (12) (1999) 1297–1311.

[56] Sundaresh N., "An empirical study of analogy based software fault prediction", Master's thesis, Florida Atlantic University, Boca Raton, FL, USA, May 2001. Advised by Taghi M. Khoshgoftaar.

[57] Takahashi R., Muraoka Y., Nakamura Y., "Building software quality classification trees: Approach, experimentation, evaluation", in: *Proceedings of the 8th International Symposium on Software Reliability Engineering, Albuquerque, NM, USA*, IEEE Computer Society, November 1997, pp. 222–233.

[58] Vasudevan C., Ganesan K., "Case-based path planning for autonomous underwater vehicles", *Journal of Autonomous Robots* **3** (1996) 79–89.

[59] Votta L.G., Porter A.A., "Experimental software engineering: A report on the state of the art", in: *Proceedings of the 17th International Conference on Software Engineering, Seattle, WA, USA*, IEEE Computer Society, April 1995, pp. 277–279.

[60] Wohlin C., Runeson P., Host M., Ohlsson M.C., Regnell B., Wesslen A., *Experimentation in Software Engineering: An Introduction*, in: *Kluwer International Series in Software Engineering*, Kluwer Academic Publishers, Massachusetts, 2000.

[61] Xu Z., Khoshgoftaar T.M., "Software quality prediction for high assurance network telecommunications systems", *The Computer Journal* **44** (6) (December 2001) 557–568.

[62] Xu Z., Khoshgoftaar T.M., Allen E.B., "Application of fuzzy linear regression modeling to predict the number of program faults", in: Pham H., Lu M. (Eds.), *Proceedings of the 6th ISSAT International Conference on Reliability and Quality in Design, Orlando, FL, USA*, August 2000, pp. 96–101.

Data Management Technology for Decision Support Systems[1]

SURAJIT CHAUDHURI

Microsoft Research
Redmond, WA
USA
surajitc@Microsoft.com

UMESHWAR DAYAL

Hewlett-Packard Labs
Palo Alto, CA
USA
dayal@hp.com

VENKATESH GANTI

Microsoft Research
Redmond, WA
USA
vganti@Microsoft.com

Abstract

Developing, deploying, and maintaining an effective decision support system is a daunting task—one that requires an enormous effort. In this paper, we review various components of a decision support system: loading, maintenance, and analysis of data. We briefly discuss the key issues underlying each one of these components, current research on these issues, and the support provided by commercial database and data warehousing systems.

---

[1] Portions reprinted, with permission, from the article "Database technology for decision support systems", *IEEE Computer* **34** (12) (December 2001).

ADVANCES IN COMPUTERS, VOL. 62
ISSN: 0065-2458/DOI 10.1016/S0065-2458(03)62007-3

293

1. Introduction

On-line transaction processing (OLTP) systems have enabled organizations to collect large volumes of point-of-sales data during their daily business activity. The ability to analyze and explore the data thus collected has gained prominence in the recent past because of the consequent business gains that can be had by making the right business decisions, say, for managing inventory and for coordinating a mail order campaign.

Data is collected at various independent touch points in a business. Enabling analytical tools to take advantage of such data requires that data be consolidated into a single location—called the *data warehouse*. A data warehouse is a "subject-oriented, integrated, time-varying, non-volatile collection of data that is used primarily in organizational decision making [28]." Typically, the data warehouse is maintained separately from the organization's operational databases because the functional and performance requirements of analytical applications are quite different from those of OLTP applications traditionally supported by operational databases.

OLTP applications typically automate data processing tasks such as order entry and banking transactions that are the bread-and-butter day-to-day operations of an organization. These tasks are structured and repetitive, and consist of short, atomic, isolated transactions. The transactions require detailed, up-to-date data, and read or update a few (tens of) records accessed typically on their primary keys.

Data warehouses, in contrast, are targeted for decision support applications. Historical, summarized and consolidated data is more important for analysis than detailed, individual records. Data warehouses contain data consolidated, from several operational databases, over potentially long periods of time. Hence, they tend to be orders of magnitude larger than operational databases; enterprise data warehouses are projected to hundreds of gigabytes to terabytes in size. The workloads consist of mostly ad hoc, complex queries that can access millions of records and perform a lot of scans, joins, and aggregates. Query response times are more important than transaction throughput.

In this chapter, we survey the various components—tools to consolidate data into the data warehouse, systems to store and manage a large data warehouse, analytical tools leveraging the data warehouse—that a successful decision support system must contain. However, we do not intend to provide comprehensive descriptions of all products in every category. We encourage the interested reader to look at recent issues of trade magazines[2] and vendors' web sites for more details of commercial products, white papers, and case studies.

2.   Decision Support System: Overview

We now introduce a running example, which we will use to illustrate the various components required for building and maintaining a decision support system. First, we introduce the setting of the example database and then describe a set of canonical tasks that a decision support system can accomplish for such a company.

Consider a company called the *Footwear Sellers Company* (FSC) that manufactures and sells footwear to end-customers directly as well as through resellers. Each sales transaction involves the participation of several *entities*—a customer, a sales person, a product, an order, the date when the transaction happened, and the city

---

[2]E.g., *Databased Advisor, Database Programming and Design, Datamation,* and *DBMS Magazine.*

where it happened. Besides, each transaction is also associated with a set of *measure* attributes: the number of units sold and the total amount paid by the customer. Informally, data warehouses and analytical tools are targeted towards exploring and modeling the distribution of measure attributes with other entities. Also, some entities are associated with *hierarchies.* A hierarchy is a multi-level grouping where each level consists of a disjoint grouping of the values in the level immediately below it. For instance, all products can be grouped into a disjoint set of *categories*, which are themselves grouped into a disjoint set of *families*.

FSC's marketing executives must be able to perform the following tasks after the data warehouse has been built.

(1) List the 5 states that reported the highest increases in sales of product categories released for the youth in the last year.
(2) Chart by product family the total footwear sales in New York City within the last month.
(3) Find the 50 cities with the highest number of *unique* customers.
(4) Identify a million customers who are *most likely* to buy the new "Walk-on-air" model of shoes.

To accomplish the above tasks, we have to resolve the following three fundamental issues. First, what data do we gather and how do we conceptually model the data and manage its storage? Second, how do we analyze data? Third, how do we load data frequently coming in from several independent sources? We now present the architecture of a decision support system before discussing each of these issues in detail.

2.1 Architecture

A decision support system has three broad components. First, the data is stored and maintained in a main *data warehouse server.* In addition to the main warehouse, there may be several departmental data marts, which provide a partial view of the data warehouse. Second, a variety of tools like online analytical processing (OLAP) or data mining sit on top of the data warehouse or data marts enabling sophisticated data analysis. The third component consists of the back end tools (extraction, transformation, load tools) for populating the data warehouse from several independent external data sources. Figure 1 presents the architecture of a decision support system.

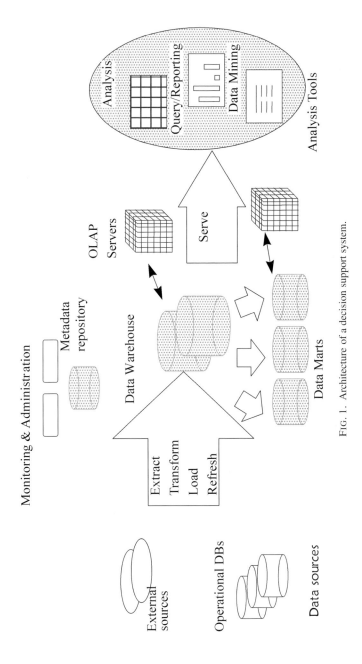

FIG. 1. Architecture of a decision support system.

3.   Data Warehouse Servers

All decision support tasks such as the ones outlined in the previous section have to be accomplished using the *data* gathered by an organization during its daily operation or from other external sources. So, the first issue to address is what information do we gather? The second issue is that of storing and managing it.

Most data warehouses leverage the robust, reliable, and efficient relational database technology for storing and managing large volumes of data. We now discuss the flavor of the logical and the physical schema designs typical of data warehouses that use a relational database management system.

3.1   Logical Database Design

Consider the tasks to be accomplished in our FSC example in Section 2. All of them require that we record information about each sales transaction. In this section, we discuss the nature of appropriate schema for representing the sales transactions that would facilitate analytical tasks.

Schemas for data warehouses often follow the so-called *star schema design*. The database consists of a *fact table* that describes all (sales) transactions that ever happened and a *dimension* table for each *entity*. Each tuple in the fact table consists of a pointer[3] to each of the entities that participate in a transaction, and also consists of the numeric measures associated with the transaction (e.g., sales, profit, etc.). Each dimension table consists of columns that correspond to attributes of the corresponding entity. Computing the join between a fact table and a set of dimension tables is much more efficient than computing a join among arbitrary relations.

Star schemas, however, do not explicitly provide support for attribute hierarchies. *Snowflake schemas* provide a refinement of star schemas where a dimensional hierarchy is explicitly represented by normalizing the dimension tables. Figure 2 depicts a snowflake schema for the FSC data warehouse.

3.2   Physical Database Design

Data warehouses may contain large volumes of data. Therefore, efficiently answering complex queries requires the right data access methods and query processing techniques. For efficient query processing, database systems use redundant structures such as indices and materialized views. A challenge here is to effectively use existing indices and materialized views to answer queries, e.g., [15,20]. While for data-selective queries, index lookups and scans may be very effective, data-intensive

---

[3] Such a pointer represents a *foreign key* that often uses a generated key for efficiency.

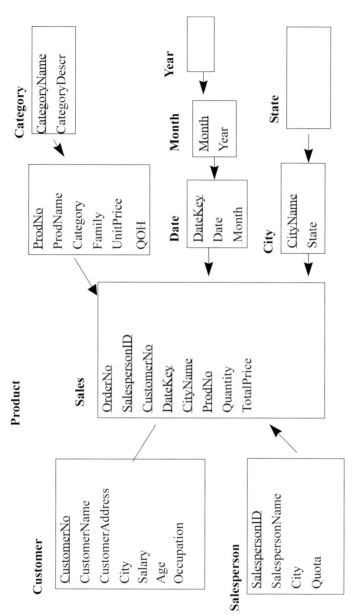

FIG. 2. Star schema for FSC.

queries may require sequential scans of an entire relation or vertical partitions of a relation. Thus, improving the efficiency of table scans is very important. Finally, parallelism has to be exploited to reduce query response times. We will now briefly touch upon the current technology within each of these issues.

Index Structures and Their Usage

Query processing techniques in current commercial database systems rely heavily on indexes to efficiently answer queries involving predicates that are very selective. For instance, an index on Customer.CustomerName can be used to efficiently answer a query requiring all customers in Seattle whose name is 'John Smith.' Further, advanced query processing techniques even exploit indexes through index intersection and union to answer queries on multiple predicates. In particular, the selectivities of multiple conditions can be exploited through index intersection. These index operations can significantly reduce, and in many cases, eliminate the need to access base tables if all projection columns are available via index scans. For example, if we have a query of the form $column1 = d$ & $column2 = d'$, then we can identify the qualifying records by taking the AND of the indexes on column1 and column2.

In addition to indices on single tables, the specialized nature of star schemas makes master-detail *join indices* especially attractive for decision support. While traditionally indices map the value in a column to a list of rows with that value, a join index maintains the relationship between a foreign key with its matching primary keys. In the context of a star schema, a join index can relate the values of one or more attributes of a dimension table to matching rows in the fact table. For example, consider the schema of Fig. 2. There can be a join index on City that maintains, for each city, a list of RIDs of all sales tuples in the Sales table that correspond to sales in that city. Essentially, this join index precomputes a binary join, i.e., a join between two relations (Customer and Sales), and indexes it. Multikey join indices generalize binary join indexes by precomputing n-way joins and indexing them.

Finally, data warehouses contain a significant amount of descriptive text, and so indices to support text search are useful as well. The full text search feature of Microsoft SQL Server, the IBM Text Extender, and Oracle InterMedia are examples of systems that provide this functionality.

The Index Selection Problem

As discussed earlier, appropriate indexes can be used to significantly speed up query answering. However, indexes require significant additional storage space and incur maintenance overhead whenever base tables are updated. Therefore, building too many indexes is in fact detrimental because of excessive costs of maintaining a number of indexes for each update. The natural question then is which set of indexes do we build? The space of indexes from which we have to select the right set of indexes is very large. For example, the number of indexes over a relation with n indexable attributes is $n!$. And, if we consider join indexes then the space is even larger. Consequently, determining a small set of appropriate indexes is a very important and a challenging aspect of the physical database design problem.

We now briefly discuss the intuition behind current approaches for solving the automatic *index selection problem* [3]. The index selection problem can be formalized as that of identifying the *optimal* set of indexes which would occupy no more than an allotted amount of space and which would most reduce the running time of queries that the database system is expected to process—typically characterized by a query workload. Update queries in the workload would force the solution to trade the gain in efficiency from building indexes with the cost of maintaining them under updates.

Solutions to the index selection problem search through the space of indexes evaluating *candidate* sets of indexes, also called *index configurations*, against a workload for identifying the optimal set. However, a naïve methodology of evaluating a candidate index configuration would require us to actually build the indexes and process a set of queries. For instance, evaluating the benefit of indexes on Product.ProdName, Customer.City, and Sales.DateKey on our FSC database may require these indexes to be built. However, actually building a large number of candidate indexes and evaluating them is undesirable because of the inordinately long time and large disk space it would take for building all indexes. Therefore, a significant challenge in developing an efficient and scalable solution to the index selection problem is to the evaluation of candidate indexes without actually building them.

A general approach (first described in [3]) for evaluating index configurations without actually building them is based upon the insight of using *what-if* indexes. What-if indexes exploit the query optimizer in a database system to evaluate index configurations without building them. Recall that the goal of a query optimizer is to produce the best execution strategy for any query and for a given physical database design. Therefore, an effective way of evaluating an index configuration (and other aspects of the physical database design), which is also the intuition behind what-if indexes, is to simulate the existence of these indexes for the query optimizer. That is, the query optimizer is led to believe that these indexes exist even when they are not actually present. What-if indexes effectively answer the following fundamental index evaluation question: will the optimizer use a set of indexes if we were to build them? Once we are able to evaluate an index configuration without building indexes we can in principle efficiently search the space of all indexes using standard search strategies. The architecture of this general index selection approach based upon what-if indexes is shown in Fig. 3.

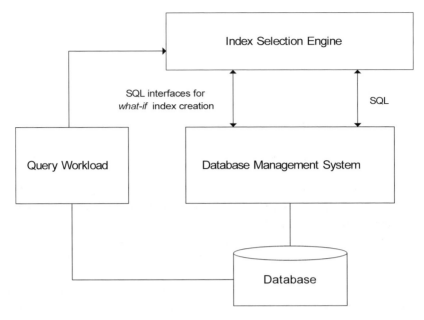

FIG. 3. A general architecture for index selection.

Among popular commercial database systems, the Index Tuning Wizard in Microsoft SQL Server, the Index Tuning Wizard in Oracle, and DB2 Advisor provide the functionality of automatically choosing indices.

Materialized Views and Usage

Many queries over data warehouses require summary data and, therefore, use aggregates. Hence, in addition to indices, materializing summary data can help accelerate many common queries. In our FSC example from Section 2, two views (1) the total sales grouped by (product families, city) and (2) the total number of customers grouped by city can be used to efficiently answer Tasks 1, 2, and 3 listed in Section 2.

The challenges in exploiting materialized views are not unlike those in exploiting indices: (a) identify the views to materialize, (b) exploit the materialized views to answer queries, and (c) efficiently update the materialized views during load and refresh. Since the space of materialized views is extremely large, currently adopted industrial solutions to these problems only consider materializing a restricted class of structurally simple views. Relational database systems like IBM DB2, Microsoft SQL Server, and Oracle support materialized views.

Materialized View Selection

The problem of automatically selecting a best set of views for answering queries is similar to that of the index selection problem. The goal is to identify the best of views to materialize that would most reduce the query answering time for a given set of workload queries. However, the space of views to search over is much larger than the space of indexes due to the rich view definition structure, which can have selection predicates and group by clauses over attributes in a relation as well as over joins of relations. In fact, an index can logically be viewed as a single-table, projection-only materialized view over the relation on which the index was built. However, the equivalent materialized view has to be indexed before it can be effectively searched. Thus the space of all materialized views is much larger than the space of all indexes. Furthermore, the interaction between the choices of views and indexes to build has a significant bearing on the quality of the overall physical design.

The solutions for the view selection problem can be classified into two categories. The first category of solutions addresses the view selection problem in isolation independent of the choice of indexes to build, e.g., [23,26]. The second category of solutions recognizes the interaction between the index selection and the view selection problems and develops a unified solution, e.g., [3]. The index tuning wizard in Microsoft SQL Query takes the unified approach of recommending the right indexes and views to build for a given workload of queries.

Data Marts

Many organizations want to implement an integrated enterprise warehouse that collects information about all subjects (e.g., customers, products, sales, assets, personnel) spanning the whole organization. However, building an enterprise warehouse is a long and complex process, requiring extensive business modeling, and may take many years to succeed. Some organizations are settling for *data marts* instead, which are departmental subsets focused on selected subjects (e.g., a marketing data mart may include customer, product, and sales information) present in the warehouse. These data marts enable faster roll out, since they do not require enterprise-wide consensus, but they may lead to complex integration problems in the long run.

Usually, such data marts are independently managed, developed, and deployed. When new data are added to these data marts, it is possible that the conventions of data flow and quality assurance followed within any data mart may evolve to be different from those across the rest of the organization. When this happens, it becomes very difficult to share or re-integrate data across data marts without an expensive effort. Therefore, it is better to put in a unified and complete business process model while developing and maintaining data marts.

4. OLAP

Consider the Task 1 in our FSC example in Section 2. The query asks for a set of interesting aggregate measures over the sales transactions accumulated in the last year. Note that "state" and "year" are ancestors of the city and date entities, respectively. Such a query aggregating a *numeric measure* at higher levels in the dimensional hierarchies is typical of *online analytical applications (OLAP)*.

In the context of our FSC data warehouse, a typical OLAP session of an analyst understanding the *regional* sales of athletic shoes in the last quarter may proceed as follows. The analyst starts by viewing the distribution of sales of athletic shoes in the last quarter across all countries (by issuing a "select sum(sales) group by country" query). After isolating a country (say, the country with the highest or the lowest total sales value relative to the market size), the analyst issues another query to compute the total sales within each state of that country so as to understand the reason for its exceptional behavior. It may be that a particular state or set of states may be associated with really high (or really low) sales values. If so, the analyst repeats the process on this small set of states. Thus the analyst traverses down the hierarchy associated with the city dimension. Such a downward traversal of the hierarchy from the most summarized to the most detailed level is often called *drill-down*. Occasionally, the analyst may prefer to go one level upwards (say, from the state level to the country level) in a dimensional hierarchy. Such an operation is called *rollup*. OLAP analysis may also involve more complex statistical calculations like moving averages, percentage change of an aggregate within a certain period over that of a different time period.

In the rest of the section, we discuss three issues: the conceptual data model exposed by OLAP tools, server architectures for enabling OLAP analysis, and a few common approaches for improving the functionality and performance of such servers.

4.1   The OLAP Conceptual Data Model

We now discuss a popular aggregation-centric conceptual data model called the *multidimensional model* (Fig. 4), exposed to analysts by OLAP tools. In this data model, there is a set of *numeric measures* (similar to the measure attributes in a star schema) that are the objects of analysis. Examples of such measures are *sales, profit, budget, cost, inventory,* etc. Each of the numeric measures depends on a set of *dimensions* (similar to the dimension tables in a star schema). The dimensions describe the entities involved in a (sales) transaction. For example, the dimensions associated with a sale amount in our FSC example are the customer, the salesperson, the city, the product name, and the date when the sale was made. The dimensions

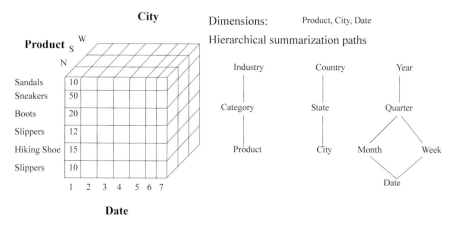

FIG. 4. Multidimensional data.

together are assumed to *uniquely* determine the measure. Thus, the multidimensional data model treats a measure as a value in the *multidimensional space* of dimensions.

As in the case of the star schema, each dimension is described by a set of attributes. For example, the Product dimension may consist of four attributes: the *product name, category,* the *family* of the product, and the average profit margin. For example, the product "running shoe 2000" may belong to the category *athletics* and the family "shoe," may have been introduced in the year 2000, and may have an average profit margin of 80%. The attributes of a dimension may be related via a hierarchy of relationships. In our example, the product name is related to its category and the family attribute through such a hierarchical relationship.

Given the multidimensional view of the data, drill-down and rollup operations can logically be viewed as operations on the cube. Other popular operations include *comparing* two measures (e.g., sales and budget) aggregated by the same dimensions.

Time is a dimension that is of particular significance to decision support (e.g., trend analysis). Often, it is desirable to have built-in knowledge of calendars and other aspects of the time dimension and its special *sequential* characteristics. Knowledge of the sequential characteristics may be used to perform sophisticated trend analysis. For example, market analysts may want to discover periodic patterns or spikes in sales of a class of athletic shoes before or after certain major national athletic meets. A list of other such operations on the multidimensional cube has been defined [7].

4.2   Server Architectures for OLAP

Traditional relational servers were not geared towards processing complex OLAP queries and other requirements for supporting multidimensional views of data. However, all relational DBMS vendors have now moved rapidly to support these additional requirements. In addition to traditional relational servers, there are three other categories of servers that were developed specifically for decision support.

MOLAP Servers

MOLAP servers directly support a multidimensional view of data through a multidimensional storage engine. This makes it possible to implement multidimensional queries on the storage layer through direct mapping. An example of such a server is Hyperion Essbase. Such an approach has the advantage of excellent indexing properties, but provides poor storage utilization, especially when the data is sparse. Many MOLAP servers adopt a 2-level storage representation to adapt to sparse datasets and use compression extensively. In the two-level storage representation, a set of one or two dimensional sub-arrays that are likely to be dense are identified, through the use of design tools or by user input, and are represented in the array format. Traditional indexing structures are then used to index these "smaller" arrays. Many of the techniques that were devised for statistical databases appear to be relevant for MOLAP servers. Even though MOLAP servers offer really good performance and good functionality, they do not scale very well for extremely large data sizes.

ROLAP Servers

These are middleware servers that sit between a relational back end server (where the data in the warehouse is stored) and client front-end tools. Microstrategy is an example of such servers. They extend traditional relational servers with specialized middleware to efficiently support multidimensional OLAP queries, and they typically optimize for specific back end relational servers. They identify the views that are to be materialized, rephrase given user queries in terms of the appropriate materialized views, and generate multi-statement SQL for the back end server. They also provide additional services such as scheduling of queries and resource assignment (e.g., to prevent runaway queries). The main strength of ROLAP servers is that they exploit the scalability and the transactional features of relational systems. However, intrinsic mismatches between OLAP-style querying and SQL can become performance bottlenecks for OLAP servers. On the other hand, the gap is decreasing with the inclusion of OLAP-specific extensions (like the window construct) into standard SQL.

HOLAP Servers

These servers take the best-of-both-worlds approach, and combine ROLAP and MOLAP technologies. Microsoft Analysis Services is an example of this class of servers. ROLAP servers are better when the data is extremely sparse, while MOLAP servers are better when the data is reasonably dense. The hybrid HOLAP servers identify sparse and dense regions of the multidimensional space and take the RO-LAP approach for sparse regions and the MOLAP approach for dense regions. Given a query, the HOLAP servers split it into multiple queries and issue them against the relevant portions of the data, combine them, and then present it to the user. Other issues about selective view materialization, selective index building, query and re-source scheduling remain similar to the MOLAP and ROLAP counterparts.

4.3   Performance Enhancement Techniques

We now discuss two popular approaches for enhancing the performance and func-tionality of OLAP servers.

4.3.1   SQL Extensions

Several extensions to SQL that facilitate the expression and processing of OLAP queries have been implemented in relational servers, such as Oracle, IBM DB2, and Microsoft SQL Server. Some of these extensions, like the *window* construct, have been included in the SQL-99 standard.

The family of aggregate functions has been extended with functions like *median, mode, rank,* and *percentile*. Features like aggregate computation over *moving windows, running totals,* and *breakpoints* aimed at enhancing the support for reporting applications have also been added. These aggregate functions when applied in con-junction with appropriate group by clauses can be used to express a wide variety of analysis queries. Further, operators for easily succinctly expressing several group by clauses together have also been introduced.

Multiple Group-By: Multidimensional spreadsheets require aggregating the same measure attribute and aggregation function over different sets of attributes. Recently, two new operators, *Rollup* and *Cube,* have been proposed to augment SQL to ad-dress this requirement [21]. Their semantics are illustrated by the following exam-ples. *Rollup* of the list of dimensions (*Product, Year, City*) over a dataset results in multiple answer sets with the following applications of group by keeping the aggre-gation function and the measure attribute constant: (a) group by (Product, Year, City) (b) group by (Product, Year), and (c) group by Product. On the other hand, given a list of k dimensions, the *Cube* operator provides a group-by for each of the 2^k com-binations of dimensions. Such aggregate measures are useful for generating reports and analyzing an aggregate measure (say, total sales) across one or more dimensions. Such multiple group-by operations can be executed efficiently by recognizing commonalties among them [9,14].

4.3.2   Pre-computation

Independent of what category the underlying OLAP server belongs to, the processing of OLAP queries may benefit from pre-computing several aggregate measures and materializing them as views. For instance, Task 2 of our FSC example can be efficiently answered if we materialize the number of customers per city. However, different types of queries (say, total sales per product family in the month of June) require different aggregate measures to be pre-computed, and the number of such aggregates can be very large. Hence, it is not usually possible to pre-compute and maintain all possible aggregate measures. The challenge therefore is to identify the *right* set of aggregate measures to pre-compute such that a broad class of OLAP queries may be answered efficiently. This is similar to the materialized view selection problem except that the classes of queries here are ad hoc OLAP-style queries useful for (exploratory) data analysis. Further, due to the adhocness of queries, it is usually not possible to assume that a workload of queries upon which most materialized view selection approaches rely is given. Significant amount of research focused on the task of identifying the *best* aggregate measures, which can be stored within a given amount of disk space.

The fundamental idea guiding most approaches for identifying a subset of aggregates to pre-compute is that many aggregate queries can be answered using the results of other aggregate queries [26]. For example, a query "*select City, Year, sum(TotalPrice) from R group by City, Year*" asking for the total sales per city per year can be answered if we have the result of the query "*select ProductNo, City, Year, sum(TotalPrice) from R group by ProductNo, City, Year*" where R is the join of the fact table with all dimensional tables. The latter query result can also be used to answer other queries, say, "*select sum(TotalPrice) from R.*" In general, the set of aggregate queries in the data cube where two queries are related if one of them can be computed from the result of the second forms a lattice. Figure 5 shows an example lattice where we only consider three dimensions: *Customer* (C), *Product* (P), *and Date* (D). A node labeled by a set S of attributes in Fig. 5 denotes the result of grouping the join R of the fact table and the dimensional tables on S and computing the aggregate function f on the measure attribute M over each group. That is, each node denotes the result of the query "*select S, f (M) from R group by S.*" A query on the node labeled {C} can be answered from the result of {C, P, D}, {C, P}, and {C} itself. And, the directed edges between these nodes denote these relationships. For clarity, we did not include self edges and edges that can be deduced by the transitivity of the *answered-by* relationship in Fig. 5.

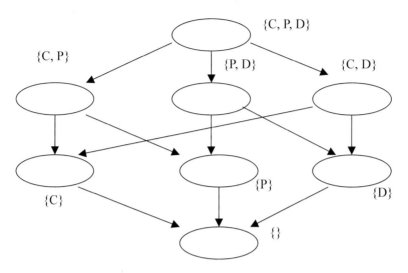

FIG. 5. A lattice of aggregate queries.

Observe that the query at {C, P, D} returns the base relation, the join of the fact table with all dimension tables, which is already available. As we would expect all nodes in the lattice can be answered by the result of this node. The query at node {C} can be answered using either the result of the node {C, P} or the node {C, P, D}. However, it is more efficient to use the result of {C, P} because the size of the result {C, P} is less than the size of the result {C, P, D}. Thus, the additional benefit of materializing the result of {C, P} is that we are able to answer queries on its descendants more efficiently than using the base data {C, P, D}. Therefore, pre-computing and materializing the result of a query in the lattice has a *cost*—the disk space for storing the result—and a *benefit*—the reduction in cost of answering queries on itself and its descendants. Therefore, the goal of the problem of pre-computing the best set of aggregate measures is to identify a set of nodes in the lattice with the best benefit whose total storage cost is less than the available disk space. This problem has been shown to be NP-hard [26]. However, the good news is that several good approximate solutions to this problem have been developed [26,30].

Most commercial OLAP engines provide support for selectively materializing views for improving the efficiency of answering queries over the data cube. In addition, Microsoft SQL Server can select a set of views to materialize for an arbitrary workload of SQL queries.

While materializing such pre-computed views, OLAP servers may leverage support that the backend data warehouse server may provide for materialized views. For example, warehouse servers (like Microsoft SQL Server, IBM DB2, and Oracle) are able to generate query plans that exploit materialized views within the server. Consequently, an OLAP server might actually store a view within the warehouse server. Since the warehouse server's query optimization engine is able to exploit such views then the ROLAP server does not need to split an incoming query into parts that can exploit existing views.

5.   Data Mining

Suppose FSC wants to launch a catalog mailing campaign subject to the constraint that the overall campaign cost is less than a million dollars. Given this constraint, we want to identify the best set of customers who are likely to respond to and buy from the catalog. This goal corresponds to the Task 4 listed in Section 2. *Data mining* tools provide such advanced predictive, analytical functionality. In general, data mining assists analysts in discovering distribution patterns and characteristic behaviors within data to achieve a specific goal, say, that of understanding which type of customers buy a specific class of products.

The end-to-end process of specifying and achieving a goal through an iterative data mining process—sometimes called the knowledge discovery process—typically consists of three phases: *data preparation, model building and evaluation, and model deployment.* For example, SAS Enterprise Miner allows users to create such a staged iterative exploratory process flow.

5.1   Data Preparation

In the data preparation phase, an analyst prepares a dataset that has enough information for building accurate models in subsequent phases. Considering Task 4 in Section 2, we want to prepare a dataset so that we can build an accurate model for predicting whether a customer is likely to buy products advertised in a new catalog. Since potential factors influencing purchases of customers are their demographic information and their past response history, an example of such a dataset is: the set of all customers who responded to mailed catalogs in the last three years, their demographic information, the set of 10 most expensive products each customer purchased during this period, and the information about the catalog each of them responded to.

Support for Executing Complex Queries

Data preparation may involve very complex queries with large result sizes. For instance, the preparation of the dataset in the above example involves joins between the customer relation and the sales relation as well as identifying the top 10 products for each customer. All the issues discussed in the context of efficiently processing decision support queries are equally relevant in this context as well. In fact, data mining platforms (e.g., Microsoft Analysis Services) use OLAP or relational servers to serve their data preparation requirements.

Support for sampling

Data mining process typically involves iteratively building models on a prepared dataset before an analyst finally decides to deploy one or more models. Since model building on large datasets can be expensive, analysts often work with samples of the prepared dataset. Only after deciding on the model to be deployed, a model is built on the entire prepared dataset rather on a sample. Thus, data mining platforms need to provide support for computing *samples* over data and over complex queries.

5.2   Building and Evaluating Mining Models

The *model building* phase involves building models on the prepared dataset. The goal of a model is to identify patterns that determine a *target* attribute. An example of a target attribute in the prepared FSC dataset mentioned above is whether a customer purchased at least one product from the catalog mailed to her. Several classes of models have been proposed in the literature to predict both explicitly specified and hidden attributes. The accuracy of the model and the efficiency of the algorithm for constructing it over large datasets are two important issues while choosing an appropriate mining model.

5.2.1   Variety of Models

Several classes of mining models—in the Statistics and the Machine Learning literature—have been proposed and studied. We now briefly and informally describe a few classes of mining models without describing how they are constructed. For a survey of several popular data mining models and their construction algorithms, we refer the reader to books and surveys [25,17,19].

Classification Models.   *Classification models* are predictive models, which when given a new tuple, predict whether the tuple belongs to one among a set of target classes. For example, in our FSC catalog mailing application, a classification model determines whether a customer purchases or does not purchase from the catalog before mailing a catalog to her. Many classification models have been developed. We briefly illustrate, through an example, the *decision tree models* which are a popular class of classification models—because of their ease of understandability

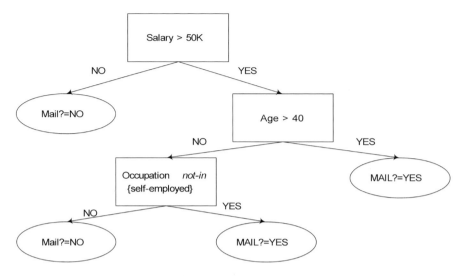

FIG. 6. Sample decision tree for catalog mailing.

arising from their intuitive representation, classification accuracy, and availability of scalable model building algorithms—in Fig. 6, which is perhaps useful for deciding whether or not to mail a catalog to a customer.

A decision tree model is a tree-structured model. Each internal node of a decision tree is labeled with a predicate called the *splitting predicate* and each leaf node is labeled with a *target class label.* The number of edges originating out of an internal node is equal to the range size of the splitting predicate. In the sample decision tree (as in several common decision tree models), the range size is equal to 2 for all internal nodes. The splitting predicates have the property that any record will take a unique path from the root to exactly one leaf node.

Regression Models.   Consider the catalog mailing task that FSC wants to launch and the sample decision tree in Fig. 6. The first attribute required to evaluate whether a particular customer needs to be mailed a catalog or not is the Salary attribute. And, if the salary information is missing for a specific customer then the decision tree cannot predict whether she is a good target for sending out a catalog. In such scenarios where we need to predict numeric attributes *regression models* can be employed.

Models that predict numeric attributes like *salary* or *age* are called *regression models. Regression tree models* [cart] are an example class of regression models. Like decision tree models, they also have a tree structure where internal nodes are

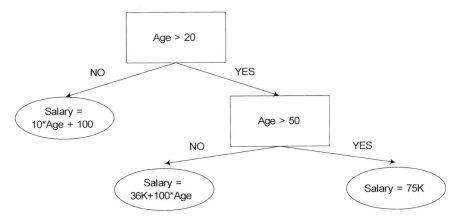

FIG. 7. Sample regression tree for predicting salary.

associated with splitting predicates. However, the leaf nodes in regression tree models are labeled with functions which take the input tuple, e.g., customer, and predict a value for the target attribute, e.g., the customer's salary. An example regression tree model which predicts the salary of customers is shown in Fig. 7. The predicted salary values can presumably be used for deciding via the decision tree in Fig. 6 whether or not to send a catalog to the customer in question.

Clustering Models.   In some applications, we do not explicitly know the set of target classes, and hence consider them to be *hidden*. In these scenarios, we have to determine the appropriate set of classes and then classify a new tuple into one of these discovered classes. *Clustering models* achieve this goal by grouping tuples such that "similar" tuples are placed in the same groups, called *clusters*. The notion of "similarity" between tuples is quantified by *similarity functions* or *distance functions*. An example of a commonly used function is the *Euclidean distance* function. Informally, clustering models partition the input data tuples into "compact" clusters such that a tuple is more similar to tuples in its own cluster than to those in other clusters. The notion of compactness or quality of clustering is usually quantified by a *criterion* function, e.g., sum of mean squared distances over all clusters. The goal of any clustering algorithm is to identify a partitioning of the input relation into K— usually user-specified—clusters that optimizes the criterion function. The clustering problem has been studied in many fields, including machine learning, statistics, biology, and with an additional emphasis on scalability in data mining.

Association Rule Models. In some other applications, we may be interested in exploring whether the purchase of a certain set of footwear products is indicative, with some degree of confidence, of a purchase of another product or set of products. The large collection of individual customer transactions involving FSC products at various retail FSC outlets can be effectively used to achieve this goal by mining *association rules models* [10]. An example of an association rule, which indicates that people who buy Nike shoes and t-shirts are also likely to buy Nike socks, is [*Nike shoes, Nike t-shirt*] → [*Nike socks*]. Such a rule is considered significant if a reasonably large percentage of transactions in the database containing Nike shoes and t-shirt purchases also contain purchases of Nike socks. The percentage of transactions that contain all items or products (Nike shoes, Nike t-shirts, and Nike socks) participating in the rule is often called the *support* of the rule or the set of items. The ratio of the support, *support({Nike shoes, Nike t-shirts, Nike socks})*, of the set of all items participating in the rule with the support, *support({Nike shoes, Nike t-shirts})*, of the rule is called the *confidence.* An association rule model over a dataset consists of all association rules whose support and confidence are above user-specified constants, called the *support* and *confidence thresholds.* Several efficient algorithms for discovering such significant association rules have been proposed. The Apriori algorithm provided an early solution, which subsequent algorithms built upon [11].

The Apriori algorithm mines for association rules in two phases. In the first phase, it discovers the set, called the set of *frequent itemsets*, of all sets of items whose supports are above the support threshold. That is, each of these sets is contained by at least a certain number of customer transactions. Apriori exploits the *monotonicity property* that the support of a set of items is above a threshold only if supports of all its subsets are also above the threshold. For example, if the support of a set of items {Nike shoes, Nike t-shirts, Nike socks} is above the support threshold then the supports of all subsets {Nike shoes}, {Nike t-shirts}, {Nike socks}, etc. are also above the threshold. Alternatively, if the support of {Nike shoes, Nike t-shirts, Nike socks} is below the threshold, then the supports of all its supersets are below the threshold. Thus, whenever Apriori discovers that the support of a set S of items is below the threshold, it *prunes* away all supersets of S and does not count their supports. In the second phase, Apriori uses the set of all frequent itemsets to discover association rules whose support and confidence are above the required thresholds.

5.2.2 Scalability

Even though data analysts may build models over random samples in the exploratory phase of model building, they ultimately want to build the final model on the entire dataset. This is because statistically it is well known that the accuracy of most models improves with the amount of data used. Therefore, it is imperative that algorithms for inducing mining models are very *efficient and scalable* to process very large datasets within a reasonable amount of time. Surveys on scalable data mining exist, e.g., [19]. Considerable amount of research went into scaling up algorithms for constructing popular classes of models like decision trees, cluster models, and association rules. Most of these algorithms just involve scanning the prepared dataset multiple times.

5.2.3   Extensibility & APIs for User-Defined Models

Data mining platforms support the construction of several classes of models so that analysts can evaluate several models. Data mining platforms like the SAS Enterprise Miner, IBM Intelligent Miner, Epiphany E5, Microsoft Analysis Services, and Oracle allow users to create multiple classes of models. Even though data mining platforms provide support for constructing a wide variety of models, it is quite likely that some applications require custom models which are not provided by the platform. Suppose an analyst exploring the FSC data warehouse wants to build her own correlation model, which is not supported by the data mining platform. To handle such requirements, mining platforms must support extensibility. Microsoft Analysis Services, which publishes an open API, *OLE DB for DM*, and Oracle, which publishes a Java-based API are examples of such extensible platforms.

5.3   Mining Model Deployment

In the third *model deployment* phase, we apply these models on datasets for which we want to predict the target attribute whose value is unknown. Considering our FSC example, for each of the current set of customers, we want to predict whether they will purchase a product from the new catalog. The result of the deployment of a model on an input dataset may be another dataset (a subset or partitioning of the input dataset) that the analyst can act upon. In the context of FSC example, the model deployment phase leads to identifying a subset of customers each of whom will be mailed a catalog.

Efficiency

Depending on the application, the time required to deploy a model on each tuple of the input dataset may have to be limited. In an application of a model that personalizes the placement of advertisement banners when a user visits a website, we want the deployment time to be as short as possible. Also, in the case when an input dataset is extremely large (say, the set of all customers in a data warehouse), we want the deployment strategy to be very efficient. In such cases strategies to filter (using indexes on the input relation) out tuples that will not be in the result of the deployment may be very important. However, such strategies require tighter integration between database systems and model deployment.

Mining Model Interoperability.   Many commercial products build models for specific domains (e.g., IBM Intelligent Miner for Text). However, the actual database on which this model needs to be deployed may be in a different database system. Either the model or the target database needs to be moved to the other's location. Since mining models are typically much smaller than the datasets on which they are being deployed, it is much more efficient to transfer the model to the database platform which holds the target dataset. Therefore, there is a strong requirement for data mining platforms and database servers to interchange models between them.

Data Mining Group [4] has recently proposed an XML-based standard, called *PMML (predictive model markup language)*, for interchanging several popular classes of predictive models. The idea is that any model described in this standard can be imported and deployed by any database vendor that supports the standard. For example, IBM Intelligent Miner Scoring, which is an add-on to IBM Intelligent Miner, enables DB2 to import and execute several classes of predictive models that conform to the PMML standard.

6.   OLAP and Data Mining: Other Issues

We now briefly discuss other issues that are important in the context of OLAP and data mining technology.

6.1   Reporting Tools

Several analysts repeatedly evaluate the same set of queries to periodically assess sales performance of a product. (E.g., "select sum(sales) from FactTable group by state, product category where state = 'New York' ".) Consequently, routine but sophisticated functionality like moving averages, comparison of aggregates in a time period with the same aggregate over a different time period, and similar specialized temporal analysis may be provided by *canned, parameterized queries. Reporting tools* focus on the development of such queries. Typically, reports have easy-to-use user interfaces for specifying input parameters (like the value "New York" in the above example) as well as explanatory visual charts depicting a clear comparison of the results. The key features of a good reporting tool are the high-level OLAP functionality it encapsulates, the user interface, and the visualization front-end for displaying the reports. Crystal Reports from Crystal Decisions is an example of such a reporting tool.

6.2   Packaged Applications

Developing a complete analysis solution either in the OLAP space or in the data mining space requires a series of complex queries and/or building, tuning, and deploying complex data mining models.

Several commercial tools try to bridge this gap between the actual solution requirements for well-understood domains and the support from any given OLAP or data mining platform. By exploiting the knowledge of a vertical domain, packaged applications and reporting tools can make it much easier for end users to develop complete solutions by providing them higher-level domain-specific abstractions. Oracle Financials, PeopleSoft Budgeting, BlueMartini Commerce, Crystal Reports, and Epiphany Campaign Management are some examples of solutions for vertical domains. Comprehensive lists of domain-specific solutions are provided by data warehousing information center [5] and KDD Nuggets [6].

Businesses like FSC can now purchase solutions instead of developing home-grown analysis solutions. Solutions developed for a vertical domain are limited by the feature set of the particular solution. Hence, there is always a downside that a solution's feature set may not satisfy all the analysis needs of a business as it grows.

6.3   Platform APIs and the Impact of XML

In order to enable solution-providers, several OLAP and data mining platforms (e.g., Microsoft Analysis Services, DB2 OLAP, and DB2 Intelligent Miner) provide APIs to enable custom solutions to be built. Microsoft Analysis Services provides OLE DB for OLAP and OLE DB for DM APIs for building OLAP and data mining solutions, respectively. Similarly, Oracle provides Java-based APIs for OLAP and data mining. IBM provides the Essbase API for OLAP.

Solution-providers (ISVs) typically have to program against a variety of OLAP or data mining engines in order to provide an engine-independent solution. The advent of web-based services through XML is driving the scenario to a point where it is possible for all OLAP engines to agree on a common XML-based interface, which can be used by solution providers. Recently, Microsoft and Hyperion published *XML for Analysis* [8], which is a Simple Object Access Protocol (SOAP)-based XML API, designed specifically for standardizing the data access interaction between a client application and an analytical data provider (OLAP and Data Mining) working over the Web. ISVs can now program using a single XML API instead of multiple vendor-specific APIs. Such an open API enables ISVs to enhance the functionality (say, support for time-series and temporal analysis) of any OLAP engine easily.

In the context of data mining models, *PMML* is emerging as the potential standard for interchanging classes of predictive models.

6.4 Approximate Query Processing

Processing complex aggregate queries typically require accessing large portions of the data warehouse. For example, computing the average sales of FSC across all cities requires the entire data in the warehouse to be scanned. However, many times a reasonably accurate approximate answer could be computed very fast. The basic idea is to summarize the underlying data as concisely as possible and then answering aggregate queries using the summary instead of the actual data (e.g., [1,2]). Several approaches have been proposed for summarizing large relations. Sampling, wavelets, and histograms are a few among them. However, there is no clear verdict yet on which approach is better for any given domain or dataset. Another important outstanding issue is that of measuring the quality of an approximate answer for an arbitrary SQL query. How does the answer computed from the summary compare with the exact answer? The challenge here is that quality measures have to be calculated without computing the exact answer.

6.5 OLAP and Data Mining Integration

As discussed earlier, OLAP tools help analysts in determining the interesting portions of the data. Mining models may be used to effectively enhance such functionality. For example, if the increase in sales of FSC products does not meet the targeted rates, then we want to discover the *anomalous* regions and categories of products, which resulted in not meeting the target. To help such an exploratory analysis for discovering anomalies, we require a technique that marks an aggregate measure at a higher level in a dimensional hierarchy with an *anomaly score* that computes the overall deviation of the actual aggregate values from corresponding "expected" values over all its descendants [29,24]. Data mining models (like regression models) can be used to compute expected values.

6.6 Web Mining

Nowadays, almost all major businesses have created a web presence where customers can browse, enquire, and purchase products. Since each customer has a "one-on-one" contact with the business through the web site, it is possible to *personalize* her experience on the web site. For example, the web site may *recommend* products, services, or articles belonging to the category of interest to the particular customer. Amazon.com has been a pioneer in deploying such *personalization* systems. Blue Martini Commerce is an example of a personalization solution. Developing and deploying such personalization systems requires the two issues of *data collection* and *personalization* techniques.

Customers visiting business websites leave a trail of their activities. Businesses can collect such trails, called *web logs.* Demographic information about customers may also be collected when they register. Since web log data is collected automatically, it can be cleaner than manually entered demographic data. However, several customers accessing the website from the same ISP or from behind a firewall may share the same IP address preventing precise customer identification using IP addresses.

Web log data may be analyzed for determining typical behavioral patterns, e.g., users who purchase athletic shoes also purchase socks. Therefore, if a customer purchased an athletic shoe, then the business may also offer her a deal on socks. Such patterns can also be used to *personalize* web pages shown to a particular user with the goal of increasing sales (or other target metrics) by placing appropriate product advertisements. Data mining models discussed earlier may be used to discover such patterns. Over a period of time, a large community of users may develop. In such cases, behavioral patterns of a user in conjunction with those of "similar" users can be used for recommending products to the user. For instance, if Lisa is similar in behavior to Anita, then products that Anita purchased may be recommended to Lisa. Once again, data mining models may be used to identify such similar classes of users.

7. Tools for Populating a Data Warehouse

Until now, we discussed solutions for data warehouse management and decision support tools that sit on top of data warehouses. We now discuss the technology required for building such large data warehouses by consolidating data from various operational databases and other independent data sources.

Building a large data warehouse from independent data sources requires the *extraction* of data from each source, *transforming* it to conform to the warehouse schema, *cleaning,* and then *loading* into the warehouse. This sequence of operations is often called *ETL (extract, transform, load) process.* Two fundamental problems have to be addressed in the ETL process. First, the schema of the data sources is typically different from the target schema. Hence, the conversion needs to be well defined and automated. Second, since we are consolidating data from several data sources, the same customer may be reported by two or more sources. Due to differences in conventions followed within data sources and due to data entry errors, the attribute values corresponding to duplicate customer records may not match exactly across different data sources. Reconciling such differences is the second problem.

Data warehousing systems use a variety of ETL tools. Pure Extract and Pure Integrate from Oracle, Data Transformation Services from Microsoft, DB2 Data Joiner from IBM are just a few examples of tools for addressing parts of the ETL process. The data warehousing information center provides a fairly comprehensive list of such tools [5].

7.1   Extraction and Transformation

Suppose a distributor of FSC reports sales transactions as a flat file of records where each record describes all entities, besides the number of units, involved in the transaction. Also suppose the distributor splits each customer's name into first name, middle initial, and last name. When incorporating sales information into the FSC data warehouse with the schema shown in Fig. 2, we first have to *extract* records, and then for each record *transform* all three name-related source columns to derive a value for the "customer name" attribute.

The goal of the data extraction step is to bring data from sources into a database that can be modified so that data may be incorporated into the data warehouse. Data from operational OLTP databases or from flat files within the organization may be extracted through bulk copy operations or through functions provided by the relational database system. Data extraction from "foreign" sources is usually implemented via gateways and standard interfaces, most notably ODBC. The goal of the subsequent data transformation step is to address discrepancies in schema and attribute value conventions. Transforming data from an input schema to the destination schema is typically specified through a set of rules and scripts. Most of the ETL tools mentioned at the beginning of this section can be used for this task.

7.2   Data Cleansing

Consider Task 3 listed in Section 2. It is possible that due to data entry errors and differences in schema conventions that a customer may have several tuples corresponding to her in the Customer dimension table. Such errors can result in incorrect answers to tasks such as Task 3, and may also cause incorrect mining models to be built. For example, if each of several customers in New York City is recorded with multiple tuples in the Customer table, then New York City may incorrectly appear in the list of top 5 cities with the highest number of unique customers. Such a result is not desirable if the analyst goes on to use the results for a direct mailing campaign. Data mining models that predict the importance of a customer based on the amount of money they spent on FSC products may not give accurate results because the total amount spent by a single customer may be split among several records corresponding to her. Therefore, tools that help detect data anomalies and correct them can have a high payoff. Data cleaning also becomes necessary when the input sources share inconsistent field lengths, inconsistent descriptions, inconsistent value assignments, missing entries, and violation of integrity constraints. Not surprisingly, optional fields in data entry forms are significant sources of inconsistent data.

Several domain-specific commercial solutions, especially for the domain of names and addresses, have been developed. PureIntegrate from Oracle, Integrity from Vality, ETI*DataCleanse from ETI, and Centrus from Sagent are just a few of the many tools for the address cleansing domain. Recent research focused on the problems of duplicate elimination (e.g., [27]) and data cleaning frameworks (e.g., [18]).

7.3   Loading

After extracting and transforming, data must be loaded into the warehouse. Additional preprocessing may still be required: checking integrity constraints; sorting; summarization, aggregation and other computation to build the derived tables stored in the warehouse; building indices and other access paths. Typically, batch load utilities are used for this purpose. In addition to populating the warehouse, a load utility must allow the system administrator to monitor status, to cancel, suspend and resume a load, and to restart after failure with no loss of data integrity.

The load utilities for data warehouses have to deal with much larger data volumes than for operational databases. Hence, pipelined and partitioned parallelism is typically exploited [12]. Performing a full load has the advantage that it can be treated as a long batch transaction building up a new database. While it is in progress, the current database can still support queries; when the load transaction commits, the current database is replaced with the new one. Using periodic checkpoints ensures that if a failure occurs during the load, the process can restart from the last checkpoint.

Many database vendors enhance SQL with additional operations that can be leveraged by the load process. For instance, Oracle provides multi-table inserts and upserts (in-place updates), which can be used to avoid multiple SQL update queries for each input tuple.

7.4   Refresh

In our FSC example, distributors of FSCs footwear products periodically (say, every week) report all the transactions that were generated by the sale of FSCs products. Therefore, we have to periodically *refresh* the data warehouse with new data during the typically small nightly downtime windows. Refreshing a warehouse consists of propagating updates on source data to correspondingly update the base tables and derived data—materialized views and indexes—stored in the warehouse. There are two sets of issues to consider: *when* to refresh, and *how* to refresh.

The warehouse is refreshed periodically (e.g., daily or weekly). Only if some OLAP queries need current data (e.g., up to the minute stock quotes), it is necessary to propagate every update. The refresh policy is set by the warehouse administrator, depending on user needs and traffic, and may be different for different sources. The refresh cycles have to be properly chosen so that the volume of data does not overwhelm the incremental load utility.

Most commercial utilities (e.g., Change Data Capture from Oracle) use incremental loading during refresh to reduce the volume of data that has to be incorporated into the warehouse. Only the updated tuples are inserted if the data sources support extracting relevant portions of data. However, the load process now is harder to manage because the incremental update has to be coordinated with ongoing transactions. The incremental load may conflict with ongoing queries, so it is treated as a sequence of shorter transactions (which commit periodically, e.g., after every 1000 records or every few seconds), but now this sequence of transactions has to be coordinated to ensure consistency of derived data and indices with the base data.

Refresh techniques may also depend on the characteristics of the source and the capabilities of the database servers. Extracting an entire source file or database is usually too expensive, but may be the only choice for legacy data sources. Most contemporary database systems provide replication servers that support incremental techniques for propagating updates from a primary database to one or more replicas. Such replication servers can be used to incrementally refresh a warehouse when the sources change.

In addition to propagating changes to the base data in the warehouse, the derived data also has to be updated correspondingly. The problem of constructing logically correct updates for incrementally updating derived data (materialized views) has been the subject of much research [13,22,31,16]. For data warehousing, the most significant classes of derived data are summary tables, single-table indices, and join indices.

8.   Metadata Management

Creating and managing a warehousing system is hard because a data warehouse reflects the business model of an enterprise. Any information required for managing the
data warehouse is called *metadata*. An essential element of a warehousing architecture is metadata management. Many different kinds of metadata have to be managed.
Administrative metadata includes all of the information necessary for setting up and
using a warehouse. *Business* metadata includes business terms and definitions, ownership of the data, and charging policies. *Operational* metadata includes information
that is collected during the operation of the warehouse: the lineage of migrated and
transformed data; the currency of data in the warehouse (active, archived or purged);
and monitoring information such as usage statistics, error reports, and audit trails.

Often, a *metadata repository* is used to store and manage all the metadata associated with the warehouse. The repository enables the sharing of metadata among
tools and processes for designing, setting up, using, operating, and administering a
warehouse. Commercial examples include Microsoft Repository, Platinum Repository and Prism Directory Manager.

Many different classes of tools are available to facilitate different aspects of metadata management. Development tools are used to design and edit schemas, views,
scripts, rules, queries, and reports. Planning and analysis tools are used for what-
if scenarios such as understanding the impact of schema changes or refresh rates,
and for doing capacity planning. Warehouse management tools (e.g., HP Intelligent
Warehouse Advisor, IBM Data Hub, Prism Warehouse Manager) are used for monitoring a warehouse, reporting statistics and making suggestions to the administrator:
usage of partitions and summary tables, query execution times, types and frequencies
of drill downs or rollups, which users or groups request which data, peak and average workloads over time, exception reporting, detecting runaway queries, and other
quality of service metrics. System and network management tools (e.g., HP Open-
View, IBM NetView, Tivoli) are used to measure traffic between clients and servers,
between warehouse servers and operational databases, and so on.

9.   Conclusions and Future Directions

Decision support systems form the core of the IT infrastructure of businesses because of the business gains from the information that can potentially be extracted
from them. Creating, populating, maintaining, and analyzing a large data warehouse
is a mammoth task and involves substantial technical challenges.

Substantial technological progress has been made due to concerted efforts of the
industry as well as the academia. The efforts are reflected in the number of commer-

cial tools that exist for each of the three major tasks: populating the data warehouse from independent operational databases, storing and managing the data warehouse, and analyzing the data to make intelligent business decisions. Good sources of references on data warehousing technology as well as standardization efforts are the OLAP Council [7] and the Data Warehousing Information Center [5]. The data mining group [4] and KDD nuggets [6] are similar sources of information for data mining tools and technology.

Despite the plethora of commercial tools, there are still several interesting avenues for research. We will only touch on a few of these here. Data cleaning is a problem that is reminiscent of heterogeneous data integration, a problem that has been studied for many years. But here the emphasis is on *data* inconsistencies instead of schema inconsistencies. Though there is some recent work on data cleaning, much more work needs to be done before domain independent tools that can solve a variety of data cleaning problems faced during data warehouse development are available.

Most research in data mining has focused on developing algorithms for either building more accurate models or for building equally accurate models faster. The other two stages of the knowledge discovery process—data preparation and model deployment—have been ignored to a large extent. Both these stages have several outstanding problems. When pointed to a data warehouse and given a specific goal, how does an analyst prepare a "good" dataset to achieve the application's goals? What is an efficient way to deploy models over the results of arbitrary SQL queries? Addressing these issues requires a tighter integration between database systems and data mining technology.

REFERENCES

[1] "The approximate query processing project", http://www.research.microsoft.com/dmx/ApproximateQP.
[2] "The AQUA project", http://www.bell-labs.com/project/aqua.
[3] "The AutoAdmin project", http://www.research.microsoft.com/dmx/AutoAdmin.
[4] The data mining group, http://www.dmg.org.
[5] The data warehousing information center, http://www.dwinfo.org.
[6] KDD nuggets, http://www.kdnuggets.com/solutions/index.html.
[7] Olap Council, http://www.olapcouncil.org.
[8] "XML for analysis specification", http://www.essbase.com/downloads/XML_Analysis_spec.pdf.
[9] Agarwal S., Agarwal R., Deshpande P.M., Gupta A., Naughton J.F., Ramakrishnan R., "On the computation of multidimensional aggregates", in: *Proceedings of the VLDB 96*, 1996, pp. 506–522.

[10] Agrawal R., Imielinski T., Swami A., "Mining association rules between sets of items in large databases", in: *Proceedings of the ACM SIGMOD Conference on Management of Data, Washington, D.C.*, May 1993, pp. 207–216.

[11] Agrawal R., Srikant R., "Fast Algorithms for Mining Association Rules", in: *Proceedings of the 20th International Conference on Very Large Databases, Santiago, Chile*, September 1994.

[12] Barclay T., Barnes R., Gray J., Sundaresan P., "Loading datasets using dataflow parallelism", *SIGMOD Record* **23** (4) (December 1994).

[13] Blakeley J.A., Coburn N., Larson P., "Updating derived relations: Detecting irrelevant and autonomously computable updates", *ACM TODS* **4** (3) (1989).

[14] Chatziantoniou D., Ross K., "Querying multiple features in relational databases", in: *Proceedings of the VLDB Conference*, 1996.

[15] Chaudhuri S., Krishnamurthy R., Potamianos S., Shim K., "Optimizing queries with materialized views", in: *Proceedings of the International Conference on Data Engineering*, 1995.

[16] Roussopoulos N., et al., "The Maryland ADMS project: Views R Us", *Data Engineering Bulletin* **18** (2) (1995).

[17] Fayyad U.M., Piatetsky-Shapiro G., Smyth P., Uthurusamy R. (Eds.), *Advances in Knowledge Discovery and Data Mining*, AAAI/MIT Press, 1996.

[18] Galhardas H., Florescu D., Shasha D., Simon E., Saita C., "Declarative data cleaning: Language, model, and algorithms", in: *Proceedings of the 27th International Conference on Very Large Databases, Roma, Italy*, September 11–14, 2001, pp. 371–380.

[19] Ganti V., Gehrke J., Ramakrishnan R., "Mining very large datasets", *IEEE Computer* **32** (9) (1999) 38–45.

[20] Goldstein J., Larson P., "Optimizing queries using materialized views: A practical, scalable solution", in: *Proceedings of the 2001 ACM SIGMOD Conference on the Management of Data, Santa Barbara, CA*, 2001.

[21] Gray J., Chaudhuri S., Bosworth A., Layman A., Pellow F., Pirahesh H., "Data cube: A relational aggregation operator generalizing group-by, cross-tab and sub-totals", *Data Mining and Knowledge Discovery* **1** (1) (1997) 29–53.

[22] Gupta A., Mumick I.S., "Maintenance of materialized views: Problems, techniques, and applications", *Data Engineering Bulletin* **18** (2) (1995).

[23] Gupta H., Harinarayan V., Rajaraman A., Ullman J.D., "Index selection for OLAP", in: *Proceedings of the ICDE Conference*, 1997.

[24] Han J., "Olap mining: An integration of OLAP with data mining", in: *Proceedings of the IFIP Conference On Data Semantics*, 1997.

[25] Han J., Kamber M., *Data Mining: Concepts and techniques*, Morgan Kaufmann, 2000.

[26] Harinarayan V., Rajaraman A., Ullman J., "Implementing data cubes efficiently", in: *Proceedings of the ACM SIGMOD*, 1996.

[27] Hernandez M., Stolfo S., "The merge/purge problem for large databases", in: *Proceedings of the ACM SIGMOD, San Jose, CA*, May 1995, pp. 127–138.

[28] Inmon W.H., *Building the Data Warehouse*, John Wiley & Sons, 2002.

[29] Sarawagi S., "User adaptive exploration of olap data cubes", in: *Proceedings of 26th International Conference on Very LargeData Bases, Cairo, Egypt*, 2000.

[30] Shukla A., Deshpande P., Naughton J., "Storage estimation for multidimensional aggregates in the presence of hierarchies", in: *Proceedings of VLDB*, 1996.

[31] Zhuge Y., Garcia-Molina H., Hammer J., Widom J., "View maintenance in a warehousing environment", in: *Proceedings of the ACM SIGMOD*, May 1995.

Author Index

Numbers in *italics* indicate the pages on which complete references are given.

A

Abowd, G., *248*
Abrahamsson, P., 2, *63*
Abran, A., 252, *288*
Abts, C., 226, *247*
Agarwal, R., 308, *324*
Agarwal, S., 308, *324*
Agrawal, G., 112, 117, 121, *172*
Agrawal, H., 109, 111, 148, *172*
Agrawal, R., 314, *325*
Aha, D.W., 252, *287*
Al-Said, M., 217–219, *247*
Alberg, H., 251, *289*
Allen, E.B., 251–253, 256, 258, 259, 264, 266, 283, *287–289, 291*
Allen, J., 187, *201*
Allen, R., 209, 216, *247*
Ambler, S., 22, 23, 25–27, 32, 40, 42, *63*
Andersen, L.O., 153, *172*
Atkinson, D.C., 110, 122, 134, 139, 143, 150, 153, 154, *172, 176*
Aud, S.J., 266, *288*

B

Babcock, C., *247*
Ball, T., 111, *172*
Banavar, G.S., 187, 193, 194, *201, 202*
Bankert, R.L., 252, *287*
Barclay, T., 321, *325*
Bareiss, R., 252, *287*
Barletta, R., 252, *289*
Barnes, R., 321, *325*
Bartsch-Spoerl, B., 252, *287*
Basili, V.R., 3, 27, 34, *63–65*, 71, 81, 87, 100, *102, 103*

Bass, L., *248*
Beck, J., 187, 193, *201*
Beck, K., 2–4, 7, 8, 11, 13, 27, 28, 41, *63*, 71, 86, 91, *102, 103*
Beedle, M., 29, *65*
Beigi, M., 194, *202*
Bell, B., 252, *287*
Benlarbi, S., 252, *288*
Bent, L., 143, 153, 154, *172*
Berenson, M.L., 254, 272, 286, *287*
Berners-Lee, T., 190, 191, *201*
Bernstein, A., 186, 187, *201*
Beszédes, A., 132, *172*
Bieman, J.M., 131, 158, *172*
Binkley, D.W., 106–110, 112–114, 117, 119, 120, 122, 124, 145, 146, 148, 154, 155, 157, 158, 166–168, 170, *172–176, 178*
Blakeley, J.A., 322, *325*
Boehm, B.W., 4, 9, 25–28, 34, *63–65*, 70, 71, 89, *102*, 204, 206, 208, 209, 211, 224, 226–228, 239, *247, 248*
Bose, P., *248*
Bosworth, A., 307, *325*
Bowers, P., 11, *63*
Brant, J., 91, *103*
Bratko, I., 281, *289*
Briand, L.C., 250, 252, 266, *287*
Briggs, R., 228, *247*
Brooks, A., 119, *176*
Brooks, F.P., 81, *103*
Brown, A.W., 27, *65*
Brown, W., 208, 239, *247*
Busboom, J.C., 259, *288*

C

Calliss, F.W., 107, *177*
Campbell, R.H., 194, *202*

327

Subject Index

333

Contents of Volumes in This Series